Object-Oriented Software Development Using

Java™

Object-Oriented Software Development Using

Java™

principles, patterns, and frameworks

Xiaoping Jia

 ADDISON-WESLEY

An imprint of Addison Wesley Longman, Inc.

Reading, Massachusetts · Menlo Park, California · New York · Harlow, England
Don Mills, Ontario · Sydney · Mexico City · Madrid · Amsterdam

Acquisitions Editor: Maite Suarez-Rivas
Senior Production Editor: Amy Rose
Packager: Trillium Project Management
Composition: TechBooks
Copyeditor: Jerry Moore
Proofreader: Trillium Project Management
Art source: TechBooks
Cover designer: Renee Sartell/Lynne Reed

Access the latest information about Addison-Wesley books from our World Wide Web site: http://www.awlonline.com

Many of the designations used by manufacturers and sellers to distinguish their products are claimed as trademarks. Where those designations appear in this book, and Addison-Wesley was aware of a trademark claim, the designations have been printed in initial caps or all caps.

The programs and applications presented in this book have been included for their instructional value. They have been tested with care, but are not guaranteed for any particular purpose. The publisher does not offer any warranties or representations, nor does it accept any liabilities with respect to the programs or applications.

Library of Congress Cataloging-in-Publication Data

Jia, Xiaoping.
    Object-oriented software development in Java : principles, patterns, and frameworks / Xiaoping Jia.
        p.   cm.
    ISBN 0-201-35084-X
    1. Object-oriented programming (Computer science)   2. Computer software—Development.   3. Java (Computer program language)
    I. Title.
    QA76.64.J53   2000
    005.13′3—dc21   99-14184
                                                          CIP

Reprinted with corrections, June 2000

2 3 4 5 6 7 8 9 10-MA-020100

To Ai-Ling and Robin

Preface

Object-oriented software development has been evolving for nearly twenty years and has matured significantly during the past several years. Advances in the following areas have played crucial roles in the maturing of this technology.

- The convergence of object-oriented modeling techniques and notations resulted in the *Unified Modeling Language* (UML) as the de facto standard.
- The development of object-oriented frameworks and design patterns led to publication of the *Design Patterns* catalog by Gamma et al.
- The evolution of object-oriented programming languages culminated in the emergence of Java.

Object-oriented technology in general—and Java in particular—enjoy unprecedented popularity today. However, the rapid pace of development presents educational challenges to computer science and software engineering students and software development professionals alike. This book is intended to provide a reasonably broad and coherent coverage of object-oriented technology, including object-oriented modeling using UML, object-oriented design using design patterns, and object-oriented programming using Java—with the primary focus on design and programming. This book may be used for an introductory level graduate or an advanced level undergraduate course in computer science and software engineering, as well as in professional development courses. It is not intended for an introductory course on programming in Java; students should have some previous experience in programming, preferably in C or C++.

In the object-oriented paradigm, programming and design are two distinct tasks; however, they are more tightly intertwined than in the conventional programming paradigm. Learning object-oriented software development using Java involves more than just learning Java's syntax and libraries. Object-oriented development is a dramatic departure from conventional programming, and to master it requires a new way of thinking. In this book I attempt to instill the object-oriented way of thinking in those who use it through the use of design patterns, exploration of the design of the Java class libraries, and illustration of incremental software development. I am both an educator and a practitioner in software engineering and object-oriented development. My intent is to provide a balanced view of object-oriented software development from different perspectives—academia and industry, theory and practice.

Complete coverage of the Java language and the Java class library is beyond the scope of this book. Therefore my focus is on

▪ the most important and commonly used features of the language and the class libraries, and

▪ the use of the Java class libraries to illustrate the applications of object-oriented design principles and design patterns.

To complement this book, I recommend the following books from the Java Series published by Addison Wesley Longman.

1. *Java Programming Language*, 2d ed., by Ken Arnold and James Gosling.

2. *The Java Class Libraries*, 2d ed., Volumes 1 and 2, by Patrick Chan and Rosanna Lee.

3. *The Java Tutorial* by Mary Campione and Kathy Walrath.

4. *The Java Language Specification* by James Gosling, Bill Joy, and Guy Steele.

Notations and Conventions

The following fonts are used in presenting program code.

(a) Code fragments that can be copied verbatim are set in `Monotype`. Code fragments in **`Boldface Monotype`** font are important or of particular interest.

(b) Code fragments in upright Roman font are pseudocode, which are informal descriptions of program logic.

(c) Entities in angle brackets, such as

⟨method `doSomething()` on page 108⟩

represent placeholders. Code fragments that are defined elsewhere should be inserted here. The page numbers refer to the pages on which the code fragments to be inserted are defined.

(d) Italicized names, such as *var*, may be replaced by any other specific and distinct names.

Online Supplements

All programs in this book were developed using The Java Development Kit (JDK) 1.2.[1] The JDK and the complete API documentation is available for downloading at

---

[1] Some of the programs require only JDK 1.1.

```
http://java.sun.com
```

The source code of all the examples in this book, as well as related information that will be useful to both students and teachers, can be found at the book's companion Web site at

```
http://www.awl.com/cseng/titles/0-201-35084-X
```

Acknowledgements

Writing this book has been a long journey. The rapid evolution of Java has made the journey both challenging and exciting. Throughout this journey, I was fortunate to have had the help and contributions of many people. I am deeply indebted to them. I'd like to thank my editor at Addison Wesley Longman, Maite Suarez-Rivas. This book would not have been possible without her continued encouragement, support, and guidance. I am especially grateful to Robert Pasenko, who helped tremendously to make this a better book.

Thanks are extended to the staff at Addison Wesley Longman: Amy Rose (production editor), Molly Taylor (assistant editor), Michael Hirsch (marketing manager), and Jarrod Gibbons (marketing assistant). They have made this long journey a pleasant one. I'd also like to thank Jerrold Moore (copyeditor) for his thorough editing job. I appreciate the efforts of the reviewers: J. D. Baker (Chapman University), Jim Bieman (Colorado State University), Frank P. Coyle (Southern Methodist University), Joan Peckham (University of Rhode Island), Larry F. Sells (Oklahoma City University), and Shih-Ho Wang (University of California, Davis). Their comments and suggestions have greatly improved this book. Also thanks go to Ted Pearson and Sotiris Skevoulis for their many contributions.

I'd like to thank the School of Computer Science, Telecommunication, and Information Systems, DePaul University, for supporting me in bringing Java technology to the classroom in its early days. And to all my students in SE 450 during the past few years: Your enthusiasm for Java and my lectures convinced me to embark on this journey. Your feedback on my lectures and early drafts of the book were enormously helpful. I always considered you as my companions on this journey and I truly enjoyed your company.

Request for Comments

I would appreciate any suggestions and feedback on any aspect of this book that may help me to improve it. Please send your comments via e-mail to

```
xjia@cti.depaul.edu
```

Contents

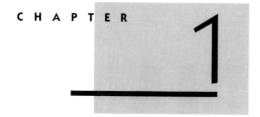

CHAPTER 1

Object-Oriented Software Development

CHAPTER OVERVIEW

In this chapter we provide an overview of object-oriented software. We start with a general discussion of software development and the desirable qualities of software products. Next, we discuss what makes software development difficult and the difference between software engineering and other, more established engineering practices. Then we introduce the basic principles, concepts, processes, and techniques of the object-oriented development approach. We also introduce a graphical notation for object-oriented analysis and modeling and conclude the chapter with a case study of object-oriented analysis and modeling.

The software industry was one of the most successful industries during the 1980s and 1990s. Not only was its growth in market value exponential, but it also was able to deliver technologically advanced and innovative products at an unrelenting pace. Today, computer software has become prevalent in every aspect of life. Societies are becoming more and more dependent on software systems, from autopilot systems of jetliners to computerized trading systems of stock markets to personal organizers on palm-top computers. However, software is expensive. The cost of purchasing, developing, maintaining, and upgrading software systems has become the largest single expenditure for many large corporations. This continuing cost contrasts sharply to the dramatic decrease in hardware costs and the equally dramatic increase in hardware performance and capacities. The object-oriented software development approach can significantly improve current software development practice, and the software industry has widely embraced it in recent years.

1.1 SOFTWARE DEVELOPMENT

The software industry has produced many technologically advanced, innovative, and successful products. However, the process of creating these successful products (i.e., software development) is a difficult, time-consuming, and costly endeavor. For example, the initial version of the Microsoft Windows NT operating system consisted of 6 million lines of code, cost $150 million to develop, and took 200 developers, testers, and technical writer 5 years to complete. The struggle to create Windows NT is vividly presented in *Show-Stopper* [Zachary 1994]. Furthermore, software systems tend to be "buggy"; that is, they contain glitches that hamper or even disrupt their performance. Minor glitches can be merely annoying, but serious glitches can be disastrous.

- On January 15, 1990, the AT&T long-distance telephone network broke down, interrupting nationwide long-distance telephone services in the United States for more than 8 hours. An ill-placed `break` statement in the switching software, written in the C language, was to blame for the breakdown.
- On June 4, 1996, the maiden flight of the new and improved Ariane 5 communication satellite launcher developed by the European Space Agency exploded 37 seconds after lift-off. An incorrectly handled software exception resulting from converting a 64-bit floating point to a 16-bit signed integer caused the disaster.

Although such catastrophic failures are rare, minor glitches are common in almost all software. In other words, buggy software is the norm. Despite the phenomenal success of the software industry in delivering technologically advanced and innovative software products, it still faces challenges in terms of complexity, longevity and evolution, and high user expectations.

The software systems being built are large and complex. Complexity is dictated by the problems the systems are intended to solve and the services they are intended to provide. Both requirements are beyond the control of software developers. The complexity involved in a large software system is so great that no individual can comprehend every detail of the system. To build such a complex system, it must be broken down into manageable parts and requires the cooperative efforts of a team of developers rather than the efforts of an individual. Methodologies, techniques, and tools that work well for small systems developed by individuals usually are not effective for large systems developed by teams.

Because of economic, political, and other constraints, software systems are often in service for very long periods of time. Today, some legacy systems have been operating for more than 20 years. During their lifetimes, software systems must constantly evolve to accommodate changes in users' needs and environments. However, making changes to software systems (i.e., maintenance) is a difficult task. The widely publicized Year 2000 (Y2K) problem shows the enormous magnitude of efforts required to accommodate the coming of the new Christian millennium with legacy software systems. Furthermore, maintenance is not only costly and time-consuming, but it also usually degrades the quality of the systems being maintained. On average, the maintenance cost of a software system over its lifetime is far more than its initial development cost.

In the past, the majority of software systems users had the technical skills to handle glitches they might encounter while using those systems. Today, the majority of software users are nontechnical, ordinary people. Computer software is viewed more and more as a consumer product and is expected to perform with the same dependability as household appliances. Occasional glitches that once were considered acceptable are now intolerable. Software systems are expected to be "bug-free," which is next to impossible.

1.1.1 An Engineering Perspective

The term *software engineering* was coined at a NATO workshop in 1968. It represented an aspiration to build the practice of software development on a solid scientific foundation and to attain the level of reliability and productivity associated with well-established engineering disciplines, such as civil and mechanical engineering. There is little consensus on the precise definition of *software engineering*, and even the legitimacy of using *software engineer* as a professional title is still being debated. As Shaw and Garlan pointed out, software engineering is a label that

> refers to a collection of management processes, software tooling, and design activities for software development. The resulting practice, however, differs significantly from the practice of older forms of engineering [Shaw and Garlan 1996].

A close examination of traditional, well-established engineering disciplines reveals that several essential characteristics of those practices are absent in today's software development practice.

Analysis of Designs

Over the centuries, craftsmanship clearly has proved capable of building magnificent structures, such as the Egyptian pyramids, Roman aqueducts, and Notre Dame Cathedral. However, modern engineering offers assurance, predictability, and efficiency that craftsmanship cannot match. One of the key differences between engineering and craftsmanship is that the success of engineering projects can be assured beforehand through scientific analysis of their designs, whereas the success of craftsmanship projects is attained through trial and error during current and prior construction.

Civil engineers depend on mechanics to help them predict with confidence before construction begins that a newly designed bridge or building will stand and function as it is supposed to. Aerospace engineers depend on aerodynamics and simulation to help them predict with confidence before it is built that a newly designed airplane will fly.

In contrast, software developers largely depend on testing and debugging (i.e., trial and error) to establish confidence in their products. Software development is like building modern skyscrapers with craftsmanship, with the success of software development projects rarely assured beforehand.

Nonrecurrence of Failures

Failures, sometimes catastrophic, also occur in well-established engineering fields. Perhaps one of the most spectacular failures in the history of engineering was the collapse of the Tacoma Narrows Bridge in 1940. The design of the bridge was unconventional and innovative and was dramatic and elegant in appearance. Careful analysis was performed to ensure that the bridge would behave well under its own weight with anticipated traffic loads and winds as high as 45 miles per hour. However, the designer did not foresee that the slender bridge deck would act like an airplane wing in a moderate crosswind of less than 40 miles per hour, which twisted the bridge apart. As soon as the cause of the collapse was known, measures were developed to prevent such failures in the future. Hence in well-established engineering fields, the same type of failure is rarely repeated.

In software development, the same types of failures recur all the time. Few practical measures can be taken to ensure the absence of certain types of faults in software systems. The sad truth about software development is that no one can ensure that the type of failure that occurred in Ariane 5 will never occur again.

Codification of Knowledge

The success of well-established engineering fields is due largely to the accumulation and codification of knowledge and the reuse of prior solutions. Design knowledge and solutions often are organized and presented in manuals and handbooks to make common and routine design not only easier and faster, but also more reliable, dependable, and manageable. Designers often find solutions in handbooks and then adapt and assemble these solutions to their specific design problems. Only rarely are original and innovative solutions needed. Usually, the codified knowledge includes what to avoid as well as what to do.

In software development, although a lot of design knowledge and experience has been accumulated, very little has been systematically codified. Without the benefit of prior design solutions, each design of a software system is treated as an original. Therefore it is no surprise that software design is difficult, time-consuming, and unreliable.

Thus software development is quite different from the traditional engineering disciplines. At most, it is an immature engineering discipline. For software development to become a true engineering discipline, software developers must have mechanisms to carry out the analysis of designs, ensure nonrecurrence of known failures, and codify design knowledge.

1.1.2   Desirable Qualities of Software Systems

Let's now turn our attention to the products of software development—software systems. The following are the most desirable qualities of software systems.

Usefulness: Software systems should adequately address the needs of their intended users in solving problems and providing services.

Timeliness: Software systems should be completed and shipped in a timely manner. Otherwise, they may be less useful or even useless owing to changes in users' needs and operating environments. This factor is also important in the software maker's ability to remain competitive.

Reliability: Software systems should perform as expected by users in terms of the correctness of the functions being performed, the availability of services, and an acceptable level of failures.

Maintainability: Software systems should be easily maintained, that is, making corrections, adaptations, and extensions without undue costs.

Reusability: Components of software systems should not be designed as ad hoc solutions to specific problems in specific contexts; rather they should be designed as *general* solutions to a class of problems in different contexts. Such general components can be *adapted* and *reused* many times.

User Friendliness: Software systems should provide user-friendly interfaces tailored to the capabilities and the background of the intended users to facilitate easy use and access to the full extent of the systems' capabilities.

Efficiency: Software systems should not make wasteful use of system resources, including processing time, memory, and disk space.

Not all of these desirable qualities are attainable at the same time, nor are they of equal importance. A crucial part of software development is to deal with the trade-offs among these different qualities to achieve a reasonable balance. Obviously, the object-oriented development approach cannot directly improve all of these qualities. It focuses primarily on improving the maintainability and reusability of software systems. Maintainability should be the focus of the development process for three main reasons. First, for software systems with long lifetimes, maintenance costs will far exceed initial development costs. It is imprudent to compromise maintainability because any savings that may result initially will undoubtedly be dwarfed by maintenance cost penalties over the long run. Second, current development technology doesn't yield high reliability in the initial release of software systems. Reliability is usually attained through repeated corrections during the development phase and throughout the lifetimes of software systems. Software system reliability can be severely hampered by poor maintainability. Third, high maintainability requires flexibility in the design and implementation of software systems. Such flexibility facilitates the kind of incremental development that enhances reliability, usefulness, and user friendliness, as well as the ability to contain costs.

Several factors contribute to the maintainability of software systems.

Flexibility: Flexibility means that various aspects of software systems should be easily changeable. The correctness of the changes can be verified locally, and the impact of the changes can be confined to small regions.

Simplicity: Human beings are fallible. It is impossible for people to avoid making mistakes. However, when things are simple, people are much less error-prone, and making sure that things are working properly is much easier. If there are errors, they become more obvious and correcting them is easier. Complex software systems can be simplified by the effective use of the divide-and-conquer technique.

Readability: A prerequisite for maintainability is readability, or
understandability, because software systems must be understood before
they can be modified. Readability depends on the clarity and the simplicity
of the design and the program code, the clarity and completeness of the
accompanying documentation, and a simple and consistent style of design,
implementation, and documentation.

These factors are the focus of our discussion of many methods and techniques in later
chapters.

1.2   REAL-WORLD SOLUTIONS

The main goal of software development is to build software systems that provide
services to people and enhance their abilities to solve problems in the real world. A
software system usually consists of two essential components: a *model*, which is a
representation of a pertinent part of the real world; and an *algorithm*, which captures
the computations involved in manipulating or processing the model.

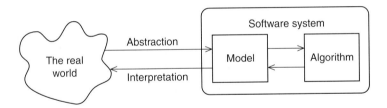

The real world is enormous and complex. Many of its aspects are fuzzy, un-
known, or intangible. In contrast, the models in software systems must be precise
and relatively small. A model is necessarily an *abstraction* of the real world. It captures only the essential and relevant characteristics of the real world from a particular
perspective and ignores others. Models are intended to be manipulated or processed,
and their behaviors should mimic those of the real world to reflect the chosen perspectives reasonably accurately. The results of manipulations can be fed back to the
real world through *interpretation* (i.e., the assignment of meanings to the entities in
the models) and often represent solutions to real-world problems.

Programming languages are the main tools used by software developers to describe computer models. The evolution of programming languages and programming
methodologies is driven by the need to build more and more sophisticated and effective models. That need in turn is driven by the ever-increasing power of modern
computers and the desire to utilize this power.

One of the fundamental problems in software development is: *How does someone
model the real world?* The answer largely depends on the problems to be solved.
One way to look at the evolution of software development methodologies is through
the changing views of computer models.

In the 1950s and 1960s, the focus of software systems developers was on the algorithm. As a result, the main concerns at that time were solving computation problems, designing efficient algorithms, and controlling the complexity of *computation*. The models used were computation-oriented models, and the decomposition of complex systems was primarily based on *control flow*.

In the 1970s and 1980s, different types of software systems emerged to address the complexity of the *data* being processed. These systems were centered on data entities and data flows, with computation becoming a secondary concern. The models used were data-oriented models, and the decomposition of complex systems was primarily based on *data flow*.

Object-oriented models represent a balanced view of the data and computation aspects of software systems. Object-oriented models are composed of *objects*, which contain data and make computations. The decomposition of complex systems is based on the structure of objects, classes, and the relationships among them.

The origin of object-oriented software development dates back to late 1960s. A computer simulation language called Simula was the first programming language that included some important features of object-oriented programming, such as class. The first full-blown and perhaps the best known object-oriented programming language was Smalltalk developed by Xerox PARC in the 1970s. Object-oriented technology grew tremendously during the 1980s, with the emergence of several more sophisticated object-oriented programming languages, including C++, Objective-C, and Eiffel. It also evolved from a programming methodology to a software development methodology that addresses the analysis, design, testing, and debugging phases of software development in addition to the implementation phase. Despite its long history of development, only recently has the object-oriented development approach matured and become widely accepted by the mainstream software industry. This acceptance is largely due to recent advances in object-oriented programming languages, object-oriented analysis and modeling notations, and frameworks and design patterns.

The object-oriented software development approach represents a dramatic departure from conventional software development approaches. It looks at the world from a rather different perspective.

1.3   PRINCIPLES AND CONCEPTS

In this section, we discuss the basic concepts and the principles of object-oriented development. We also introduce a graphical notation for describing object-oriented analysis and design models, which is based on the *Unified Modeling Language* (UML) [Grady, Booch and Jacobson 1999].[1] We use a subset of UML notations, with minor adaptations in syntax for consistency with Java.

---

[1] UML is a proposed standard for object-oriented modeling notations currently under consideration by the Object Management Group (OMG), an industrial consortium on object technologies.

1.3.1 Classes and Objects

Definitions

Objects and *classes* are two of the fundamental concepts in object-oriented development. Objects and classes have two different aspects: their *representation* in the object-oriented model and their *interpretation* in the real world. The representation of objects and classes dealt with in the object-oriented model (including programs) is only an approximation of the objects and classes in the real world. We define objects and classes in terms of how they are interpreted in the real world and their representation in the model.

	Interpretation in the real world	Representation in the model
Object	An *object* represents anything in the real world that can be distinctly identified.	An *object* has a unique identity, a state, and behaviors.
Class	A *class* represents a set of objects with similar characteristics and behavior. These objects are called the *instances* of the class.	A *class* characterizes the structure of states and behaviors that are shared by all its instances.

The state of an object is composed of a set of *fields*, or *attributes*, and their current values. The behavior of an object is defined by a set of *methods*, which may access or manipulate the state. The *features* of an object refer to the combination of the state and the behavior of the object.

A class serves as a template for creating its instances. Instead of defining the features of individual objects, common practice is to define the features of the classes to which these objects belong. The terms *object* and *instance* are often interchangeable. *Methods* are sometimes called *operations*, and we consider these two terms to be synonymous.

Let's look at a simple class `Point` that represents points in a two-dimensional space. The Java code defining the class is shown on the right-hand side.

		```class Point {```
Class name	Point	`    int x, y;`
Attributes	x, y	`    public void move(int dx, int dy) {`
		`        // ...`
Method	move	`    }`
		`}`

Graphical Notations

The graphical notation for classes is a rectangular box with as many as three compartments.

ClassName
field₁
...
fieldₙ
method₁
...
methodₘ

The top compartment shows the class name.

The middle compartment contains a list of the fields of the class.

The bottom compartment contains a list of the methods of the class.

Several variations of this graphical notation are used to show different levels of detail.

- The middle compartment, the bottom compartment, or both the bottom and the middle compartments can be omitted.
- The fields can be described with the following syntax:[2]

  [*Visibility*] [*Type*] *Identifier* [**=** *InitialValue*]

- The methods can be shown with the following syntax:

  [*Visibility*] [*Type*] *Identifier* **(** [*ParameterList*] **)**

The visibility, or accessibility, of fields and methods can be *public*, *protected*, *private*, or *package*. We discuss the visibility of attributes and methods in Section 3.4.1 [p. 70]. The following are some examples.

Fields
```
Date birthday
public int duration = 100
```
Methods
```
void move(int dx, int dy)
public int getSize()
```

The `Point` class shown earlier can be represented graphically as follows, at different levels of detail.

Point
int x
int y
public void move(int dx, int dy)

Point
x
y
move

Point

The graphical notation for objects is a rectangular box with either one or two compartments.

---

[2] The notation *Foo* (e.g., *Type*) denotes a nonterminal symbol. Terminal symbols are shown in boldface **Courier** font (e.g., **=**). The entities between [ ] (e.g., [*Type*]) are optional.

```
┌─────────────────────────────┐
│   objectName : ClassName    │
├─────────────────────────────┤
│       field₁ = value₁       │
│            . . .            │
│       fieldₙ = valueₙ       │
└─────────────────────────────┘
```

The top compartment shows the name of the object and its class. The object and class names are underlined to distinguish object notation from class notation.

The bottom compartment contains a list of the fields and their values.

Variations in syntax for the top compartment include:

- objectName
  Omission of the colon and the class name denotes an object named objectName whose class is of no interest.

- : ClassName
  Omission of the object name denotes an anonymous object of class ClassName, which can be identified only through its relationship with other objects.

The fields and their values in the bottom compartment are described with the following syntax:

$$[\ Type\ ]\ Field = Value$$

The bottom compartment may be omitted altogether if the attributes and values of an object are of no interest.

For example, instances of the Point class, with fields (0, 0) and (24, 40), can be represented graphically as follows.

```
┌─────────────────┐   ┌─────────────────┐       Point p1 = new Point( );
│   p1 : Point    │   │   p2 : Point    │       p1.x = 0;
├─────────────────┤   ├─────────────────┤       p1.y = 0;
│     x = 0       │   │     x = 24      │       Point p2 = new Point( );
│     y = 0       │   │     y = 40      │       p2.x = 24;
└─────────────────┘   └─────────────────┘       p2.y = 40;
```

Message Passing

Objects communicate with one another via *message passing*. A message represents a command sent to an object—known as the *recipient* (also known as the *receiving object* or the *receiver*) of the message—to perform a certain action by invoking one of the methods of the recipient. A *message* consists of the receiving object, the method to be invoked, and (optionally) the arguments to the method. Message passing is also known as *method invocation*. The following is a message to instruct the recipient, point p1, to move 10 units and 20 units in the *x* and *y* direction, respectively, by invoking the method move.

	Recipient	p1
p1.move(10, 20)	Method	move
	Arguments	10, 20

1.3.2 Modularity

One of the fundamental principles of the object-oriented approach is the principle of modularity. It is intended to control the complexity of large-scale systems through the use of the divide-and-conquer technique.

Principle *Modularity*

A complex system should be decomposed into a set of highly cohesive but loosely coupled *modules*.

Decomposition of complex software systems into modules is one of the most intriguing tasks in software development and is more an art than a science. The reason is that most of the entities in a software system are intricately interconnected like a web and must be untangled. The basic criteria for decomposition are two of the best known and most elusive concepts in software development—cohesion and coupling.

- *Cohesion* refers to the functional relatedness of the entities within a module.
- *Coupling* refers to the interdependency among different modules.

A system may be extremely complex in its totality, but a *modular decomposition* of the system aims to break it down into modules so that

- each module is relatively small and simple (i.e., highly cohesive) and
- the interactions among modules are relatively simple (i.e., loosely coupled), ensuring that—by examining the module *within*, not *without*—each module will be well-behaved and that, if all the modules are well-behaved, the entire system also will be well-behaved.

Typically, modular decompositions are hierarchical (i.e., a module may contain other modules).

The concepts of modules, cohesion, and coupling all predate the object-oriented approach. The forms of modules have evolved over time. In the structured development approach, the modules take the form of routines and functions. In the object-oriented approach, modules take the form of classes and packages.[3]

1.3.3 Abstraction and Encapsulation

Abstraction and encapsulation are powerful tools for deriving modular decompositions of systems.

---

[3] Packages are mechanisms for grouping classes (see Section 3.5 [p. 99]).

Abstraction

In its purest sense, *abstraction* means to separate the essential from the nonessential characteristics of an entity. The result is a simpler but sufficiently accurate approximation of the original entity, obtained by removing or ignoring the nonessential characteristics. The abstraction principle in software development can be described in the following manner.

Principle *Abstraction*

The behaviors, or functionalities, of a module should be characterized in a succinct and precise description known as the *contractual interface* of the module. In other words, the contractual interface captures the essence of the behavior of the module. The contractual interface is an abstraction of the module.

We can view a module as a *service provider* and other modules that use the services provided by the module as *clients* of the module. We can view the contractual interface as the *service contract* between the service provider and its clients. A service contract need only describe *what* services can be provided, not *how* the services are to be provided. Therefore, despite the fact that the services to be provided are very complex, the service contract may be very simple. With a simple service contract and an assurance by the service provider of honoring the contract, the clients need only understand the simple contract in order to use the complex services. The contractual interface allows the clients to use the services and not be concerned with the complexity of the services. In other words, the complexity of the module is hidden within it.

Let's consider the example of the telephone. The mechanism for providing telephone service is a rather complex one. It involves routing and connecting calls, converting voice to electronic signals and back to voice, transmitting the signals in analog or digital mode, and possibly encrypting and decrypting the signals for security reasons. However, telephone users (i.e., the clients of a telephone service) don't need to understand the mechanics of a phone system. All the users need to understand is the manual that comes with the telephone set, which includes instructions on dialing, speaking, and hanging up. The user's manual in this case is the contractual interface of the telephone service, and it serves as an abstraction of the telephone service from the user's perspective.

Encapsulation

A closely related and complementary principle is *encapsulation*, which stipulates that the clients need know nothing more than the service contract while using the service.

Principle *Encapsulation*

The implementation of a module should be separated from its contractual interface and hidden from the clients of the module.

Hence this principle is also known as *information hiding*. Encapsulation is intended to reduce coupling among modules. The less the clients know about the implementation of the module, the looser the coupling between the module and its clients can be. An important benefit of encapsulation is that, if the clients know nothing beyond the contractual interface, implementation can be modified without affecting the clients, so long as the contractual interface remains the same.

Telephone service is a good example of an application in which the contractual interface and implementation are separated. In the past, signals were transmitted in analog mode. Over time, telephone service has been upgraded until, nowadays, the signals can be transmitted in digital mode with encryption. Although the implementation of telephone service has changed, the contractual interface remains the same. The only effects on telephone users are that they enjoy better sound quality and greater security.

Interface

If a contractual interface is completely separated from implementation, the contractual interface can exist on its own. A contractual interface without any implementation associated with it is known as an *abstract data type* or *interface* in Java terminology. A module can be represented by two separate entities: an *interface* that describes the contractual interface of the module and a *class* that implements the contractual interface.

The graphical notation for interfaces is the same as the graphical notation for classes, except that the names of interfaces and their methods are italicized. The *implementation* relationship between interfaces and classes is represented by a dashed link from the class to the interface, with a hollow triangle pointing toward the interface.

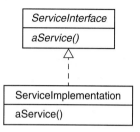

Polymorphism

Several different service providers can honor the contractual interface. Moreover, these service providers can be interchanged without affecting the clients. The ability to interchange modules dynamically without affecting the clients is known as *poly-morphism.*[4]

Let's take the telephone service example one step further and consider cellular telephone service. Digital cellular service uses more advanced technologies but has smaller service regions than does the more established analog cellular service. The dual-model analog/digital cellular phone is an example of polymorphism. It provides a single contractual interface for using the phone but employs two different technologies to provide the service. Users need not be concerned with—and certainly are not affected by—which technology is used to provide the service at any given moment. The dual-mode cellular phone dynamically switches (a *soft switch*) between the digital and analog modes as the user crosses the boundary of the digital/analog service regions. We discuss polymorphism in more detail in Section 4.2.2 [p. 124].

Style Convention   *Class and Object Names*

Class and interface names should begin with uppercase letters, as in `Point`. Attribute and method names should begin with lowercase letters, as in `point`. If a name consists of multiple words, it is formed by concatenating the words and capitalizing each word except the first, as in

- a long class name, `CheckBoxMenuItem`, and

- a long object name, `printOptionMenu`.

In class diagrams, the regular class, field, and method names are shown in roman fonts, as in `MyClass`. The names for abstract classes, interfaces, and abstract methods are shown in italic fonts, as in *`MyInterface`*.

1.3.4   Inheritance

Inheritance defines a relationship among classes. When class C2 *inherits* from, or *extends*, class C1, class C2 is known as a *subclass* or an *extended class* of class C1, and class C1 is known as a *superclass* of C2. The graphical notation for inheritance is a solid link from the subclass to the superclass with a hollow triangle pointing toward the superclass as shown in Figure 1.1.

Conceptually, inheritance models the *is-a(n)* relationship in the real world; that is, if C2 is a subclass of C1, then every instance of C2 *is an* instance of C1, and everything that applies to instances of C1 also applies to instances of C2.

---

[4] The word *polymorphism* means an entity with multiple forms. In this particular context, it refers to a contractual interface with multiple interchangeable implementations.

Figure 1.1

Inheritance
relationship.

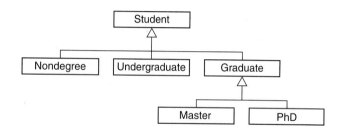

Inheritance allows the implementation (i.e., the fields and methods) of a super-class to be *shared* or *reused* by its subclasses. For example, consider the classes that represent different students groups in a university, as shown in Figure 1.1.

Class	Description
Student	Students in general
Graduate	Graduate students
Undergraduate	Undergraduate students
Nondegree	Nondegree students

The `Graduate` class is a subclass of `Student`, as every graduate student *is a* student, and everything that applies to a student also applies to a graduate student. Other inheritance relationships are determined similarly.

A class can inherit from multiple superclasses, often referred to as *multiple inheritance*. However, many object-oriented programming languages, including Java, support only a restricted form of inheritance known as *single inheritance*, in which each class may inherit from only one superclass. The implementation relationship between classes and interfaces can also be considered as a special form of inheritance. Java supports a limited form of multiple inheritance by allowing classes to implement multiple interfaces. We discuss issues related to single and multiple inheritance in Section 4.3 [p. 135].

Classes and interfaces represent abstractions and the inheritance relationship organizes the classes and interfaces into different levels of abstractions.

Principle *Levels of Abstraction*

Abstractions can be ordered into different levels. The higher the level, the more general the abstraction is. The lower the level, the more specialized the abstraction is.

Figure 1.2

Association
relationship.

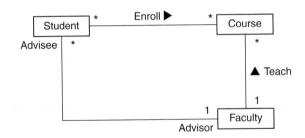

In other words, the superclasses represent more general abstractions and the subclasses represent more specialized abstractions. Consider again the example of students shown in Figure 1.1. The inheritance hierarchy shows different levels of abstractions of students in a university. The Student class represents the most general abstraction of students, whereas its subclasses represent various specialized abstractions of students. The leaf classes (i.e., classes with no subclasses) represent the most specialized abstractions of students.

1.3.5 Association

Associations represent general binary relationships among classes. The graphical notation for association is simply a solid line between the two classes involved with optional adornments attached to either end. Figure 1.2 shows several associations among the Student, Faculty, and Course classes.

Each association may have an optional label that describes it. In Figure 1.2, *teach* and *enroll* are the labels of the association between Faculty and Course, and between Student and Course, respectively. The direction arrows next to the labels simply indicate that "a student enrolls in a course," not that "a course enrolls in a student."

Each class involved in an association may also have a role name associated with it. In Figure 1.2, *advisor* and *advisee* are the role names associated with Faculty and Student, respectively, in the association between Faculty and Student.

Each class involved in an association may also have a multiplicity specification associated with it. The multiplicity specification consists of a comma-separated sequence of integer intervals. An integer interval can be one of the following:

l . . u   *l* is the lower bound, and *u* is the upper bound. Both the lower bound and upper bound are integer literals, specifying a closed range of integers. The upper bound may also be the asterisk character (*), which indicates an unlimited upper bound.

i   *i* is an integer literal, specifying an integer range that contains a single integer.

*   * specifies the entire nonnegative integer range: 0, 1, 2, 3, . . .

Here are some examples of multiplicity specifications:

0 .. *	0 or more
1 .. *	1 or more
2 .. 5	2 to 5
2, 5, 7	2, 5, and 7
1, 3, 5 .. *	1, 3, and 5 or more

In Figure 1.2, the *enroll* association is many-to-many; that is, a student may enroll in any number of courses, and a course may have any number of students enrolled in it. The *teach* association is one-to-many; that is, each course has only one faculty member to teach it, but a faculty member may teach any number of courses. The *advisor–advisee* association is also one-to-many; that is, each student has one advisor, but an advisor may have any number of advisees.

Aggregation

Aggregation is a special form of association. It represents the *has-a* or *part-of* relationship. A stronger form of aggregation is called *composition*, which implies exclusive ownership of the component class by the aggregate class. Graphically, aggregation is indicated by a diamond, called the *aggregation indicator*, attached to the end of the aggregate class. A filled diamond indicates the composition relationship. The aggregation indicator may not appear at both ends of an aggregation.

Figure 1.3 shows the aggregation relationships among the `Department`, `Faculty`, and `Student` classes. Both the *chairman of* and *member of* relations are of type composition because a faculty member can be the chairman of only one department and a faculty member can belong to only one department. In contrast, a department has students, but students do not necessarily belong to just one department. The graphical notations for various relationships among classes and interfaces are summarized in Figure 1.4.

1.3.6 Modeling Dynamic Behavior

Class diagrams describe the *static* relationships among classes. However, another important aspect of software systems—*dynamic behavior*—involves the interactions

Figure 1.3

Aggregation relationship.

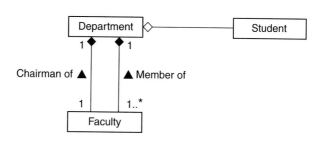

Figure 1.4

Graphical notations for relationships among classes and interfaces.

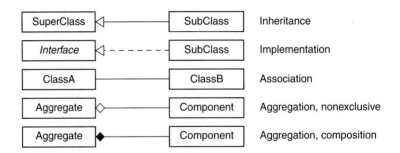

Figure 1.4

Graphical notations for relationships among classes and interfaces.

among objects and the ordering of events and actions related to the object. In this section, we discuss two popular graphical notations for modeling the dynamic behavior of software systems: the sequence diagram and the statechart.

Sequence Diagrams

Sequence diagrams depict object interaction by highlighting the time ordering of method invocations. The objects that participate in the interaction are represented by columns in a sequence diagram. The object that initiates the interaction is usually placed in the leftmost column, with increasingly subordinate objects shown on the right. A vertical dashed line shows the lifeline of an object. The horizontal arrows indicate the invocation and return of methods. Method invocations are arranged in ascending time order vertically. A tall, thin rectangular box depicts the time period during which an object executes a method. The sequence diagram shown in Figure 1.5 depicts the flow of execution when a client issues a request to print a document. It indicates the following sequence of method invocation.

Figure 1.5

A sequence diagram.

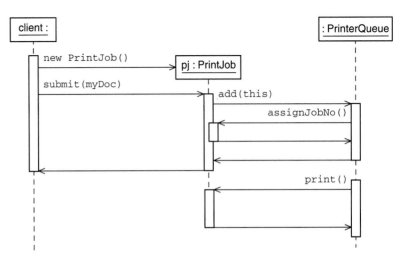

1. An object `client` creates an instance of `PrintJob`.
2. The object `client` invokes the `submit()` method of `PrintJob` to print a documentation (`myDoc`).
3. The `PrintJob` object adds itself to a queue, which is an instance of `PrinterQueue`.
4. The `PrinterQueue` object invokes the `assignJobNo()` method of `PrintJob` to assign a number to the new print job being added to the queue.
5. The `assignJobNo()` method returns.
6. The `add()` method returns.
7. The `submit()` method returns.
8. When the print job becomes the first in the printer queue, the `print()` method of `PrintJob` is invoked to print to document.
9. The `print()` method returns.

Statecharts

Statecharts depict the flow of control, using the concepts of *states* and *transitions*. Statecharts are generalizations of the traditional *finite state machines* (FSM). A *state* is a condition or situation in the life of an object during which it satisfies some condition, performs some actions, or waits for some events. A *transition* is a relationship between two states indicating that an object in the first state (the source state) will perform certain actions and enter the second state (the destination state) when a specified event occurs and certain conditions are satisfied. An *event* is an occurance of a stimulus that can trigger a state transition. Each transition may have one or more events attached to it that will trigger the transition. When no event is attached to a transition, the transition is triggered without an event. Optionally, conditions, known as *guards*, can also be attached to transitions. An *entry action* and an *exit action* may be attached to each state.

In statecharts, states can be composite, or *hyperstates*. A hyperstate contains a nested statechart. If a transition enters a hyperstate, it enters the initial state of the enclosed statechart. If a transition originates from a hyperstate, the transition may originate from any of the states enclosed in the hyperstate.

Graphically, states are drawn as round-cornered rectangles. A filled small circle represents an initial state. Transitions are shown as links (arrows) between states. Transitions can be labeled with events and optional conditions. Conditions are represented as Boolean expressions and are placed inside brackets ([ ]).

The life of an object begins in a designated *initial state*. It follows a series of transitions to reach various states. The life of the object ends when it reaches a *final state*. The following are rules for the state transitions.

■ If an unlabeled transition originates from the current state, the transition is triggered and the object enters the destination state of the unlabeled transition.

■ Otherwise, the object waits for some events to occur. When an event ocurrs, if a transition originates from the current state, the event that occurred matches one of the events attached to the transition, and if the conditions attached to the

Figure 1.6

A statechart.

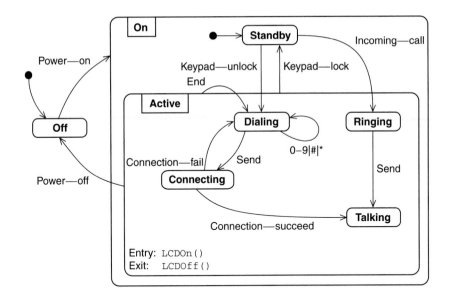

transition are all satisfied, the transition is triggered and the object enters the destination state of the transition. Otherwise, the object remains in the current state.

When the object enters a state, the entry action attached to the state, if any, is performed. When the object leaves a state, the exit action attached to the state, if any, is performed.

Figure 1.6 is a statechart describing the operation of a cellular phone. Operation starts in the initial state, which leads to the Off state. The *Power—on* event triggers a transition that leads to the On state. As the On state is a hyperstate, the cellular phone enters the initial state of the statechart enclosed in the On state, which leads to the Standby state. The transition labeled *Power—off* originates from another hyperstate Active. Hence this transition may originate from any of the states inside the Active state. Note that the Active state has both entry and exit actions attached to it. Thus, whenever the cellular phone enters the Active state, the LCDOn() method (i.e., the entry action) is invoked to turn on the LCD screen and that whenever the cellular phone leaves the Active state, the LCDOff() method (i.e., the exit action) is invoked to turn off the LCD screen. The statechart inside the Active state depicts the flow of both making a call and receiving a call. To make a call requires the following sequence of events.

- From the Standby state, unlock the pad (the *Keypad—Unlock* event) to enter the Dialing state in Active.
- In the Dialing state, dial the phone number by using the number keys (0–9) or # or *, and the cellular phone remains in the Dialing state.
- From the Dialing state, push the send key (the *Send* event) to enter the Connecting state.

- From the Connecting state, if the connection succeeds (the *Connection—succeed* event), the cellular phone enters the Talking state. If the connection fails (the *Connection—fail* event), the cellular phone returns to the Dialing state.

To receive a call requires following the sequence of events.

- From the Standby state, an incoming call (the *Incoming—call* event) triggers a transition that leads to the Ringing state in Active.
- From the Ringing state, push the send key (the *Send* event) to enter the Talking state.

Note that the transition labeled *End* originates from the hyperstate Active. Hence from any state in the Active state, pushing the end key (the *End* event) triggers this transition and the cellular phone enters the Dialing state. Similarly, from any state in the Active state, locking the keypad (the *Keypad—lock* event) triggers the transition labeled *Keypad—lock*, which leads to the Standby state.

1.4 OBJECT-ORIENTED DEVELOPMENT

In this section, we first discuss the micro and macro processes of object-oriented software development. Then we present a case study to illustrate these processes.

1.4.1 The Micro and Macro Processes

In contrast to the traditional waterfall software life-cycle model, Booch [Booch 1994] suggests that the object-oriented software development process should be *iterative*. That is, a development process should consist of successive iterations to identify the classes, identify the semantics (i.e., attributes and behaviors) of the classes, identify the relationships among the classes, and define the class interface and then implement the classes. Each iteration deals with relatively small increments of the system being developed. Thus the system is developed incrementally, not as a monolithic piece, and the iterative process continues until the entire system is complete. This approach is known as the *micro* process.

Booch also suggests a *macro* process that serves as the "controlling framework of the micro process." The macro process consists of the following phases.

Conceptualization: The goal of the conceptualization phase is to establish the vision and the core requirements of the software system to be developed.

Analysis and Modeling: The goal of the analysis and modeling phase is to build a model of the system's desired behavior. The model is intended to capture the essential relevant aspects of the real world and to define the services to be provided and/or the problems to be solved.

Design: The goal of the design phase is to create an architecture for implementation. Designs are represented in terms of objects and classes and the relationships among them. Key concerns of an object-oriented design include: (a) Does the design satisfy all the stated requirements and constraints and provide all the desired services adequately? (b) Is the design flexible enough to accommodate future changes and enhancement? and (c) Is the design feasible for implementation and, if so, can it be implemented efficiently?

Implementation: The goal of the implementation phase is to implement the design by using an object-oriented programming language, such as Java, through successive refinements. Implementation involves coding, testing, and debugging. Key concerns of object-oriented implementation include: (a) Is the implementation correct? (b) Is the implementation efficient and maintainable? and (c) Is the implementation robust, that is, capable of tolerating faults and recovering from failures?

Maintenance: The goal of the maintenance phase is to manage postdelivery evolution. The primary maintenance tasks include removing bugs, enhancing functionalities, and adapting the system to evolving needs and environments.

1.4.2 Case Study: An Online Bookstore

In this case study, we develop an object-oriented model for an *online bookstore* to illustrate some of the activities in the object-oriented development approach.

Conceptualization

The conceptualization phase is not intended to establish *complete* system requirements. Rather it is to establish the system's *vision* and *core* requirements. A prototype could be developed as a proof-of-concept demonstration and to validate important assumptions.

The core requirements of the online bookstore are to allow its customers to browse and order books, music CDs, and computer software through the internet. The main functionalities of the system are to provide information about the titles it carries to help customers make purchasing decisions; handle customer registration, order processing, and shipping; and support management of the system, such as adding, deleting, and updating titles, updating customer information, and the like.

This core requirements statement allows us to start the analysis phase. Many aspects of the requirements need to be elaborated upon and refined. We do so through several iterations.

Identifying Classes

The first step in the analysis phase is to identify the classes involved in the system. This step is one of the more perplexing tasks in object-oriented analysis and modeling. The questions are What can be a class? and What features (i.e., attributes and methods) should a class have?

The answers largely depend on the domain and the problem to be solved. The following are some simple guidelines. Classes represent entities, not actions, and can represent many different types of entities, including

- physical objects, such as equipment, devices, and products;
- people, such as students, faculty, and customers, and the roles they play;
- organizations, such as universities, companies, and departments;
- places, such as buildings, rooms, and seats;
- events, such as mouse clicks, service requests, and purchase orders; and
- concepts, such as multidimensional spaces, transactions, and weather maps.

Actions should be modeled as the methods of classes. A simple rule is that class names should be noun phrases and that method names should be verb phrases.

Only the classes and features of classes that are relevant to the problem to be solved need be included in the model. One of the most straightforward methods of identifying classes is known as the *noun–verb analysis of requirements*:

> Describe the requirements of the system in a natural language, such as English. Then underline the verbs and nouns in the natural language description of the requirements. The nouns are the candidates for classes or attributes, and the verbs are the candidates for methods.

By simply identifying the nouns in the core requirements of the online bookstore, we can at least identify the following classes.

Class	Description
OnLineBookstore	The entire system
Customer	Customers
Book	Books
MusicCD	Music CDs
Software	Computer software

Another useful technique in identifying classes is called *scenario analysis*. A scenario is a view of the system from the user's perspective, including an event sequence of the interaction between the user and the system. A scenario can be represented in a two-column table, in which the left-hand column describes the user's actions and the right-hand column describes the system's response. A typical scenario for a registered customer of the online book store can be described as follows.

User action	System response
Logon	Display a welcome message and request customer ID and password
Enter customer ID and password	Validate customer ID and password; validation succeeds

Repeat the following until done:
    Search and browse titles
    Select a title to buy
	Show information about the titles
	Add to the shopping cart

Done with shopping	Display shopping cart contents and shipping and billing addresses
Confirm order and payment method	Process order, issue a electronic receipt, and notify warehouse for shipping
Logoff	

Additional information and details are often generated through scenario analysis, and the information and details often lead to additional class-related behaviors.

By analyzing the preceding scenario, we can identify additional classes.

Class	Description
ShoppingCart	A temporary list of titles that a customer intends to buy
Order	An order by a customer
Address	Customer's address

Identifying the Semantics of Classes

In this phase, for each class that we have identified, we try to identify all the relevant attributes and the behaviors. For example, for the online bookstore, let's start with the Customer classes. We identify the attributes by analyzing the requirements and the scenarios to find the relevant attributes associated with customers.

```
Customer
name
customerID
password
shippingAddress
billingAddress
```

The list is incomplete, but it is a start. As we go through more iterations, attributes that belong to the Customer class should become clear. The attributes shipping-

Address and billingAddress in Customer are both instances of the Address class. To identify the attributes of the Address class, we simply rely on common sense and knowledge of actual forms of addresses.

Address
street
city
state
country
postalCode

Now, let's move on to books, music CDs, and computer software.

Book
title
author
publisher
yearPublished
edition
volume
ISBN
price

MusicCD
title
artist
publisher
yearPublished
volume
ISBN
price

Software
title
publisher
yearPublished
version
ISBN
price

Obviously, some attributes are common to all three classes. The commonalities are not coincidental because when calculating the total price of a mixed order of books, CDs, and software, each entity should be treated the same way. The three classes then should be subclasses of a common superclass, and the common attributes of the three classes should belong to their common superclass. Thus another way of identifying classes is by identifying commonalities among existing classes and extracting the commonalities to a common superclass. The following are the revised classes after extracting the common attributes to the Item superclass.

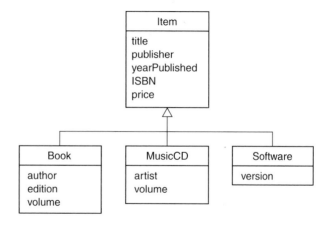

Identifying Relationships Among Classes

Now, let's consider the `ShoppingCart` class, which seems simply to contain a set of items. However, some customers might want to order multiple copies of the same items. A shopping cart therefore should be allowed to contain multiple copies of the same items. Thus an auxiliary class `ItemOrder` is needed. Each instance of the `ItemOrder` class includes the item and quantity ordered, and an instance of the `ShoppingCart` class contains a set of instances of `ItemOrder`.

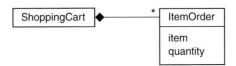

Each instance of the `Order` class also has a set of instances of `ItemOrder`.

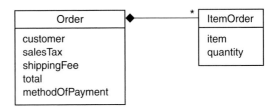

Now, let's consider the main class `OnLineBookStore`, which represents the entire system. Obviously, the system has to keep records of a variety of things, including all the items on sale, all the customers, and all the orders that have been placed. The relationships among the classes identified so far are shown in the following diagram.

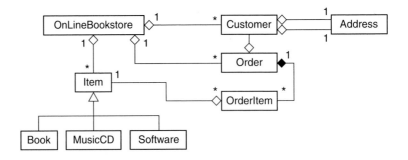

This step completes the *initial* version of the analysis model of the online bookstore. An initial model captures the most important and obvious aspects of the system but often is rather incomplete. Several iterations usually are necessary to derive a complete analysis model. A useful technique for deriving complete analysis models is the use of *class/responsibility/collaborator* (CRC) *cards*. A CRC card is simply a 3 × 5 inch index card on which a class, its responsibilities, and its collaborators are described. The idea is to enumerate and analyze all the scenarios, assign responsibilities to classes, and identify the collaborators of each class. This approach usually leads to identifying new responsibilities for existing classes or identifying new classes. The process continues until all the responsibilities have been assigned and all the collaborators have been identified. CRC cards can also be spatially arranged to represent the patterns of collaboration.

In the online bookstore example, additional responsibilities and classes can be identified by analyzing additional scenarios, such as new customer logon and customer logoff without checking out, but saving the contents of the shopping cart; and by expanding the requirements for inventory management, order processing, and so on. We leave derivation of a more complete analysis model of the online bookstore to an exercise on your own.

CHAPTER SUMMARY

- Despite the phenomenal success of the software industry in delivering technologically advanced and innovative software products, the software development process remains a difficult, time-consuming, and costly endeavor. Challenges include finding ways of reducing the costs of both system development and maintenance and developing methods of minimizing, if not eliminating, software system bugs (i.e., glitches) that hamper or even disrupt the functioning of software.

- The main causes of problems in software development are complexity, longevity, evolution, and high user expectations.

- Software development lacks some key characteristics of well-established engineering disciplines, including analysis of designs, nonrecurrence of failures, and codification of knowledge. Software development is an immature field of engineering.

- The desirable qualities of software systems include usefulness, timeliness, reliability, maintainability, reusability, user friendliness, and efficiency. Of these qualities, maintainability is the most crucial and deserves the most attention during development. Factors contributing to maintainability include flexibility, simplicity, and readability. The object-oriented development approach focuses primarily on improving the maintainability and reusability of software systems.

- Object-oriented software development consists of analysis and modeling, design, and implementation.

- Object-oriented analysis and modeling involves describing the essential and relevant aspects of the problem domain and the problems to be solved in terms of objects, classes, and their relationships.

- The fundamental principles of object-oriented development are modularity, abstraction, encapsulation, and levels of abstraction. Their purpose is to reduce complexity and enhance flexibility.

- The basic criteria for decomposition are two well-known but elusive concepts in software development: cohesion and coupling. Cohesion refers to the functional relatedness of the entities within a module. Coupling indicates the interdependency among different modules.

- The important relationships among classes and interfaces include inheritance, implementation, association, aggregation, and composition.

- The micro process of object-oriented development includes the following phases: identifying classes, determining the semantics of these classes, identifying the relationships among classes, and defining the class interfaces and subsequent implementation of the classes. The macro process of object-oriented development serves as the controlling framework for the micro process. It includes the following phases: conceptualization, analysis and modeling, design, implementation, and maintenance.

EXERCISES

1.1. Develop an object-oriented model for an airline reservation system.

(a) Write a one-paragraph description of the system. Then underline all the nouns and verbs in your paragraph. Use the nouns to determine the classes and the verbs to determine the methods needed to implement this system.

(b) Develop a list of scenarios for the system. From these scenarios try to determine additional classes.

(c) Now that you have a list of classes for the system, identify a set of methods and attributes for each class.

(d) Describe how these classes relate to each other and illustrate the relationships among them with class diagrams.

2

Introduction to Java

CHAPTER OVERVIEW

In this chapter we discuss the key characteristics of Java and examine its architecture and execution model. We compare this architecture and execution model to the approaches used for other programming languages. We also discuss the use of Java in Web pages. We use two very simple programs, an app and an applet, to illustrate the basic structure of Java programs and use of the Java development tools and environment.

Java is an object-oriented programming language that was developed by a research team led by James Gosling at Sun Microsystems. Java is suitable for developing a wide range of applications, including graphical user interfaces (GUIs) and multimedia, network, database, and numerical applications. Java's popularity is due partly to the fact that it is largely based on proven technologies. Its key characteristics are that the language is:

- *Object-oriented.* Java is the most recent in a family of object-oriented programming languages. It not only supports object-oriented programming in the strongest sense, as does Smalltalk and Objective-C, but it also prohibits many "bad" programming styles and practices.

- *Distributed.* Java is designed for developing distributed applications, which consist of multiple autonomous programs residing on different computers, or hosts, in a computer network and cooperating with one another. It provides a variety of mechanisms to support communication and interoprability.

- *Platform independent.* The most unique characteristic of Java is that compiled Java programs can run on almost all platforms with functionally identical behavior. This capability makes Java an ideal choice for operating in heterogeneous networks, such as the Internet, and eliminates the need for porting programs to different platforms.

From the software engineering perspective, Java is a superior programming language because it supports many features that facilitate the development of large-scale and reliable software systems. These include strong type checking, packages, exception handling, and garbage collection. These features make software development with Java much more manageable than with other languages.

2.1 THE ARCHITECTURE OF JAVA

Java is designed for distributed computing in a heterogeneous network environment, such as the Internet and the World Wide Web. The primary goals of Java's architecture design are platform independence, security, and efficiency.

2.1.1 Platforms

The Internet is a heterogeneous, open, and self-organizing anarchy. It consists of a vast number of computers with different CPUs running different operating systems. The combination of the CPU and operating system of a computer is referred to as the *platform* of the computer,[1] which defines the key characteristics of the operating environment of that machine. Popular platforms include the Sun Sparc CPU with the Sun Solaris operating system (Sparc/Solaris); the Intel Pentium CPU with the Microsoft Windows NT operating system (Pentium/NT); and the PowerPC CPU with the MacIntosh operating system (PowerPC/MacOS).

Programs usually are *platform specific*; that is, a program developed and compiled for one platform will not automatically run on a different platform, unless the two platforms are *compatible* or one platform can emulate the other.[2] Most of the time, when a program needs to run on different platforms, special versions of the program must be developed and compiled for each environment. Converting a program to run on a different platform is called *porting*. In general, porting is a nontrivial task. One of Java's advantages is that it is platform independent; Java programs are designed to run on different platforms without porting.

2.1.2 Security

Owing to its open nature, the Internet is inherently insecure. Common security breaches include break-ins to computers connected to the Internet. Such intrusions may

---

[1] Sometimes, the phrases *hardware platform* and *software platform* are used to refer to the CPU and the operating system of the computer, respectively.
[2] There are a number of DOS/Windows emulators for MacOS and Solaris.

lead to unauthorized access or modification of data and possibly to the destruction of software and hardware. Others involve eavesdropping on messages, such as e-mail and online transactions involving the use of credit cards.

A completely secure but open environment is unattainable. However, some effective methods in network technology and cryptography have been developed to reduce significantly the risk of security breaches. Java is designed to prevent break-ins by running a special class of Java programs called *applets*.

2.1.3 Conventional Approaches to Executing Programs

There are two conventional approaches to executing programs: compilation and interpretation.

Compilation

In compilation a *compiler* translates, or compiles, the source code of a program into machine code, allowing the machine code to be executed directly by the operating systems and the hardware. The compilation approach is invariably used in programming languages intended for developing large-scale, efficient, and reliable systems, such as C, C++, Ada, and Eiffel. The compilation approach has several important advantages.

- Modern compilers perform extensive static analysis, such as *strong type checking* and *dataflow analysis*, to detect many potential errors in programs at compile time.
- Modern compilers apply sophisticated optimization techniques, such as *common expression extraction* and *loop strength reduction*, before generating machine code. Optimization produces efficient code and eliminates the need for hand-optimization, so programmers can focus on the functionality and maintainability of the programs, not their efficiency.
- Executing machine code generated by compilers is far more efficient than interpreting source code directly.
- For commercial software vendors, software can be delivered to customers in binary executable form, thus protecting the source code as a trade secret.

The main deficiency of the compilation approach is that the executables are platform dependent. Two options are available for allowing a program to run on different platforms, but neither one is appealing. The first option is to port and compile the source code for each platform. However, porting source code to different platforms is tedious, time-consuming, and error-prone. In addition, the number of different platforms is potentially large, and porting to all of them may not be economically feasible. Netscape, Inc., adopted this approach for its Netscape browser, which is mostly written in C and ported to every major platform.

The second option is to provide source code and porting instructions to allow customers to port programs themselves to the platforms they use. This approach shifts the burden to the customers and causes the original developer to lose control over software quality and compatibility. This approach also exposes the source code to outsiders. However, it is often adopted for noncommercial products, such as the Linux operating system and the GNU project of the Free Software Foundation. These are large-scale and industrial strength software systems that have been ported to different platforms.

Interpretation

In interpretation an *interpreter* directly parses and executes the source code of a program without generating machine code. The main advantage of the interpretation approach is its quick turnaround of edit–run cycles. Thus the interpretation approach is often adopted for programming languages used for prototyping, or *rapid application development* (RAD), such as BASIC, LISP, and Smalltalk.[3] This technique requires no compilation, and errors can be discovered only at run time. The interpretation approach is platform independent because programs exist only in their source form. However, software products developed with interpretive languages must be delivered as source code. The main disadvantages of the interpretation approach are the loss of static analysis and code optimization and the much slower execution speeds than those generally achieved with compiled executables.

2.1.4   The Java Execution Model

Neither of the conventional approaches to program execution can accomplish platform independence and efficiency. Java presents a different approach to executing programs, which is a compromise between the conventional compilation and interpretation approaches, as illustrated in Figure 2.1. Java programs are executed in two stages.

Stage 1—Compilation of the Source Code to Byte-Code

Java is a compiled language. However, unlike the conventional compilers, the Java compiler compiles the source code to the machine code of the *Java virtual machine* (JVM) [Lindholm and Yellin 1996]. The JVM is an abstraction of the CPU of a real computer. But it shares many common characteristics of a real CPU and thus can be implemented on a real CPU in a relatively straightforward way. The machine code of the JVM is known as *byte-code*.

Stage 2—Execution of Byte-Code

Byte-code is platform independent and can be executed on different platforms. There are three ways of executing Java byte-code:

---

[3] Some of these languages also have compilers. For example, Microsoft Visual BASIC includes both an interpreter and a compiler.

Figure 2.1

Execution of Java programs.

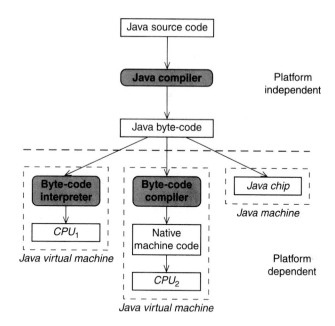

1. *Interpretation.* On a given platform, an interpreter of the Java virtual machine interprets the JVM instructions and executes them.[4] This approach is the original one supported by Sun.

2. *JIT compilation.* On a given platform, a more *just-in-time* (JIT) *compiler* compiles the Java byte-code to the native machine code on the fly and then executes the native machine code. This approach is being used increasingly in Java products.

3. *Direct execution.* Special platforms can be built by using *Java chips*, which have Java byte-code as their native machine code. On such platforms, Java byte-code can be executed directly without a compiler or interpreter. The first generation Java chips are expected to be available soon. They will be used in embedded systems in electronic devices, such as cable set-top boxes and cellular phones.

The Java execution model essentially maintains all the advantages of the compilation approach and accomplishes platform independence. The execution of byte-code is far more efficient than the direct interpretation of source code, but it still is not as efficient as the direct execution of native machine code.[5] With further improvements

---

[4] Sometimes, we simply use the term *Java virtual machine* to refer to the interpreter of the Java virtual machine.

[5] Java wasn't the first to be based on this approach. P-code for PASCAL developed at the University of California at San Diego in the late 1970s was the first platform independent, or *portable*, intermediate

in byte-code optimization and compilation, as well as improvements in the JVM, the efficiency of Java will approach that of compilation languages targeting native machine code, such as C++.

2.1.5   Java Byte-Code and Virtual Machine

Java byte-code refers to the instructions of the Java virtual machine. A JVM instruction consists of a 1-byte *opcode* (hence the name byte-code) and zero or more *operands*, which are the parameters of the instruction. Operands vary in length, and the number and lengths of the operands are determined by the opcode.

opcode (1-byte)
operand$_1$
operand$_2$
. . .

The core of the JVM involves a loop that can be described roughly as follows:

```
do {
    fetch the opcode byte of the current instruction;
    fetch the operands, depending on the value of the opcode byte;
    execute the instruction;
} while ( not done );
```

The JVM executes byte-code much like a simple reduced instruction set computer (RISC) CPU does, using several 32-bit registers.

- The pc (program counter) register contains the address of the next instruction to be executed.
- The optop register points to the top of the operand stack.
- The vars register points to a set of local variables of the current method.
- The frame register points to the execution environment structure.

The JVM also uses a garbage-collected heap to store all objects at run time.

The JVM instructions take operands from the operand stack, operate on them, and return the results to the stack. The operand stack is 32-bits wide. The JVM instructions perform the following functions:

- stack manipulation,
- array management,
- arithmetic and logical operations,

code for high-level languages. A few other languages, such as Emacs LISP, also compile source code to byte-code.

- method invocation and return,
- exception handling, and
- synchronization of multiple threads.

A detailed specification of the JVM and the format of the .class file are presented in [Lindholm and Yellin 1996].

2.1.6 Java Apps and Applets

There are two categories of Java programs: *apps* (shorthand for applications) and *applets*. An app is a full-fledged program with full access to system resources. An applet is a program embedded in a Web page with restricted access to system resources to prevent break-ins to the host that runs the applet.

A Java app must be explicitly invoked, like any other program, by issuance of a command on the command line or selection of the command from a menu. Therefore an app can be invoked only by an authorized user of a host, unless the security of the host has already been compromised. Java imposes no restrictions on the behavior of apps and their access to the host environment. Presumably, authorized users are responsible for the consequences of executing apps.

Applets are embedded in Web pages and are invoked automatically when the Web pages containing the applets are loaded by Java-enabled browsers. Most of the time, a user is unaware of the contents and behavior of the applets embedded in a Web page before it is loaded in a browser. Thus, ensuring that executing applets will not compromise the security of the host on which the browser and the applet are running is imperative. Otherwise, Web surfing for whatever purpose would be dangerous and could result in disaster.

2.1.7 Security of Applets

Java has several layers of defense against potential security attacks through applets.

Shielded Memory Addresses

The Java language does not allow direct manipulation of memory addresses. There is no way for someone to access a specific memory cell or forge a pointer to an address. Memory allocation and deallocation are handled automatically and transparently by the JVM at run time.

Verification of Byte-Code

The JVM enforces *verification* of the byte-code before it is executed. Verification involves looking for any improper structures and control flows in the byte-code, any violation of access restrictions, and any violation of the type system. The purpose of the verification is to ensure that the byte-code is the output of a legitimate Java compiler, is generated from a consistent version of the source code, and has not been tampered with.

Run-Time Security Manager

While executing an applet, the JVM consults a *security manager* whenever a potentially insecure operation is about to be performed. The security manager decides whether to allow the operation. The security manager is customizable to allow implementation of different security policies. In fact, browsers from different vendors implement slightly different security policies.

Commonly implemented security policies include the following restrictions on applets.

- An applet usually is not allowed to read or write files on the host that is executing it. Some browsers allow certain exceptions.
- An applet is not allowed to communicate with hosts other than the one that it comes from.
- An applet is not allowed to start other programs, execute operating system commands, or inquire about certain system properties of the host.

These Java security measures form the so-called sand box, within which all applets are confined. McGraw [McGraw and Felton 1997] discusses the security issues involving Java applets in detail. Schneier 1996 gives an excellent general introduction to cryptography and computer security.

2.2   SIMPLE PROGRAMS

In this section we present two simple Java programs—an app and an applet—to illustrate the basic structures of Java programs and the fundamentals of compiling and running Java programs.

2.2.1   A Simple App

As the Internet has reached almost everywhere on Earth, the next logical step would be an interplanetary Internet. NASA is planning to have the first Internet host beyond planet Earth online early in the twenty-first century. Imagine how exciting it would be to receive a greeting from a close neighbor—Venus.

EXAMPLE 2.1   The Hello from Venus! App

PURPOSE

To illustrate the basic structure of Java programs.

DESCRIPTION

This app displays a greeting message: *Hello from Venus!* The message is in plain text and is sent to the standard output (i.e., the command console from which the app is invoked).

SOLUTION

The following steps are used to build and run the app, assuming that you have installed the Java Development Kit on your system.

1. Type in and save the following Java source code in a file named `Hello.java`.

Hello from Venus! app: Hello.java

```
// Filename: Hello.java

/**
A Java app that prints the message: "Hello from Venus!"
 */
class Hello {
   public static void main (String[] args) {
      System.out.println ("Hello from Venus!");
      /* System.out refers to the standard output */
   }
}
```

2. Compile the Java source code, using the Java compiler `javac`:

```
venus% javac Hello.java
```

If the compilation is successful, a file named `Hello.class` will be generated. This is the Java byte-code file.

3. Execute the app by invoking the Java byte-code interpreter `java`:

```
venus% java Hello
Hello from Venus!
```

Note that the argument of `java` is the class name, not the file name, that is, without the extension `.java` or `.class`. ▪

Basic Program Structure

The Hello from Venus! app illustrates two essential elements of Java programs.

1. A program—app or applet—comprises one or more classes. In this case, the program comprises a single class, `Hello`.
2. An app must contain a class that implements the `main` method. The `main()` method is similar to the `main()` function of C and C++ programs. As the

entry point of a Java app, the `main()` method must be declared as shown in Example 2.1:

```
public static void main (String[] args) {
    ⟨body of the main() method⟩
}
```

In this case, class `Hello` has only one method—the `main()` method. (See Section 3.4.5 [p. 79] for discussion of the `main()` method.)

The `main()` method of `Hello` simply prints out following message to the console, or standard output:

```
Hello from Venus!
```

`System.out` refers to the standard output. The `println()` method prints a string and appends a newline character at the end.

Source Files

Java programs are stored in *files*. Unlike many other languages, Java enforces certain rules about how classes should be placed in files and how files should be named. A simplified version of the rules is as follows.

- All Java source files must have the extension `.java`.
- Usually, each file should contain a single class. However, Java allows a single file to contain multiple classes, but with certain restrictions. (See Section 3.5 [p. 99] and Section 4.5 [p. 145] for details.)
- The file name should match the class name. Java is case sensitive.

These rules make it easy to locate the source code of a class by simply listing or searching the file names.

Comments

There are three kinds of comments in Java: C-style, C++-style, and documentation comments. *C-style comments* can span multiple lines; characters between /* and */, including the delimiters, are ignored by the Java compiler. *C++-style comments* are short one-liners; characters from // to the end of the line are ignored by the Java compiler. *Documentation comments* serve a special purpose. They are used by a documentation generation utility called `javadoc` to generate HTML-style documentation automatically by extracting information from the source code; characters between /** and */, including the delimiters, are ignored by the Java compiler. (We discuss the use of documentation comments and the `javadoc` tool in Section 4.5 [p. 145].) Example 2.1 illustrates the use of all three types of comments.

2.2.2 Applet and the World Wide Web

Java apps must be invoked from command consoles. Java applets can be embedded in Web pages. They are downloaded via the World Wide Web and invoked by Java-enabled browsers.

EXAMPLE 2.2 Hello from Venus! Applet

PURPOSE

To illustrate the basic structure of Java applets and the basic graphics capability of displaying text and choosing font, size, style, and color.

DESCRIPTION

This applet displays the greeting message from Venus graphically. It consists of a text message and an image of the planet Venus.

SOLUTION

The following steps are used to build and run the applet.

1. Type in and save the following Java source code in a file named `HelloFromVenus.java`.

Hello from Venus! applet: HelloFromVenus.java

```java
import java.awt.*;
import java.applet.Applet;

public class HelloFromVenus extends Applet {

   public void paint(Graphics g) {
      Dimension d = getSize( );
      g.setColor(Color.black);
      g.fillRect(0,0,d.width,d.height);
      g.setFont(new Font("Sans-serif", Font.BOLD, 24));
      g.setColor(new Color(255, 215, 0)); // gold color
      g.drawString("Hello from Venus!", 40, 25);
      g.drawImage(getImage(getCodeBase( ), "Venus.gif"),
                  20, 60, this);
   }
}
```

2. Compile the Java source, using the Java compiler to generate the byte-code file `HelloFromVenus.class`.

```
venus% javac HelloFromVenus.java
```

3. Type in and save the following HTML source in a file named `HelloDemo.html`. We may name the HTML file anything we want to.

HTML source: HelloDemo.html

```
<html>
   <head>
      <title> Hello from Venus Applet </title>
   </head>
   <body bgcolor=black text=white>
      <center>

         <applet code="HelloFromVenus.class"
            width=300 height=350>
         </applet>

      </center>
      <hr>
      <a href="HelloFromVenus.java">The source.</a>
   </body>
</html>
```

Be sure that the HTML file, the Java source file, and the byte-code file are in the same directory. The image of planet Venus is stored in a separate file named `Venus.gif`. Be sure to place the image file in the same directory with the other files.

4. One way to view the applet is to use the applet viewer in JDK:

```
venus% appletviewer HelloDemo.html
```

Note that the argument of `appletviewer` is the HTML file name.

5. Another way to view the applet is to use a Java-enabled browser, such as the Netscape Communicator:

```
venus% netscape HelloDemo.html
```

The result of the applet is shown in Figure 2.2.

Basic Applet Structure

The Hello from Venus! applet illustrates several essential elements of Java applets. In general, an applet must extend the `Applet` class (either directly or indirectly), does not need a `main()` method, and should at least implement the `paint()` method. An applet is rather different from an app. It is indirectly invoked through the applet viewer or, more commonly, a Java-enabled browser. An applet is not a top-level program. Therefore the `main()` method is not needed. An applet is invoked in an *applet context*, usually a browser. An applet must interact with its applet context according to a set of prescribed conventions (i.e., *contracts*).

Figure 2.2

The Hello from Venus! applet.

The contract regarding the paint() method of an applet includes the following.[6]

- Each applet is assigned a rectangular region on the Web page in which it is embedded. The dimension of this rectangular region is set in the applet tag in the HTML file.

- An applet implements the paint() method to *paint* the appearance of the applet in the rectangular region. The origin (0, 0) is located at the upper left corner of the rectangular region, as shown in Figure 2.3.

- The paint() method is invoked by the applet context whenever the applet is active and the rectangular region designated to the applet becomes visible. This implies that the paint() method will be invoked when the applet is initially loaded in a browser.

Later we discuss in detail most of the language features and classes involved in this applet. A cursory understanding of what is going on in the paint() method of the HelloFromVenus applet is sufficient at this point. Line by line, each statement in the paint() method

1. gets the dimension of the rectangular region designated to the applet;

2. sets the pen color to black;

[6] The paint() method is a member of the Component class, which is a superclass of Applet. See Section 4.6 [p. 157] for details about the paint() method.

Figure 2.3

Viewing area of applets and the Java coordinate system.

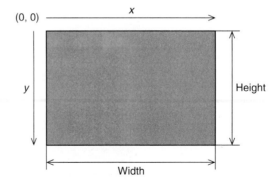

3. fills the entire rectangular region with black color, which paints the background;

4. sets the font to sans serif, boldface style, and 24-point size;

5. sets the pen color to gold;

6. draws the text message at the top in gold color; and

7. draws the image of the planet Venus below the message. The image is stored in a file named `Venus.gif`.

Embedding Applets in Web Pages

Applets are embedded in Web pages by using the `applet` tag, which is included in the official specification of HTML.[7] The simplest form of the `applet` tag is

```
<applet code=class_filename
        width=pixels
        height=pixels>
</applet>
```

consisting of three required *attributes*, which are key-value pairs.

Attribute	Description
`code`	Specify the name of the byte-code file containing the applet
`width`	Specify the width of the applet in pixels
`height`	Specify the height of the applet in pixels

[7] Raggett et al. 1998 gives a complete and definitive description of HTML 4.0, the current standard. The most up-to-date information about HTML can be obtained from the W[3] Consortium at

```
http://www.w3.org
```

The applet tag for the `HelloFromVenus` applet is highlighted in the `HelloDemo.html` file in step 3 of Example 2.2. For a complete description of the `applet` tag see Summary of the `Applet` tag [p. 465].

Placing Applets on the World Wide Web

To make your applets accessible on the World Wide Web, you simply put Web pages, the applet class files, and other related files (e.g., image or audio files) on a host that is connected to the Internet and has a *Web server* (i.e., an *HTTP server*).

An applet may involve several files. For example, an applet might have several class files, as well as image and audio files. To run an applet that resides on a remote server requires that all the related files be downloaded to the host that is running the applet. By default, a single connection to a remote HTTP server will download only one file. Therefore an applet that involves multiple files requires several connections to the same server in order to download all the files needed to run the applet. Multiple connections to the remote server involve significant overhead and may cause substantial delays in downloading the files. An archive and compression utility, called `jar`, is provided in the JDK. Using `jar`, we can pack all the files involved in an applet into a single compressed archive file. Hence the files needed to run an applet can be downloaded with a single connection to the remote server, reducing download time and network load.

The Hello from Venus! applet contains two files: the class file `HelloFrom-Venus.java` and the image file `Venus.gif`. To take advantage of the `jar` utility, we first pack and compress these two files,

```
venus% jar cf Hello.jar HelloFromVenus.class Venus.gif
```

which creates a *Java archive* (JAR) file named `Hello.jar`.[8] In order to use the JAR file, we must specify the JAR file name in the `applet` tag, using the `archive` attribute:

```
<applet code="HelloFromVenus.class
         archive="Hello.jar"
         width=300 height=350>
</applet>
```

A browser that supports the `archive` tag will download the JAR file instead of the class file. The JAR file will be decompressed and the class and image files will be extracted from the JAR file.

---

[8] Use of command-line utility `jar` is similar to use of the UNIX `tar` utility. Its syntax is

```
jar [ options ] destination input files
```

See JDK tools documentation for details.

Symptoms	Possible causes and/or fixes
You are unable to invoke JDK tools such as `javac`, `java`, or `appletviewer`.	Be sure that the `PATH` environment variable includes the JDK `bin` directory.
You get deprecation messages while compiling programs.	The programs contain features that are deprecated. The programs were developed for an older version of Java compiler than the one you are using. As of Java 2, deprecation is only a warning, so programs using deprecated features should still run without problems. However, you should remove deprecated features from programs because they may not be supported in future JDK releases.
Your applets run fine when you use the applet viewer but do not run in a browser.	Be sure that the version of JVM in your browser is equal to or higher than the version of JDK you used to compile your programs. When transferring files to a Web host via FTP, be sure that you transfer the class files in binary mode and that the file names are intact, not truncated or converted to all uppercase.

CHAPTER SUMMARY

- Java is object-oriented, distributed, and platform independent.
- The primary architecture design goals of Java are platform independence, efficiency, and security.
- The Java execution model is a compromise between the conventional approaches of executing programs through compilation or interpretation. Java source code is compiled to byte-code and executed by the Java virtual machine (JVM).
- The JVM is an abstract computing machine that executes Java byte-code. It can be implemented as interpreters, just-in-time (JIT) compilers, or Java chips—hardware implementations of the JVM. The instructions of the Java virtual machine are called byte-code. The Java compiler compiles Java source code to Java byte-code and stores the resulting code in files with the extension `.class`.

■ The two common categories of Java programs are apps and applets. Apps (applications) are full-fledged Java programs with full access to system resources. Applets are programs that are embedded in Web pages with restricted access to system resources to prevent break-ins to the hosts that run the applets.

EXERCISES

2.1. Write a Java application similar to the `Hello.Java` app in Example 2.1. This new program should contain a class named `MyFavoritePoem`. It should call `System.out.println()` to display a poem that you like. (*Hint:* Look ahead to Chapter 3 for information on the Java printing features that can be used to display this poem neatly and elegantly.)

2.2. Develop an applet similar to the `HelloFromVenus` applet in Example 2.2. Your new applet should display an image of your choice. Change the color, size, and textual display of the image as necessary.

3

Elements of Java

In this chapter we discuss the basic elements of Java, including operators and expressions, data types, garbage collection, control structures, class declaration, parameter passing, packages, and exceptions. We also discuss some of the more commonly used classes in the Java Class Library. We present several simple programs to demonstrate string manipulation and simple input and output. Finally, we develop a simple animation applet.

Java is the most recent entry in the evolution of object-oriented programming languages. It has benefited tremendously from the lessons learned from its predecessors, most notably C++ [Ellis and Stroustrup 1990; Stroustrup 1994; Stroustrup 1997], Smalltalk [Goldberg and Robson 1983; Goldberg 1985], Objective C [Pinson and Wiener 1991], Modula3 [Harbison 1992], Eiffel [Meyer 1992; Meyer 1997], and Ada [Booch 1987]. Java is a well-designed language comprising constructs that have been used in other languages and have proved effective. Java bears some resemblance to its direct ancestor—C++. However, their similarities are largely syntactical and superficial, whereas their differences are more fundamental. One of the most striking differences between Java and C++ is in their design philosophies. C++ is designed to be a rather comprehensive, expressive, and permissive language—and most important to allow *very efficient* implementation. Many of its features were developed with good intentions and sound justifications but often are subject to misuse and bad programming practices, partly because of backward compatibility with C. In contrast,

Java is designed to be (a) more selective and restrictive—to prevent bad programming practices, even at the cost of sacrificing expressiveness and convenience in some cases; (b) easy to use, and versatile; and (c) suitable for a variety of tasks, including object-oriented programming, numeric computation, and system programming.

Java differs from other object-oriented programming languages in several important respects.

- Unlike C++, Java is purely object-oriented. All nonstatic methods in Java are polymorphic (i.e., virtual in C++ terminology). It does not allow global variables and stand-alone functions, as C++ does.

- Unlike Smalltalk, in which everything is an object, including values of primitive types, such as `int` and `char`, in Java, values of primitive types are not objects.

- Unlike C++, Java does not support multiple inheritance in general. Like Objective-C, only a limited form of multiple inheritance, accomplished by the use of *interfaces*, is supported in Java.

- Unlike most other procedural and object-oriented programming languages, in Java the `goto` statement was eliminated.

- Unlike most other programming languages, Java utilizes 16-bit characters instead of 8-bit characters to support internationalization.

- Java supports exception handling, garbage collection, and multithreaded programming. These mechanisms are considered to be essential in object-oriented programming.

Perhaps the most notable feature of Java is its support for *distributed computing*. Unlike most other programming languages that depend on platform dependent add-on utilities to support distributed computing, Java provides built-in language constructs and standard libraries for distributed computing.

3.1 LEXICAL ELEMENTS

Lexical elements are basic building blocks of programming languages. We begin with a look at Java's characters, identifiers, and literals. Then we discuss the operators and expressions used in Java.

3.1.1 Character Set

Java programs are written in *Unicode*,[1] an international standard of 16-bit character sets that contain encodings of characters of most languages used in the world today.

---

[1] *The Unicode Standard 2.0* is defined in [The Unicode Consortium 1996]. Unicode related information, including various tables and programs, can be obtained from the Unicode Consortium at

http://www.unicode.org

The commonly used 7-bit ASCII character set is equivalent to the first 128 characters of Unicode, known as the International Standardization Organization's (ISO's) Latin-1 character set. The Java development environment can be localized to accommodate many different locales. A *locale* is a country or region with distinct characteristics in culture and language. The most wildly distributed version of the Java Development Kit (JDK) is localized to U.S. English. It performs the conversion between ASCII and Unicode characters on the fly; that is, the U.S. English version of JDK reads and writes ASCII files by default.

3.1.2 Identifiers

A Java identifier begins with a letter, which includes the underscore (_) and the dollar sign ($) followed by letters or digits. Because Java programs are written in Unicode, you may use the following as identifiers in Java:[2]

多语言   πολυγλωσσικο

3.1.3 Primitive Types and Literals

Java provides the primitive types:

- boolean type: `boolean`;
- integer types: `byte`, `short`, `int`, and `long`;
- character type: `char`; and
- floating-point types: `float` and `double`.

The constant values of each type are expressed as *literals*.

Boolean Type

The `boolean` type consists of two boolean literals: `true` and `false`. In Java, the `boolean` type is not compatible with integer types. The results of comparisons are of type `boolean`, not integer as in C and C++. The conditions of control statements, such as `if` and `while` statements (see Section 3.3.4 [p. 66]), are expected to be of type `boolean`, not integer types.

Integer Types

Java provides integer types of different sizes.

---

[2] These are the word "multilingual" in Chinese and Greek, respectively.

Type	Size	Minimum value	Maximum value
byte	8-bit	−128	127
short	16-bit	−32768	32767
int	32-bit	−2147483648	2147483647
long	64-bit	−9223372036854775808	9223372036854775807

However, Java provides no unsigned integer types. Integer literals can be written in decimals, octals, and hexadecimals. A *decimal integer literal* begins with a nonzero decimal digit, followed by decimal digits (e.g., 30). An *octal integer literal* begins with a leading zero (0), followed by octal digits (e.g., 036). A *hexadecimal integer literal* begins with a leading 0x or 0X, followed by hexadecimal digits (e.g., 0x1E and 0X1e). An integer literal may also be followed by a 1 or an L to indicate that it is of type long (e.g., 0x1L). The letter L is preferred for 1 to avoid confusion with the integer 1.

Floating-Point Types

Java provides two floating-point types.

Type	Size	Description
float	32-bit	Single precision IEEE-754 floating-point
double	64-bit	Double precision IEEE-754 floating-point

Floating-point literals are written as a decimal number with an optional exponent. Numbers may be followed by f or F to indicate float type or by d or D to indicate double type. Some examples of floating-point literals are

```
23.f     .5     0.0     3.1415     1e-9d     1E1D
```

Character Type

Most programming languages provide a single-byte (8-bit) character type that is capable of encoding up to 256 printable characters and control characters. Although it is adequate for Western languages, which all have small alphabets, it is quite inadequate for some Oriental languages, such as Chinese and Japanese. Modern Chinese consists of more than 15,000 characters, of which some 6,000 are in common daily use. For languages with large alphabets a double-byte character type capable of encoding as many as 65,536 printable characters and control characters is needed.

In the past, the vast majority of commercial software was developed and available only in English. As nations' economies become more and more global, the huge market potentials of non-English–speaking countries, such as the People's Republic of China, have prompted commercial software vendors to port their software to other languages. Microsoft, for example, released its Windows 98 package in several different languages almost simultaneously. Owing to the different size requirements of characters, however, porting the English version of software (where 8-bit characters were used) to Oriental languages (where 16-bit characters are necessary) has proved to be extremely tedious and costly.

To support the internalization of software, Java provides a single character type `char` that is 16-bit unsigned and uses the Unicode 2.0 character encoding.

Character Literals

ASCII characters can be written directly (e.g., a or C). Non-ASCII characters can be written in their hexadecimal or octal codes. In hexadecimal code \u is followed by four hexadecimal digits, as in \u00E6 (æ, from Greek), and \u5496 \u5561 (咖啡, coffee in Chinese). In octal code \ is followed by one to three octal digits, as in \040. Octal character code may not exceed \377 (\u00FF).

The following special characters can be written by using *escape sequences*.

Escape sequence	Unicode	Description
\n	\u000A	Newline
\t	\u0009	Tab
\b	\u0008	Backspace
\r	\u000D	Return
\f	\u000C	Form feed
\\	\u005C	Backslash
\'	\u0027	Single quote
\"	\u0022	Double quote

Character literals such as the following appear between single quotes:

```
'a'   'C'
'\u00E6'   '\u5496'   '\u5561'
'\040'
'\n'   '\t'   '\\'   '\''   '\"'
```

String Literals

The `string` type is not a primitive type in Java; it is a class. However, string constants can be written as literals. A string literal consists of a sequence of characters, including escape sequences, enclosed by a pair of double quotes, as in the following examples.

String literal	Value
`"A string literal"`	A string literal
`"\u5469 \u5561"`	咖啡
`"\"A quote\""`	"A quote"

See also *String Concatenation* in Section 3.1.4 [p. 54] and Section 3.4.8 [p. 86] for operations on strings.

3.1.4 Operators and Expressions

Java provides operators that are very similar to those in C and C++. These operators and expressions are summarized in Table 3.1. The leftmost column indicates the precedence of the operators, with 1 as the highest precedence and 14 the lowest. A *numeric* type is either an integer or a floating-point type. All operators that can be applied to integer types can also be applied to type `char`. All the binary operators, except the assignment operators, are left-associative. The assignment operators are right-associative. Note the following examples.

Expression	Interpreted as	Reason
`u + v * w`	`u + (v * w)`	* has higher precedence than +.
`x - y + z`	`(x - y) + z`	+ and – have the same precedence and are left-associative.
`a = b = c`	`a = (b = c)`	Assignment operators are right-associative.

Arithmetic Operators

The following arithmetic operators can be applied to all integer and floating-point types.

Infix binary		Prefix unary	
+	Addition	+	Positive sign
−	Subtraction	−	Negative sign
*	Multiplication		
/	Division		
%	Remainder		

TABLE 3.1

Operators and expressions.

	Expression	Operand types	Description
1.	exp ++	Numeric	Postfix increment; result is the value before
	exp −−	Numeric	Postfix decrement; result is the value before
2.	++ exp	Numeric	Prefix increment; result is the value after
	−− exp	Numeric	Prefix decrement; result is the value after
	+ exp	Numeric	Unary positive
	− exp	Numeric	Unary negative
	~ exp	Integer, boolean	Bitwise complement
	! exp	Boolean	Logical negation
3.	exp_1 * exp_2	Numeric	Multiplication
	exp_1 / exp_2	Numeric	Division
	exp_1 % exp_2	Numeric	Remainder, modulus
4.	exp_1 + exp_2	Numeric	Addition
		String	String concatenation
	exp_1 − exp_2	Numeric	Subtraction
5.	exp_1 << exp_2	Integer	Left shift, filling with 0s
	exp_1 >> exp_2	Integer	Signed right shift, filling with the highest bit
	exp_1 >>> exp_2	Integer	Unsigned right shift, filling with 0s
6.	exp_1 < exp_2	Numeric	Less than
	exp_1 > exp_2	Numeric	Greater than
	exp_1 <= exp_2	Numeric	Less than or equal to
	exp_1 >= exp_2	Numeric	Greater than or equal to
7.	exp_1 == exp_2	Any	Equality
	exp_1 != exp_2	Any	Inequality

TABLE 3.1

Operators and expressions (continued).

	Expression	Operand types	Description
8.	exp_1 & exp_2	Integer, boolean	Bitwise and
9.	exp_1 ^ exp_2	Integer, boolean	Bitwise exclusive or (xor)
10.	exp_1 | exp_2	Integer, boolean	Bitwise inclusive or
11.	exp_1 && exp_2	Boolean	Conditional and
12.	exp_1 || exp_2	Boolean	Conditional or
13.	exp_1 ? exp_2 : exp_3	exp_1: boolean exp_2, exp_3: any	Conditional expression
14.	$var = exp$	Any	Assignment
	$var\ {+}{=}\ exp$	Numeric, string	
	$var\ {-}{=}\ exp$	Numeric	$var\ op{=}\ exp$
	$var\ {*}{=}\ exp$	Numeric	is equivalent to
	$var\ {/}{=}\ exp$	Numeric	$var = (\ var\ )\ op\ (\ exp\ )$ except that
	$var\ \%{=}\ exp$	Numeric	var is evaluated only once
	$var\ {<}{<}{=}\ exp$	Integer	
	$var\ {>}{>}{=}\ exp$	Integer	
	$var\ {>}{>}{>}{=}\ exp$	Integer	
	$var\ \&{=}\ exp$	Integer, boolean	
	$var\ {\char`^}{=}\ exp$	Integer, boolean	
	$var\ |{=}\ exp$	Integer, boolean	

Integer addition, subtraction, and multiplication follow the customary rules. Integer division truncates the result toward zero. The integer remainder is defined as

```
x % y == x - (x / y) * y
```

The examples below show integer division and remainder and their relationship.

Expression	Result	Relationship
`7 / 3`	2	$7 == 3 * 2 + 1$
`7 % 3`	1	
`(-7) / 3`	-2	$(-7) == 3 * (-2) + (-1)$
`(-7) % 3`	-1	

Java integer arithmetic never overflows or underflows. If a value exceeds the range of its type, it will be wrapped modulo the range.

For expressions `x / y` and `x % y`, an `ArithmeticException` is thrown when y is 0 (see Section 3.6 [p. 104] for a discussion of exceptions).

Java floating-point arithmetic conforms to the IEEE-754-1985 standard [IEEE 1985]. One advantage of this type of arithmetic is that an exception will not be generated under any circumstance. In other words, your program will not crash, even when you divide a floating-point number by zero. The IEEE-754 standard defines two magic numbers: infinity and NaN (representing *not a number*). Floating-point arithmetic is closed with the addition of infinity and NaN. Two rules govern floating-point multiplication and division.

1. If neither operand is NaN, then the results are as follows.

x	y	x / y	x * y
Finite	±0.0	±∞	±0.0
Finite	±∞	±0.0	±∞
±0.0	±0.0	NaN	±0.0
±∞	Finite	±∞	±∞
±∞	±∞	NaN	±∞
±0.0	±∞	±0.0	NaN

2. If either operand is NaN, then the result is NaN.

The floating-point remainder is defined much the same as the integer remainder, or

$$x \% y == x - (x / y) * y$$

See *The* `Float` *and* `Double` *Classes* [p. 96] and *Mathematical Constants and Functions* [p. 96] in Section 3.4.9 for floating-point constants and commonly used mathematical functions.

String Concatenation

The + operator can also be used to concatenate two strings. If one of the operands is a string and the other is of some other type, the nonstring operand will be converted to a string representation of its value and concatenated to the string operand, as in the following examples:

Expression	Result
"object" + "-" + "oriented"	Object-oriented
"object" + '-' + "oriented"	Object-oriented
"Mail Stop" + 205	Mail Stop 205
123 + ' ' + "Oak Street"	123 Oak Street

The conversion of primitive type values to their string representations follows customary conventions. The conversion of objects to their string representation is carried out by the `toString()` method, which we discuss in Section 3.4.8 [p. 89].

Increment and Decrement Operators

The increment operator `++` and the decrement operator `--` can be applied to all integer and floating-point types. Both operators can be either prefix or postfix. For example, `i++` and `++i` increment the value of i by 1; `i--` and `--i` decrement the value of i by 1. The result of the postfix increment or decrement expression is the value of i *before* the increment or decrement, respectively. The result of the prefix increment or decrement expression is the value of i *after* the increment or decrement, respectively. For example, if we let the initial value of i be 8, the effects of the postfix/prefix and increment/decrement expressions are as shown in the following table. (These expressions are evaluated independently, not consecutively.)

Expression	Result of the expression	Value of i afterward
i++	8	9
++i	9	9
i--	8	7
--i	7	7

Relational Operators

The equality operator `==` and the inequality operator `!=` can be applied to any type. The comparison operators `<` (less than), `<=` (less than or equal to), `>` (greater than), and >= (greater than or equal to) can be applied only to numeric types. All relational expressions yield `boolean` results. The meaning of relational expressions on primitive types follows customary conventions. We discuss the meaning of equality and inequality of nonprimitive types in Section 3.2.3 [p. 62].

Logical Operators

The logical operators ! (negation), && (and), and | | (or) can be applied to operands of type `boolean`. The binary logical operators are *conditional*. That is, in expression exp_1 && exp_2, exp_2 is evaluated only when exp_1 evaluates to `true`. Similarly, in expression exp_1 | | exp_2, exp_2 is evaluated only when exp_1 evaluates to `false`.

Bitwise and Shift Operators

Bitwise operators can be applied to both integer and `boolean` types. The following bitwise operators are supported in Java.

Bitwise expression	Description
~ x	Bitwise complement of x
x & y	Bitwise and of x and y
x | y	Bitwise inclusive or of x and y
x ^ y	Bitwise exclusive or of x and y

Unlike the conditional logical operators, when the bitwise operators &, |, and ^ are applied to operands of type `boolean`, both operands are always evaluated.

The shift operators can be applied only to integer types. The following shift operators are supported in Java.

Shift expression	Description
x << k	Shift the bits in x k places to the left, filling in with 0 bits on the right-hand side.
x >> k	Shift the bits in x k places to the right, filling in with the highest bit (i.e., the sign bit) on the left-hand side.
x >>> k	Shift the bits in x k places to the right, filling in with 0 bits on the left-hand side.

The following examples illustrate use of the bitwise and shift operators.

Expression	Description
~0x0	All bits are set to 1.
0x1 << k	All except the kth bit are set to 0.
~(0x1 << k)	All except the kth bit are set to 1.
x << k	The result is $x * 2^k$.
x >> k	The result is $x/2^k$.

Conditional Operators

A conditional expression takes the form

$$exp_1 \; ? \; exp_2 \; : \; exp_3$$

where exp_1 must be of type boolean, and exp_2 and exp_3 can be of any type. The value of the conditional expression shown is exp_2, if exp_1 evaluates to true, and exp_3, if exp_1 evaluates to false. Examples of conditional expressions include the following.

Expression	Description
(x < y) ? x : y	The minimum of x and y
(x >= 0) ? x : -x	The absolute value of x

Assignment Operators

An assignment operator is either the simple = or one of these:

```
+=    -=    *=    /=    %=    <<=    >>=    >>>=    &=    ^=    |=
```

These operators are formed by concatenating a binary operator with =. The assignment expression

$$var \; op= exp$$

is equivalent to

$$var = (\, var \,) \; op \; (\, exp \,)$$

except that *var* is evaluated only once in the original expression. When *var* is a simple variable, these two expressions are always equivalent. However, they may yield different results when *var* has side effects. That typically occurs when array indexes are involved. Let's assume that a is an integer array and that the initial value of i is 2. The assignment expressions a[i++] += i and a[i++] = a[i++] + i will have different effects.

Expression	Effect
a[i++] += i	a[2] = a[2] + 3
a[i++] = a[i++] + i	a[2] = a[3] + 4

The following are examples of assignment expressions.

Expression	Description
b |= (0x1 << k)	Set the *k*th bit of *b* to 1.
b &= ~(0x1 << k)	Set the *k*th bit of *b* to 0.

3.2   VARIABLES AND TYPES

A *type* denotes the set of all the legal values of that type. A *variable* refers to a location in memory where a value can be stored. Each variable is associated with a type. The variable type restricts the values that the variable may hold. Variables and their types are declared in variable declarations.

3.2.1   Variable Declarations

The basic syntax of *variable declarations* is

$$Type\ VarName_1\ [= InitialValue_1\ ]\ ,\ VarName_2\ [= InitialValue_2\ ]\ \ldots\ ;$$

It declares one or more variables, $VarName_1$, $VarName_2, \ldots$, to be of type *Type*. When a declaration contains more than one variable, the variables are separated by commas (,). Optionally, each variable can be assigned an initial value. A variable declaration determines the type and the scope of the variables in the declaration at compile time. We discuss the scope of variables in more detail later (see Sections 3.3.3 and 3.4.6).

Java supports two kinds of types: *primitive types* and *reference types*. We discussed all the primitive types in Section 3.1.3 [p. 48]. Recall that a primitive type variable holds a value of the type, whereas a reference type variable holds a reference to an object or array.

Default Initial Values

Each type has a *default initial value*. These values are used in initializing objects and arrays. The default initial values of various types are summarized as follows.

Type	Default initial value
Integer	0
Floating-point	0.0
char	\u0000
boolean	false
Reference	null

3.2.2   Type Compatibility and Conversion

Type compatibility is an important relationship.

Definition 3.1   *Type Compatibility*

Type T_1 is *compatible* with type T_2 if a value of type T_1 can appear wherever a value of type T_2 is expected, and vice versa.

Type conversion is the conversion of values of one type to values of another type. We discuss the conversion of primitive types here and the conversion of reference types in Section 4.2.2 [p. 126]. Conversions between different numeric types are allowed. There are two different forms of conversion.

Definition 3.2   *Widening and Narrowing (the Primitive Type)*

Converting a type of a smaller range to a type of a larger range is called *widening*. Converting a type of a larger range to a type of a smaller range is called *narrowing*.

The sizes of ranges of numeric types are ordered from small to large:

```
byte    short    int    long    float    double
```

Examples of widening include converting int to long or int to double. Examples of narrowing include converting long to int or float to long. On the one hand, widening is carried out implicitly whenever necessary. On the other hand, narrowing may result in overflow or loss of precision. Therefore explicit casts are necessary for narrowing.

```
int i = 10;
long m = 10000L;
double d = Math.PI;
i = (int) m;   // narrowing, cast necessary
m = i;         // widening, no cast necessary
m = (long) d;  // narrowing, cast necessary
d = m;         // widening, no cast necessary
```

3.2.3   Reference Types

A reference type is a *class* type, an *interface* type, or an *array* type. A reference variable (i.e., a variable of a reference type) may hold references to objects or arrays.[3] A reference variable may also hold a special value, null, which indicates that no object or array is being referenced.

References in Java are implemented as 32-bit pointers. Reference variables do not directly hold values, as variables of primitive types do. Instead, reference variables hold *indirect references* to object or array instances, as illustrated in Figure 3.1.

Figure 3.1

Primitive and reference types.

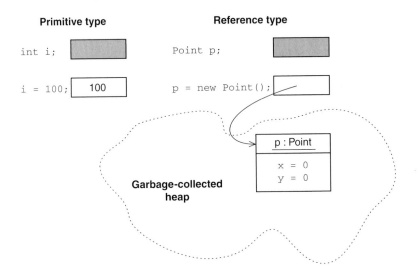

_____
[3] Arrays are actually objects too. See Section 4.2.2 [p. 129].

Java references are very different from pointers in C and C++ in two respects. First, in C and C++, pointers can be cast to any type, modified through pointer arithmetic, and assigned arbitrary values. In Java, none of that is allowed: Java prohibits the direct manipulation of reference variables. Second, in C and C++, pointers usually reference chunks of memory that are dynamically allocated from a heap. Programmers assume full responsibility for managing allocation and deallocation of memory. In Java, reference variables point to memory space that is dynamically allocated from a garbage-collected heap. Programmers are thus freed from the responsibility of managing the allocation and deallocation of memory.

Garbage Collection

Garbage collection refers to a mechanism that automatically deallocates unreferenced or unreachable objects (i.e., garbage). It is one of the most important features of Java. Garbage collection not only simplifies the programming task, but it also eliminates one of the major sources of faults in programs involving memory leaks and dereferencing invalid pointers, which are common and notoriously difficult to trace and remove. Garbage collection significantly reduces the amount of effort and time associated with programming, testing, and debugging.

Whether to use garbage collection is perhaps one of the most hotly debated issues in programming language design. Despite its obvious and significant advantages, garbage collection imposes rather severe penalties on the performance of programs of which it is a part.

Most garbage collection techniques involve exhaustive examination of the *entire* memory space, either all at once or rotating through segments of the memory space one at a time. Even with various improvements, such as *generational* garbage collection, garbage collection techniques are inherently time-consuming. Those that do not involve exhaustive examination of memory space, such as *reference counting*, often incur per-use penalties (i.e., a small penalty every time a variable is referenced), which can become a significant cumulative penalty. Techniques such as reference counting also suffer from various limitations, such as circular references. In addition, the garbage collection process could start at any moment, the timing of which is unpredictable and usually beyond the control of the programmer. Therefore programming languages containing garbage collection are not suitable for developing hard real-time systems that require the assurance of completing certain tasks within a specified period of time.

To summarize, Java does not require the programmer to keep track of objects created and destroy these objects when no longer needed. Java uses garbage collection to manage automatically the deallocation of objects. Garbage collection does impose some additional demands on hardware components. But, with the continuing increase of CPU speed and drop in CPU and memory costs, the penalty on performance becomes at least acceptable, if not negligible, for the vast majority of software systems. The benefits of garbage collection far outweigh any penalty on performance imposed by this mechanism.

Creating Objects and Arrays

Declaring a variable of a primitive type creates a storage location for its values. However, declaring a variable of a reference type does *not* create a storage location for an object or an array. Only a storage location for the *reference* is created. The object or array to which the reference variable refers must be created, or allocated, using the new operator or an *initializer*. See Sections 3.2.4 and 3.4 for the details of creating objects and arrays.

Equality of References

For two reference variables r1 and r2, r1 == r2 refers to the equality of the two *references*, not the equality of the *states* of the objects or arrays referred to by them. In other words, r1 == r2 tests the equality of the identities of the objects or arrays. To test the equality of the states of the objects or arrays, the equals() method should be used, such as r1.equals(r2). See the discussion of the equals() method in Section 4.5 [p. 145].

3.2.4 Arrays

An array variable holds a reference to an array. An array is a fix-sized sequential collection of elements of identical types. Arrays are created with the new operator or array initializers. The storage space for arrays is allocated from the garbage-collected heap.

One-Dimensional Arrays

The elements in a one-dimensional array are indexed by the integers 0 to $n - 1$, where n is the size of the array. A one-dimensional array of size n can be created and initialized with either of the following methods.

1. Using the new operator:

$$\text{new } \textit{Type } [\ n \ ]$$

   In this case the size of the array must be specified, and all the elements in the array are initialized to the default initial values (see Section 3.2.1 [p. 59]) based on the type of the elements.

2. Using the one-dimensional array initializer:

$$\{ \ v_0, v_1, \ldots, v_{n-1} \ \}$$

   The values $v_0, v_1, \ldots, v_{n-1}$ are the initial values of the elements in the array. The size of the array is determined by the number of initial values provided in the array initializer.

Examples of creating and initializing one-dimensional arrays include:

```
int ia1[] = new int[3];
```
Create an integer array of size 3; all elements are initialized to 0.

```
int ia2[] = {1, 2, 3};
```
Create an integer array of size 3; elements are initialized to 1, 2, and 3, respectively.

```
Point pa[] = new Point[10];
```
Create a point array of size 10; all elements are initialized to `null`.

If we assume that a is an one-dimensional array, the common operations on arrays are as follows.

Operation	Description
a.length	The length of array a
a[i]	The *i*th element of array a

One of the main differences between the arrays in Java and those in C and C++ is that Java arrays are always bound-checked. Array bound-checking will automatically detect a major source of faults in programs, that is, exceeding the bounds of arrays while accessing or manipulating their elements. An `IndexOutOfBoundsException` will be thrown when you attempt to access an array with an out-of-bound index (see Section 3.6 [p. 104] for a discussion of exceptions).

Multidimensional Arrays

A multidimensional array is treated simply as an array of arrays. A k-dimensional array can be created with either of the following methods.

1. Using the `new` operator:

    $$\text{new } Type \ [\ n_1 \ ] \ [\ n_2 \ ] \ \cdots \ [\ n_k \ ]$$

    The size of each dimension is $n_1, n_2, \ldots, n_k$, respectively. All the elements in the array are initialized to the default initial values [p. 59] based on the type of the elements.

2. Using the k-dimensional array initializer:

    $$\{ \ I_1, I_2, \ldots, I_k \ \}$$

    where each $I_1, I_2, \ldots, I_k$ is a $(k-1)$-dimensional array initializer.

The following are examples of creating and initializing two-dimensional arrays:

```
double mat1[][] = new double[4][5];
```

Create a 4 × 5 two-dimensional array. All elements are initialized to 0.0.

```
int mat2[][] = {{1, 2, 3}, {4, 5, 6}};
```

Create a 2 × 3 two-dimensional array. The elements are initialized as

```
mat2[0][0] = 1, mat2[0][1] = 2, mat2[0][2] = 3
mat2[1][0] = 4, mat2[1][1] = 5, mat2[1][2] = 6
```

3.3   STATEMENTS

The syntax and semantics of statements in Java are nearly identical to those of C and C++. There is one exception: The `goto` statement was eliminated. As early as 1966, Böhm and Jacopini [Böhm and Jacopini 1996] pointed out that the `goto` statement is unnecessary. That is, any program containing `goto` statements can be converted to a functionally equivalent program without `goto` statements. In 1968, Dijkstra made perhaps the best known assertion about the `goto` statement, considering it to be harmful [Dijkstra 1968]. Nearly 30 years later, the `goto` statement remains in almost every programming language in use because occasionally it is useful. However, Java's developers eliminated the `goto` statement by providing some sensible alternatives: multilevel break and continue (see Section 3.3.5 [p. 69]) and exception handling (see Section 3.6 [p. 106]).

3.3.1   Statement Labels

Each statement can have an optional label, which is simply an identifier. A labeled statement has the syntax

[*StatementLabel* **:**] *Statement*

Labels can be used in `break` and `continue` statements. In Java, although it is legal to attach a label to any statement, it is only meaningful to attach a label to a statement block, a `switch` statement, or a `loop` statement. In the following program segment `Loop1` and `Loop2` are labels:

```
Loop1: while (i-- > 0) {
    Loop2: while (j++ < 100) {
        // ...
    }
}
```

3.3.2   Statement Blocks

A *statement block* simply consists of a sequence of statements or local variable declarations (which are also considered statements) enclosed by a pair of braces, { }. The statements in a statement block can be either simple or compound and are executed sequentially:

```
{
    Statement₁
    Statement₂
        ⋮
    Statementₙ
}
```

For example,

```
{
    int i = 0;
    prime[i++] = 2;
    prime[i++] = 3;
    prime[i++] = 5;
}
```

3.3.3   Simple Statements

The simple statements in Java include *expression* statements, *declaration* statements, *break* statements, *continue* statements, and *return* statements. Simple statements must be terminated by a semicolon (;).

Expression Statements

Assignment expressions and increment/decrement expressions can be made into statements by appending a terminating semicolon. For example, the following are expression statements.

```
x = 5;
m <<= k;
i++;
--j;
```

Expressions for object creation and method invocation can also be made into statements by appending a semicolon to the expressions, as in

```
point1 = new Point();
point1.move(10, 10);
ia = new int[3];
```

We discuss object creation and method invocation in Sections 3.4.2 [p. 73] and 3.4.4 [p. 76].

Declaration Statements

Variable declarations also can be made into statements by appending a terminating semicolon. Declaration statements can occur anywhere in a statement block and can be intermixed with other statements. The variables declared in the declaration statements are *local variables*. The scope of a local variable begins at its declaration and extends to the end of the immediate enclosing statement block. For example,

```
{
    ...
    int i;       // i's scope begins here
    i = 10;
    int j = 10;  // j's scope begins here
    i += j;
    ...
}               // both i's scope and j's scope end here
```

Local variables are not automatically initialized. They must be assigned values explicitly.

The break and continue Statements

A break statement abruptly terminates an enclosing compound statement. A continue statement must be enclosed in a loop statement, completing the current iteration of one of the enclosing loop statements. The syntax of the break and continue statements is

break [*StatementLabel*];

continue [*StatementLabel*];

An unlabeled break statement must be enclosed in a loop statement or a switch statement, terminating the immediate enclosing iteration or switch statement. A labeled break statement must be enclosed by a labeled statement, which it terminates. An unlabeled continue statement completes the current iteration of the immediate enclosing loop statement and starts a new iteration. A labeled continue statement must be enclosed by a labeled loop statement. It completes the current iteration of the labeled enclosing iteration statement and starts a new iteration. We discuss the use of break and continue statements shortly under *Selection Statements*. We discuss the use of labeled break and continue statements in Section 3.3.5 [p. 69].

The return Statement

The return statement terminates the execution of a method and returns control to its caller. The syntax of the return statement is

return [*Expression*];

The type of the expression must match the return type of the method that contains the return statement. The return statement may not have an expression if the return type of the method that contains the return statement is void. (See Section 3.4.4 for a discussion of methods.)

3.3.4   Compound Statements

Compound statements are statements composed of other statements. They include statement blocks, selection statements, loop statements, and try-catch statements.

We have already discussed statement blocks (see Section 3.3.2). We discuss the try-catch statement in Section 3.6 [p. 106].

Selection Statements

Java has two types of selection statements: the **if** statement,

```
if ( Condition )          if ( Condition )
    Statement                 Statement₁
                          else
                              Statement₂
```

and the **switch** statement,

```
switch ( Expression ) {

case CaseLabel₁:

    Statement₁

         ⋮

case CaseLabelₙ:

    Statementₙ

default:

    Statementₙ₊₁

}
```

The expression following the `switch` keyword must be an integer expression. The *case labels* in `switch` statements are different from statement labels. Case labels must be *constant* integer expressions. Each branch in a `switch` statement may have one or more labels. Although the `default` branch is optional, you should include the `default` branch at the end.

The execution of a `switch` statement begins with evaluation of the integer expression and comparison of the result with each case label sequentially. The first branch with a matching case label will be executed. If none of the case labels match the result of the expression, the default branch will be executed. If the default branch is absent, the entire `switch` statement is skipped. Each branch is usually terminated by a `break` statement, in which case execution continues with the statement following the `switch` statement. If a branch is not terminated by a `break` statement, execution will fall through and continue with the next branch of the `switch` statement. This *fall-through* feature allows several branches to share common code.

Loop Statements

There are three types of loop statements: the **while** loop,

```
while ( Condition )
    Statement
```

the **do** loop,

> **do**
>
> > *Statement*
>
> **while** (*Condition*) **;**

which is equivalent to

> > *Statement*
>
> > while (*Condition*)
>
> > > *Statement*

wherein the two occurences of *Statement* refer to the same statement, and the **for** loop,

> **for** (*InitExpr* **;** *Condition* **;** *IncrExpr*)
>
> > *Statement*

which is equivalent to

> > *InitExpr;*
>
> > while (*Condition*) {
>
> > > *Statement*
> >
> > > *IncrExpr;*
>
> > }

EXAMPLE 3.1

Assume the following declaration of a one-dimensional integer array:

```
int a[];
```

The following program segment calculates the sum of the values in the array.

```
int sum =0;
for (int i = 0; i < a.length; i++) {
  sum += a[i];
}
System.out.println("The sum is: " + sum);
```

EXAMPLE 3.2

Assume the same declaration of a one-dimensional integer array:

```
int a[];
```

The following program segment—utilizing the *bubble sort* algorithm—sorts the array in ascending order and prints the sorted array.

```
for (int i = a.length; --i >= 0; )
    for (int j = 0; j < i; j++) {
        if (a[j] > a[j+1]) {
            int temp = a[j];
            a[j] = a [j + 1];
            a[j + 1] = temp;
        }
    }
}
// print the sorted array
for (int k = 0; k < a.length; k++) {
    System.out.println("a[" + k + "]: " + a[k]);
}
```

3.3.5   Multilevel Breaking

Multilevel breaking is used to break out of a loop that is not the immediate enclosing loop statement, as for example in

```
outer: while (cond1) {
    inner: while (cond2) {
        // ...
        break;
        // ...
    }
}
```

With the preceding pair of nested loops, the break statement will break out of the inner loop but not the outer loop. Using a break statement to break out of an inner loop and outer loop simultaneously also is known as multilevel breaking. Sometimes, multilevel breaking is desirable. Let's consider the two dimensional array

```
double matrix[][];
```

We try to determine whether all the values are nonnegative. The following is a solution in C and C++, which uses a goto statement to break out the nested loop.

```
boolean nonNegative = true;
for (int i = 0; i < matrix.length; i++) {
    for (int j = 0; j < matrix[i].length; j++) {
        if (matrix[i,j] < 0.0) {
            nonNegative = false;
            goto Done;
        }
    }
}
Done: // ...
```

One way of eliminating the `goto` statement requires a new boolean variable, `isDone`, and a more complicated loop condition for the outer loop.

```
boolean nonNegative = true;
boolean isDone = false;
for (int i = 0; !isDone && i < matrix.length; i++) {
    for (int j = 0; j < matrix[i].length; j++) {
        if (matrix[i,j] < 0.0) {
            nonNegative = false;
            isDone = true;
            break; // breaks out of the inner loop
        }
    }
}
```

In Java, however, the labeled `break` statement can be used for multilevel breaking.

```
      boolean nonNegative = true;
OuterLoop:
    for (int i = 0; i < matrix.length; i++) {
        for (int j = 0; j < matrix[i].length; j++) {
            if (matrix[i,j] < 0.0) {
                nonNegative = false;
                break OuterLoop; // breaks out of the outer loop
            }
        }
    }
```

A labeled `break` statement must occur within a labeled compound statement, which can be a loop statement, `switch` statement, or a statement block. The labeled `break` statement will transfer control to the statement immediately following the labeled statement.

Similarly, A labeled `continue` statement must occur within a labeled loop statement. The labeled `continue` statement will complete the current iteration of the labeled loop statement.

3.4 CLASS DECLARATIONS

Classes are the basic building blocks of Java programs. A Java program consists of one or more class declarations. A *class declaration* defines a *class*, and each class defines a reference type.

3.4.1 Class Syntax

A class declaration consists of the *class name*, and a sequence of fields, methods, and inner class declarations. The fields of a class are also known as the *variables* or *attributes* of the class. The syntax of class, field, and method declarations is summarized as follows:

> [*ClassModifiers*] **class** *ClassName*
>   [**extends** *SuperClass*]
>   [**implements** *Interface₁, Interface₂* ...] {
>   *ClassMemberDeclarations*
> }

A class declaration may begin with a list of *class modifiers*, which are summarized as follows:

	When no modifier is present, by default, the class is accessible by all the classes within the same package (see Section 3.5 [p. 99]).
public	A public class is accessible by any class.
private	A private class is accessible only by classes within the same file.
abstract	An abstract class contains abstract methods (see Section 5.2 [p. 179]).
final	A final class may not have subclasses.

Only `public` or `private` may appear in a class modifier list. Each file can contain only one public class. The name of the file and the name of the public class it contains must coincide, and the file must have the extension `.java`. For example, the class declaration of public class `Point` must be stored in a file named `Point.java`.

The `extends` clause specifies the superclass, and the `implements` clause specifies the interfaces being implemented. We discuss extending classes in Section 4.2 [p. 122], and implementing interfaces in Section 4.3 [p. 135].

The body of a class declaration consists of a list of member declarations. Member declarations can be declarations of *fields*, *methods*, and *inner classes*, which are classes nested inside a class. The field, method, and inner class declarations can be intermixed, and the order is unimportant. Thus they can be ordered in a way that is most logical and comprehensible.

A method declaration takes the form

> [*MethodModifiers*] *ReturnType MethodName* ([*ParameterList*]) {
>   *Statements*
> }

A field declaration takes the form

> [*FieldModifiers*] *Type FieldName₁* [= *Initializer₁*] ,
>   *FieldName₂* [= *Initializer₂*] ... ;

An inner class declaration has the same syntax as the top-level class declaration, with one exception: An inner class may not contain other nested inner classes.

Each class member declaration begins with an optional list of modifiers. Modifiers that can be applied to method, field, and inner class declarations include:

	When no modifier is present, by default, a member is accessible by all the classes within the same package (see Section 3.5 [p. 99]).
public	A public member is accessible by any class.

protected	A protected member is accessible by the class itself, all its subclasses (see Section 4.2 [p. 122]), and all the classes within the same package.
private	A private member is accessible only by the class itself.
static	A static field is shared by all instances of the class. A static method accesses only static fields (see Section 3.4.5 [p. 79]). A static inner class has an implicit reference to the enclosing class (see Section 3.4.6 [p. 83]).
final	A final method may not be overridden in subclasses (see Section 4.2.3 [p. 130]). A final field has a constant value, which may not be changed (see Section 3.4.5 [p. 79]).

Modifiers that can be applied only to method declarations include:

abstract	An abstract method has deferred implementation (see Section 5.2 [p. 179]).
synchronized	A synchronized method is atomic in a multithread environment (see Section 8.2.1 [p. 378]).
native	A native method is implemented in C and C++.

Modifiers that can be applied only to field declarations include:

volatile	A volatile field may be modified by nonsynchronized methods in a multithread environment. (see Section 8.2.1 [p. 378]).
transient	A transient field is not part of the persistent state of the instances (see Section 6.4.1 [p. 291]).

Only one public, protected, or private modifier may appear in a member list. Member accessibility is summarized in Table 3.2.

TABLE 3.2

Accessibility of class members.

	Public	Protected	Package	Private
The class itself	Yes*	Yes	Yes	Yes
Classes in the same package	Yes	Yes	Yes	No†
Subclasses in a different package	Yes	Yes	No	No
Non-subclasses in a different package	Yes	No	No	No

* Yes: Accessible.
† No: Not accessible.

Method Declarations

The return type of a method is required. If a method does not return a value, the return type should be specified as `void`. A method may take a list of parameter declarations separated by commas (the list could be empty). Parameters are declared in the form

> [**final**] *Type ParameterName*

A final parameter is one that cannot be assigned a value inside the method (see *Pitfall: Final Parameters* in Section 3.4.4 [p. 78]).

The following declaration is of a simple `Point` class, which represents points in a two-dimensional space.

```
public class Point {
  public double x, y;

  public void move(double dx, double dy) {
    x += dx; y += dy;
  }
}
```

3.4.2   Creating and Initializing Objects

There are four ways of initializing the fields of a class: an explicit initializer in a declaration, default initial values, an initialization block, or constructors.

Explicit Initializer

A field can be assigned an initial value in the declaration with an *explicit initializer*. For example, the x and y in the `Point` class can be explicitly initialized as

```
public double x = 0.0, y = 0.0;
```

Default Initial Values

If the fields are not explicitly initialized, they are implicitly initialized to their default initial values [p. 59].

Constructors

Another way to initialize fields is to use constructors. *Constructors* are special methods that have the same name as the class; their return type must be omitted. A class may have multiple constructors, provided that they take different numbers of arguments or arguments of different types.[4] The following is an enhanced `Point` class declaration with two constructors.

---

[4] Constructors can be *overloaded.* See Section 4.1 [p. 118].

```
public class Point {
  public double x, y;

  public Point() {  // no-arg constructor
    x = 0.0; y = 0.0;
  }

  public Point(double init_x, double init_y) {
    x = init_x; y = init_y;
  }

  public void move(double dx, double dy) {
    x += dx; y += dy;
  }
}
```

A constructor that takes no parameters is known as a *no-arg constructor* (short-hand for a no-arguments constructor). Instances of a class can be created with the new operator followed by an invocation of one of the constructors of the class. For example,

```
Point p1 = new Point();           // using the no-arg constructor
Point p2 = new Point(20.0, 20.0); // using the other constructor
```

If no constructor is provided for a class, a default no-arg constructor with an empty body is provided implicitly. In other words, even if none of the constructors of the Point class in the preceding example were provided, creating instances of the Point class with the no-arg constructor would still be legal, as in

```
Point p3 = new Point();
```

The instance p3 would be initialized to (0, 0) by virtue of the default initial values. When constructors are provided explicitly, the no-arg constructor is no longer provided implicitly. It must be provided explicitly if it is desired. In other words, if the no-arg constructor of Point class were removed but the other constructor remained, new Point() would be illegal. Hence the no-arg constructor should be provided for all classes.

Initialization Block

Fields can be also initialized by means of an *initialization block*, which is a statement block directly enclosed in the class declaration. The initialization block is executed before the body of any constructor is executed. The initialization block can be used to avoid duplicating identical statements for initializing fields in several constructors. These identical statements can be factored to the initialization block. This block is needed only when the initializations are too complicated for initializers, such as those that require loops. For example, the following Card and Deck classes model the cards and decks used in card games such as bridge.

```
public class Card {
  // the following are symbolic constants
  public static final byte CLUBSUIT    = 0;
  public static final byte DIAMONDSUIT = 1;
```

```
public static final byte HEARTSUIT   = 2;
public static final byte SPADESUIT   = 3;

public byte suit; // range: CLUBSUIT - - SPADESUIT
public byte rank; // range: 2 - - 14
                  //     11=Jack, 12=Queen, 13=King, 14=Ace
}
public class Deck {
   public Card[] cards = new Card[52];

   { // initialization block
      int i = 0;
      for (byte suit = Card.CLUBSUIT; suit <= Card.SPADESUIT; suit++) {
         for (byte rank = 2; rank <= 14; rank++) {
            cards[i] = new Card();
            cards[i].suit = suit;
            cards[i].rank = rank;
            i++;
         }
      }
   }

   // constructors and methods ...
}
```

The initialization of `cards` is more suited to the use of loops than enumerating all 52 cards in an array initializer. The `Deck` class may have several constructors. Placing the initialization of `cards` in the initialization block avoids duplication of code in several constructors.

3.4.3 Accessing Members

After an instance has been created, the fields and methods of the instance can be accessed as follows:

objectReference.method **(** *Parameters* **)**
objectReference. *field*

For example,

```
Point p1 = new Point();
double x1 = p1.x; // the value is 0.0
double y1 = p1.y; // the value is 0.0
p1.move(10.0, 20.0);
double x2 = p1.x; // the value is 10.0
double y2 = p1.y; // the value is 20.0
```

Comparison with C++

In C++ variables of a class type can be declared in three different ways.

```
Point p1;   // an object
Point *p2;  // a pointer to an object
Point &p3;  // a reference to an object
```

```
p1.x        // access a field of an object directly
p2->x       // access a field of an object through a pointer
p3.x        // access a field of an object through a reference
```

Memory space for object variables is automatically allocated and deallocated on the stack. No explicit allocation using the `new` operator is necessary. Memory space for pointer variables is also allocated on the stack. The memory space for objects referenced by the pointer variable must be explicitly allocated on the heap, using the `new` operator, and explicitly deallocated, using the `delete` operator. Reference variables serve as aliases for objects either on the stack or on the heap.

In Java, a variable of a class type can be declared in only one way.

```
Point p1; // a reference to an object
p1.x;      // access a field of an object through a reference
```

In terms of Java reference variables, memory space for objects must always be explicitly allocated on the garbage-collected heap by the `new` operator. Java reference variables are analogous to C++ pointer variables but use the syntax of C++ object variables for accessing members. In Java deallocation of memory space is automatically handled through garbage collection. No explicit deallocation is necessary. Hence there is no Java counterpart of the C++ destructor, whose main responsibility is to deallocate memory space.[5]

3.4.4   Method Invocation and Parameter Passing

Implementing Methods

The body of a method is simply a block statement. If the return type of a method is `void`, the `return` statements in the method body may not return values. If the return type of a method is not `void`, *all* the paths of the method body must be terminated by a `return` statement with an expression that matches the return type. The following `calculateItemTotal()` method will cause a compilation error because the path of `quantity < 0` is not terminated by a `return` statement.

```
public class PurchaseOrder {
  // ...
  public double calculateItemTotal(double unitPrice, int quantity) {
    if (quantity >= 0) {
      return unitPrice * quantity;
    }
  }
}
```

To correct this error, we must add a `return` statement to return a value when the `quantity` is negative or an exception must be thrown (see Section 3.6 [p. 104]).

The local variables declared in method bodies are not automatically initialized to their default initial values. Local variables must be explicitly initialized on all paths

---

[5] When some cleanup must to be done before an object is deallocated, such as closing files or flushing changes to files, the `finalize()` method in the `Object` class can be used.

that lead to their uses. For example, the following `calculateItemTotal` method will cause a compilation error because the local variable `total` is not initialized on the path of `quantity < 0`.

```
public class PurchaseOrder {
  // ...
  public double calculateItemTotal(double unitPrice, int quantity) {
     double total;
     if (quantity >= 0) {
        total = unitPrice * quantity;
     }
     return total;
  }
}
```

This error can be corrected in one of two ways:

```
public class PurchaseOrder {
  // ...
  public double calculateItemTotal(double unitPrice, int quantity) {
     double total = 0.0;
     if (quantity >= 0) {
        total = unitPrice * quantity;
     }
     return total;
  }
}
```

or

```
public class PurchaseOrder {
  // ...
  public double calculateItemTotal(double unitPrice, int quantity) {
     double total;
     if (quantity >= 0) {
        total = unitPrice * quantity;
     } else {
        total = 0.0;
     }
     return total;
  }
}
```

Parameter Passing

In Java, all parameters of methods are passed *by value*. In other words, modifications to parameters of primitive types inside a method will be made on copies of the actual parameters and will have no effect on the actual parameters themselves. Consider the example of class C1,

```
public class C1 {
   public void inc(int i) { i++; }
}
```

and an invocation of the `inc` method,

```
C1 c1 = new C1();
int k = 1;
c1.inc(k);  // k is still 1 afterward
```

For parameters of reference types, the fields of the actual parameters can indeed be affected inside a method. Consider the example of class C2,

```
public class C2 {
    public void pointInc(Point p) { p.x++; p.y++; }
}
```

and an invocation of the `pointInc` method,

```
C2 c2 = new C2();
Point p = new Point(10.0, 10.0);
c2.pointInc(p);  // now p is (11.0, 11.0)
```

Hence parameters of reference types can serve as in–out parameters. In order for a parameter of primitive type to do so, it must be wrapped inside a class. Consider the example of an integer wrapped in the `IntRef` class so that it may act as an in–out parameter,

```
class IntRef {
    public int val;
    public IntRef(int i) { val = i; }
}

public class C3 {
    public void inc(IntRef i) { i.val++; }
}
```

and an invocation of the `inc` method,

```
C3 c3 = new C3();
IntRef k = new IntRef(1);
c3.inc(k);  // now k.val is 2
```

Usually, a method passes values back to its caller via the return value of the method. In–out parameters are necessary only when the method needs to pass multiple values back to the caller.

Pitfall: Final Parameters

The notion of final parameters in Java is rather weak. A final parameter of a method may not be assigned a new value in the body of the method. However, if the parameter is of reference type, it is allowed to modify the object or array referenced by the final parameter. Let's consider the following method.

```
void aMethod(final IntRef i) {
    // ...
    i = new IntRef(2);  // not allowed
}
```

This code segment will cause a compilation error because it is not allowed to assign a final parameter a new value. However, the following method is allowed.

```
void aMethod(final IntRef i) {
    // ...
    i.val++; // ok.
}
```

Java final parameters are not the same as `const` parameters in C++. Furthermore, there is no Java counterpart of C++ `const` methods, which do not modify the state of the receiving object.

3.4.5   Static Fields and Methods

By default the fields declared in a class are *instance fields*, which means that each instance of the class carries its own copy of these fields, and modifications to the fields of one instance will not affect any other instances. In contrast, *static fields* are shared by all the instances of the same class. There is only one copy of each static field for the class. Modifications to static fields will affect all the instances of the class. If a method accesses only static fields, it can be declared as a *static method*. Static methods are also called *class methods*, and nonstatic methods are also called *instance methods*.

Instance fields and methods can be accessed only through an object reference. Static fields and methods may be accessed through either an object reference or the class name.

objectReference.staticMethod **(** *Parameters* **)**
objectReference.staticField

ClassName.staticMethod **(** *Parameters* **)**
ClassName.staticField

Static fields and methods should be accessed through class names, not object references. Then instance fields and methods can easily be distinguished from static fields and methods by the way they are accessed.

Static and instance fields and methods are subject to the same accessibility controls. Another version of the `Point` class with two new fields involves an instance field, `moveCount()`, that counts the total number of moves made by each instance and a static field, `globalMoveCount()`, that counts the total number of moves made by *all* instances of the `Point` class. The method `getGlobalMoveCount()` is declared static because it accesses only static fields.

```
public class Point {
    public double x, y;
    private int moveCount;
    static private int globalMoveCount;

    public void move(double dx, double dy) {
        x += dx; y += dy;
        moveCount++;
        globalMoveCount++;
    }
```

```
public int getMoveCount() {
    return moveCount;
}

static public int getGlobalMoveCount() {
    return globalMoveCount;
}
}
```

The following code segment illustrates the invocation of static methods.

```
Point p1 = new Point();
Point p2 = new Point();
p1.move(20.0, 10.0);
p1.move(10.0, 20.0);
p2.move(10.0, 10.0);
int count1, count2, count3;
count1 = p1.getMoveCount(); // count1 is 2
count2 = p2.getMoveCount(); // count2 is 1
// The next three statements will get the same result.
count3 = p1.getGlobalMoveCount();      // count3 is 3
count3 = p2.getGlobalMoveCount();      // count3 is 3
count3 = Point.getGlobalMoveCount(); // count3 is 3
```

Initialization of Static Fields

Static fields can exist without any instances of the class being created. In fact, static fields are initialized before any of the instances of the class are created and before any of the static fields or methods are accessed. The lifetime of static fields extends until the program terminates. With respect to lifetime, static fields are similar to the global variables of C and C++.

Static fields can be initialized

1. with default initial values.
   This is how globalMoveCount() is initialized in the preceding example. It is initialized to the default initial value 0.
2. with an explicit initializer in its declaration.
   The globalMoveCount() field in the preceding example can also be initialized with an explicit initializer.

```
public class Point {
    // ...
    static private int globalMoveCount = 0;
    // ...
}
```

3. by the static initialization block.
   The static initialization block is similar to the instance fields initialization block, except that it begins with the keyword static. The globalMoveCount() field in the preceding example can also be initialized with a static initialization block.

```
public class Point {
   // ...
   static private int globalMoveCount;

   static {
      globalMoveCount = 0;
   }

   // ...
}
```

Static fields should not be initialized in constructors, as constructors are executed only when instances are created. Therefore constructors are used for initializing instance fields only.

Constants

In Java, constants are declared as static final fields. For example, several integer constants for specifying font styles are defined in the Font class.

```
public class Font {
   public final static int PLAIN  = 0;
   public final static int BOLD   = 1;
   public final static int ITALIC = 2;
   // ...
}
```

We may also define constant objects. In the Color class, some commonly used colors are declared as follows.

```
public class Color {
   public final static Color black  = new Color(0, 0, 0);
   public final static Color blue   = new Color(0, 0, 255);
   public final static Color gray   = new Color(128, 128, 128);
   public final static Color white  = new Color(255, 255, 255);
   public final static Color yellow = new Color(255, 255, 0);
   // ...
}
```

Style Convention   *Constant Names*

Constants of primitive types have their names in all uppercase letters (e.g., the constants in the Font class).

Constants of reference types are named following the usual naming convention of instance names (e.g., the constants in the Color class).

The main() Method

Each class can have a special static method main(), which must be declared as

```
public static void main(String[] args) { ... }
```

The `main()` method serves as the entry point for the Java virtual machine (JVM) to invoke a Java app. Java apps are invoked as

```
venus% java ClassName [ Arguments ]
```

ClassName.`main()` is invoked to start an app. When the app starts, no instance of *ClassName* has been created, so only a static method can be invoked. Thus the start-up method `main()` must be static.

The command line arguments, not including `java` or the class name, are passed to the `main` method through the `args` parameter.

EXAMPLE 3.3

The following program prints out the command line arguments.

Print command line arguments

```java
public class Arguments {

    public static void main(String[] args) {
        if (args.length > 0) {
            for (int i = 0; i < args.length; i++) {
                System.out.println("args[" + i + "]: " + args[i]);
            }
        } else {
            System.out.println("No arguments.");
        }
    }

}
```

If the program is invoked as

```
venus% java Arguments foo bar
```

the result is

```
args[0]: foo
args[1]: bar
```

Singleton Classes

Some classes should not be allowed more than one instance at a time. Examples are the top-level window of an application and the timer of an entire system. Classes that can have no more than one instance at a time are called *singleton classes*. Using static fields and methods, we can ensure that no more than one instance of a singleton class exits at the same time. The following is a schematic implementation of a singleton class.

```java
public class Singleton {
    static public Singleton getInstance() {
        if (theInstance == null) {
            theInstance = new Singleton();
        }
```

```
                return theInstance;
        }

        protected Singleton() {
                // initializing instance fields
        }

        // instance fields and methods

        private static Singleton theInstance = null;
}
```

The unique instance of the `Singleton` class is stored in a static variable, `theInstance`, which is initialized to `null`. Note that the constructor of the `Singleton` class is *protected*. Therefore clients are prohibited from creating an instance of the `Singleton` class by doing

```
            myInstance = new Singleton();
```

The only way for clients to obtain an instance of the `Singleton` class is to use the static method `getInstance()`:

```
            myInstance = Singleton.getInstance();
```

Hence just one instance of the `Singleton` class can be created!

3.4.6   Object Reference this

The keyword `this` can be used inside instance methods to refer to the *receiving object* (also known as the *receiver* or the *recipient*) of the method, that is, the object instance through which the method is invoked. The object reference `this` may not occur inside static methods. The two common uses of `this` are (a) to pass the receiving object instance as a parameter and (b) to access instance fields shadowed, or hidden, by local variables.

Passing this as a Parameter

Let's consider the composition relationship between `Faculty` and `Department`, as shown previously in Fig. 1.3. The relationship can be implemented as follows.

```
public class Faculty {
    protected Department dept;
    protected String name;

    public Faculty(String n, Department d) {
        name = n; dept = d;
    }

    public Department getDepartment() {
        return dept;
    }

    // ... other methods
}
```

Each faculty member has a name and a reference to the department to which the faculty member belongs.

```
public class Department {
   protected String name;
   protected Faculty facultyList[] = new Faculty[100];
   protected int numOfFaculty = 0;

   public Department(String n) {
      name = n;
   }

   public void newFaculty(String name) {
      facultyList[numOfFaculty++] =
         new Faculty(name, this);
   }
   // ... other methods
}
```

Each department has a name and a list of faculty members who belong to the department. Maintaining the following consistency is important:

If a faculty member a occurs in the `facultyList` of department d, then `a.dept` should refer to d.

This consistency requirement is maintained in the `newFaculty()` method by passing the `this` reference—the department to which the new faculty member belongs—as the parameter to the constructor of the `Faculty` class.

Accessing Shadowed Fields

A field declared in a class can be *shadowed*, or *hidden*, inside a method by a parameter or a local variable of the same name, as in the following code segment.

```
public class MyClass {
   int var; // an instance variable

   void method1() {
      float var; // the local variable var shadows the instance variable
      // ...
   }

   void method2(int var) {
      // the parameter var also shadows the instance variable
      // ...
   }

}
```

Java utilizes the usual scope rule: When a name in an outer scope is shadowed by a name in an inner scope, the name in the outer scope is hidden. However, the hidden variable can be accessed as `this.var`. In general, the shadowing of variable names in outer scopes is a bad programming practice and should be avoided, as it is a common source of program bugs. In contrast, the shadowing of variables of a class from within its methods is an acceptable and common practice, if the local variables are indeed copies of the variables of the same class. The purpose is to avoid the confusion of introducing a new set of variable names to mirror the variables of the class. The following program segment is another version of the Point class.

```
public class Point {
    public double x, y;

    public Point() {}

    public Point(double x, double y) {
        // the parameters x and y are simply the initial values of
        // fields x and y of class Point
        this.x = x; this.y = y;
    }

    public void adjustPosition(...) {
        double x = this.x, y = this.y;
        // do calculation using the local x and y
        // commit the changes when done
        this.x = x; this.y = y;
    }

    // ... other methods
}
```

In the preceding constructor, parameters x and y represent the initial values of the corresponding instance fields of class Point. The expressions this.x and this.y refer to the instance variables. In method adjustPosition(), the instance fields are copied to the local variables with the same names. Calculations are performed on these local copies. Only when the calculations have been completed will the results be committed to the instance fields of class Point. Therefore no intermediate values are ever stored in the instance fields. The advantages of this approach are to avoid leaving intermediate results in the instance variables, in case an exception is encountered (see Section 3.6 [p. 104]) and to avoid synchronizing an entire method of a multithreaded program. Only the reading and writing of instance fields should be synchronized. The calculation portion can be unsynchronized (see Section 8.2.1 [p. 378]).

Hint   *Shadowing Variables*

Avoid shadowing variables. Shadow only the class fields with local variables that serve as temporary copies of the class fields in a method. Always copy the local variables back to the class fields before leaving the method.

3.4.7   Interfaces and Abstract Classes

Interfaces can be thought of as a special form of class, which declares only the features to be supported by the class. Java interfaces provide no implementation.

Implementation is deferred to the classes that implement the interface. The syntax of an interface declaration is

> [*ClassModifiers*] **interface** *InterfaceName*
> [**extends** *Interface*$_1$, *Interface*$_2$ ...] {
> *InterfaceMemberDeclarations*
> }

Interface members can be either *abstract methods* or constants (i.e., static and final fields). Implementation of abstract methods is deferred to subclasses. Abstract methods are declared as

> *MethodModifiers ReturnType MethodName* **(** [*ParameterList*] **)** **;**

All interfaces are public, and all methods and constants declared in interfaces are public. The `public` modifier can be omitted in interface declarations.Static methods are not allowed in interfaces. Interfaces have no constructors and no instances of interfaces are allowed. The two commonly used interfaces in Java are the `Runnable` interface,

```
interface Runnable {
   void run();
}
```

and the `Iterator` interface,

```
interface Iterator {
   boolean hasNext();
   Object  next();
   Object  remove();
}
```

Classes can implement an interface by overriding the methods declared in the interface. Classes may also declare abstract methods by using the modifier `abstract`.

> `abstract` *MethodModifiers ReturnType MethodName* ([*ParameterList*]);

An *abstract class* is a class that includes or inherits at least one abstract method. In other words, an abstract class is a class with partial implementation. Although the presence of an abstract method in a class implies that the class is abstract, the class must still be declared abstract explicitly; that is, the class modifier `abstract` must be present for the sake of readability. Like interfaces, an abstract class may not have instances. We discuss the implementation, extension, and use of interfaces in detail in Chapters 4 and 5.

3.4.8 Strings

A *string* is a sequence of characters. The `string` type is not a primitive type in Java; it is a class type. Java provides two classes to support strings: (a) the `String` class, whose instances are immutable (i.e., constant strings), and the `StringBuffer` class, whose instances are mutable strings. The rationale for distinguishing mutable from immutable strings is that in a typical program most strings are immutable.

Immutable strings allow simpler implementation and a more compact representation than do mutable strings.

The String class is special in the sense that it enjoys some unique privileges not shared by ordinary classes.

- A string can be created using *string literals* (see *String Literals* in Section 3.1.3 [p. 51]).
- Operators + and += can be applied to strings (see *String Concatenation* in Section 3.1.4 [p. 54]).

The characters in a string are indexed by integers 0 to $n - 1$, where n is the length of the string. The common operations on strings are summarized in Table 3.3.

TABLE 3.3

Methods of operation on strings.

Method	Description
s.length()	Return the length of string s.
s.charAt(i)	Return the ith character of string s.
s.indexOf(c)	Return the index of the first occurance of character c, return -1 if c does not occur in s.
s.indexOf(c, i)	Return the index of the first occurance of character c after (including) index i; return -1 if c does not occur in s after index i.
s.indexOf(s1)	Return the index of the first occurance of string s1; return -1 if s1 does not occur in s.
s.indexOf(s1, i)	Return the index of the first occurance of string s1 after (including) index i; return -1 if s1 does not occur in s after index i.
s.substring(i)	Return the substring of s from i to the end.
s.substring(i, j)	Return the substring of s from i to $j - 1$, inclusive.
s.toLowerCase()	Return a string with all the characters in s converted to lowercase.
s.toUpperCase()	Return a string with all the characters in s converted to uppercase.
s.trim()	Return a string with all the leading and trailing white space of s removed.
s1.endsWith(s2)	Return true if s2 is a suffix of s1.
s1.startsWith(s2)	Return true if s2 is a prefix of s1.

The `StringBuffer` class provides an overloaded `append()` method that appends the text representation of its arguments to the string buffer.

String Comparison

For two string variables `s1` and `s2`, `s1 == s2` indicates the equality of the two references, not the equality of the strings referenced by them. Thus `s1 == s2` is `true` if and only if both `s1` and `s2` reference the same string (i.e., point to the same memory location). The equivalence of two strings can be tested in several ways:

`s1.equals(s2)` returns a boolean value,

`true`	if `s1` and `s2` are identical in content (case-sensitive).
`false`	otherwise.

`s1.equalsIgnoreCase(s2)` is the same as `equals()`, except that the comparison is case-insensitive.

`s1.compareTo(s2)` compares the two strings lexicographically, according to Unicode; the comparison is case-sensitive and returns an integer value of

`< 0`	if `s1` is lexicographically less than `s2`.
`0`	if `s1` and `s2` are equal.
`> 0`	if `s2` is lexicographically less than `s1`.

The different ways of comparing strings shown here

will yield the following results.

Expression	Result
`str1 == str2`	`true`
`str1 == str3`	`false`
`str1.equals(str2)`	`true`
`str1.equals(str3)`	`true`
`str1.compareTo(str2)`	`0`
`str1.compareTo(str3)`	`0`

The `toString()` Method

The `toString()` method of a class allows it to define a string representation of the class. For example, we can add the following `toString()` method to the `Point` class.

```
public class Point {
  public double x, y;

  // other methods ...

  public String toString() {
    return "(" + x + ", " + y + ")";
  }
}
```

If we assume that `str` is a string variable and that `obj` is a variable of class type, the expression

```
str + obj
```

is interpreted as

```
str + obj.toString()
```

Now, having added the `toString()` method to the `Point` class, we may do the following.

```
Point p = new Point(10.0, 20.0);
System.out.println("A point at" + p);
```

The output will be

```
A point at (10.0, 20.0)
```

String and `char` Array

Unlike those in C and C++, strings in Java are not `char` arrays. However, strings can be converted to `char` arrays and vice versa.

```
char data[] = {'F', 'o', 'o'};
String str = new String(data);
```

is equivalent to

```
String str = "Foo";
```

and

```
String str = "Bar";
char data[] = str.toCharArray();
```

is equivalent to

```
char data[] = {'B', 'a', 'r'};
```

More sophisticated methods for string–char array conversions are available also.

Reading and Writing Strings

We begin with an example of how strings can be read and written from the standard input and output streams. These streams are declared as static fields in the System class.

```
public class System {
    public static final InputStream in;   // the standard input
    public static final PrintStream out;  // the standard output
    public static final PrintStream err;  // the standard error output
    // ...
}
```

The Java input and output mechanism is both versatile and nontrivial (We discuss it in detail in Section 6.4 [p. 291]). However, operations that read and write strings are fairly simple.

EXAMPLE 3.4

The following program simply copies standard input to standard output, line by line.

Copy from standard input to standard output

```
import java.io.*;

public class Copy {

    public static void main(String[] args) {
        try {
            BufferedReader in = new BufferedReader(
                            new InputStreamReader(System.in));
            String line;
            while ((line = in.readLine()) != null) {
                System.out.println(line);
            }
        } catch (IOException e) {}
    }

}
```

We discuss the BufferedReader and InputStreamReader classes in Section 6.4 [p. 291]. The readLine() method simply reads a line from a character input stream. It returns null when the end of the stream is reached. Standard input and output can be redirected to files. The following invocation of the Copy class copies infile.txt to outfile.txt.

```
venus% java Copy < infile.txt > outfile.txt
```

Reading and writing text files directly is also quite easy.

EXAMPLE 3.5

The following program simply copies the contents of one text file to another text file, line by line.

Copy a text file

```java
import java.io.*;

public class CopyTextFile {

   public static void main(String[] args) {
      if (args.length >= 2) {
         try {
            BufferedReader in = new BufferedReader(
                             new FileReader(args[0]));
            PrintWriter out = new PrintWriter(
                             new BufferedWriter(
                             new FileWriter(args[1])));
            String line;
            while ((line = in.readLine()) != null) {
               out.println(line);
            }
            out.flush();
            out.close();
         } catch (IOException e) {}
      }
   }

}
```

Again, we discuss the `FileReader`, `FileWriter`, `PrintWriter`, and `BufferedWriter` classes in Section 6.4 [p. 291]. The following invocation copies a text file named `infile.txt` to `outfile.txt`.

```
venus% java CopyTextFile infile.txt outfile.txt
```

Working with Strings

We often need to divide strings into smaller pieces, known as *tokens*, that are separated by *separators* or *delimiters*. For example, it may be useful to break strings that represent sentences or paragraphs into words that are separated by spaces or some type of punctuation. The following colon-delimited records could be divided into fields.

```
Michael:Owen:123 Oak Street:Chicago:IL:60606
James:Gosling:456 Sun Blvd.:Mountain View:CA:45454
```

Each of these name and address records consists of fields that are delimited by colons (`:`). One way to break these strings is to use the `indexOf()` and `substring()` methods of the `String` class.

EXAMPLE 3.6

The following program reads colon-delimited records from standard input and breaks each record into fields.

Break colon-delimited records

```
import java.io.*;

public class BreakRecords {
  public static void main(String[] args) {
    BufferedReader in = new BufferedReader(
             new InputStreamReader(System.in));
    try {
      String record, field;
      char delim =':'; // the delimiter
      for (int n = 1; (record = in.readLine()) != null; n++) {
        System.out.println("Record " + n);
        int begin, end, i;
        begin = 0;
        for (i = 0; (end = record.indexOf(delim, begin)) >= 0; i++) {
          field = record.substring(begin, end);
          begin = end + 1; // skip the delimiter
          System.out.println("\tField " + i + ": " + field);
        }
        field = record.substring(begin); // the last field
        System.out.println("\tField " + i + ": " + field);
      }
    } catch (IOException e) { }
  }
}
```

The following output of the program is obtained when the two name and address records are used as input.

```
Record 1
        Field 0: Michael
        Field 1: Owen
        Field 2: 123 Oak Street
        Field 3: Chicago
        Field 4: IL
        Field 5: 60606
Record 2
        Field 0: James
        Field 1: Gosling
        Field 2: 456 Sun Blvd.
        Field 3: Mountain View
        Field 4: CA
        Field 5: 45454
```

The second approach separates the strings with the help of the StringTokenizer class.

EXAMPLE 3.7

The following program reads text from standard input and breaks the text into words.

Break text into words

```
import java.io.*;
import java.util.*;

public class Words {
   public static void main(String[] args) {
      BufferedReader in = new BufferedReader(
               new InputStreamReader(System.in));
      try {
         String line, word;
         String delim = " \t \n.,:;?!-/()[]\"\'";  // spaces and punctuations
         while ((line = in.readLine()) != null) {
            StringTokenizer st = new StringTokenizer(line, delim);
            while (st.hasMoreTokens()) {
               System.out.println(st.nextToken());
            }
         }
      } catch (IOException e) {}
   }
}
```

The constructor call in Example 3.7 creates an instance of the String-Tokenizer class that discards the delimiters indicated by the string delim. The StringTokenizer class has two other constructors. All three String-Tokenizer constructors are summarized in the following table. Parameter *str* is the string to be tokenized, *delim* is a string of delimiters, and *keep* is a boolean value indicating whether the delimiters should be returned as tokens.

Constructor	Description
StringTokenizer(*str*)	Tokens are delimited by one or more white spaces, and the delimiters are discarded.
StringTokenizer(*str*, *delim*)	Tokens are delimited by any character in *delim*, and the delimiters are discarded.
StringTokenizer(*str*, *delim*, *keep*)	Tokens are delimited by any character in *delim*. The delimiters are returned as tokens if *keep* is true. Otherwise, the delimiters are discarded.

The methods of the `StringTokenizer` class are summarized as follows.

Method	Description
hasMoreTokens()	Return `true` if there are remaining tokens.
nextToken()	Return the next token and advance.
countTokens()	Return the number of remaining tokens.

3.4.9 Wrapper Classes

Because values of primitive types are not objects, a *wrapper* class is provided to "wrap" the values of primitive types into objects. The wrapper classes are shown for each of the primitive types.

Primitive type	Wrapper class
boolean	Boolean
byte	Byte
char	Character
double	Double
float	Float
int	Integer
long	Long
short	Short

Wrapper classes provide useful methods and constants for manipulating the values of primitive types. They also allow values of primitive types to be used in places where objects are expected, as in the elements of collection classes such as `List` or `Hashtable` (we discuss collections in Section 6.2 [p. 236]). Seemingly, instances of wrapper classes could also be used for in–out parameters for primitive types. Unfortunately, however, they may not. The reason is that instances of wrapper classes are immutable; that is, they provide no way to modify the state of their instances.

If we let *Type* be a wrapper class of primitive type named *type*, for each wrapper class *Type* at least two constructors are provided. One takes a value of *type*, and the other takes a string representation of a literal of *type*. For example, the Integer class has the constructors

```
Integer(int value)

Integer(String value)
```

Instances of wrapper classes can also be created by using the static method `valueOf()`. The `valueOf()` method of wrapper class *Type* takes a string representation of a literal of *type* and returns an instance of *Type*. Each wrapper class also provides methods for retrieving its value in primitive types.

Wrapper class	Method of retrieving values
Boolean	booleanValue()
Character	charValue()
Byte	byteValue()
Double	doubleValue()
Float	floatValue()
Integer	intValue()
Long	longValue()
Short	shortValue()

For a string representation of a literal of primitive type *type*, the value represented by the literal can be obtained as

Type`.valueOf(`*literal*`).`*type*`Value()`

For example, the following expressions give the results shown.

Expression	Result
Integer.valueOf("100").intValue()	100
Double.valueOf("1E3").doubleValue()	1000.0

The static method `parseInt()` of the `Integer` class can also be used to parse integers. It parses a string representation of an integer literal and returns an `int` value. For example the expression `Integer.parseInt("100")` produces the result 100.

The `Float` and `Double` Classes

Classes `Float` and `Double` provide some useful constants and methods for floating-point arithmetic. Among them are *constants* such as

In Double	In Float	Description
double POSITIVE_INFINITY	float POSITIVE_INFINITY	$+\infty$
double NEGATIVE_INFINITY	float NEGATIVE_INFINITY	$-\infty$
double NaN	float NaN	NaN

instance methods, which can be used to test whether the value wrapped in the instance is NaN or infinity, such as

In Double	In Float
boolean isNaN()	boolean isNaN()
boolean isInfinite()	boolean isInfinite()

and *static methods*, which can be used to test whether a parameter is NaN or infinity, such as

In Double	In Float
boolean isNaN(double v)	boolean isNaN(float v)
boolean isInfinite(double v)	boolean isInfinite(float v)

Mathematical Constants and Functions

Table 3.4 shows the commonly used mathematical constants and functions defined in class `Math`. All the methods are static. The following are some simple examples of the use of these functions.

```
Point p1, p2;
double dx = (p2.x - p1.x);
double dy = (p2.y - p1.y);
// the distance between p1 and p2
double distance = Math.sqrt(dx * dx + dy * dy);
// the angle between the line connecting p1 and p2 and the X axis
double angle = Math.atan2(dy, dx);
```

TABLE 3.4

Mathematical constants and functions.

Constant/Method	Description
`double E`	$e = 2.7182818284590452345$
`double PI`	$\pi = 3.14159265358979323846$
`double sin(double a)`	$\sin(a)$, a an angle in radians
`double cos(double a)`	$\cos(a)$, a an angle in radians
`double tan(double a)`	$\tan(a)$, a an angle in radians
`double asin(double a)`	$\arcsin(a)$, result in $[-\pi/2, \pi/2]$
`double acos(double a)`	$\arccos(a)$, result in $[0, \pi]$
`double atan(double a)`	$\arctan(a)$, result in $[-\pi/2, \pi/2]$
`double atan2(double a, double b)`	$\arctan(b/a)$, result in $[-\pi, \pi]$
`double exp(double a)`	e^a
`double pow(double a, double b)`	a^b
`double log(double a)`	$\ln(a)$, the natural logarithm of a
`double sqrt(double a)`	$\sqrt{a}$, the square root of a
`double rint(double a)`	truncated integer value of a
`double random()`	a pseudorandom number in $[0.0, 1.0)$
`double ceil(double a)`	$\lceil a \rceil$, the ceiling of a
`double floor(double a)`	$\lfloor a \rfloor$, the floor of a
`int round(float a)`	$\lfloor a + 0.5 \rfloor$, the rounding of a
`int round(double a)`	
`int abs(int a)`	$|a|$, the absolute value of a
`long abs(long a)`	
`float abs(float a)`	
`double abs(double a)`	

TABLE 3.4

Mathematical constants and functions (continued).

Constant/Method	Description
int max(int a, int b)	max(a, b), the maximum of a and b
long max(long a, long b)	
float max(float a, float b)	
double max(double a, double b)	
int min(int a, int b)	min(a, b), the minimum of a and b
long min(long a, long b)	
float min(float a, float b)	
double min(double a, double b)	

EXAMPLE 3.8

Assume the one-dimensional integer array

```
int a[];
```

The following program segment finds the minimum value of an array.

```
int min = a[0];
for (int i = 1; i < a.length; i++) {
   min = Math.min(min, a[i]);
}
System.out.println("The minimum value is " + min);
```

EXAMPLE 3.9

Assume the following declaration of a matrix of doubles.

```
double mat[][];
```

The following program segment finds the max–min value of a two-dimensional array, that is, the maximum of the minimums of each column, or

$$\max_{0 \le j \le m} \min_{0 \le i \le n} mat[i][j]$$

where n and m are the number of rows and columns, respectively.

```
int n = mat.length;
int m = mat[0].length;
double maxmin;
```

```
for (int j = 0; j < m; j++) {
  double min = mat[j][0];
  for (int i = 1; i < n; i++) {
    min = Math.min(min, mat[i][j]);
  }
  if (j == 0) {
    maxmin = min;
  } else {
    maxmin = Math.max(maxmin, min);
  }
}
System.out.println("The max-min is " + maxmin);
```

3.5 PACKAGES

Classes are the basic building blocks of Java programs, and a Java program consists of one or more classes. Classes should be relatively small and comprise highly cohesive functionalities. A large program may consist of thousands of classes. Therefore providing a mechanism for logically organizing large programs is necessary. Java provides two such mechanisms:

1. *files*, which may contain a main public class and possibly a few nonpublic helper classes; and

2. *packages*, which comprise many related classes, interfaces, or other packages.

Files are the *compilation units* of Java; that is, each file can be compiled separately. Packages support hierarchical organization and are used to organize large programs into logical and manageable units.

3.5.1 Using Packages

Style Convention *Package Names*

Package names are all in lowercase letters, such as
`java.awt.datatransfer`
Packages intended to be widely available should use the reverse of the Internet domain as the prefix of the package name so that it will be unique globally—for example,
`com.sun.java.swing`

In Java each class belongs to a package. Package declaration is file based; that is, all classes in the same source file belong to the same package. Each source file may contain an optional *package declaration*, such as

package *package-name*;

Let's consider the source file `Point.java`, for example.

```
package geometry;

public class Point {
    public double x, y;
    // ...
}
```

The package declaration at the top of the source file declares that the `Point` class belongs to the package named `geometry`. When the package declaration is absent from a file, all the classes contained in the file belong to an *unnamed* package.

Packages serve as a useful mechanism for grouping closely related classes and interfaces. The classes that belong to a package should be closely related because a class may access not only the public fields and methods of other classes belonging to the same package, but also all except the private fields and methods of these classes.

A class in a named package can be referred to in two different ways.

1. Using the fully qualified name,

    package-name . *class-name*

    we can refer to the `Point` class in package `geometry` as

    `geometry.Point`

2. Importing the class and using the simple class name. We can import a class in the designated package using

    import *package-name.class-name*;

    or, we can import all the classes in the designated package using

    import *package-name.**;

    ...

The `Point` class in package `geometry` can simply be referred to as `Point` when either of the following `import` clauses occur at the top of the source file.

```
import geometry.Point;
```

```
import geometry.*;
```

3.5.2 Partitioning Name Space

Packages serve as a useful mechanism for partitioning name space and preventing name collisions. When they belong to different packages, classes with the same name can be included in the same class file without causing name collision. The Java Class Library, for example, contains another `Point` class, whose fields x and y are

Figure 3.2

Graphical notation of packages.

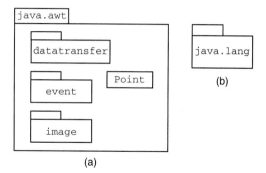

(a)

(b)

declared as type int instead of type double. This other version of the Point class is defined in package java.awt. However, both classes can be included in the same file by using their fully qualified names.

```
geometry.Point = new geometry.Point(10.0, 20.0);
java.awt.Point = new java.awt.Point(10, 20);
```

Alternatively, we can use the import clause to import one of the classes so that it can be directly referenced by its class name.

```
import geometry;
Point = new Point(10.0, 20.0); // this refers to geometry.Point
java.awt.Point = new java.awt.Point(10, 20);
```

3.5.3 Graphical Notation of Packages

The graphical notation of packages is shown in Figure 3.2. A package is represented by a rectangular container with a tab at the upper left corner. The classes and sub-packages that belong to a package are sometimes depicted within the rectangular container. In that case, the package name is placed in the tab, as in Figure 3.2(a). When the package contents are not included, as in Figure 3.2(b), the package name can be placed inside the rectangular container.

3.5.4 Packages and the Directory Structure

When packages are used, source and class files must be placed in directories whose structures match the structures of the packages. Several directory paths are important to the Java compiler, javac, as described in Table 3.5.

For example, let's let *srcdir* be the source directory root and *classdir* be the destination directory root. Let's assume that we have a class Foo in package package1.package2. In this case, the source file Foo.java must be located at

srcdir/package1/package2/Foo.java

After compilation, the class file will be located at

classdir/package1/package2/Foo.class

TABLE 3.5

Directory paths.

Path	Description
The source directory root	This is where the compiler looks for the source files. The default is the current working directory.
The destination directory root	This is where the compiler places the class files (i.e., the files that the compiler generates). The default is the current working directory. It can be specified on the command line by using the `-d` option.
The `CLASSPATH`	A list of directories and/or files. The compiler will look here for any precompiled class files it needs. These files may be in `zip` or `jar` format. The `CLASSPATH` can be set as an environment variable or specified on the command line by using the `-classpath` option. The `CLASSPATH` is also used by the Java Virtual Machine to load classes.*

* Consult the JDK/JRE installation guide for instructions on setting the `CLASSPATH` environment variable on specific platforms.

To compile the program, we change the working directory to the *source* directory root (i.e., *srcdir*) and do the following.

```
venus% javac package1/package2/Foo.java
```

To run the program, we change the working directory to the *destination* directory root (i.e., *classdir*) and do the following.

```
venus% java package1.package2.Foo
```

If we want a different program to use the precompiled class `package1.package2.Foo.class`, we must include the *classdir* in the `CLASSPATH` for that program.

3.5.5 Organization of the Java Class Library

An integral part of Java is the *Java Class Library*, which in Java 2 is comprised of more than 1900 classes. The Java Class Library consists of the *core packages*, or those whose names begin with the prefix `java`, and the *extension packages*, or those whose names begin with the prefix `javax`. These classes are organized as a hierarchy of packages according to their functionalities. Table 3.6 presents a brief summary of all the packages in Java 2.

TABLE 3.6

Java packages.

Package	Description
java.applet	Support for applets
java.awt	*AWT (Abstract Window Toolkit)* for graphical user interfaces
java.beans	Support for pluggable components
java.io	Support for input and output
java.lang	Basic language and run-time support, including manipulation of simple data types, common mathematical functions, threads, security, and system resource management
java.math	Support for large numbers
java.net	Support for network communication
java.rmi	Support for *remote method invocation*
java.security	Support for data encryption and digital signature
java.sql	Support for Java database connectivity (JDBC)
java.text	Support for text processing and formatting
java.util	Support for common utilities, including collections, time management, and data compression
java.vecmath	Support for tuples and matrixes
javax.activation	Support for the JavaBean Activation Framework
javax.mail	Support for electronic mail
javax.media	Support for a variety of formats of multimedia data, including streaming and stored audio and video
javax.naming	Support for Java naming and directory services (JNDI)
javax.servlet	Support for servlets, which are like applets but run on the server side within a "sandbox"
org.omg.CORBA	Support for common object request broker architecture (CORBA)

3.6 EXCEPTIONS

Exceptions are *unexpected* conditions in programs. The Java exception handling mechanism facilitates recovery from unexpected conditions or failures. There are at least three reasons for having a special mechanism to handle exceptions instead of using the regular control statements. First, the location at which an exception usually occurs is not where it can be reasonably dealt with. Therefore handling exceptions disrupts the normal flow of execution and provides a legitimate excuse for using `goto` statements. Second, mixing the logic of error handling with the logic of regular tasks makes a program unnecessarily large and complex and thus more difficult to read and maintain. Finally, ad hoc methods for error handling, such as `longjmp` (a common way of handling exceptions in C), are often platform specific and nonportable.

Moreover, when systems require high reliability and fail-safe processing, an effective exception handling mechanism is essential in the effort to deliver such assurance. An exception handling mechanism should be an integral part of a programming language if that language is to support effectively the development of large-scale, complex, and reliable software systems.

3.6.1 Sources of Exceptions

When an exception occurs in a Java program, the normal flow of execution is interrupted and we say that an exception has been *thrown*. Exceptions originate from two sources:

1. the run-time environment (i.e., the JVM). Performing an illegal operation, such as dereferencing a null pointer or accessing an array with an out-of-bound index, causes a *run-time exception* to be thrown.
2. Java programs, including the Java Class Library. When a unexpected condition is encountered in a program, an exception can be explicitly thrown with the `throw` statement. A variety of exceptions are defined in the Java Class Library. Programmers may also introduce their own exceptions.

3.6.2 Hierarchy of Exceptions

Exceptions are objects, and the different kinds of exceptions are organized in a class hierarchy. The syntax of the `throw` statement is

$$\textbf{throw}\ [\ \textit{exception}\ ]\ ;$$

where *exception* is an instance of a class that is a subclass of `Throwable`. There are several major categories of throwables.

Category	Description
Error	A subclass of `Throwable`. Errors are serious and fatal problems in programs. Errors are thrown by the JVM.
Exception	A subclass of `Throwable`. Exceptions can be thrown by any program. All user-defined exceptions should be a subclass of `Exception`.
RuntimeException	A subclass of `Exception`. Run-time exceptions are caused by illegal operations and thrown by the JVM.

Errors and run-time exceptions are called *unchecked exceptions*. All others are called *checked exceptions*. The following are the most common run-time exceptions.

Exception	Common causes
ArithmeticException	Dividing an integer by zero
ClassCastException	Casting an object to a wrong class (see Section 4.2.2 [p. 230])
IndexOutOfBoundsException	Accessing an array with an out-of-bound index, that is, an index that is negative, greater than or equals the length of the array
NullPointerException	Deferencing a reference variable that is `null`

A method *must* declare the checked exceptions that it *may* throw, using the `throws` clause, as follows.

> [*MethodModifiers*] *ReturnType MethodName* ([*ParameterList*])
>   [throws *Exception, Exception, ...*]
> {
>   *Statements*
> }

Statements that can throw a checked exception must be placed in either of two contexts: in a try-catch statement with a matching catch block for the exception such as

```
try {
  // ...
  throw new MyException();
  // ...
} catch (MyException e) {
  // handle MyException
}
```

or in a method that declares the exception in its throws clause such as

```
void aMethod() throws MyException {
    // ...
    throw new MyException();
    // ...
}
```

3.6.3 Catching Exceptions

The main purpose of the Java exception handling mechanism is to allow an exception to be caught and handled by a code segment located elsewhere, perhaps a good distance from the error's source. When an exception is thrown, the exception handling mechanism will attempt to locate and transfer control to a matching *exception handler*. The exception handler determines whether the exception can be handled and if so, how. Statements that may throw exceptions must be enclosed in a try-catch statement.

```
try {

    (statements that may throw exceptions)

} catch (Exception1 e1) {

    (exception handler 1)

} catch (Exception2 e2) {

    (exception handler 2)

} finally {

    (finish up)

}
```

A try-catch statement can have one or more `catch` blocks (i.e., exception handlers) and an optional `finally` block. Each catch block can take a single parameter, whose type must be `Throwable` or one of its subclasses. When an exception is thrown, the catch blocks of the immediate enclosing try-catch statement are searched *sequentially* for a match. A catch block matches the exception thrown if the type of the exception thrown matches the parameter type of the catch block or one of its subclasses. If a match is found, control is transfered to the matching catch block. If a `finally` block is present, it will be executed just before control leaves the try-catch statement, whether or not an exception is thrown. The catch clause

```
catch (Exception e)
```

would catch all checked and unchecked exceptions, as they are instances of classes that are subclasses of the `Exception` class.

3.6.4 Exception Handling

Let's consider the following `PurchaseOrder` class, which contains a method `calculateItemTotal()` that attempts to calculate the total amount of an order based on the unit price of the item and the quantity sold. A precondition of the method is that the quantity must be greater than or equal to zero. If the quantity is negative, it is an exception; an error must have occurred somewhere. The `calculateItem-Total()` method cannot proceed after a negative quantity is detected. The only reasonable thing to do is to notify the caller that an exception has occurred. The following solution doesn't use the exception handling mechanism.

```
public class PurchaseOrder {
   public static final double ERROR_CODE1 = ...;

   public double calculateItemTotal(double unitPrice, int quantity) {
      if (quantity < 0) {
         // exception
         return ERROR_CODE1;
      } else {
         // normal condition
         return unitPrice * quantity;
      }
   }
   // ...
}
```

The caller might catch the exception as follows.

```
PurchaseOrder anOrder;
// ...
double total = anOrder.calculateItemTotal(...);
if (total == PurchaseOrder.ERROR_CODE1) {
   // handle the exception
   ...
} else {
   // the normal condition
   ... total ...
   // ...
}
```

This solution is rather inelegant. Various error conditions might complicate what started as a simple calculation. Moreover, the error condition is returned to the caller through a programmer-defined error code named ERROR_CODE1, which must be carefully chosen. Otherwise, it could be confused with a legitimate value. In addition, the caller must check the return value for the error code before it can be used. Otherwise, it could cause more serious problems by treating the error code as a regular value and using it in other computations.

Using the exception handling mechanism, we have a simpler and more elegant solution.

```
public class PurchaseOrder {
   public double calculateItemTotal(double unitPrice, int quantity) {
      if (quantity < 0) {
         // exception
         throw new IllegalArgumentException("negative quantity");
      }
```

```
                          // normal condition
                          return unitPrice * quantity;
                   }
                   // ...
            }
```

Now the caller can catch the exception.

```
       PurchaseOrder anOrder;
       try {
           // ...
           double total = anOrder.calculateItemTotal( ... );
           ... total ...
           // ...
       } catch (IllegalArgumentException e) {
           // handle exception
       }
```

Now, the code for handling normal conditions is separated from the code that handles exceptions. The logic flow under the normal condition can be written more clearly and succinctly.

There are several options in handling exceptions: (a) Recover from the exception and resume execution with the statement immediately following the try-catch statement; (b) throw another exception, and pass the responsibility to another exception handler; or (c) terminate the program gracefully when unable to recover from the exception. In any case, the `finally` block, if present, will be executed before leaving the try-catch statement.

3.7 A SIMPLE ANIMATION APPLET

Java programming is quite different from conventional programming. Not only it is object-oriented, but it also is framework-*based*.

3.7.1 Framework-Based Programming

A *framework* provides the basic structure and utilities for applications, allowing the application development effort to be reduced significantly. A framework is extendable and flexible and hence can accommodate a broad range of application requirements and functionalities. However, using a framework also means that the conventions and styles adopted by the framework must be followed and that applications do not have full control of the system. The top-level control of the system usually resides in the framework, which is often called the *inversion of control*. Applications must cooperate with the framework to perform their tasks.

3.7.2 Interaction Styles

The way in which typical Java programs interact with users can be categorized in the following manner.

Active: Programs in this category run actively without input or intervention from the user. The most common type of active programs are animation programs, such as the applet that we present in Example 3.10.

Reactive: Programs in this category perform tasks in reaction to user input, such as key strokes, mouse clicks, and menu selections. The *Drawing Pad* program discussed in Chapter 7 [p. 319] is an example of such a program.

Hybrid: Hybrid programs combine features from the first two categories. These programs function by themselves and also react to user input. The *Bouncing Ball with Controls* program discussed in Chapter 6 [p. 277] is an example of a hybrid program.

EXAMPLE 3.10 A Digital Clock Applet—The Initial Version

PURPOSE

To illustrate animation applets.

DESCRIPTION

This applet simply displays the current time in hours, minutes, and seconds in the following format (see Figure 3.3):

$$HH:MM:SS$$

The life cycle of applets is illustrated in Figure 3.4.

SOLUTION

An applet does not require a `main()` method, but it must be a subclass of `java.applet.Applet`. The `Applet` class is actually a skeletal implementation of an applet. A subclass can extend and customize the applet by overriding some of the following methods.

Figure 3.3

The digital clock applet.

Figure 3.4

The life cycle of
applets.

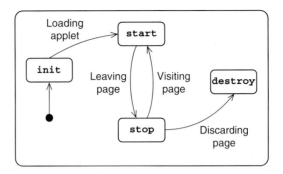

Method	Purpose	Invoked
init()	Initialize the applet.	When the applet is initially loaded
start()	Activate the applet.	When entering the Web page that contains the applet
stop()	Deactivate the applet.	When leaving the Web page that contains the applet
destroy()	Destroy the applet.	When the Web page that contains the applet is discarded

In the digital example, we override three of these four methods, init(), start(), and stop(), and define two other methods: paint() and run().

All applets are graphical applications, so the graphical appearance of the applet must be defined. An easy way of doing so is to use the paint() method to paint the appearance of the applet directly. Because this is an active applet, requiring a thread, it must implement the Runnable interface. It must also define a run() method, which is the main body of the thread. The run() method of a thread is analogous to the main() function of a program.

We begin with the following class declaration, which shows the overall structure of the program. We present the details of the methods later in the example.

Digital clock applet: DigitalClock.java

```
import java.awt.*;
import java.util.Calendar;

public class DigitalClock
    extends java.applet.Applet implements Runnable {
```

```
protected Thread clockThread = null;
protected Font    font = new Font("Monospaced", Font.BOLD, 48);
protected Color   color = Color.green;

(start() and stop() methods on page 111)

(run() method on page 111)

(paint() method on page 112)
}
```

The `font` and `color` fields specify the font and color to be used in drawing the numbers. We use a 48-point boldface monospace font and the color green.

The field `clockThread` is the thread that keeps the clock running. We discuss threads in detail in Chapter 8 [p. 368]. However, the use of threads is nearly identical in all animation applets, and will be captured as an idiom (see 4.6.2). The `start()` and `stop()` methods activate and deactivate the applet by creating and killing the thread.

**Methods of class `DigitalClock`:
`start()` and `stop()`**

```
public void start() {
   if (clockThread == null) {
      clockThread = new Thread(this);
      clockThread.start();
   }
}

public void stop() {
   clockThread = null;
}
```

It is important to deactivate the applet by killing the animation thread. Otherwise, the applet would keep running and consuming CPU and memory resources even after you leave the Web page that contains the applet.

The `run()` method contains an infinite loop that periodically invokes the `re-paint()` method. The rate of update, also called the *refresh rate*, is controlled by the argument of the `sleep()` method. It specifies the sleep duration in milliseconds. As the digital clock shows only hours, minutes, and seconds, it needs to be updated only once every second. Therefore the animation thread can sleep 1 second (1000 milliseconds) after each update. Also note that the `sleep()` method may throw an `InterruptedException`; therefore the `sleep()` method must be invoked inside a try-catch statement.

Method of class `DigitalClock`: `run()`

```
public void run() {
   while (Thread.currentThread() == clockThread) {
      repaint();
      try {
```

```
                Thread.currentThread().sleep(1000);
            } catch (InterruptedException e){}
        }
    }
```

Note that the `run()` method, calls the `repaint()` method, not `paint()`, and the `paint()` method is not explicitly invoked. The missing link is provided by the framework. The `paint()` method will be invoked indirectly when `repaint()` is invoked. We discuss the details of the interaction between these methods in Section 4.6 [p. 157]. The following conventions are important.

▪ Call the `repaint()` method, not `paint()`, to change the applet's appearance.
▪ Override the `paint()` method, not `repaint()`, to describe how the applet should be drawn.

We use the `Calendar` class in our `paint()` method to obtain the current hour, minute, and second. For obvious reasons, `Calendar` is a singleton class. An instance of `Calendar` must be obtained with the `getInstance()` method, not the `new` operator.

Method of class `DigitalClock:  paint()`

```
public void paint(Graphics g) {
    Calendar calendar = Calendar.getInstance();
    int hour = calendar.get(Calendar.HOUR_OF_DAY);
    int minute = calendar.get(Calendar.MINUTE);
    int second = calendar.get(Calendar.SECOND);
    g.setFont(font);
    g.setColor(color);
    g.drawString(hour +
                ":" + minute / 10 + minute % 10 +
                ":" + second / 10 + second % 10,
                10, 60);
}
```

The `drawString()` method takes three arguments:

drawString(*str*, x, y)

where *str* is the string to be drawn and (*x*, *y*) specifies the *x* and *y* coordinates of the left end of the string on the baseline, as illustrated in the following diagram.

Baseline

A sample string

(*x, y*)

The HTML source code for the `DigitalClockDemo` page follows.

HTML source: `DigitalClockDemo.html`

```
<!--DigitalClockDemo.html-->
<html>
   <head>
      <title>Digital Clock Applet</title>
   </head>
<body bgcolor=white>
<h1>The Digital Clock Applet</h1><p>
<applet code=DigitalClock.class
        width=250 height=80>
</applet>
<p><hr>
<a href=DigitalClock.java>The source</a>
</body>
</html>
```

3.7.3 The `java.awt.Color` Class

Instances of the `Color` class represent colors. The `Color` class is capable of representing roughly 1.6 million 24-bit colors. The following common colors are predefined as constants.

Constant	Description
black	The color black
blue	The color blue
cyan	The color cyan
darkGray	The color dark gray
gray	The color gray
green	The color green
lightGray	The color light gray
magenta	The color magenta
orange	The color orange
pink	The color pink
red	The color red
white	The color white
yellow	The color yellow

We can create an arbitrary color with

```
new Color(r, g, b)
```

where *r*, *g*, and *b* are the values of the red, green, and blue components, respectively. They fall in the range 0 to 255.

3.7.4 The `java.awt.Font` Class

We can create a font with

```
new Font(name, style, size)
```

where *name*, *style*, and *size* are the font family name, font style, and font size, respectively. If a font that exactly matches the description cannot be found, an available font that closely matches the description will be returned. The attributes of fonts are as follows.

Name: A string value indicating the family name of the font. The following font families are available:[6]

```
Serif    Sans-serif    Monospaced    Dialog    DialogInput
```

Style: An integer value indicating the style of the font. It can be one of the following constants, defined in the `Font` class:

```
Font.PLAIN    Font.BOLD    Font.ITALIC
```

Combination styles can be obtained by joining two or more of the style constants using bitwise-or. For example, the bold and italic style can be specified as:

```
Font.BOLD | Font.ITALIC
```

Size: A positive integer value indicates the size of the font in printer's points; a point is approximately 1/72 inch.

CHAPTER SUMMARY

- Java supports two kinds of types: primitive types and reference types. A primitive type variable holds a value of the type. A reference type variable holds a reference

---

[6] For backward compatibility, the font families also available, but deprecated, are `TimesRoman`, `Helvetica`, and `Courier`.

to an object or array. Wrapper classes convert values of primitive types to objects.

- Java supports the primitive types `boolean`, `byte`, `short`, `int`, `long`, `char`, `float`, and `double`. Each type has default initial values for initializing variables.

- Conversion of a type of a narrower range to a type of a broader range is called widening. Conversion of a type of a broader range to a type of a narrower range is called narrowing.

- Java expression and statement syntax is very similar to that of C++.

- Objects and arrays are stored on a garbage-collected heap. They must always be created explicitly by using the `new` operator, array initializer, or string literals.

- Arrays are objects and are bound-checked.

- Equality of references and equality of object states are two distinct concepts. For the reference variables `r1` and `r2`, `r1 == r2` refers to the equality of the references, and `r1.equals(r2)` refers to the equality of the state of the two objects.

- The `goto` statement was eliminated in Java. Multilevel breaking and the exception mechanism are used to handle situations in which `goto` may have been used in other languages.

- Classes are the basic building blocks of Java programs. A Java program consists of one or more class declarations. A class declaration defines a class. Each class defines a reference type. A class declaration comprises declarations of fields, methods, and inner classes.

- Class fields can be initialized via explicit initializers, default initial values, initialization blocks, and constructors.

- Parameters are passed by value. Values of primitive types must be wrapped inside a class in order to serve as in–out parameters.

- Strings are objects, not `char` arrays. The `String` class is immutable, and the `StringBuffer` class is mutable.

- The `toString()` method of each class is implemented to convert the instances of the class to string representations.

- Interfaces declare features but do not provide implementation. Abstract classes are classes with partial implementation.

- Packages are used to organize large programs into logical and manageable units. A package may contain classes, interfaces, or other packages.

- Exceptions are unexpected conditions in programs. The exception handling mechanism facilitates recovery from unexpected conditions or failures. A statement that may throw an exception must be placed inside a try-catch statement that catches the exception or in a method that declares the exception in its `throws` clause.

EXERCISES

3.1. Write Java code segments to do the following.

    (a) Calculate the factorial of an integer i, using iteration (not recursion). The factorial function $n!$ is defined as

$$0! = 1$$
$$n! = n * (n - 1)!$$

    (b) Calculate the average of the floating-point numbers stored in the array

```
double[] a;
```

3.2. Implement the `toString()` method for the `Card` class in Section 3.4.2. Each suit of cards should be represented by a single letter:

    S for ♠   H for ♡   D for ◇   C for ♣

When the rank of a card is no higher than 10, it should be represented by its numeric value. When the rank of a card is higher than 10, it should be represented as

    J for Jack   Q for Queen
    K for King   A for Ace

For example, the ♠ King should be represented as SK.

3.3. Write a Java application that uses the data from a text file named `students.txt` to create a file called `studmail.txt`. The input file will contain data in the following format.

```
Jordan:Michael:326502626
Pippen:Scotty:366901818
Kerr:Stephen:232098282
Longley:Lucas:293823848
Rodman:Dennis:312092827
Harper:Ronald:322198438
Brown:Randy:264092343
Kukoc:Tony:333013994
Burrell:Scott:232096996
Wennington:Bill:201399928
Buechler:Judd:323097538
```

The output file contains student e-mail IDs generated from the information in the input file. Each input record will be converted to an e-mail ID in the following format:

the first character of the first name +
the first character of the last name +
the last 4 digits of the social security number +

    `"@"` +
    `"cs.depaul.edu"`

For example, Michael Jordan's new e-mail ID would be

    `mj2626@cs.depaul.edu`

Note that no uppercase letters are allowed in the new e-mail IDs and that the output file should contain one e-mail ID per line.

3.4. Write Java code segments to do the following.

    (a) Given a point p and a circle centered at c with radius r, determine whether p is inside the circle.

    (b) Given the center and radius of two circles, determine whether the two circles touch or overlap.

3.5. Implement a `shuffle()` method for the `Deck` class in Section 3.4.2 to shuffle the deck of cards. Use `Math.random()` to emulate the randomness of shuffling. Then implement a `deal()` method to deal the cards in the shuffled deck to four hands and use the `toString()` method in Exercise 3.2 to print out the hands.

3.6. The `Calendar` class also provides methods to get the current year, month, date, and the day of the week. Enhance the digital clock applet to do the following.

    (a) Display the current year, month, date, and day of week.

    (b) Display the time, using the 12-hour format instead of the 24-hour format.

For example, the display might be

    `3:05:28 PM`
    `5 May 1998 Tue`

3.7. Assume that you have a student record file. It is a text file in which each line contains a single record, and each record consists of the following colon-delimited fields.

last name **:** *first name* **:** *project 1* **:** *project 2* **:** *project 3* **:** *midterm exam* **:** *final exam*

The scores of the projects and exams are recorded as integers between 0 and 100, as in the record

```
Johnson:Phil:100:90:95:84:91
```

The total score of each student is calculated by using the formula

Total = (project 1) × 10% + (project 2) × 10% + (project 3) × 10% + (midterm exam) × 30% + (final exam) × 40%

The total score is then converted to a letter grade by using the chart

Total $\geq$ 90	A
90 > total $\geq$ 80	B
80 > total $\geq$ 70	C
70 > total $\geq$ 60	D
Total < 60	F

Write a Java app that will read the student record file from standard input and do the following.

(a) Calculate the total score and the letter grade for each student. Print the results to standard output in the format

last name   first name   total   grade

(b) Calculate the highest, lowest, and average scores of the student projects, exams, and total scores, and print the results to standard output.

(c) Count the number of students in each letter grade range and print the count to standard output.

Assume that the input file contains no more than 100 records.

4

Classes and Inheritance

CHAPTER OVERVIEW

In this chapter we discuss overloading, inheritance, overriding, hiding, subtytpes, polymorphism, and casting. In addition, we examine issues involved in designing and implementing classes and offer some design guidelines. We also present several more sophisticated animation applets to illustrate techniques and idioms commonly used in animation.

4.1 OVERLOADING METHODS AND CONSTRUCTORS

The methods and constructors of a class can be overloaded.

Definition 4.1 *Overloading*

Overloading refers to the ability to allow different methods or constructors of a class to share the same name. The name is said to be *overloaded* with multiple implementations.

The legality of overloading depends on the *signatures* of the methods or constructors being overloaded. The signature of a method or constructor is a sequence that consists of types of its parameters. Note that the return type, parameter names, and final designations of parameters are not part of the signature. Parameter order, however, is significant. The following are some examples of methods and their signatures.

Method	Signature
`String toString()`	`()`
`void move(int dx, int dy)`	`(int, int)`
`void move(final int dx, final int dy)`	`(int, int)`
`void paint(Graphics g)`	`(Graphics)`

The condition under which overloading is allowed is stated as the following rule.

The Rule of Overloading

If two methods or constructors in the same class have different signatures, then they may share the same name; that is, they may be overloaded on the same name.

The following class declaration illustrates overloaded constructors and overloaded methods.

```
public class Point {

   protected double x, y;

   public Point() {
      x = 0.0; y = 0.0;
   }

   public Point(double x, double y) {
      this.x = x; this.y = y;
   }

   /** calculate the distance between this point and the other point */
   public double distance(Point other) {
      double dx = this.x - other.x;
      double dy = this.y - other.y;
      return Math.sqrt(dx * dx + dy * dy);
   }

   /** calculate the distance between this point and (x,y) */
   public double distance(double x, double y) {
```

```
        double dx = this.x - x;
        double dy = this.y - y;
        return Math.sqrt(dx * dx + dy * dy);
    }

    /** calculate the distance between this point and (x,y) */
    public double distance(int x, int y) {
        double dx = this.x - (double) x;
        double dy = this.y - (double) y;
        return Math.sqrt(dx * dx + dy * dy);
    }

    /** calculate the distance between this point and the origin */
    public double distance() {
        return Math.sqrt(x * x + y * y);
    }

    // other methods
}
```

When an overloaded method is called, the number and the types of the arguments are used to determine the signature of the method that will be invoked. Overloading is resolved at compile time, as in the following code segment.

```
Point p1 = new Point();            // invoke Point()
Point p2 = new (20,0, 30.0);       // invoke Point(double,double)
p2.distance(p1);                   // invoke distance(Point)
p2.distance(50.0, 60.0);           // invoke distance(double,double)
p2.distance(50, 60);               // invoke distance(int,int)
p2.distance();                     // invoke distance()
```

4.1.1 Operator Overloading

In Java, operators are overloaded only on built-in operations on primitive types. For example, the arithmetic operators (+, −, *, /, %) are overloaded on all numeric types. The only exception is that the operator + is also overloaded on class String for concatenation. No other classes are allowed to overload operators.

Operator overloading is a characteristic of C++. When used properly, it allows computations to be expressed naturally and succinctly while maintaining the conventional meaning of the operator. Operators should be defined in accordance with their usual and conventional meanings. However, there is nothing to prevent operator overloading in misleading ways. Furthermore, as we learned from C++, too much operator overloading can hamper program readability. Thus the potential pitfalls of operator overloading overshadow any possible benefits. For this reason, Java restricts operator overloading to its primitive data types and strings.

4.1.2 To Overload or Not to Overload

Overloading is, for the most part, a convenience, not a necessity. It allows methods to be named naturally and logically. However, the same functionality can often be accomplished without the use of overloading. Care must be exercised not to overuse or misuse overloading, which would hamper program readability.

Design Guideline   *Use Overloading Judiciously*

Overloading should be used only in two situations:

1. when there is a general, nondiscriminative description of the functionality that fits all the overloaded methods; and
2. when all the overloaded methods offer the same functionality, with some of them providing default arguments.

In the first case, all the overloaded methods have the same number of parameters but with different types. An example is the overloaded `append()` methods in the class `StringBuffer`.

```
public class StringBuffer {
    StringBuffer append(String str) { ... }
    StringBuffer append(boolean b) { ... }
    StringBuffer append(char c) { ... }
    StringBuffer append(int i) { ... }
    StringBuffer append(long l) { ... }
    StringBuffer append(float f) { ... }
    StringBuffer append(double d) { ... }
    // ...
}
```

All the overloaded methods fit the following general description:

> A string representation of the argument is appended to the end of the current contents of the string buffer.

Another example in this category is the overloaded `max()` method in the class `Math`.

```
public class Math {
    public static int max(int a, int b) { ... }
    public static long max(long a, long b) { ... }
    public static float max(float a, float b) { ... }
    public static double max(double a, double b) { ... }
    // ...
}
```

Again, all the the overloaded methods fit the following general description:

> The result is the maximum of the two arguments.

In the second case, the overloaded methods have different numbers of parameters. Usually the one with the most parameters is the base method. Base methods implement functionality. All other overloaded methods simply delegate the task to the base method. An example is the overloaded `substring` method in the class `String`.

```
public class String {
    public String substring(int i, int j) {
        // base method: return substring [i .. j − 1]
    }
    public String substring(int i) {
        // provide default argument
        return substring(i, length);
    }
    // ...
}
```

Both methods provide the same functionality: They return a substring. The method with two parameters is the base method. The method with a single parameter simply delegates the task to the base method by supplying a default second argument. Overloading should be avoided in all other situations.

4.2   EXTENDING CLASSES

Inheritance defines a relationship among classes. When class C2 *inherits* from, or *extends*, class C1, class C2 is called a *subclass* or an *extended class* of class C1, and class C1 is called a *superclass* of C2. Inheritance is a mechanism for reusing the implementation and extending the functionalities of superclasses. All the public and protected members of the superclass are accessible in the extended classes.

The extension relationship among classes is the strict form of inheritance, in the sense that the implementation of the superclass is actually inherited or reused in the subclasses. Two other relationships can be viewed as weak forms of inheritance: interface extension and interface implementation (see Section 4.3 [p. 135]). Java supports only single inheritance for class extension; that is, each class may not have more than one superclass. The extension relation among classes forms a hierarchy with the class `Object` as its root. Every class other than `Object` has a unique superclass. If no superclass is explicitly declared, `Object` is assumed to be the superclass. The `Object` class is the only class with no superclass. Multiple inheritance is supported for interface extension and implementation. We discuss the extension and implementation of interfaces in Section 4.3 [p. 135].

Again, the syntax of class declaration is as shown in the following fragment. The `extends` clause specifies the superclass, and the `implements` clause specifies the interfaces implemented by the class.

> [*ClassModifiers*] **class** *ClassName*
>   [**extends** *SuperClass*]
>   [**implements** *Interface$_1$*, *Interface$_2$* ...] {
>   *ClassMemberDeclarations*
> }

4.2.1 Constructors of Extended Classes

The initialization of an extended class consists of two phases: (a) the initialization of the fields inherited from the superclass and (b) the initialization of the fields declared in the extended class. One of the constructors of the superclass must be invoked to initialize the fields inherited from the superclass. The constructors of the extended class are responsible for initializing the fields declared in the extended class. The following code fragment illustrates the use of several typical constructors of extended classes. The ColoredPoint class extends the Point class to include a new color field.

```java
import java.awt.Color;
public class ColoredPoint extends Point {
  public Color color;

  public ColoredPoint(final double x,
                      final double y, final Color color) {
    super(x, y);
    this.color = color;
  }

  public ColoredPoint(final double x, final double y) {
    this(x, y, Color.black); // default value of color
  }

  public ColoredPoint() {
    color = Color.black;
  }
}
```

The fields inherited from the superclass, x and y, should be initialized by invoking one of the constructors of the Point class. The new field in the extended class, color, should be initialized in the constructors of the ColoredPoint class. The constructors of the superclass are invoked with the keyword super.

- In the first constructor of the ColoredPoint class, super(x, y) invokes the constructor of the Point class with a matching signature: Point(double, double). The invocation of super(...) must be the first statement in the constructor of the extended class.

- In the second constructor of the ColoredPoint class, another constructor of the same class is invoked with the keyword this. The constructor invoked is the one with the matching signature: ColoredPoint(double,double, Color). It supplies a default value for the color field. The invocation of this(...) must be the first statement in the constructor.

- In the third constructor of the ColoredPoint class, no explicit invocation using super or this is made. In this case, the no-arg constructor of the superclass is invoked implicitly.

If no constructor is defined in the extended class, the no-arg constructor is provided by default. The default no-arg constructor simply invokes the no-arg constructor of the superclass. For example, the following no-arg constructor will be provided implicitly for the `Extended` class, when no constructor is provided explicitly.

```
public class Extended extends Super {

    public Extended() {
        super();
    }

    // methods and fields
}
```

If the `Super` class does not provide a no-arg constructor, a compilation error will result. If another constructor of the `Extended` class is present, the no-arg constructor is *not* provided implicitly.

The extended class may also use explicit initializers or the default initial values to initialize the fields. The following order of initialization applies to the fields in both the superclass and the extended class.

1. The fields of the superclass are initialized, using explicit initializers or the default initial values.

2. One of the constructors of the superclass is executed.

3. The fields of the extended class are initialized, using field initializers or the default initial values.

4. One of the constructors of the extended class is executed.

For example, let's consider the classes `Super` and `Extended`.

```
public class Super {
    int x = ...; // executed first

    public Super() {
        x = ...; // executed second
    }

    // ...
}
public class Extended extends Super {
    int y = ...; // executed third

    public Extended() {
        super();
        y = ...; // executed fourth
    }

    // ...
}
```

When `new Extended()` is invoked to create an instance of the extended class, initialization proceeds as indicated by the comments.

4.2.2 Subtypes and Polymorphism

One of the most important characteristics of object-oriented programming languages is the dynamic binding of methods. *Dynamic binding of methods* refers to the binding

Figure 4.1

Different views of inheritance: (a) Extending the superclass; and (b) inclusion of instance sets.

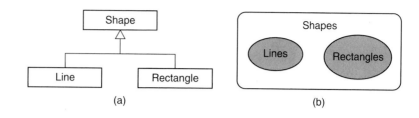

(a) (b)

of a method invocation to a specific implementation of the method at *run time* rather than at *compile time*.

Variables and Types, Objects and Classes

Before getting into the details of dynamic binding, we need to take a closer look at some commonly used terms: variable, object, class, and type. A *variable* is a storage location having an associated *type*. The type of a variable is determined at compile time, that is, statically, based on the declaration of the variable. The type of a variable is also known as its *declared type*. An *object* is an *instance* of a *class*. The class of an object is determined when the object is *created*, at run time. A variable of reference type holds a reference to an object. As we demonstrate shortly, the variable may hold references to objects of different *classes*, subject to the *Rule of Subtypes*. The class of the object referred to by a reference variable cannot always be determined at compile time. Sometimes it can be determined only at run time.

Subtypes

Inheritance can be viewed in various ways, as illustrated in Figure 4.1(a). A subclass *extends* the capability of its superclass; the subclass inherits features from its superclass, and adds more features. Moreover, a subclass is a *specialization* of its superclass; every instance of a subclass is an instance of the superclass, not vice versa. For example, every line is a shape but not every shape is a line. Some features are available in the subclass but not in the superclass. There is yet another view of classes and inheritance: Each class defines a type. All the instances of the class constitute the set of the legitimate values of that type. As every instance of a subclass is also an instance of its superclass, the type defined by the subclass is a subset of the type defined by its superclass.

The set of all the instances of a subclass is included in the set of all the instances of its superclass, as shown in Figure 4.1(b). The subset relation between the value set of types is known as the *subtype* relation.

Definition 4.2 *Subtype*

Type T_1 is a *subtype* of type T_2 if every legitimate value of T_1 is also a legitimate value of T_2. In this case, T_2 is the *supertype* of T_1.

That T_1 is a subtype of T_2 is not the same as T_1 and T_2 being compatible. The compatible type relation is symmetric, whereas the subtype relation is not. If T_1 is a subtype of T_2 and T_2 is also a subtype of T_1, then T_1 and T_2 are compatible.

The inheritance relation among classes is a subtype relation. Moreover, each interface also defines a type, and the interface extension and implementation relations are also subtype relations (see Section 4.3 [p. 135]).

Rule of Subtypes

A value of a subtype can appear wherever a value of its supertype is expected.

To rephrase this rule in the context of classes and objects: An instance of a subclass can appear wherever an instance of its superclass is expected.

Conversion of Reference Types

The conversion of reference types is governed by the subtype relation. The concept of widening and narrowing can be extended to reference types.

Definition 4.3 *Widening and Narrowing (Reference Type)*

The conversion of a subtype to one of its supertypes is called *widening*. The conversion of a supertype to one of its subtypes is called *narrowing*.

Widening of reference types is always allowed and is carried out implicitly whenever necessary. In other words a reference to an object of class C can be implicitly converted to a reference to an object of one of the superclasses of C. Narrowing of reference types requires explicit casts and is always allowed at compile time. However, narrowing is not always safe and may result in run-time exceptions.

There is also an important difference between the conversions of primitive types and reference types. The conversion of primitive types results in a change of the representation of the values being converted. For example, converting an int to double results in representing the int value in double format. The conversion of an object reference *does not* affect the representation of the object. Its identity and state remain the same.

Polymorphic Assignment

In static programming languages, such as C, the rule of assignments is that the left-hand side and the right-hand side of an assignment must be of compatible types. In object-oriented languages a more powerful form of assignment, known as *polymorphic assignment*, is allowed.

Rule of Assignment

The type of the expression at the right-hand side of an assignment must be a subtype of the type of the variable at the left-hand side of the assignment.

This rule means that the variable on the left-hand side may hold objects of different classes. In other words, if class E extends class B, any instance of E can *act as* an instance of B. In the following code fragment the Student class has two subclasses Undergraduate, and Graduate.

```
class Student { ... }
class Undergraduate extends Student { ... }
class Graduate extends Student { ... }
```

Now we create two instances.

```
Student student1, student2;
student1 = new Undergraduate(); // polymorphic assignment, okay
student2 = new Graduate();      // polymorphic assignment, okay
```

In the assignments shown, the types of the expressions on the right-hand side are Undergraduate and Graduate, respectively. They are subtypes of the type of the variable on the left-hand side, Student. Therefore no explicit cast is necessary. However, attempting to do the following will result in a compilation error.

```
Graduate student3;
student3 = student2; // compilation error
```

An error will be generated because the right-hand side type is Student and the left-hand side type is Graduate. Even though student2 actually holds a reference to an instance of Graduate, the declared type of student2 is Student, which is not a subtype of the left-hand side type Graduate. Type checking is carried out at compile time and is based on the declared types of variables. An explicit cast is necessary here:

```
student3 = (Graduate) student2; // explicit cast, okay
```

Casting a variable to a subtype of its declared type is called *downcasting*. Java allows explicit casting of any reference type to any other reference at compile time. The validity of an explicit cast is always checked at run time. If the cast is invalid, a ClassCastException will be thrown.

In this case, a run-time check will be performed to determine whether student2 actually holds a reference to an object that is an instance of Graduate or its subclasses. If not, a `ClassCastException` will be thrown:

```
student3 = (Graduate) student1; // compilation okay, run-time exception
```

This statement will not result in a compilation error. However, as `student1` actually holds an instance of `Undergraduate`, which is not a subtype of `Graduate`, a `ClassCastException` will be thrown at run time.

There are two proper ways of downcasting.

1. Use the `instanceof` operator before downcasting. The expression

$$exp \text{ instanceof } Type$$

returns a boolean value indicating whether *exp* is an instance of a class or an interface type named *Type*. The following program segment uses `instanceof` to prevent a potential run-time exception.

```
if (student1 instanceof Graduate) {
   Graduate gradStudent = (Graduate) student1;
} else {
   // student1 is not a graduate student
}
```

2. Catch the `ClassCastException` exception, as follows.

```
try {
   // ...
   Graduate gradStudent = (Graduate) student1;
   // ...
} catch (ClassCastException e) {
   // student1 is not a graduate student
}
```

Failing to downcast in either of these ways may lead to run-time failure of the program.

Why Is Downcasting Needed?

Let's assume that the `Graduate` class defines a method `getResearchTopic()` that is not defined in the `Student` class.

```
Student student1 = new Graduate();
// ...
student1.getResearchTopic(); // compilation error
// ...
```

Invocation of the `getResearchTopic()` method through `student1` results in a compilation error because the declared type of `student1` is `Student`—not `Graduate`—even though `student1` holds an instance of `Graduate`.

The validity of method invocation is checked statically at compile time and is based on the declared types of variables, not the actual classes of the objects. Therefore `student1` must be downcast to `Graduate` before the `getResearchTopic()`

method can be invoked.

```
Student student = new Graduate();
// ...
if (student1 instanceof Graduate) {
   Graduate gradStudent = (Graduate) student;
   gradStudent.getResearchTopic(); // okay
   // ...
}
```

Then the question is: Why not declare `student` to be `Graduate` in the first place? The possible reasons are that

- `student` is a parameter. The actual object refered to by `student` is created in some other part of the program and may be an instance of any subclass of `Student`.

- `student` is an element retrieved from a collection object, such as a `Map` or a `Set`. The declared type of elements in collections is usually `Object`. Downcasting the elements retrieved from a collection to their actual classes is often necessary (see Section 6.2 [p. 236]).

- `student` is returned by the `clone()` method. The return type of the `clone()` method is declared as `Object`. Hence a cloned object needs to be downcast to its actual class.

Array Types

Java arrays are objects. The subtype relationship among array types are defined as follows. First, all array types are subtypes of `Object` (e.g., `int[]` and `double[]` are subtypes of `Object`). Second, if class or interface `Y` is a subtype of class or interface type `X`, then `Y[]` is also a subtype of `X[]`.

The following diagram illustrates the subtype relation among array types.

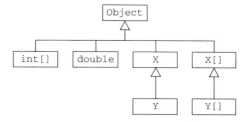

The following sequence is allowed.

```
Student sa1[];
Graduate sa2[] = new Graduate[40];
// ...
sa1 = sa2; // polymorphic assignment
Student student4 = sa1[0];
Graduate student5 = sa2[0];
```

However,

```
Graduate student6 = sa1[0]; // compilation error
```

causes a compilation error, so an explicit downcast is necessary:

```
Graduate student6 = (Graduate) sa1[0]; // okay
```

4.2.3 Overriding Methods

Overriding is different from overloading. Overriding refers to methods of *different* classes that have an inheritance relationship. In overriding, methods share the *same* name, signature, and return type. In contrast, overloaded methods are part of the *same* class, but have *different* signatures.

Definition 4.4 *Overriding*

Overriding refers to the introduction of an instance method in a subclass that has the same name, signature, and return type of a method in the superclass. Implementation of the method in the subclass *replaces* the implementation of the method in the superclass.

We can illustrate the distinction between overloading and overriding in the following manner. In

```
class A {
    public void m1() {...}
    public void m1(int i) {...}
}
```

class A contains two *overloaded* methods. An instance of A can access both methods, depending on the arguments of the method invocation, so

```
A a = new A();
a.m1();    // invoke m1()
a.m1(1);   // invoke m1(int)
```

Now, let's assume that we have the two classes

```
class B {
    public void m2() {...}
}
```

```
class C extends B {
    public void m2() {...}
}
```

Implementation of method m2() in class B is *overriden* by another implementation of method m2() in class C. For a given object, one but not both of the implementations of method m2() is available, depending on the class of the object.

```
B b = new B();
C c = new C();
b.m2(); // invoke the m2() in class B
c.m2(); // invoke the m2() in class C
```

Overriding a method with another method of different signature or return type is not allowed. For example, the following code segment will cause a compilation error.

```
class B {
   public void m3(int i) {...}
}

class C extends B {
   public void m3(char c) {...}
}
```

Method m3 () in class B is *not* overloaded with method m3 () in class C because they are not in the same class. In C++ this is legal, and it is interpreted as method m3 () in class C *hiding* method m3 () in class B (see Section 4.4 [p. 143] on hiding). Such permissiveness in C++ offers little help but adds to the complexity of its semantics. Most likely, the signature of m3 () in class C is a mistake. It could actually be intended to override method m3 () in class B with the same signature. A C++ compiler would let it go unnoticed, but the Java compiler would generate an error message.

Let's expand the preceding example with the following declarations for Student, Graduate, and Undergraduate.

```
class Student {
   public Student(String name) {
      this.name = name;
   }

   public String toString() {
      return "Student: " + name;
   }

   protected String name;
}

class Undergraduate extends Student {
   public Undergraduate(String name) {
      super(name);
   }

   public String toString() {
      return "Undergraduate student: " + name;
   }
}

class Graduate extends Student {
   public Graduate(String name) {
      super(name);
   }

   public String toString() {
      return "Graduate student: " + name;
   }
}
```

Note that the instance method toString() of Student is overridden in both of its subclasses. Because a variable of Student may hold a reference to an instance of Student, Graduate, or Undergraduate, implementation of method `toString()`, which will be invoked in the following method invocation, cannot be determined at compile time.

```
Student student;
// student is assigned some value
student.toString();
```

Which implementation of method `toString()` will be invoked depends on the actual class of the object referenced by the variable at run time, not the declared type of the variable. This is known as a *polymorphic method invocation*, in which implementation of a method is bound to an invocation *dynamically* at run time. For a polymorphic method invocation

```
var.m(...);
```

dynamic binding proceeds as follows:

> *Step 1. currentClass* = the class of the object referenced by var.
> *Step 2.* **if** method m() is implemented in *currentClass*
> > **then** the implementation of m() in *currentClass* is invoked.
> > **else** *currentClass* = the superclass of *currentClass*, and repeat Step 2.

Now, we illustrate the use of polymorphic method invocation in class `Course`, which provides an `enroll()` method to enroll a student in the course and a list method to list all the students currently enrolled in the course.

```
public class Course {
   public void enroll(Student s) {
      if (s != null && count < CAPACITY)
         students[count++] = s;
   }

   public void list() {
      for (int i = 0; i < count; i++)
         System.out.println(students[i].toString());
   }

   protected static final int CAPACITY = 40;
   protected Student students[] = new Student[CAPACITY];
   protected int count = 0;
}
```

Figure 4.2 shows the relationship between the classes. Note that the assignment in `enroll`,

```
students[count++] = s;
```

is a polymorphic assignment and that the method invocation in `list`,

```
students[i].toString()
```

is a polymorphic method invocation. Now, we enroll some students—both graduate and undergraduate—in a course.

```
Course c = new Course();
c.enroll(new Undergraduate("John"));
c.enroll(new Graduate("Mark"));
c.enroll(new Undergraduate("Jane"));
c.list();
```

Figure 4.2

Students and courses.

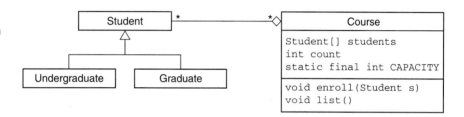

The output is

```
Undergraduate student: John
Graduate student: Mark
Undergraduate student: Jane
```

Note that the expression `students[i].toString()` was executed three times. Twice it was bound to the implementation in the `Undergraduate` class, and once it was bound to the implementation in the `Graduate` class.

Final Methods

A method that is declared as `final` cannot be overridden in a subclass. Final methods are useful in preventing a subclass from accidentally overriding methods that should not be overridden. Usually, such methods collaborate with some other methods or objects and are expected to follow certain conventions. Accidental overriding of these methods could violate the conventions for collaboration and cause a program failure. (See Section 5.2 [p. 179] for a discussion of the `initAnimator()` method of the `DBAnimationApplet` class.) Final methods also allow the Java compiler and JVM to optimize byte-code.

Invoking Overridden Methods

Sometimes it is desirable to invoke the implementation of a method that has been overridden. Suppose that we have defined an `equals()` method for the `Point` class.

```
class Point {
  public boolean equals(Object other) {
    if (other != null &&
        other instanceof Point) {
      Point p = (Point) other;
      return (x == p.x) && (y == p.y);
    } else {
      return false;
    }
  }

  // other declarations
}
```

Now, we try to define the method `equals()` for the class `ColoredPoint`, which extends the class `Point`. The `equals()` of `ColoredPoint` overrides the `equals()` of `Point`. However, we do not want to repeat implementation of the method `equals()` of `Point`. We want to use the method `equals()` of `Point` to check the equality of the inherited fields and check only the equality of the fields declared in `ColoredPoint` in the `equals()` method of `ColoredPoint`. The `equals()` method of `Point` can be invoked via the `super` reference.

```
public class ColoredPoint extends Point {

    public boolean equals(Object other) {
        if (other != null &&
            other instanceof ColoredPoint) {
          ColoredPoint p = (ColoredPoint) other;
          return (super.equals(p) &&
                      color.equals(p.color));
        } else {
          return false;
        }
    }

    // other declarations
}
```

The keyword `super` represents an object reference having the same value as `this`, but it behaves as if it were a reference to the superclass.

4.2.4   Restriction

In the following scenario, we have a `Polygon` class.

```
public class Polygon {
    public void move(int dx, int dy) { ... }
    public void scale(double factor) { ... }
    public void addVertex(Point p) { ... }
}
```

We want to define a `Rectangle` class, and it is natural to think that `Rectangle` should extend the `Polygon` class. However, the `addVertex()` method clearly does not apply to rectangles because rectangles have a fixed number of vertices. Thus it is reasonable to make the `addVertex()` method unavailable to instances of the `Rectangle` class. Such extensions are called *restrictions*. Although a restriction is desirable in some circumstances, it is also problematic. A restriction is not a subtype of its superclass.

Handling Restrictions in Java

Java does not directly support restrictions. However, restrictions can be handled in Java by overriding the restricted method with an empty body, as in

```
public class Rectangle extends Polygon {
   public void addVertex(Point p) {}
   // ...
}
```

and overriding the restricted method and throwing an exception, as in

```
public class Rectangle extends Polygon {
   public void addVertex(Point p)
       throws MethodNotSupported {
     throw new MethodNotSupported("addVertex");
   }
   // ...
}
```

In the latter case, the `throws` clause must be included in the method declaration of the superclass. (See the discussion of the `throws` clause in Section 3.6 [p. 104].)

4.3   EXTENDING AND IMPLEMENTING INTERFACES

Interfaces declare features but provide no implementation. Classes that implement an interface should provide implementation for all the features (i.e., methods) declared in the interface. Interfaces are intended to capture the common characteristics and behavior of the classes that implement the interfaces. Two relationships involving interfaces may be considered to be weak forms of inheritance. In the *implementation relationship* among classes and interfaces a class may implement zero or more interfaces. A class does not inherit any implementation from an interface; it provides implementation for the features declared in the interface. In the *extension relationship* among interfaces the extended interface does not inherit any implementation from the base interface because interfaces contain no implementation. The extended interface contains all the features declared in the base interface. An interface can only extend other interfaces, not classes.

Java allows only *single inheritance* for class extension but *multiple inheritance* for interface extension and interface implementation. A class may implement multiple interfaces, and an interface may extend multiple interfaces. Although the `Object` class is the root of the inheritance hierarchy among classes, there is no single root for the interface extension and implementation relationships.

A class that implements an interface provides implementation for the abstract methods declared in the interface by overriding those methods, as illustrated by the following program fragment.

```
interface MyInterface {
   void aMethod(int i); // an abstract method
}

class MyClass implements MyInterface {
```

```
public void aMethod(int i) {
    // implementation
}
// ...
}
```

If a class implements multiple interfaces, it should override all the abstract methods declared in all the interfaces.

4.3.1 Subtypes Revisited

Each interface defines a type. The interface extension and implementation are also subtype relations. Now, we can define the complete subtype relations in Java.

- If class C_1 extends class C_2, then C_1 is a subtype of C_2.
- If interface I_1 extends interface I_2, then I_1 is a subtype of I_2.
- If class C implements interface I, then C is a subtype of I.
- For every interface I, I is a subtype of Object.
- For every type T, reference or primitive type, T[] (array of type T) is a subtype of Object.
- If type T_1 is a subtype of type T_2, then T_1[] is a subtype of type T_2[].

These relations also imply that, for every class C that is not Object, C is a subtype of Object.

Implementing multiple interfaces allows a class to assume different roles in different contexts. Suppose that we have the following two interfaces, one for students and one for employees.

```
interface Student {
    float getGPA();
    // ... other methods
}

interface Employee {
    float getSalary();
    // ... other methods
}
```

The FulltimeStudent and FulltimeEmployee classes in the following program segment implement the Student and Employee interfaces, respectively.

```
public class FulltimeStudent implements Student {
    public float getGPA() {
        // calculate GPA
    }
    protected float gpa;
    // ... other methods and fields
}

public class FulltimeEmployee implements Employee {
    public float getSalary() {
```

```
                        // calculate salary
                    }
                    protected float salary;
                    // ... other methods and fields
                }
```

A class can also implement both interfaces.

```
public class StudentEmployee implements Student, Employee {
    public float getGPA() {
        // calculate GPA
    }
    public float getSalary() {
        // calculate salary
    }
    protected float gpa;
    protected float salary;
    // ... other methods and fields
}
```

The `StudentEmployee` class is a subtype of both `Student` and `Employee`, as illustrated in Figure 4.3. Hence instances of `StudentEmployee` can be treated either as students or as employees. In one context, a student employee can be viewed as a student.

```
Student[] students = new Student[...];
students[0] = new FulltimeStudent();
students[1] = new StudentEmployee(); // a student employee as a student
// ...
for (int i = 0; i < students.length; i++) {
    ... students[i].getGPA() ...
}
```

In the other context, a student employee can be viewed as an employee.

```
Employee[] employees = new Employee[...];
employees[0] = new FulltimeEmployee();
employees[1] = new StudentEmployee(); // a student employee as an employee
// ...
for (int i = 0; i < employees.length; i++) {
    ... employees[i].getSalary() ...
}
```

Therefore a student employee can play two different roles in two different contexts. This dichotomy is the key advantage for allowing a class to have multiple supertypes via interface implementation.

Figure 4.3

Implementation of interfaces.

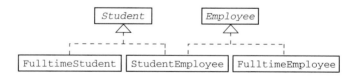

4.3.2 Single Versus Multiple Inheritance

Whether to support single or multiple inheritance is one of the most hotly debated issues in object-oriented programming language design. C++ supports true multiple inheritance, whereas Java supports only a limited form of multiple inheritance through interface extension and implementation. In the preceding example, the `Student-Employee` class implements two interfaces but inherits no *implementation* from the interfaces, as interfaces have no implementation. As a consequence, the `getGPA()` method is implemented separately in the `FulltimeStudent` and the `Student-Employee` classes. Similarly, the `getSalary()` method is implemented separately in the `FulltimeEmployee` and the `StudentEmployee` classes. With the type of true multiple inheritance supported by C++, besides the subtype relationship that allows the instances of a subclass to play different roles, a subclass can also *inherit* (i.e., *reuse*) implementation from multiple superclasses. For example, with true multiple inheritance, we could do the following.

```java
public class Student {
    public float getGPA() {
        // calculate GPA
    }
    protected float gpa;
    // ... other methods and fields
}

public class Employee {
    public float getSalary() {
        // calculate salary
    }
    protected float salary;
    // ... other methods and fields
}

public class FulltimeStudent extends Student {
    // implementation of getGPA( ) is inherited
    // ... other methods and fields
}

public class FulltimeEmployee extends Employee {
    // implementation of getSalary( ) is inherited
    // ... other methods and fields
}

// the following is illegal in Java!
// multiple inheritance of classes
public class StudentEmployee extends Student, Employee {
    // implementation of both getGPA( ) and getSalary( ) is inherited
    // ... other methods and fields
}
```

Although multiple inheritance among classes supports implementation reuse in addition to the subtype relation, it is much more complicated than the Java inheritance model. It is more difficult to implement, less efficient, and difficult to use

Figure 4.4

Diamond-shaped
multiple inheritance
relationship.

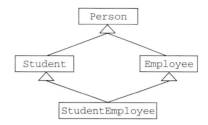

when the inheritance relation becomes complicated. Let's extend the preceding example a bit. Conceivably, both the Student and Employee classes should be subclasses of a more general class Person. This type of inheritance relation is known as *diamond-shaped multiple inheritance*, as illustrated in Figure 4.4, because of its shape. Diamond-shaped multiple inheritance is not a problem, and in fact it is rather common.

```java
public class Person {
   public String getName() {
      // ...
   }
   protected String name;
}

public class Student extends Person {
   public float getGPA() {
      // calculate GPA
   }
   protected float gpa;
   // ... other methods and fields
}

public class Employee extends Person {
   public float getSalary() {
      // calculate salary
   }
   protected float salary;
   // ... other methods and fields
}

// the following is illegal in Java!
// multiple inheritance of classes
public class StudentEmployee extends Student, Employee {
   // implementation of both getGPA() and getSalary() is inherited
   // ... other methods and fields
}
```

Now, the question is: How many names does a student employee have? Both the Student and Employee classes inherit a copy of the name field from the Person class, and the StudentEmployee class in turn inherits all the fields from both of its superclasses. Therefore each instance of the StudentEmployee class contains two copies of the name field. When we try to access the name field of a student employee, which copy is accessed? Is it possible to access both copies?

Figure 4.5

Implementation
reuse through
delegation.

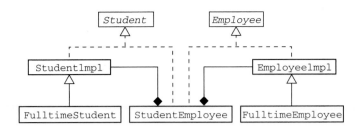

Common sense tells us that there should be only one copy of the name field instead of two for each student employee. These issues must be addressed when we use true multiple inheritance in C++, whose semantics are further complicated by name resolution features and virtual base classes. The complicated semantics of C++ make the implementation and use of multiple inheritance difficult.

The restricted form of multiple inheritance in Java is much simpler. Furthermore, the reuse of implementation can be accomplished by using an alternative mechanism, as shown in Figure 4.5. Assume that we have two interfaces.

```
interface Student {
    public float getGPA();
}

interface Employee {
    public float getSalary();
}
```

We can have two classes to implement these interfaces.

```
public class StudentImpl implements Student {
    public float getGPA() {
        // calculate GPA
    }
    protected float gpa;
}

public class EmployeeImpl implements Employee {
    public float getSalary() {
        // calculate salary
    }
    protected float salary;
}
```

The implementation in StudentImpl and EmployeeImpl can be directly reused in the full-time student and employee classes by utilizing class extension.

```
public class FulltimeStudent extends StudentImpl {
    // method getGPA() and field gpa are inherited
    // .. other methods and fields
}

public class FulltimeEmployee extends EmployeeImpl {
    // method getSalary() and field salary are inherited
    // .. other methods and fields
}
```

In addition, a student employee class can be implemented as follows to reuse the implmentation in StudentImpl and EmployeeImpl.

```java
public class StudentEmployee implements Student, Employee {
   public StudentEmployee() {
      studentImpl = new StudentImpl();
      employeeImpl = new EmployeeImpl();
      // ...
   }

   public float getGPA() {
      return studentImpl.getGPA(); // delegation
   }

   public float getSalary() {
      return employeeImpl.getSalary(); // delegation
   }

   protected StudentImpl studentImpl;
   protected EmployeeImpl employeeImpl;

   // ... other methods and fields
}
```

The implementation technique used in the getGPA() and getSalary() methods is known as *delegation* because each method simply delegates the task to another object, studentImpl and employeeImpl, respectively. The implementation in the StudentImpl and EmployeeImpl classes is reused through delegation.

The simple and restricted form of multiple inheritance adopted in Java coupled with the delegation technique can accomplish everything that can be accomplished by using true multiple inheritance.

4.3.3 Resolving Name Conflicts Among Interfaces

In Java, a class may extend one class and implement multiple classes, and an interface may extend multiple interfaces. Names inherited from one interface may collide with names inherited from another interface or class. However, name collisions are fairly easy to resolve in Java.

Two methods that have the same name offer the following possibilities.

- If they have different signatures, they are considered to be overloaded.
- If they have the same signature and the same return type, they are considered to be the same method. In other words, the two methods collapse into one.
- If they have the same signature but different return types, a compilation error will result.
- If they have same signature and the same return type but throw different exceptions, they are considered to be the same method, and the resulting throws list is the union of the two original throws lists.

For example, let's consider two interfaces and a class that implements both.

```
interface X {
    void method1(int i);
    void method2(int i);
    void method3(int i);
    void method4(int i) throws Exception1;
}

interfaces Y {
    void method1(double d);
    void method2(int i);
    int method3(int i);
    void method4(int i) throws Exception2;
}

public class MyClass implements X, Y {
    void method1(int i) { ... }    // overrides method1 in X
    void method1(double d) { ... } // overrides method1 in Y

    void method2(int i) { ... }    // overrides method2 in X and Y

    void method4(int i)            // overrides method4 in X and Y
        throws Exception1, Exception2 { ... }
}
```

The two methods named `method1()` in `MyClass` are overloaded. The two methods named `method3()` in `X` and `Y` will cause a compilation error.

Two constants having the same name is always allowed. They are considered to be two separate constants, as in

```
interface X {
    static final int a = ... ;
}

interfaces Y {
    static final double a = ... ;
}

public class MyClass implements X, Y {
    void aMethod() {
        ... X.a ...  // the int constant a in X
        ... Y.a ...  // the double constant a in Y
    }
}
```

4.3.4   Marker Interfaces

Marker interfaces are empty interfaces, that is, interfaces that declare no methods or constants. They establish a subtype relationship between themselves and the classes that implement them. They are intended to mark classes as having certain properties. The most commonly used marker interface is the `Cloneable` interface. The `Cloneable` interface is used to distinguish classes that can be cloned from those that cannot be cloned. Only those classes that implement the `Cloneable` interface can be cloned.

4.4 HIDING FIELDS AND STATIC METHODS

When a subclass declares a field or static method that is already declared in its superclass, it is not overriden; it is hidden.

Definition 4.5 *Hiding*

Hiding refers to the introduction of a field or a static method in a subclass that has the same name as a field or a static method in the superclass.

Overriding and hiding are different concepts.

- Instance methods can only be overridden. A method can be overridden only by a method of the same signature and return type.
- Static methods and fields can only be hidden. A static method or field may be hidden by a static method or a field of a different signature or type.

The following example illustrates these differences.

```
class A {
   int x;
   void y() { ... }
   static void z() { ... }
}

class B extends A {
   float x;                    // hiding
   void y() { ... }            // overriding
   static int z() { ... } // hiding
}
```

There is a crucial distinction between overriding and hiding. When an overridden method is invoked, the implementaton that will be executed is chosen at *run time*. However, when a hidden method or field is invoked or accessed, the copy that will be used is determined at *compile time*. In other words, the static methods and fields are *statically bound*, based on the declared type of the variables. Let's consider the following variation of the Point and ColoredPoint example.

```
class Point {
   public String className = "Point";

   static public String getDescription() {
      return "Point";
   }
   // other declarations
}
```

```
class ColoredPoint extends Point {
  public String className = "ColoredPoint";

  static public String getDescription() {
    return "ColoredPoint";
  }
  // other declarations
}
```

The instance field `className` of the `ColoredPoint` class hides the field of the same name of the `Point` class. The static method `getDescription()` of the `ColoredPoint` class hides the method of the same name of the `Point` class.

```
ColoredPoint p1 = new ColoredPoint(10.0, 10.0, Color.blue);
Point p2 = p1;

System.out.println(p1.getDescription());
System.out.println(p2.getDescription());
System.out.println(p1.className);
System.out.println(p2.className);
```

The output is

```
ColoredPoint
Point
ColoredPoint
Point
```

Although, both `p1` and `p2` refer to the same object, the binding of the static methods and fields is based on the declared types of the variables at compile time. The declared type of `p1` and `p2` are `ColoredPoint` and `Point`, respectively. Hence the result.

If the preceding example looks confusing, that is the reason to avoid hiding. Hiding fields and static methods offers little help but hampers the readability of programs. The rules of hiding are intended to resovle *coincidental* name collisions, that is, unrelated features that happen to have the same name in subclasses and superclasses.

Design Guideline   *Avoid Hiding*

Avoid hiding fields and static methods. Use different field names and static method names for unrelated features.

Moreover, it is better to invoke static methods through class names instead of object references. So instead of

```
System.out.println(p1.getDescription());
System.out.println(p2.getDescription());
```

we should write

```
System.out.println(ColoredPoint.getDescription());
System.out.println(Point.getDescription());
```

Even though `ColoredPoint.getDescription()` still hides `Point.get-Description()`, at least it is less confusing.

4.5 DESIGNING CLASSES

In this section we examine the issues involved in designing classes. We discuss guidelines for class design, including avoiding public fields; separating implementation from interface; organizing files; using the canonical form of public classes, which involves the no-arg constructor, object equivalence, hash code, cloning, string representation, and serialization; and organizing classes. We also briefly discuss the use of the `javadoc` utility and unit testing.

4.5.1 Avoiding Public Fields

Design Guideline   *Avoid Public Fields*

There should be no nonfinal public fields, except when a class is final *and* the field is unconstrained.

For a field named *attr*, an accessor called *getAttr( )* should be provided to access the value of the field. Optionally, a modifier of the field *setAttr( )* can be provided to modify the value of the field. When a field is of type `boolean`, its accessor should be named *isAttr( )*.

Therefore in the `Point` class, instead of making `x` and `y` public, they should be nonpublic, and accessors and modifiers should be provided for them.

```
public class Point {
  public Point() {}

  public Point(final double x, final double y) {
    this.x = x; this.y = y;
  }

  public double getX() {
    return x;
  }

  public double getY() {
    return y;
  }

  public void setX(final double x) {
    this.x = x;
  }
```

Figure 4.6

Rectangular and
polar coordinates.

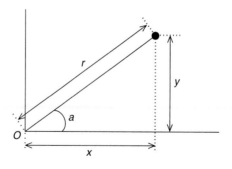

```
public void setY(final double y) {
    this.y = y;
}

protected double x, y;
}
```

You may think that public fields such as x and y in Point are straightforward and harmless and that accessors and modifiers are overkill. However, that isn't so. Let's consider the class PolarPoint. It extends the Point class and represents a point in both rectangular coordinates (x, y) and polar coordinates (r, a), where r is the radius (the distance from the point to the origin) and a is the angle between the x axis and the line that connects the point and the origin, as depicted in Figure 4.6.

```java
public class PolarPoint extends Point {

    public PolarPoint() {}

    public PolarPoint(final double r, final double a) {
        this.r = r; this.a = a;
        polarToRectangular();
    }

    public double getRadius() {
        return r;
    }

    public double getAngle() {
        return a;
    }

    public void setRadius(final double r) {
        this.r = r;
        polarToRectangular();
    }

    public void setAngle(final double a) {
        this.a = a;
        polarToRectangular();
    }

    public void setX(final double x) {
        this.x = x;
        rectangularToPolar();
    }
```

```
            public void setY(final double y) {
                this.y = y;
                rectangularToPolar();
            }

            protected double r, a;

            protected void polarToRectangular() {
                x = r * Math.cos(a);
                y = r * Math.sin(a);
            }

            protected void rectangularToPolar() {
                r = Math.sqrt(x * x + y * y);
                a = Math.atan2(y, x);
            }
        }
```

Now, the fields in `PolarPoint` are *constrained*; they must satisfy the constraint[1]

$$x = r * \cos(a) \land y = r * \sin(a)$$

If the fields r and a were public, a client could do the following and leave the object in an inconsistent state.

```
            PolarPoint p = new PolarPoint();
            p.r = 100.0; // p could be inconsistent
```

Using modifiers `setR()` and `setA()`, we can adjust fields x and y accordingly when field r or a is modified, maintaining the constraints. Making fields r and a nonpublic and requiring clients to use `setR()` and `setA()` to modify these fields ensures that the instances of `PolarPoint` remain in consistent states.

```
            PolarPoint p = new PolarPoint();
            p.setR(100.0); // p remains consistent
```

If the fields x and y were public in `Point`, the `Point` class wouldn't be harmed because x and y are unconstrained. However, that would allow the clients of `PolarPoint` to modify directly the fields x and y, resulting in an inconsistent state.

```
            PolarPoint p = new PolarPoint();
            p.x = 100.0; // p could be inconsistent
```

Thus seemingly harmless public fields can hinder the ability of subclasses to maintain consistency. However, when the x and y fields are nonpublic, their modifiers, `setX()` and `setY()`, can be overridden in `PolarPoint` to ensure consistency.

4.5.2 Separating Interface from Implementation

Now, let's design and implement a list, which is an ordered collection of elements that can be accessed through an index. The size of the list can grow as needed. Such a list can be implemented in various ways, such as a linked list or dynamic array. In this case, we should separate the list interface from the list implementation.

---

[1] Such constraints are also known as the *invariants* of the class.

Design Guideline *Separate Interface from Implementation*

When the functionality supported by a class can be implemented in different ways, it is advisable to separate the interface from the implementation.

The advantages of separating interface from implementation are (a) the implementation details are completely hidden from the clients, so changes in implementation will not affect clients; and (b) switching to a completely different implementation without affecting clients is possible. For example, the functionality of the list can be defined by the following interface `List`.

Interface List

```
public interface List {
    // accessors
    public int getCount();
    public boolean isEmpty();
    public Object elementAt(int pos);
    public Object elementAtHead();
    public Object elementAtTail();

    // modifiers
    public void insertElementAt(Object element, int pos);
    public void insertAtHead(Object element);
    public void insertAtTail(Object element);
    public Object removeHead();
    public Object removeTail();
    public Object removeElementAt(int pos);
}
```

Implementation of the list can be provided in several different classes, all of which implement the `List` interface. For example, both of the following classes, `LinkedList` and `DynamicArray`, implement the `List` interface, but their implementation can be entirely different.

```
public class LinkedList implements List {
    (body of LinkedList)
}

public class DynamicArray implements List {
    (body of DynamicArray)
}
```

Separating an interface from the implementation of a class in Java is similar to separating a class into a header file and an implementation file in C++. However, there are a few subtle differences between Java and C++ in this regard. In C++ the header and the implementation files are two parts of a class. In Java, however, the interface and the class are two separate entities that have an implementation relation.

In C++ the header file contains the interface and some of the implementation of the class. All the fields—even protected or private—must be declared in the header file. Inline methods must also be defined in the header file. In Java, however, an interface contains no implementation. The implementation is entirely encapsulated in the class that implements the interface.

4.5.3 Organizing Files

There are two kinds of classes. The first kind comprises classes for general use, which should be public. A public class should reside in a file whose name coincides with the class name. For example, the public class `Point` should reside in a file named `Point.java`. The second kind comprises classes that are used solely for implementing other classes. These classes are called *auxiliary*, or *helper*, *classes*. They should not be public, nor should they reside in separate files; they should reside in the same file as the class they support. Take for example, the `LinkedList` class, which implements the `List` interface with a doubly linked list. It is a public class and resides in a file named `LinkedList.java`. The `LinkedList` class requires an auxiliary class `Node`, which represents the nodes in the doubly linked list. The `Node` class is used only in implementation and should not be exposed to clients. The `Node` class should not be public and should reside in the same file as the `LinkedList` class (i.e., `LinkedList.java`). There are two options for the `Node` class.

1. The `Node` class can be a separate class. In file `LinkedList.java`,

```
public class LinkedList implements List {
    protected Node head, tail;
    protected int count;
    // ...
    // implementation of linked list
}

class Node {
    Object element;
    Node next, prev;
}
```

2. The `Node` class can be an inner class of the `LinkedList` class. In file `Linked-List.java`,

```
public class LinkedList {
    protected Node head, tail;
    protected int count;
    static protected class Node {
        Object element;
        Node next, prev;
    }
    // ...
    // implementation of linked list
}
```

The difference between the two is that in option (1) the Node class is not accessible to any subclass of LinkedList, whereas in option (2) the Node class is accessible to subclasses of LinkedList.

4.5.4 Using the Canonical Form

The *canonical form* of public classes ensures that instances of those classes will be well behaved when they are manipulated by the Java run-time environment and the classes in the Java Class Library, such as the collection classes (see Section 6.2 [p. 236]).

Design Guideline *Canonical Form of Public Classes*

Classes intended for general use should follow the *canonical form*.

> Provide a public no-arg constructor.
> Override the equals() and hashCode() methods.
> Override the toString() method.
> Implement the Cloneable interface, and override the clone() method when necessary.
> If the instances of the class are to be saved in files or transfered over the network, implement the java.io.Serializable interface and override the readObject() and writeObject() methods when necessary.

Object Equivalence

The equals() method defines the equivalence of objects on a per-class basis. The default implementation of the equals() method in the Object class is the equality of object identity; that is, o1.equals(o2) if and only if both o1 and o2 refer to the same object. Most classes should override this method and define the notion of equality based on contents—the state of the objects, not their identities. The following program segment is an implementation of the equals() method of the LinkedList class. Two lists are considered equal if they are of the same length and the elements at the same position of the two lists are pairwise equal. Note that the list referenced by parameter other does not need to be a linked list.

```
public boolean equals(Object other) {
    if (other != null &&
        other instanceof List) {
        List otherList = (List) other;
        if (this.getCount() == otherList.getCount()) {
            for (int i = 0; i < this.getCount(); i++) {
                Object thisElement = this.elementAt(i);
                Object otherElement = otherList.elementAt(i);
```

```
                    if (thisElement == null) {
                       if (otherElement != null) {
                          return false;
                       }
                    } else {
                       if (!thisElement.equals(otherElement)) {
                          return false;
                       }
                    }
                 }
                 return true;
              }
           }
           return false;
        }
```

Hash Code

The hashCode() method is used by collection classes that implement hash tables such as HashMap and HashSet (see Section 6.2.3 [p. 242]). Overriding the equals() method requires overriding the hashCode() method also. The rule is that, if two objects are equal according to the equals() method, they must return the same hashcode; that is,

```
        o1.equals(o2) must imply o1.hashcode() == o2.hashcode()
```

Two unequal objects are *not* required to return different hash codes. The following code segment is an implementation of the hashcode() method for the Linked-List class that is consistent with the equals() method.

```
        public int hashcode() {
           int sum = 0;
           int i = 0;
           Node node = head;
           while (i < 4 && node != null) {
              if (node.element != null) {
                 sum <<= 8;
                 sum |= node.element.hashcode() & 0xFF;
              }
              node = node.next;
           }
           return sum;
        }
```

Cloning

The clone() method returns a clone of the object itself. It is analogous to the copy constructor in C++. The clone() method requires that

▪ the clone must not be the same object as the original (i.e., o.clone() != o); and

▪ the clone must be equal to the original object (i.e., o.clone().equals(o)).

The Object class provides a default implementation of the clone() method. However, for a class to support or override the clone() method, it must implement the `Cloneable` interface, which is a marker interface. Otherwise, a `CloneNot-SupportedException` will be thrown. Often, all that is needed to support cloning is to implement the `Cloneable` interface and override the `clone()` method.

```
public class Point implements Cloneable {
    public Object clone() throws CloneNotSupportedException {
        return super.clone();
    }

    // ...

}
// client code
Point p1 = new Point();
Point p2 = (Point) p1.clone();
```

Overriding the `clone()` method is necessary when the objects need to be cloned in a non-subclass in a different package, since the default `clone()` method in `Object` is protected.

The default implementation of the `clone` method in the `Object` class creates a *shallow copy* of the original object instead of a *deep copy*. In other words, the fields of the clone are initialized with the values of the corresponding fields of the original object. The contents of the fields are not cloned. The difference between shallow and deep copies is illustrated in Figure 4.7 for the `LinkedList` example. To support a deep cloning of a list, all the elements in the list must be cloneable and the `clone()` method must be public. In our example, the elements of the list must be instances of classes that implement the following interface if deep cloning is desired.

```
public interface CloneableListElement extends Cloneable {
    public Object clone() throws CloneNotSupportedException;
}
```

The following program fragment implements the `clone()` method of the `LinkedList` class and creates a deep copy of the list.

```
public class LinkedList implements List, Cloneable {
    // ...
    public Object clone()
        throws CloneNotSupportedException {
        LinkedList l = new LinkedList();
        for (Node node = head; node != null; node = node.next) {
            Object e = null;
            if (node.element != null) {
                if (node.element instanceof CloneableListElement) {
                    e = ((CloneableListElement) node.element).clone();
                } else {
                    throw new CloneNotSupportedException();          }
                }
            }
            l.insertAtTail(e);
        }
        return l;
    }
}
```

Figure 4.7

Copies in cloning:
(a) A shallow copy;
(b) a deep copy.

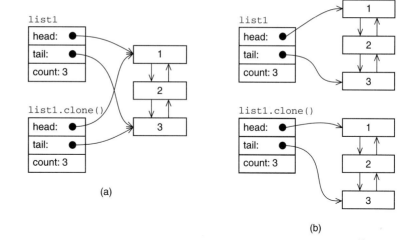

Conversion to String

We have previously discussed the `toString()` method (see Section 3.4.8 [p. 86]). It returns a string representation of objects. The following code fragment implements the `toString()` method of the `LinkedList` class.

```
public String toString() {
    StringBuffer s = new StringBuffer();
    int i = 0;
    for (Node node = head; node != null; node = node.next, i++) {
        s.append("[" + i + "] = " + node.element + "\n");
    }
    return s.toString();
}
```

Serialization

Serialization is the process of transforming an object into a stream of bytes, and *deserialization* is the reverse process. Serialization allows objects to be easily saved to files or sent to remote hosts over a network. Objects of classes that implement the `java.io.Seralizable` interface can be serialized and deserialized. Classes whose instances need to be stored in files or sent to remote hosts should implement the `java.io.Seralizable` interface. A class may customize the way its instances are serialized by overiding the the methods `readObject()` and `writeObject()`. Serialization is discussed further in Section 6.4.1 [p. 291].

4.5.5 Organizing Classes

The fields and methods of a class should be ordered according to their accessibility and roles. The methods of a class should be organized into groups appearing in the following order:

- public constructors;
- public accessors, or selectors, which are methods that do not modify the state of objects;
- public modifiers, which are methods that modify the state of objects; and
- nonpublic constructors and auxiliary methods.

A typical organization a public class is as follows.

```
public class TypicalClass {
    ⟨public constructors⟩
    ⟨public accessors⟩
    ⟨public modifiers⟩
    ⟨protected fields⟩
    ⟨protected auxiliary methods⟩
}
```

Design Guideline   *Responsibility of Public Methods*

The design of the public methods of a class should ensure the following properties.

Completeness: The public methods should provide full access to the functionality of the class.

Safety: The invocation of any public method in any given order should not result in an inconsistent state.

The following program segment shows the organization of the `LinkedList` class.

```
public class LinkedList implement List, Cloneable {
    // constructor
    public LinkedList() { ... }

    // accessors
    public int getCount() { ... }
    public boolean isEmpty() { ... }
    public Object elementAt(int pos) { ... }
    public Object elementAtHead() { ... }
    public Object elementAtTail() { ... }

    // canonical form methods
    public boolean equals(Object other) { ... }
    public int hashCode() { ... }
    public Object clone() { ... }
    public String toString() { ... }

    // modifiers
    public void insertElementAt(Object element, int pos) { ... }
    public void insertAtHead(Object element) { ... }
    public void insertAtTail(Object element) { ... }
```

```
      public Object removeHead() { ... }
      public Object removeTail() { ... }
      public Object removeElementAt(int pos) { ... }
```

```
   // fields
   protected Node head, tail;
   protected int count;
```

```
   // auxiliary inner classes
   static protected class Node {
      Object element;
      Node next, prev;
   }
}
```

4.5.6   Documenting the Source Code

Java includes an excellent means for combining source code documentation (also known as *doc comments*) with other reference materials. With the help of a Java Development Kit (JDK) utility called javadoc, a full set of reference documentation can be built in just two easy steps. First, we add a group of specially formatted comments to each class, method, and field in a program. Then we run the javadoc command on the package or class files. The javadoc utility, which comes with the JDK, parses the declarations and doc comments in a set of Java source files, generates a corresponding set of HTML pages, and stores the pages in a directory that we specify. In addition to the doc comments that we supplied, the HTML pages depict class hierarchy and "use" relationships.

Each doc comment describes a feature, which can be a class, a field, a method, a constructor, or an inner class. The doc comment must immediately precede the feature it describes. A doc comment consists of a description of the feature, which will be copied verbatim to the documentation page, followed by a list of *tags*, which will be formatted by javadoc in a consistent style. The commonly used tags are summarized in the following table. For a complete list of javadoc tags see Summary of Documentation Tags [p. 467].

Tag	Description
@author	The author(s) of the feature. Multiple author tags are allowed.
@version	The current version of the feature.
@since	When or in which version the feature first appeared.
@param	The meaning and the acceptable values of a parameter of a method. A method may have multiple param tags.
@return	The meaning and the possible values of the return value of a method.
@see	A link to the documentation of other related classes or methods.

For each public class or interface, a doc comment documenting the class or interface should be provided. The following doc comment describes the `LinkedList` class.

```
/**
 * Class LinkedList implements the interface List, which is an
 * ordered collection of elements that can be accessed through
 * an index. The size of a LinkedList can grow as needed.
 *
 * @author   Xiaoping Jia
 * @version 1.0
 * @since    JDK1.1
 */
public class LinkedList implements List {
    // ...
}
```

A doc comment should be provided for each public method or constructor. The @param tag should be used to describe each parameter of the method, and the @return tag should be used to describe the return value, if any. The following doc comment describes the `elementAt()` method of the `LinkedList` class.

```
/**
 * Retrieves an element from the LinkedList
 * at the position specified by parameter pos.
 *
 * @param pos     Represents the position of the element we want.
 * @returns       Returns an element from the LinkedList.
 * @see           #insertElementAt(Object element, int pos)
 */
public Object elementAt(int pos) {
    // ...
}
```

4.5.7 Unit Testing

The goal of *unit testing* is to test each class independently. Each class should include methods that facilitate unit testing. Usually, the `main()` method can be used to invoke these methods. The following code sequence demonstrates a simple unit test of the `LinkedList` class.

```
public static void main(String args[]) {
    LinkedList l = new LinkedList();
    l.insertAtHead(new Integer(1));
    l.insertAtHead(new Integer(2));
    l.insertAtTail(new Integer(3));
    l.insertAtTail(new Integer(4));
    l.insertElementAt(new Integer(5), 3);
    l.insertElementAt(new Integer(6), 3);
    l.insertElementAt(new Integer(7), 3);
```

```
                    System.out.println("First pass");
                    System.out.println(l);

                    l.removeHead();
                    l.removeTail();
                    l.removeElementAt(2);

                    System.out.println("Second pass");
                    System.out.println(l);
                }
```

A thorough unit test of a class should at least

- invoke *every* method directly or indirectly at least once,
- invoke every method with different combinations of possible values of parameters, and
- execute every statement and every possible path of every method at least once.

We leave the design of a thorough unit test for the LinkedList class as an exercise for you to do on your own.

4.6 APPLICATIONS—ANIMATION APPLETS

In this section, we present some animation applets to illustrate the graphics capability of Java and important techniques used in animation.

4.6.1 Getting Parameters

The initial version of the Digital Clock applet is simple but not very flexible. Nothing can be changed without modifying and recompiling the source code. The flexibility to change the appearance or behavior of applets is desirable in many situations. Applets provide this type of flexibility via the parameters supplied in the applet tag.

EXAMPLE 4.1   Digital Clock Applet—an Enhancement

PURPOSE

To illustrate getting parameters into the applet tag.

DESCRIPTION

In this example, we develop a digital clock that behaves the same as the original version (see Example 3.10) but allows the foreground color to be set as a parameter.

SOLUTION

Because we intend to preserve the behavior of the original digital clock, we simply want to extend the original version to obtain the enhanced version. The only method that needs to be overridden is the init() method, in which the display color is set.

Enhanced digital clock applet.

```
import java.awt.Color;
public class DigitalClock2 extends DigitalClock {
  public void init () {

    String param = getParameter("color");

    if ("red".equals(param)) {
      color = Color.red;
    } else if ("blue".equals(param)) {
      color = Color.blue;
    } else if ("yellow".equals(param)) {
      color = Color.yellow;
    } else if ("orange".equals(param)) {
      color = Color.orange;
    } else {
      color = Color.green;
    }
  }
}
```

The getParameter() method is a method of the Applet class. It takes a string argument—the name of the parameter to be retrieved—and returns a string that is the value of the specified parameter. The parameters are expected as part of the applet tag in the Web page. If the parameter is not set in the applet tag, a null reference is returned by the getParameter() method.

This enhanced digital clock applet allows the foreground color to be set to any of four common colors: red, blue, yellow, and orange. If the color is not specified, the color is set to green by default. The colors can easily be extended to allow more choices.

The following code fragment is a sample applet tag for the enhanced digital clock.

```
<applet code=DigitalClock2.class width=250 height=80>
<param name=color value=blue>

</applet>
```

In general, the applet tag with parameters takes the following form.

```
<applet code=class_filename

    width=pixels height=pixels >

  <param name=param_name₁   value=param_value₁ >

    ⋮

  <param name=param_nameₙ   value=param_valueₙ >

</applet>
```

4.6.2 Capturing Animation as an Idiom

The basic mechanism of animation is to display a sequence of frames. Each frame shows objects that have moved slightly from their positions in the preceding frame. When the sequence of frames is shown faster than 10 frames per second, human beings will perceive continuous motion of the objects. Motion pictures and television work in the same way but at higher frequencies, typically between 24 and 30 frames per second.

Figure 4.8

The scrolling
banner applet.

EXAMPLE 4.2 Scrolling Banner Applet—The Initial Version

PURPOSE

To illustrate animation and text drawing.

DESCRIPTION

In this example, we develop a simple animation applet. It displays a text banner that
moves horizontally from right to left. When the banner moves completely off the left
end of the viewing area, it reappears at the right end (see Figure 4.8).

SOLUTION

The fields of the `ScrollingBanner` class are summarized in the following table.

Field	Description
bannerThread	The animation thread
text	The text to be displayed
font	The font used to display the text
x, y	The current position of the text
delay	The interval between two consecutive frames in milliseconds
offset	The distance moved between two consecutive frames in pixels
d	The size of the viewing area

Scrolling banner applet

```java
import java.awt.*;

public class ScrollingBanner
        extends java.applet.Applet implements Runnable {

  protected Thread bannerThread;
  protected String text;
  protected Font font =
     new java.awt.Font("Sans-serif", Font.BOLD, 24);
  protected int x, y;
```

Figure 4.9

Drawing of the
scrolling banner.

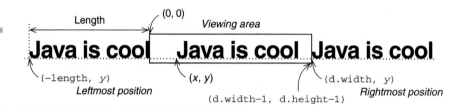

```
protected int delay = 100;
protected int offset = 1;
protected Dimension d;

⟨Method init() on page 160⟩

⟨Method paint() on page 161⟩

⟨Methods start(), stop(), and run() on page 161⟩

}
```

The notation

⟨Code segment⟩

indicates a placeholder of a code segment that is defined elsewhere.

The `init()` method handles initialization of the applet. It retrieves two parameters: `delay` and `text`. The `getSize()` method returns the size of the viewing area in the Web page. The result is of type `Dimension`, which is declared as

```
public class java.awt.Dimension {
    public int width, height;
}
```

The initial position of the text is set at the rightmost position in the viewing area. The geometry of the drawing is illustrated in Figure 4.9.

**Method `init()` of class `ScrollingBanner`
on page 158**

```
public void init() {
    // get parameters "delay" and "text"
    String att = getParameter("delay");
    if (att != null) {
        delay = Integer.parseInt(att);
    }
    att = getParameter("text");
    if (att != null) {
        text = att;
    } else {
        text = "Scrolling banner.";
    }

    // set initial position of the text
    d = getSize();
    x = d.width;
    y = font.getSize();
}
```

The paint() method paints the current frame. The key to the animation is that the position of the text has to be adjusted from the previous frame. If the text falls out of bound, it should be repositioned.

Method paint() of class ScrollingBanner on page 158

```
public void paint(Graphics g) {
    // get the font metrics to determine the length of the text
    g.setFont(font);
    FontMetrics fm = g.getFontMetrics();
    int length = fm.stringWidth(text);

    // adjust the position of text from the previous frame
    x -= offset;

    // if the text is completely off to the left end
    // move the position back to the right end
    if (x < -length)
      x = d.width;

    // set the pen color and draw the background
    g.setColor(Color.black);
    g.fillRect(0,0,d.width,d.height);

    // set the pen color, then draw the text
    g.setColor(Color.green);
    g.drawString(text, x, y);
}
```

The control portion of the applet, which consists of the bannerThread variable and the start(), stop(), and run() methods is nearly identical to that of the digital clock applet.

Methods start(), stop(), and run() of class ScrollingBanner on page 158

```
public void start() {
   bannerThread = new Thread(this);
   bannerThread.start();
}

public void stop() {
   bannerThread = null;
}

public void run() {
   while (Thread.currentThread() == bannerThread) {
      try {
         Thread.currentThread().sleep(delay);
      }
      catch (InterruptedException e){}
      repaint();
   }
}
```

Why Use init()?

Usually, initialization of an object state is done in the constructors of the class. However, you may have noticed that for applets the initialization is not done in the constructors but in the method init(). Would it be the same if the initialization were moved to a constructor of the applets? The answer is no. The reason is that an applet is not a full-blown program, and it must be invoked by another program referred to as the applet context. The *applet context* is either a Java-enabled Web browser or the appletviewer. The applet context is reponsible for interpreting the applet tag in the HTML file and initializing and executing the applet. The key factor here is timing. The applet context first creates an instance of the applet, using its no-arg constructor. At this point the applet instance has no knowledge of any information specified in the applet tag. Specifically, a call to getSize() from the no-arg constructor of an applet would return a 0 × 0 dimension, and getParameter() would return null. The information specified in the applet tag will be available to the applet only after it has been created. That is why any initialization that depends on the size and parameters specified in the applet tag must be done in the method init(). The method init() is invoked by the applet context *after* the information specified in the applet tag is processed and made available to the applet.

Idiom: Animation Applets

You may have noticed that the basic structures of the animation applets presented so far are nearly identical. That is not a coincidence. The common structure represents a general implementation of animation applets. We capture this structure as an idiom. An *idiom* is a way to represent a template implementation of a recurring problem that can be customized and adapted.

Idiom *Animation Applet*

> *Category*: Behavioral implementation idiom.
> *Intent*: For an applet to update continuously its appearance without user input or intervention.
> *Also known as*: Active applet.
> *Applicability*: Use the animation applet idiom to animate dynamic processes.

The generic structure of the top-level class of an animation applet can be described as follows.

```
public class AnimationApplet
    extends java.applet.Applet implements Runnable {
  Thread mainThread = null;
  int    delay;

  public void start(){
    if (mainThread == null) {
      mainThread = new Thread(this);
```

```
            mainThread.start();
        }
    }
    public void stop() {
        mainThread = null;
    }
    public void run() {
        while (Thread.currentThread() == mainThread) {
            repaint();
            try {
                Thread.currentThread().sleep(delay);
            }
            catch (InterruptedException e) {}
        }
    }
    public void paint(java.awt.Graphics g) {
        (paint the current frame)
    }

    (other methods and fields)
}
```

When using this idiom to create an animation applet, you should copy the code shown in `Courier` font verbatim, but you can replace the names shown in italic with any other names. Field *mainThread* is the main control thread. Field *delay* determines the refresh rate.

The `java.awt.FontMetrics` Class

The `FontMetrics` class provides the metrics for each font design. The most commonly used metrics are those illustrated in the following diagram, along with the methods for retrieving these metrics.

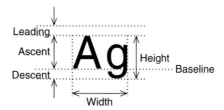

Method	Description
getAscent()	Return the ascent of the font.
getDescent()	Return the descent of the font.
getHeight()	Return the height of the font.
getLeading()	Return the leading of the font.
stringWidth(*str*)	Return the width of string *str* when it is drawn using the font.

It may seem natural for the `Font` class to provide a method, say, `getFont-Metrics()` to return an instance of the `FontMetrics` class corresponding to a given font. However, the `getFontMetrics()` method is not provided by the `Font` class, but by the `Graphics` class instead. The reason is that the metrics of a font depend not only on the font family and the size and style of the font, but also on the resolution of the graphics context in which the characters will be rendered. Therefore the metrics of a font should be obtained as follows, assuming that `g` is an instance of `Graphics`.

```
Font font = new Font(name, style, size);
g.setFont(font);
FontMetrics fm = g.getFontMetrics();
```

4.6.3 Using Double-Buffering

The `ScrollingBanner` has a minor glitch. If you pay close attention, you will notice that it flickers. To understand the cause of the flickering, we need to look more closely at how frames are painted. The animation process is controlled by the `while` loop in the `run` method. During each iteration, the thread sleeps for a short period of time before calling the `repaint()` method. The repaint() method calls another method: `update()`. The default implementation of the `update()` method

- clears the background by filling it with the background color (usually, the default background color is gray or white),
- sets the pen color to the foreground color, and
- calls the `paint()` method.

In the `paint()` method, the background is repainted—this time in black—and then the text is drawn. Because the painting is done directly on the screen, it can not be completed instantaneously. The background painting may take long enough for the human eye to notice; hence the flickering effect.

EXAMPLE 4.3   Scrolling Banner Applet—Using Double-Buffering

PURPOSE

To illustrate double-buffered animation.

DESCRIPTION

This version of the scrolling banner applet behaves basically the same as the initial version, but eliminates the flickering.

SOLUTION

The solution to flickering is quite simple. Instead of painting each frame directly on the screen, we first paint them in a temporary buffer in memory. When the frame has been completed, we copy it from the temporary buffer to the screen in a single step. The painting in progress isn't visible because it's done in a temporary buffer. Copying an image from memory to the screen is usually supported by graphics hardware so that it can be done fast, resulting in smoother motion from frame to frame. This technique is commonly called *double-buffering*, or *off-screen drawing*.

Now, we try to improve the scrolling banner applet by using double-buffering. The main functionality of the moving text remains the same, so we simply need to extend the original applet.

Double-buffered scrolling banner applet

```java
import java.awt.*;

public class ScrollingBanner2 extends ScrollingBanner {

    protected Image image;        // The off-screen image
    protected Graphics offscreen; // The off-screen graphics

    public void update(Graphics g) {
        // create the offscreen image if it is the first time

        if (image == null) {
            image = createImage(d.width, d.height);
            offscreen = image.getGraphics();
        }

        // draw the current frame into the off-screen image
        // using the paint method of the superclass
        super.paint(offscreen);

        // copy the off-screen image to the screen
        g.drawImage(image, 0, 0, this);
    }

    public void paint(Graphics g) {
        update(g);
    }
}
```

We override the default implementation of the `update()` method. Our new `update()` method uses double-buffering, which requires two additional fields.

Field	Description
image	An off-screen image that is the same size as the viewing area
offscreen	A graphics context associated with the off-screen image

An image object is simply a matrix of pixels. We cannot directly draw into an image object. A graphics object must be created for drawing into the image by calling the `getGraphics()` method. With the graphics object, drawing into an off-screen image is no different from drawing directly on the screen. ▪

EXAMPLE 4.4   The Bouncing Ball Applet

PURPOSE

To illustrate the Animation Applet Idiom, graphics drawing, and double-buffering.

DESCRIPTION

Our new animation applet shows a ball moving inside a rectangular box (see Figure 4.10). The ball reverses direction when it touches any of the four sides of the box.

SOLUTION

The fields of the `BouncingBall` class are as follows.

Field	Description
color	Color of the ball
radius	Radius of the ball in pixels
x, y	Current position of the ball
dx, dy	Distance moved between two consecutive frames in the x and y directions in pixels
image	Off-screen image
offscreen	Off-screen graphics
d	Size of the viewing area

Figure 4.10

The bouncing ball applet.

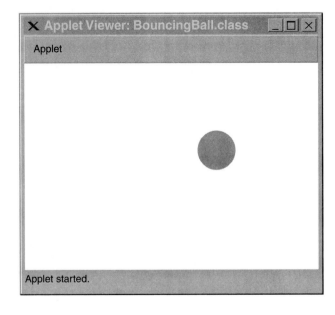

Bouncing ball applet

```java
import java.awt.*;
public class BouncingBall
   extends java.applet.Applet implements Runnable {
   protected Color color = Color.green;
   protected int radius = 20;
   protected int x, y;
   protected int dx = -2, dy = -4;
   protected Image image;
   protected Graphics offscreen;
   protected Dimension d;
   public void init() {
      String att = getParameter("delay");
      if (att != null) {
         delay = Integer.parseInt(att);
      }
      d = getSize();
      x = d.width * 2 / 3 ;
      y = d.height - radius;
   }
   public void update(Graphics g) {
      // create the off-screen image buffer
      // if it is invoked the first time
      if (image == null) {
         image = createImage(d.width, d.height);
         offscreen = image.getGraphics();
      }
      // draw the background
      offscreen.setColor(Color.white);
      offscreen.fillRect(0,0,d.width,d.height);
      // adjust the position of the ball
      // reverse the direction if it touches
      // any of the four sides
      if (x < radius || x > d.width - radius) {
         dx = -dx;
      }
      if (y < radius || y > d.height - radius) {
         dy = -dy;
      }
      x += dx;
      y += dy;
      // draw the ball
      offscreen.setColor(color);
      offscreen.fillOval(x - radius, y - radius,
                         radius * 2, radius * 2);
      // copy the off-screen image to the screen
      g.drawImage(image, 0, 0, this);
   }
   public void paint(Graphics g) {
      update(g);
   }
```

```
// The animation applet idiom
protected Thread bouncingThread;
protected int delay = 100;

public void start() {
   bouncingThread = new Thread(this);
   bouncingThread.start();
}
public void stop() {
   bouncingThread = null;
}
public void run() {
   while (Thread.currentThread() == bouncingThread) {
      try {
         Thread.currentThread().sleep(delay);
      } catch (InterruptedException e){}
      repaint();
   }
}
```

4.6.4 The `java.awt.Graphics` Class

The Graphics class is an abstraction of different displaying devices, such as screens, printers, and off-screen images. It encapsulates the details and characteristics of these devices and allows us to treat them uniformly.

The Graphics class is fairly large and provides the basic capabilities for two-dimensional graphics. More sophisticated two-dimensional graphics capabilities are provided in the Graphics2D class in JFC.

Two groups of methods are commonly used in this class: methods for setting and retrieving attributes, and methods for drawing. The methods for setting and retrieving attributes are summarized in the following table. In the parameters of the methods, color is an instance of the class Color and font is an intance of the class Font.

Method	Description
void setColor(*color*)	Set the current color.
void setFont(*font*)	Set the current font.
void setPaintMode()	Switch to the paint or overwrite mode.
void setXORMode(*color*)	Switch to the XOR mode.
Color getColor()	Get the current color.
Font getFont()	Get the current font.
FontMetrics getFontMetrics()	Get the font metrics of the current font.
FontMetrics getFontMetrics(*font*)	Get the font metrics of the specified font.

Drawing methods are divided into two categories: (a) methods that have a `draw` prefix, which draw the outlines of certain shapes with the current color; and (b) methods that have fill prefix, which fill the interior areas of certain shapes with the current color. The methods for drawing various shapes are summarized as follows.

Text string

Baseline

```
drawString(String s, int x, int y)
```

Xy

(x, y)

The ordered pair (x, y) specifies the left end of the string on the baseline.

Line segment

(x_1, y_1)

```
void drawLine(int x1, int y1,
              int x2, int y2)
```

(x_2, y_2)

The ordered pairs (x_1, y_1) and (x_2, y_2) specify the two ends of the line segment.

Rectangle

(x, y)

```
void drawRect(int x, int y, int w, int h)
void fillRect(int x, int y, int w, int h)
```

h

w

The ordered pair (x, y) specifies the upper-left corner of the rectangle; and w and h specify the width and height, respectively, of the rectangle.

Oval

(x, y)

```
void drawOval(int x, int y, int w, int h)
void fillOval(int x, int y, int w, int h)
```

h

w

The ordered pair (x, y) specifies the upper-left corner of the surrounding rectangle; and w and h specify the width and height, respectively, of the surrounding rectangle.

Round-cornered rectangle

```
void drawRoundRect(int x, int y, int w,
                   int h, int rw, int rh)
void fillRoundRect(int x, int y, int w,
                   int h, int rw, int rh)
```

The ordered pair (x, y) specifies the upper-left corner of the surrounding rectangle; w and h specify the width and the height, respectively, of the surrounding rectangle; and rw and rh specify the width and height, respectively, of the quarter ovals at the corners.

3-Dimensional highlighted rectangle

```
void draw3DRect(int x, int y, int w, int h,
                boolean raised)
void fill3DRect(int x, int y, int w, int h,
                boolean raised)
```

The ordered pair (x, y) specifies the upper-left corner of the rectangle; and w and h specify the width and height, respectively, of the rectangle. The boolean parameter `raised` has the following effects:

- `true`: Draw a raised 3-dimensional rectangle; and
- `false`: Draw a sunken 3-dimensional rectangle.

Arc

```
void drawArc(int x, int y, int w, int h,
             int rs, int ra)
void fillArc(int x, int y, int w, int h,
             int rs, int ra)
```

The ordered pair (x, y) specifies the upper-left corner of the surrounding rectangle; w and h specify the width and height, respectively, of the surrounding rectangle; and rs and ra specify the starting angle and the angle covered by the arc, respectively, in degrees.

4.6.5 Reading Files in Applets

An applet is not allowed to read or write files on the client machine—the machine on which the applet executed. However, an applet is allowed to read files from the server host—the host from which the applet is downloaded.

The URL

The URL class represents the *Universal Resource Locator* (URL). A URL takes the following form.[2]

```
http://java.sun.com:80/document/index.html#section2
```

It consists of the following components, not all of which need be present.

URL Component	Example
Protocol	http://
Host address	java.sun.com
Port	:80
Path	/document/index.html
Section reference	#section2

URLs can be constructed by using one of the following constructors of the URL class.

URL Constructor	Description
URL(*spec*)	Construct a URL represented by a string *spec*.
URL(*url, path*)	Construct a URL by giving a base URL *url* and a relative path *path* to the base URL.

For example,

```
URL url1 = new URL("http://java.sun.com/index.html");
    // Construct URL: http://java.sun.com/index.html
```

[2] The double slash (//) in a Web site address does not indicate a comment as it does in program code. When it appears in program code, it must be enclosed by double quotes as in: "http://java.sun.com/index.html"

```
URL url2 = new URL(url1, "document/intro.html");
    // Construct URL: http://java.sun.com/document/intro.html
```

The following two methods of the `Applet` class return the URL of the document page and the Java class file, respectively.

Method	Description
getDocumentBase()	Return the URL of the Web page in which the applet is emdedded.
getCodeBase()	Return the URL of the applet class file.

An applet can read a file by first constructing a URL, using the relative path of the file to be read. A text file named `filename` can be read as follows.

```
URL url = new URL(getDocumentBase(), filename);
BufferedReader in =
  new BufferedReader(new InputStreamReader(
                      url.openStream()));
String line;
try {
  while ((line = in.readLine()) != null) {
    // process line
  }
} catch (IOException e) {}
```

We discuss the `BufferedReader` and `InputStreamReader` classes in Section 6.4 [p. 291].

Images and Audio Clips

The `Applet` class also provides methods to easily access image and audio files by giving their URLs.

Method	Description
getImage(url)	Retrieve the image stored at *url*.
play(url)	Retrieve and play the audio clip stored at *url*.

COMMON PROBLEMS AND SOLUTIONS

Symptoms	Possible causes and/or fixes
Applets run fine with the applet viewer but do not run in a browser.	The most likely cause is that all the byte-code files (`.class` files) were not transfered to the Web server. Unlike C and C++ compilers, which generate a single object file for each source file, the Java compiler may generate multiple byte-code files for each source file. The Java compiler generates a `.class` file for each *class*, even when several classes are put in the same source file.

CHAPTER SUMMARY

- Java allows methods and constructors to be overloaded. Operator overloading is limited to operations on primitive types and string concatenation. Methods or constructors of the same class but with different signatures can be overloaded.

- Inheritance is a mechanism for reusing the implementation of a superclass and extending the functionality of the superclass. The class extension relation is the strict form of inheritance, in which implementation of the superclass is actually inherited or reused in the subclasses. The interface extension and implementation relations can be considered as weaker forms of inheritance, in which no implementation is inherited from the interfaces. Only single inheritance is allowed for class extension. Multiple inheritance is allowed for interface extension and implementation.

- Subtypes are relations among types. Every legitimate value of a subtype is also a legitimate value of its supertypes. A value of a subtype can appear wherever a value of its supertype is expected. The subtype relation is defined by class extension, interface extension, and implementation. Downcasting refers to casting a reference type explicitly to one of its subtypes.

- Polymorphic assignment refers to the kind of assignments allowed in object-oriented programming languages, in which the right-hand side expression of an assignment can be an object of many different types, so long as the type is a subtype of the type of the left-hand side expression of the assignment. Polymorphic method invocation refers to method invocations that can be bound to different implementations at run time. Such binding occurs when a method is overidden in subclasses.

- Overriding is different from overloading. Overriding has to do with methods in different classes having the same signature and return type. Overloading deals with methods in the same class having different signatures. Overriding is also different from hiding. Instance methods can only be overridden. Static methods and fields can only be hidden. A static method or field may be hidden by a static method or a field of a different signature or type.

- Interfaces declare class features but provide no implementation.

- Java does not support the kind of true multiple inheritance supported by C++. Java supports only a restricted form of multiple inheritance through interface extension and implementation. The Java inheritance model allows a type to have multiple supertypes. The reuse of implementation from multiple superclasses can be emulated in Java through delegation.

- Classes should be designed, organized, and implementated in a way that is easy to understand, safe to use, and provides complete functionality. Public fields should be avoided. Public classes should conform to the canonical form described in Section 4.5.

- Basic graphics capability is provided by the `Graphics` class, along with the supporting classes `Color`, `Font`, `FontMetrics`, and `Dimension`.

- Applets cannot read or write files from the client machine; they can read only from the host server.

- Double-buffering refers to a technique used in animation to reduce flickering. This technique is also called off-screen drawing. Double-buffering improves animation significantly.

EXERCISES

4.1 A polymorphic array of shapes.

(a) Implement a simple class hierarchy of *shapes*, which consists of an interface

Shape	Attributes
LineSegment	The coordinates of two end points
Rectangle	The coordinates of the upper-left corner, the width, and the height
Circle	The coordinates of the center and the radius

Shape and three classes, LineSegment, Rectangle, and Circle, that implemet

the Shape interface. Each shape has the following attributes.

All attributes are integers, and the unit is pixel. The `toString()` method should be defined for all shapes to give string representations of the shapes.

(b) Write a Java app to do the following.

i. Read a text file that contains descriptions of different shapes from standard input. Each line of the input file is a description of a shape in one of the following formats:

LineSegment	(x_1, y_1) and (x_2, y_2)
Rectangle	x and y (*width* and *height*)
Circle	(x, y) (*radius*)

All numbers are integer literals. Fields are delimited by white spaces.

    ii. Create instances of the shapes described in the input file and store them in an array of `Shapes`.

    iii. Print the string representations of all the shapes stored in the array to standard output.

Assume that the input file contains no more than 100 shapes.

4.2 Modify the `BouncingBall` applet so that it contains documentation comments that can be processed by the `javadoc` utility. Then use `javadoc` to generate HTML pages from your modified version of the `BouncingBall` applet. You should document every class, method, return type, field, and parameter. Use the tags; `author`, `version`, `since`, `param`, `returns`, and `see`.

4.3 Make the `LineSegment`, `Rectangle`, and `Circle` classes in Exercise 4.1 conform to the canonical form.

4.4 Write a java applet that uses the `getCodeBase()` and `getDocumentBase()` methods to display the applet's code base and document base, respectively. *Hint:* Use the `toString()` method of the `URL` class.

4.5 Enhance the digital clock applet to allow the font to be customized via anther parameter in the `applet` tag.

4.6 Enhance the `ScrollingBanner` applet with the following functionalities.

    (a) Allow the font and color to be set by parameters.

    (b) Allow the banner to move in different directions: left to right, upward, downward, and diagonally.

4.7 Write an applet that retrieves sales data as parameters and display the data on a pie chart. The format of the parameters is the following.

```
<param name=categories   value="cat_1
                       ... cat_n ">
<param name=cat_1    value=amount_1 >
    ⋮
<param name=cat_n    value=amount_n >
```

The amount for each category is represented as an interger. For example, the following are sample sales data for a software superstore.

```
<param name=categories
       value="education utility
entertainment reference"
<param name=education value=10000>
<param name=utility value=12000>
<param name=entertainment value=30000>
<param name=reference value=9000>
```

4.8 Write an applet that retrieves sales data as parameters in the same format as in Exercise 4.7 and display the data using a bar chart.

4.9 Write an animation applet that shows an analog clock.

4.10 Write an applet that retrieves a text file containing a list of points and do a scatterplot in a two-dimensional coordinate system. Each line of the input file contains a single point, and each point is represented by two integers that specify the x and y coordinates and are separated by white spaces.

4.11 Extend Exercise 4.1 by adding a `draw()` method to each of the shape classes that draws the respective shape. Write an applet that reads a file that contains descriptions of different shapes and draw the shapes using the `draw()` method.

5

Design by Abstraction

CHAPTER OVERVIEW

In this chapter we introduce design patterns. The main focus of this chapter is designing reusable and flexible components, using abstract classes, interfaces, and design patterns. We discuss several important design patterns for abstraction: the Template Method, Strategy, Factory, and Iterator. We also present a case study covering the animation of sorting algorithms.

One of the most tantalizing promises of object-oriented software development is reusability. Although reuse of implementations through inheritance is relatively easy, reuse on a larger scale (i.e., reuse of system designs and architectures) has proven rather difficult. Among the most important recent developments of object-oriented technologies is the emergence of *design patterns* and *frameworks*, which are intended to address reuse of design and architectures. We discuss design patterns in this chapter and frameworks in Chapter 6.

5.1 DESIGN PATTERNS

The concept of *patterns* was originally proposed by Christopher Alexander and his colleagues to describe architectural designs. In searching for the essence of great buildings, great towns, and beautiful places, Alexander proposed in *The Timeless Way of Building* [Alexander 1979] and *A Pattern Language—Towns, Buildings, Construction*

[Alexander et al. 1977], that *the* timeless way of building, which "is thousands of years old, and the same today as it has always been," can be captured in 253 *patterns*. He went on to say:

> Each pattern describes a *problem* which occurs over and over again in our environment, and then describes the core of the *solution* to that problem, in such a way that you can use this solution a million times over, without ever doing it the same way twice [Alexander et al. 1977].

In other words, each pattern represents a *generic* (i.e., reusable) solution to a recurring problem. Only a relatively small number of patterns are needed to capture the essence of all architectural designs, and they can be adapted and combined in many different ways to generate endless possibilities.

Software design resembles architectural design. Similarities between the two include the following.

- Both are creative processes that unfold within a wide range (i.e., all possible designs).
- The resulting design must satisfy the customer's needs.
- The resulting design must be feasible to engineer.
- The designers must balance many competing constraints and requirements.
- The designers must seek certain intrinsic yet unquantifiable qualities, such as elegance and extensibility.

Therefore it is natural to adapt the concept of architectural patterns to software design. *Software design patterns* are schematic descriptions of solutions to recurring problems in software design. The main purposes of using software design patterns are to (a) capture and document the experience acquired in software design in a relatively small number of design patterns to help designers acquire design expertise; (b) support reuse in design and boost confidence in software systems that use established design patterns that have been proven; and (c) provide a common vocabulary for software designers to communicate about software design.

The pioneering work in software design patterns was done by Gamma et al., who published the first software design patterns catalog, *Design Patterns* [Gamma et al. 1995]. The researchers compiled 23 of the most commonly used general purpose design patterns that are application domain independent and classified them as

1. *creational patterns*, which deal with the process of object creation;
2. *structural patterns*, which deal primarily with the static composition and structure of classes and objects; and
3. *behavioral patterns*, which deal primarily with dynamic interaction among classes and objects.

The description of each design pattern consists of some or all of the following sections.

Pattern name: The essence of the pattern.
Category: Creational, structural, or behavioral.

Intent: A short description of the design issue or problem addressed.
Also known as: Other well known names of the pattern.
Applicability: Situations in which the pattern can be applied.
Structure: A class or object diagram that depicts the participants of the pattern and the relationships among them.
Participants: A list of classes and/or objects participating in the pattern.

The *singleton class* discussed in Chapter 3 [p. 47] is one of the creational patterns in the *Design Patterns* catalog. We use the Singleton pattern to illustrate the format for describing design patterns.

Design Pattern   *Singleton*

Category: Creational design pattern.
Intent: Ensure that a class has only one instance and provide a global point of access to it.
Applicability: Use the Singleton pattern when there must be exactly one instance of a class and it must be accessible to clients from a well-known access point.

The structure of the Singleton pattern is shown in the following diagram.[1]

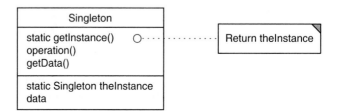

There is only one participant in the Singleton pattern:

▪ **Singleton**
   declares the unique instance of the class as a static variable, and defines a static method `getInstance()` for clients to access the unique instance.

The following program segment is an implementation of the Singleton pattern in Java.

---

[1] The rectangular box with a shaded corner denotes a note.

```
public class Singleton {
   public static Singleton getInstance() {
      if (theInstance == null) {
         theInstance = new Singleton();
      }
      return theInstance;
   }

   protected Singleton() {
      (initialize instance fields)
   }

   (instance fields and methods)

   private static Singleton theInstance = null;
}
```

In this book we focus on domain neutral design patterns. However, the concept of patterns can also be applied to other aspects of software development, such as patterns for software architecture [Shaw 1996] and object-oriented analysis [Fowler 1997], and to specific domains of software systems, such as patterns for concurrent programming in Java [Lea, 1997]. Patterns concerning implementation techniques in a specific programming language are also known as *idioms.* Coplien 1992 discusses the use of a variety of idioms in C++.

5.2 DESIGNING GENERIC COMPONENTS

By *generic components*, we mean program components, usually in the form of classes or packages, that can be adapted and used in many different contexts without having to modify their source codes. Generic components are also known as *reusable components.* In this section we discuss two basic techniques of designing generic components: factorization and generalization. The mechanisms used to build generic components are inheritance and delegation. Abstract classes and interfaces play important roles in implementing generic components.

5.2.1   Factorization

One way to discover possible generic components is by identifying recurring code segments that are identical or nearly identical. An example of such recurring code segments are the nearly identical methods start(), stop(), and run() that appear in every animation applet.

Factorization consists of

- identifying code segments in a program that implement the same logic, often in the same exact code, in many different places;

- capturing this logic in a generic component that is defined once; and
- reorganizing the program so that every occurrence of the code segment is replaced by use of the generic component.

Factorization thus eliminates code duplication and the dangers it creates for maintenance. It ensures that a bug fix or logic enhancement need be implemented only once—in the component. Without factorization, every change to recurring code must be repeated everywhere the code occurs, many instances of which may be overlooked or forgotten. Recurring code segments can easily "drift apart," adding risk to code maintenance.

Factorization must be applied only to code that actually duplicates underlying logic, however. Not all code that looks alike is alike.

Design Guideline *Factorize Recurring Code Segments*

Recurring code segments based on the same logic create a risk to maintenance. They should be factorized so that the code segment occurs only once.

The simplest form of factorization can be done through the use of *function* or *method invocation*. For example, in the following code segment, the same code sequence occurs in two different contexts.

```
class Computation {
    void method1(...) {
        // ...

        computeStep1();

        computeStep2();

        computeStep3();
        // ...

    }
    void method2(...) {
        // ...

        computeStep1();

        computeStep2();

        computeStep3();
        // ...

    }
    // ...

}
```

The common code sequence can be factorized by introducing a new method `computeAll()` that encapsulates the recurring code sequence. The code segment can be reorganized as follows.

```
class FactorizedComputation {

    void computeAll() {

        computeStep1();

        computeStep2();

        computeStep3();

    }

    void method1(...) {

        // ...

        computeAll();

        // ...

    }

    void method2(...) {

        // ...

        computeAll();

        // ...

    }

    // ...

}
```

The factorized version is functionally identical to the original version. If the code in the common sequence needs to be modified, it now has to be modified in only one place (in `computeAll()`) instead of several places, as in the original version.

Factorization by method invocation is effective only when each occurence of the recurring code segment is contained within a single method and all the methods that contain the recurring code segment belong to the same class. When the recurring code segment involves several methods, such as the methods `start()`, `stop()`, and `run()` in animation applets—or when the recurring code segment occurs in several classes—factorization can be accomplished by using inheritance or delegation.

Factorization by Inheritance

Factorization of recurring code segments in different classes can be done through *inheritance*. Consider the following example, in which an identical computation sequence occurs in two different classes.

```
class ComputationA {          class ComputationB {
   void method1(...) {            void method2(...) {
      // ...                         // ...
      computeStep1();               computeStep1();
      computeStep2();               computeStep2();
      computeStep3();               computeStep3();
      // ...                         // ...
   }    // ...                    }    // ...
}                             }
```

A common superclass of ComputationA and ComputationB is introduced. The factorized computation sequence is placed in a method computeAll() in the superclass.

```
class Common {
   void computeAll(...) {
      computeStep1();
      computeStep2();
      computeStep3();
   }
}
```

Each occurance of the code sequence in the original methods can now be replaced by invoking the method computeAll().

```
class ComputationA              class ComputationB
   extends Common {                extends Common {
   void method1(...) {            void method2(...) {
      // ...                         // ...
      computeAll();                 computeAll();
      // ...                         // ...
   }                             }
   // ...                         // ...
}                             }
```

When extracting common code sequences to a superclass, all the fields involved in the computation must also be extracted and moved to the superclass.

Factorization by Delegation

Factorization of recurring code segments in different classes can also be done through *delegation.* To factorize the recurring code sequence in the preceding example using delegation, we can introduce a helper class and place the factorized code sequence in the computeAll() method of the helper class.

```
class Helper {
   void computeAll(...) {
      computeStep1();
      computeStep2();
      computeStep3();
   }
}
```

Both `ComputationA` and `ComputationB` need to contain a reference to the helper class, and each occurence of the recurring code sequence in the original methods can be replaced by a call to `helper.computeAll()`.

```
class ComputationA                class ComputationB
   void compute(...) {               void compute(...) {
      //...                             //...
      helper.computeAll();             helper.computeAll();
      //...                             //...
   }                                 }
   Helper helper;                    Helper helper;
   //...                             //...

}                                 }
```

Factorization by inheritance and by delegation can achieve rather similar effects. Factorization by inheritance is usually simpler than by delegation. However, owing to the restriction of single inheritance among classes, factorization by inheritance may not be possible at times. When either `ComputationA` or `ComputationB` must be a subclass of a class that is not `Object`, for example, factorization by inheritance is not possible. In contrast, factorization can always be achieved through delegation.

EXAMPLE 5.1   A Generic Animation Applet

PURPOSE

This example demonstrates factorization by inheritance.

DESCRIPTION

A generic animation applet class `AnimationApplet` is defined by extracting the common elements in animation applets: the methods `start()`, `stop()`, and `run()`. The digital clock applet presented in Example 3.10 [p. 109] is reimplemented, using the `AnimationApplet` class.

SOLUTION

The relationship among the classes `Applet`, `AnimationApplet` (the generic animation applet class), and `DigitalClock3` (the reimplemented digital clock applet using the generic animation applet) are shown in Figure 5.1. The methods of `AnimationApplet` are summarized in the following table.

Method	Description
`start()`, `stop()`, and `run()`	The common methods in animation applets
`setDelay()` and `getDelay()`	Accessor and modifier of the `delay` field, which specifies the interval between two consecutive animation frames in milliseconds.

Figure 5.1

A generic
animation applet.

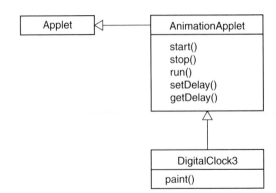

The `setDelay()` and `getDelay()` methods are introduced to make the generic animation applet class more flexible, allowing each concrete animation to set its own refresh rate. Flexibility is essential to all generic components.

Design Guideline   *Maximize Flexibility*

Rarely can components be reused without adaptation. Flexibility allows components to be adapted to different contexts. The more flexible a component is, the better is the chance that it may be reused.

The `AnimationApplet` class is defined as follows.

Generic animation applet: `AnimationApplet`

```java
import java.awt.*;

public class AnimationApplet
    extends java.applet.Applet
    implements java.lang.Runnable {
  public void start() {
    animationThread = new Thread(this);
    animationThread.start();
  }
  public void stop() {
    animationThread = null;
  }
  public void run() {
    while (Thread.currentThread() == animationThread) {
```

```
        try {
           Thread.currentThread().sleep(delay);
        } catch (InterruptedException e){}
        repaint();
      }
    }
    final public void setDelay(int delay) {
      this.delay = delay;
    }
    final public int getDelay() {
      return delay;
    }
    protected Thread animationThread;
    protected int delay = 100;
  }
```

Note that the fields used by the methods `start()`, `stop()`, and `run()` are also extracted to the superclass. The `AnimationApplet` class avoids repetition of the `start()`, `stop()`, and `run()` methods in every animation applet. A specific, or concrete, animation applet can simply extend `AnimationApplet` and override the `paint()` method to draw animation frames.

```
    public class MyAnimationApplet extends AnimationApplet {

    public void paint(Graphics g) {

        (paint a frame)

    }

    (other fields and methods)

    }
```

Using `AnimationApplet`, we can reimplement the digital clock applet in Section 3.7 [p. 109] as follows.

Concrete animation applet: `DigitalClock3`

```
import java.awt.*;
import java.util.Calendar;

public class DigitalClock3 extends AnimationApplet {
  public DigitalClock3() {
    setDelay(1000);
  }
  public void paint(Graphics g) {
    (the body is identical to that of the paint() method in DigitalClock
in Section 3.7)
  }
  protected Font font = new Font("Monospaced", Font.BOLD, 48);
  protected Color color = Color.green;
}
```

The factorization in Example 5.1 is rather straightforward. However, in reality factorization is often more complicated. Let's try to take the generic animation example one step further. Another code segment that also recurs in many animation applets deals with double-buffering. We can enhance the generic animation applet so that it can handle double-buffering when necessary. However, several aspects of double-buffering must be determined by the specific animation classes, which are subclasses of the generic animation applet.

EXAMPLE 5.2   A Double-Buffered Generic Animation Applet

PURPOSE

This example illustrates how to resolve the complications involved in factorization by inheritance. It also addresses issues of flexibility (i.e., adaptability) in the generic animation applet.

DESCRIPTION

A double-buffered generic animation applet class DBAnimationApplet is defined, using factorization by inheritance. The bouncing ball applet in Example 4.4 [p. 166] is reimplemented, using the DBAnimationApplet class.

KEY ISSUES

■ Accommodate various sizes of the view area.

■ Allow the subclasses to decide whether to use double-buffering.

■ Factorize common code segments that contain variable parts.

SOLUTION

With regard to the first key issue, in order to initialize the off-screen image buffer, we need to know the dimensions of the viewing area. The problem is that the dimensions of the viewing area are not known until the init() method is invoked. A simplistic solution to this problem is to override the init() method in the generic animation applet.

```
public class DBAnimationApplet extends AnimationApplet {
  protected Dimension dim;
  protected Image im;
  protected Graphics offscreen;

  public void init() {
    dim = getSize();
    im = createImage(dim.width, dim.height);
    offscreen = im.getGraphics();
  }
  // ...
}
```

This approach properly initializes the off-screen image buffer. However, a problem arises if a subclass of DBAnimationApplet requires additional initialization to be done in the init() method, such as getting parameters. Then it is necessary for the init() method in the subclass to call super.init() to initialize the off-screen image buffer properly.

```java
public class MyAnimation extends DBAnimationApplet {
    public void init() {
        // additional initialization specific to MyAnimation
        String param = getParameter(...);
        // ...

        // the following line is necessary
        super.init();
    }
    // ...
}
```

Not invoking super.init() will cause a null-pointer exception. The burden of following this convention is entirely on the implementer of subclasses because its violation will not be detected by the Java compiler. For various reasons, violations of such conventions are very common, and they often lead to faults, or bugs, that are difficult to trace. Although using a component without following the proper conventions is a misuse of the component, designers of reusable components must do their best to minimize the chances of the components being misused.

Design Guideline   *Minimize the Chance of Misuse*

Well-designed classes should minimize their possible misuse by clearly identifying any violation of the conventions of the classes, preferably at compile time.

Misuses can be revealed by making any violation of the component conventions detectable by the Java compiler and using assertions to detect the violation at run time.

A better solution for initializing the off-screen image buffer is to introduce a new method initAnimator() for subclasses to perform subclass specific initializations. The init() method is made *final*, so that it cannot be accidentally overridden by the subclasses. This approach ensures that initializations of dim, im, and offscreen will always be done properly. A null implementation is provided for initAnimator(). A subclass needs to override this method only when there are subclass specific initializations.

```
public class DBAnimationApplet extends AnimationApplet {
    protected Dimension dim;
    protected Image im;
    protected Graphics offscreen;

    final public void init(Graphics g) {
        dim = getSize();
        im = createImage(dim.width, dim.height);
        offscreen = im.getGraphics();
        initAnimator();
    }

    protected void initAnimator() {}
}

public class MyAnimation extends DBAnimationApplet {

    protected void initAnimator() {
        // additional initialization specific to MyAnimation
        String param = getParameter(...);
        // ...
    }
    // ...
}
```

The second key issue involves giving the subclasses the flexibility to decide whether to use double-buffering. Hence the generic animation applet should accommodate two scenarios.

1. When double-buffering is not needed, the default implementation of `update()` should be used and the `paint()` method should be overridden by the subclass to paint a frame.

2. When double-buffering is needed, the `update()` method should be overridden to paint a frame.

The generic animation class should unify the two scenarios so that it can handle both. A boolean variable can be used to control the behavior of the `update()` method.

```
public class DBAnimationApplet extends AnimationApplet {
    protected boolean doubleBuffered;

    void update(Graphics g) {
        if (doubleBuffered) {
            // do double buffering
        } else {
            super.update(g); // use the default implementation
        }
    }
    // ...
}
```

The third key issue involves the use of double-buffering. The part of the `update()` method that deals with double-buffering is common to all animation applets, whereas the part that deals with painting the frames varies from applet to applet. The generic animation class should factorize the common part and allow its subclasses to provide the variable part.

Factorization of Common Code Segments Intermixed with Context Specific Code

Let's consider a more general situation. Two methods, `method1()` and `method2()`, have some common code segments that are intermixed with some context specific code.

```
class ContextA {                      class ContextB {
   void method(...) {                     void method(...) {
     (common code segment 1)                (common code segment 1)
     (context specific code A)              (context specific code B)
     (common code segment 2)                (common code segment 2)
   }                                      }
   // ...                                 // ...
}                                     }
```

How can the common code segments be factorized? Two approaches are available. The first approach is to factorize each common code segment into a separate method by using the factorization by inheritance technique [p. 181].

```
              class Common {
                 void commonCode1() {
                    (common code segment 1)
                 }
                 void commonCode2() {
                    (common code segment 2)
                 }
              }
```

```
class ContextA                        class ContextB
    extends Common {                      extends Common {
   void method(...) {                     void method(...) {
     commonCode1()                          commonCode1()
     (context specific code A)              (context specific code B)
     commonCode2()                          commonCode2()
   }                                      }
   // ...                                 // ...
}                                     }
```

This approach works, and it is a perfectly good solution when the two common code segments are relatively independent. However, this approach is error-prone when the two common code segments are closely related and are merely pieces of a larger process. Breaking the common code segments into two separate methods breaks the logical flow and hampers the readability of the code. The invocation of `commonCode1()` and `commonCode1()` in each context must be carefully coordinated. If one of them is omitted or they are invoked in a different order, unpredictable outcomes may result.

The second, more generic, approach is to extract the entire method that contains both common and context specific code to a superclass and then factorize the context specific code by introducing a new method as a placeholder, which is intended to be overridden and customized in each subclass.

```
class Common {
    void method(...) {
        (common code segment 1)
        contextSpecificCode();
        (common code segment 2)
    }
    void contextSpecificCode() { ... }
}

class ContextA extends Common {
    void contextSpecificCode() {
        (context specific code A)
    }
    // ...
}

class ContextB extends Common {
    void contextSpecificCode() {
        (context specific code B)
    }
    // ...
}
```

The `contextSpecificCode()` method serves as a placeholder in the Common class. The question is: What implementation should be provided for `contextSpecificCode()` in class Common? The answer is that no implementation is appropriate, as Common has no knowledge of the specific context. Only the subclasses can provide sensible implementation for this method because it is an *abstract method*. The common class in the preceding code fragment is an abstract class that should be declared as follows.

```
abstract class Common {
    void method(...) {
        (common code segment 1)
        contextSpecificCode();
        (common code segment 2)
    }
    abstract void contextSpecificCode();
}
```

Figure 5.2

A double-buffered generic animation applet.

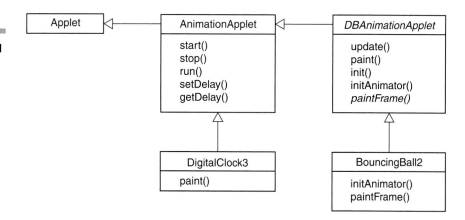

An abstract superclass provides a generic approach to the problem of recurring code segments intermixed with context specific code. The recurring code is abstracted, as before, and an abstract method is declared to serve as a placeholder for the context specific code. The Java compiler will compel the abstract method to be implemented in every derived class, allowing for insertion of the context specific code. This approach achieves a high level of encapsulation of the otherwise common and recurring code segment. All maintenance of the common code may be done in one place, out of view and without concern to the designers of the derived classes, who may focus their attention instead on the context specific code that is germane to their problem.

This approach can be used to factorize double-buffering in the `update()` method in the generic `DBAnimationApplet`. An abstract method `paintFrame()` is introduced for the subclasses to override and to paint the frames. When we put all the pieces together, we get the following program, which is the complete generic animation applet class that supports double-buffering. The structure of the program is shown in Figure 5.2.

Double-buffered generic animation applet:
DBAnimationApplet

```
import java.awt.*;

public abstract class DBAnimationApplet
      extends AnimationApplet {

   final public void update(Graphics g) {
      if (doubleBuffered) {
         paintFrame(offscreen);
         g.drawImage(im, 0, 0, this);
```

```
            } else {
              super.update();
            }
        }

        final public void paint(Graphics g) {
            paintFrame(g);
        }

        final public void init() {
            d = getSize();
            im = createImage(d.width, d.height);
            offscreen = im.getGraphics();
            initAnimator();
        }

        protected void initAnimator() {}

        abstract protected void paintFrame(Graphics g);

        protected DBAnimationApplet(boolean doubleBuffered) {
            this.doubleBuffered = doubleBuffered;
        }

        protected DBAnimationApplet() {
            this.doubleBuffered = true;
        }

        protected boolean doubleBuffered;
        protected Dimension d;
        protected Image im;
        protected Graphics offscreen;

    }
```

The initAnimator() and paintFrame() methods are protected, as they
are intended only for the subclasses to override. The update(), paint(), and
init() methods are final so that the subclasses cannot alter their implementation.
The conventions for using the double-buffered generic animation applet class are as
follows.

- A concrete animation applet should extend the DBAnimationApplet class.
  The boolean parameter of the constructor indicates whether double-buffering is
  needed.
- Each concrete animation applet must override the paintFrame() method to
  paint frames of the animation.
- The initAnimator() method may be overridden to provide subclass specific
  initializations.

The bouncing ball applet developed in Chapter 4 can be reimplemented by using the
DBAnimationApplet class.

Concrete double-buffered animation applet: `BouncingBall2`

```java
import java.awt.*;

public class BouncingBall2 extends DBAnimationApplet {

    public BouncingBall2() {
        super(true); // double buffering
    }

    protected void initAnimator() {
        String att = getParameter("delay");
        if (att != null)
            setDelay(Integer.parseInt(att));
        x = d.width * 2 / 3 ;
        y = d.height - radius;
    }

    protected void paintFrame(Graphics g) {
        g.setColor(Color.white);
        g.fillRect(0,0,d.width,d.height);
        if (x < radius || x > d.width - radius) {
            dx = -dx;
        }
        if (y < radius || y > d.height - radius) {
            dy = -dy;
        }
        x += dx; y += dy;
        g.setColor(color);
        g.fillOval(x - radius, y - radius, radius * 2, radius * 2);
    }

    protected int x, y;
    protected int dx = -2, dy = -4;
    protected int radius = 20;
    protected Color color = Color.green;
}
```

The commonalities in animation and double-buffering can also be factorized by using delegation. See Example 6.12 [p. 277] for a generic double-buffered animation class using delegation.

Design Pattern: Template Method

The preceding example also illustrates the use of an abstract class that serves as a template for classes with shared functionality. An abstract class contains behavior that is common to all its subclasses. This behavior is encapsulated in nonabstract methods, which may even be declared final to prevent any modification. This action ensures that all subclasses will inherit the same common behavior and its implementation. The abstract methods in such templates ensure the interface of the subclasses and require that context specific behavior be implemented for each concrete subclass.

The abstract method `paintFrame()` acts as a placeholder for the behavior that is implemented differently for each specific context. We call such methods *hook* methods, upon which context specific behavior may be hung, or implemented. The `paintFrame()` hook is placed within the method `update()`, which is common to all concrete animation applets. Methods containing hooks are called *template* methods.

The double-buffered generic animation applet just discussed illustrates the Template Method design pattern. The abstract method `paintFrame()` represents the behavior that is changeable, and its implementation is deferred to the concrete animation applets. We call `paintFrame()` a *hook method*. Using the hook method, we are able to define the `update()` method, which represents a behavior common to all the concrete animation applets. We call `update()` a *template method*. A template method uses hook methods to define a common behavior. Template methods describe the fixed behaviors of a generic class, which are sometimes called *frozen spots*. Hook methods indicate the changeable behaviors of a generic class, which are sometimes called *hot spots*.

Design Pattern *Template Method*

Category: Behavioral design pattern.

Intent: Define the skeleton of an algorithm in a method, deferring some steps to subclasses, thus allowing the subclasses to redefine certain steps of the algorithm.

Applicability: The Template Method pattern should be used

- to implement the invariant parts of an algorithm once and leave it to the subclasses to implement behavior that can vary and

- to factorize and localize the common behavior among subclasses to avoid code duplication.

The structure of the Template Method design pattern is depicted in the following diagram.

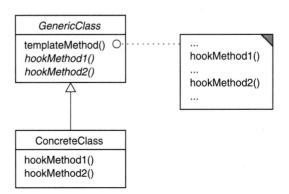

The participants in the Template Method design pattern are the

- *GenericClass* (e.g., DBAnimationApplet), which defines abstract hook methods (e.g., paintFrame()) that concrete subclasses (e.g., Bouncing-Ball2) override to implement steps of an algorithm and implements a template method (e.g., update()) that defines the skeleton of an algorithm by calling the hook methods; and the
- *ConcreteClass* (e.g., BouncingBall2), which implements the hook methods (e.g., paintFrame()) to carry out subclass specific steps of the algorithm defined in the template method.

In the Template Method design pattern, hook methods do not have to be abstract. The generic class may provide default implementations for the hook methods. Thus the subclasses have the option of overriding the hook methods or using the default implementation. The initAnimator() method in DBAnimationApplet is a nonabstract hook method with a default implementation. The init() method is another template method.

Example 5.3 illustrates the use of abstract classes and the Template Method design pattern.

EXAMPLE 5.3   A Generic Function Plotter

PURPOSE

To illustrate the use of Template Method design pattern.

DESCRIPTION

Design and implement a generic function plotter applet Plotter for plotting arbitrary single-variable functions on a two-dimensional canvas. The generic plotter should factorize all the behavior related to drawing and leave only the definition of the function to be plotted to its subclasses. A concrete plotter PlotSine will be implemented to plot the function

$$y = \sin x$$

A screen shot of PlotSine is shown in Figure 5.3.

KEY ISSUE

To represent an arbitrary single-variable function.

SOLUTION

The template method pattern offers a reasonable solution. The single-variable function to be plotted can be represented as a hook method in the generic plotter class. The function plotting method can then be defined in the generic plotter class as a template method. The generic plotter class is outlined in the following program segment.

Figure 5.3

A screen shot of
`PlotSine`.

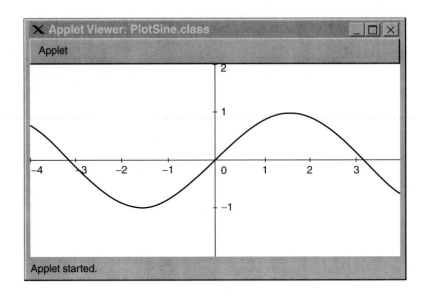

```
public abstract class Plotter {
    // the hook method
    public abstract double func(double x);

    // the template method
    protected void plotFunction(Graphics g) {
        // ...
    }
    // ...
}
```

The concrete plotter will only need to extend the generic plotter and define the function to be plotted by overriding the hook method. The program structure is shown in Figure 5.4.

The generic function plotter `Plotter` is implemented as an applet. It has the following methods.

Method	Description
init()	Initialization method to get the parameters
func()	Hook method representing the function to be plotted
paint()	Method to paint the image
plotFunction()	Template method, invoked by paint() to plot the function
drawCoordinates()	Auxiliary function called by paint() to draw the *x* and *y* axes and tick marks.

Figure 5.4

A generic function plotter.

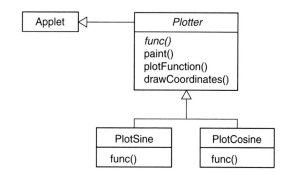

Plotter takes the following parameters set in the applet tag:

xorigin	The *x* coordinate of the origin on the canvas
yorigin	The *y* coordinate of the origin on the canvas
xratio	The number of pixels in the unit length on the *x* axis
yratio	The number of pixels in the unit length on the *y* axis

Generic plotter class **Plotter**

```
import java.awt.*;
public abstract class Plotter extends java.applet.Applet {
    public abstract double func(double x); // hook method
    public void paint(Graphics g) {
        drawCoordinates(g);
        plotFunction(g);
    }
    protected void plotFunction(Graphics g) {
        for (int px = 0; px < dim.width; px++) {
            try {
                double x = (double)(px - xorigin) / (double)xratio;
                double y = func(x);
                int py = yorigin - (int)(y * yratio);
                g.fillOval(px - 1, py - 1, 3, 3);
            } catch (Exception e) {}
        }
    }
    public void init() {
        (Get the parameters and initialize the fields)
    }
    protected void drawCoordinates(Graphics g) {
        (Draw the x and y axes and tick marks)
    }
    protected Dimension dim;
    protected Color color = Color.black;
    protected int xorigin, yorigin;
    protected int xratio = 100, yratio = 100;
}
```

The bodies of the `init()` and `drawCoordinates()` methods are left as an exercise. The complete source code is available online.

`PlotSine` is a concrete function plotter that simply extends the `Plotter` class and implements the method `func()`.

Concrete function plotter `PlotSine`

```
public class PlotSine extends Plotter {
    public double func(double x) {
        return Math.sin(x);
    }
}
```

5.2.2 Generalization

Generalization is a process that takes a solution to a specific problem and reorganizes it so that it not only solves the original problem but also solves a category of problems that are similar to the original problem.

EXAMPLE 5.4   A Generic Function Plotter That Plots Multiple Functions

PURPOSE

This example demonstrates generalization and illustrates use of the Strategy design pattern.

DESCRIPTION

In this example, the generic function plotter class `Plotter` is generalized to plot multiple single-variable functions overlaid on the same two-dimensional canvas. The new generic multiple function plotter is named `MultiPlotter`. A concrete subclass `PlotSineCosine` is implemented to plot

$$y = \sin x \qquad \text{and} \qquad y = \cos x$$

A screen shot of `PlotSineCosine` is shown in Figure 5.5.

KEY ISSUE

How to separate the functions to be plotted from the plotter.

SOLUTION

One way the generic `Plotter` class can be made to plot multiple functions is by adding more hook methods, one for each function to be plotted.

```
public class Plotter2 {
    abstract double func1(double x);
    abstract double func2(double x);
    abstract double func3(double x);
    // ...
}
```

Figure 5.5

A screen shot of
`PlotSine-
Cosine`.

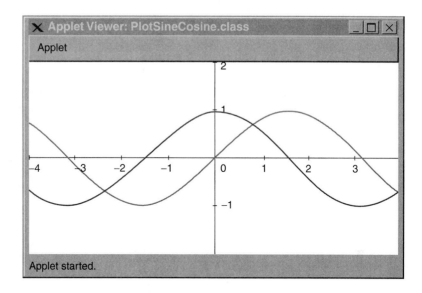

This approach is rather inflexible and inelegant, allowing only a fixed number of functions. Segments of nearly identical code will be duplicated to plot each function. The problem of this approach is that the functions to be plotted and the mechanism to plot the functions are coupled into the same class. Although the coupling is harmless for a single-function plotter, it hampers the flexibility of the plotter. A more elegent solution is to decouple the functions to be plotted from the mechanism to plot them. Instead of representing each function as a method, we can represent each function as an *object*.[2] Different functions are instances of different *function classes*. To allow uniform manipulation of the functions, all the function classes implement the following common interface.

Interface `Function`

```
interface Function {
    double apply(double x);
}
```

The functions sin *x* and cos *x* can be represented simply as follows.

Concrete functions `Sine` and `Cosine`

```
public class Sine implements Function {
    public double apply(double x) {
        return Math.sin(x);
    }
}
```

---

[2] Objects that represent functions are sometimes called *functors*.

```
public class Cosine implements Function {
  public double apply(double x) {
    return Math.cos(x);
  }
}
```

The structure of the generic multiple function plotter is shown in Figure 5.6. The `MultiPlotter` class extends `Plotter`. It uses a pair of parallel arrays to store the functions to be plotted and the colors used to plot the functions. Although there is a limit to the number of functions, `MAX_FUNCTIONS`, this limit can be easily removed without affecting any other parts of the program by using an unbounded container, such as `List` or `Set` (see Section 6.2 [p. 236]). The methods of `MultiPlotter` are summarized in the following table.

Method	Description
initMultiPlotter()	Hook method for the subclasses to set up the functions to be plotted
init()	Template method for initialization, which calls the hook method initMultiPlotter()
addFunction()	Method to add a function to be plotted
plotFunction()	Auxiliary function called by paint() to plot the functions
func()	Method inherited from class Plotter that is no longer useful in this class

Figure 5.6

Generic multiple function plotter.

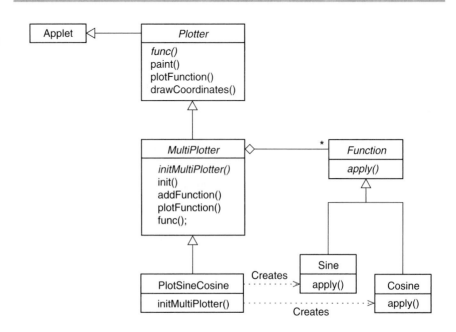

Implementation of `MultiPlotter` is shown in the following program.

Generic multiple function plotter: `MultiPlotter`

```java
import java.awt.*;

public abstract class MultiPlotter extends Plotter {

  abstract public void initMultiPlotter();

  public void init() {
    super.init();
    initMultiPlotter();
  }

  final public void addFunction(Function f, Color c) {
    if (numOfFunctions < MAX_FUNCTIONS &&
        f != null) {
      functions[numOfFunctions] = f;
      colors[numOfFunctions++] = c;
    }
  }

  protected void plotFunction(Graphics g) {
    for (int i = 0; i < numOfFunctions; i++) {
      if (functions[i] != null) {
        Color c = colors[i];
        if (c != null)
          g.setColor(c);
        else
          g.setColor(Color.black);
        for (int px = 0; px < d.width; px++) {
          try {
            double x = (double) (px - xorigin) / (double) xratio;
            double y = functions[i].apply(x);
            int py = yorigin - (int) (y * yratio);
            g.fillOval(px - 1, py - 1, 3, 3);
          } catch (Exception e) {}
        }
      }
    }
  }

  public double func(double x) {
    return 0.0;
  }

  protected static int MAX_FUNCTIONS = 5;
  protected int numOfFunctions = 0;
  protected Function functions[] = new Function[MAX_FUNCTIONS];
  protected Color colors[] = new Color[MAX_FUNCTIONS];

}
```

The following concrete subclass of `MultiPlotter` plots

$$y = \sin x \qquad \text{and} \qquad y = \cos x$$

utilizing the `Sine` and `Cosine` classes [page 199].

Concrete multiple function plotter: `MultiPlotter`

```
import java.awt.Color;

public class PlotSineCosine extends MultiPlotter {
    public void initMultiPlotter() {
        addFunction(new Sine(), Color.green);
        addFunction(new Cosine(), Color.blue);
    }
}
```

Design Pattern: Strategy

The preceding generic plotter of multiple functions illustrates the Strategy design pattern.

The structure of the Strategy design pattern is shown in the following diagram.

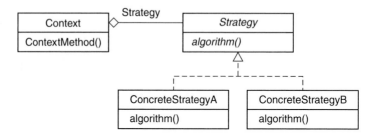

The participants in the Strategy design pattern are

- *Strategy* (e.g., `Function`), which declares an interface common to all supported algorithms;
- *ConcreteStrategy* (e.g., `Sine` and `Cosine`), which implements the algorithm using the Strategy interface; and
- *Context* (e.g., `MultiPlotter`), which maintains references to one or more Strategy objects (e.g., `functions` in `MultiPlotter`).

The Strategy design pattern can be considered as a variation of the Template Method design pattern, in which the hook method and the template method reside in

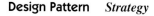

Design Pattern *Strategy*

Category: Behavioral design pattern.

Intent: Define a family of algorithms, encapsulate each one, and make them interchangeable.

Applicability: The Strategy pattern should be used when

- many related classes differ only in their behavior (e.g., plot different functions);

- different variants of an algorithm are needed (e.g., the sort algorithms in the case study in Section 5.3 [p. 212]);

- an algorithm uses data that clients shouldn't know about (e.g., the LayoutManager in AWT—see Section 6.3.2 [p. 262]); and

- a class defines many behaviors, which appear as multiple conditional statements in its methods (e.g., the TwoEndsTool in the case study in Chapter 7 [p. 318]).

two different classes. The abstract methods declared in the Strategy class are the hook methods, and the methods in the Context class that call the hook methods are the template methods.

In the MultiPlotter example, we used the Strategy design pattern to represent functions as objects (i.e., functors). Functors can be passed as parameters. This obviates the need for pointers to functions, which are commonly used in C and C++ to pass functions as parameters.

5.2.3 Abstract Coupling

The Strategy design pattern is an example of abstract coupling. *Abstract coupling* refers to a way that clients couple with service providers. A client accesses a service through an interface or an abstract class without knowing the actual concrete class that provides the service.

Let's again use the telephone service analogy. The clients are the telephone customers, and the telephone service providers are the telephone companies. Customers can be coupled to the telephone companies directly or through abstract coupling, as illustrated in Figure 5.7. Direct coupling uses each telephone company's proprietary equipment and protocols to provide services to its customers. Each customer has to choose a company for telephone service. Switching to a different company would be difficult because doing so would require replacing equipment and changing the way customers make phone calls.

Figure 5.7

(a) **Direct coupling versus (b) abstract coupling.**

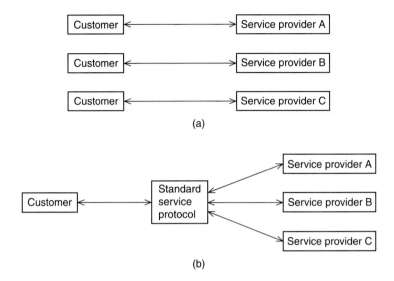

Abstract coupling is accomplished by requiring all telephone companies to use the same standard equipment and protocols. Doing so would make telephone service interchangeable and allow customers to switch easily among different companies. Customers would receive the same service without having to replace equipment or the way they make phone calls.

Abstract coupling is an important mechanism for enhancing flexibility and reusability in object-oriented design and occurs in many design patterns. Abstract coupling is also an application of the following important guideline of object-oriented design.

Design Guideline   *Program to an Interface, not to an Implementation*

Separate interface from implementation. Clients of a class should access only the functionalities of the class via its interface. Implementation should be hidden and irrelevant to the client.

Programming to an implementation yields ad hoc, context specific, and inflexible solutions. Programming to an interface yields general, flexible, and reusable solutions.

In Java, implementations are defined as the fields and methods in *classes*, and the interfaces of the implementations can be declared separately as the abstract methods in *abstract classes* or *interfaces*. An abstract method declares only the service or the feature to be provided but defines no implementation. Each abstract method also defines a *contract* of the service to be provided. The contract of an abstract method is a specification that defines the service the clients can expect but without giving an implementation. The contract also defines the responsibilities of the implementations of the service. In Java, we do not have to define the contracts of abstract methods explicitly. But we strongly recommend that the contracts of all abstract methods be made explicit and clear. Java provides a mechanism to state the contracts formally, so they can be stated either informally or semiformally.

5.2.4 Using Abstract Coupling to Enumerate Elements

Enumerating the elements in a collection object, such as a list, is one of the most common operations on any collection. Although it may seem to be a rather trivial problem, it actually is not. Let's use the simple linked list class LinkedList discussed in Section 4.5 [p. 145] as an example. Suppose that we have populated a list with instances of the Course class shown in the following program. The instances of Course represent courses offered at a university. The isPrerequisiteOf() method returns true when the receiving object represents a course that is a prerequisite of the course represented by the argument other.

Class Course

```
public class Course {
    public Course(String dept, String code, String title, int level) {
        this.dept = dept;
        this.code = code;
        this.title = title;
        this.level = level;
    }

    public String toString() {
        return (dept + " " + code + " " + title);
    }

    public boolean isPrerequisiteOf(Course other) {
        if (other != null &&
            this.dept == other.dept &&
            this.level < other.level)
          return true; {
        } else {
          return false;
        }
    }

    public String dept, code, title;
    public int level;
}
```

What we want to do is simply iterate through the list and print out the courses in the list.

Solution A: Direct Access

People who are familiar with procedural programming could easily come up with the following solution.

```
LinkedList list;
// populate the courses list
for (LinkedList.Node cur = list.head;
     cur != null;
     cur = cur.next) {
  System.out.println(cur.element);
}
```

This simple solution works. However, it requires that the fields of `LinkedList` and the inner class `Node` be accessible to the clients of `LinkedList`. This requirement means that the fields and the inner class must be public. As we discussed earlier, exposing implementation details by making the fields public not only violates the principle of encapsulation but could also compromise the integrity of the class. This solution is a poor design.

Solution B: Iterate Via Method Invocation

A better alternative is to keep the fields and the inner class `Node` nonpublic and provide public methods for iterating through the list. The `IterList` class extends `LinkedList` by adding a field `cur` that points to the current position of the iteration and providing the following methods for iterating through the list.

Method	Description
reset()	Moves the current position to the beginning of the list
next()	Retrieves the current element in the list and advances the current position
hasNext()	Returns `true` if the current position is not at the end of the list

---

Class `IterList`

```
public class IterList extends LinkedList {

  public void reset() {
    cur = head;
  }

  public Object next() {
    Object obj = null;
```

```
            if (cur != null) {
               obj = cur.element;
               cur = cur.next;
            }
            return obj;
        }

        public boolean hasNext() {
           return (cur != null);
        }


        protected Node cur;
    }
```

Now, a client can iterate through the list as follows.

```
IterList list;
// populate the courses list ...
for (list.reset(); list.hasNext();) {
   System.out.println(list.next());
}
```

This solution is clean and simple and is adequate for many situations. However, what if we want to print a table of course prerequisites that lists all the pairs of courses c1 and c2, in which c1 is a prerequisite of c2. To print out the prerequisite table requires nested loops. A logical solution seems to be the following.

```
for (list.reset(); list.hasNext();) {
   Course c1 = (Course) list.next();
   for (list.reset(); list.hasNext();) {
      Course c2 = (Course) list.next();
      if (c1.isPrerequisiteOf(c2)) {
         System.out.println(c1 + " is a prerequisite of " + c2);
      }
   }
}
```

Unfortunately, this solution doesn't work. The outer loop terminates after the first iteration. The reason is that both the outer and inner loops iterate through the same list, and when the inner loop completes one pass through the list, the cur index of the list has been moved to the end of the list, causing the outer loop to terminate. This type of iteration works only when two or more nested iterations are not on the same list.[3]

Solution C: Separate the Iterator From the List

When there are simultaneous iterations through the same list, each iteration must have its own current position index. In other words, the current position index should be decoupled from the list. The following solution uses a separate *iterator* class that contains the methods for iterating through the list and the current position index. It contains a reference to the original list.

---

[3] Simultaneous iterations may arise in unexpected situations and in much less obvious forms, such as recursion.

Iterator for linked lists: `LinkedListIterator`

```java
public class LinkedListIterator {

    public LinkedListIterator(LinkedList list) {
        this.list = list;
        cur = list.head;
    }

    public Object next() {
        Object obj = null;
        if (cur != null) {
            obj = cur.element
            cur = cur.next;
        }
        return obj;
    }

    public boolean hasNext() {
        return (cur != null);
    }

    protected LinkedList.Node cur;
    protected LinkedList list;
}
```

Now, the prerequisite table can be printed from the following code.

```java
LinkedListIterator iter1 = new LinkedListLiterator(list);
LinkedListIterator iter2 = new LinkedListLiterator(list);
while (iter1.hasNext()) {
  Course c1 = (Course) iter1.next();
  while (iter2.hasNext()) {
    Course c2 = (Course) iter2.next();
    if (c1.isPrerequisiteOf(c2)) {
      System.out.println(c1 + " is a prerequisite of " + c2);
    }
  }
}
```

Solution D: A Generalization

If all we needed to deal with were `LinkedList`, Solution C would be perfect. However, iterating through a collection is a rather common problem, and the collection could be a list, a hash table, or a tree. The implementation in Solution C is tied to a specific class—`LinkedList`—whereas the principle is applicable to iterating through all kinds of collections. We can develop a uniform way to iterate through all kinds of collections by using *abstract coupling*. In other words, clients will not deal directly with iterators tied to specific implementations; instead, clients will deal with *abstract iterators.* The Java Class Library provides two interfaces for abstract iterators.[4]

```
interface Iterator {
    boolean hasNext();
    Object next();
    void remove();
}

interface Enumeration {
    boolean hasMoreElements();
    Object nextElement();
}
```

The contracts for the methods of `Iterator` and `Enumeration` are as follows.

Method	Description
next()	Retrieves the current element in the list and advance the current position
hasNext()	Returns `true` if the current position is not at the end of the list
remove()	Removes the current element in the list and advances the current position
nextElement()	Same as `next()`
hasMoreElements()	Same as `hasNext()`

Each collection class that supports iteration should provide a *concrete iterator* that implements the `Iterator` interface. Clients will deal only with the abstract iterator and need no knowledge of the concrete iterators. They can iterate through any collection in a uniform way by using the abstract iterator.

To illustrate the implementation of an iterator, we first add the following method to the `List` interface.

```
public interface List {
    public Iterator iterator();
    // other methods ...
}
```

The `iterator()` method returns an iterator to iterate through a list. In the implementation of the `LinkedList` class, we add the implementation of the `iterator()` method, which returns a concrete iterator—an instance of the private inner class `LinkedListIterator`.

---

[4] The reason for having two abstract iterator interfaces in Java 2 is to ensure backward compatibility. The `Enumeration` interface was provided by Java 1.0. The `Iterator` interface was introduced in Java 2 and subsumes the `Enumeration` interface. The `Enumeration` interface is used mainly in Java 1.0.x classes, such as `Vector` and `Hashtable`.

Linked list class with an abstract iterator

```
public class LinkedList implements List {

   // other methods and constructors

   public Iterator iterator() {
      return new LinkedListIterator();
   }

   private class LinkedListIterator implements Iterator {

      public boolean hasNext() {
         return cur != null;
      }

      public Object next() {
         Object obj = null;
         if (cur != null) {
            obj = cur.element;
            cur = cur.next;
         }
         return obj;
      }

      public void remove() {
         throw new UnSupportedOperationException();
      }

      private LinkedList.Node cur;

      LinkedListIterator() {
         cur = head;
      }

   }

}
```

Clients iterate through a list by using abstract iterators.

```
List list = new LinkedList();
// populate the course list
Iterator iter1 = list.iterator();
for (; iter1.hasNext(); ) {
   Course c1 = (Course) iter1.next();
   Iterator iter2 = list.iterator();
   for (; iter2.hasNext(); ) {
      Course c2 = (Course) iter2.next();
      if (c1.isPrerequisiteOf(c2)) {
         System.out.println(c1 + " is a prerequisite of " + c2);
      }
   }
}
```

Note that the concrete iterator class is private. Clients of the `LinkedList` class need to know nothing about the concrete iterator.

Design Pattern: Iterator

The use of abstract iterators to iterate uniformly through different concrete collections is expressed as the following design pattern.

Design Pattern   *Iterator*

> *Category*: Behavioral design pattern.
> *Intent*: Provide a way to access the elements of a collection sequentially
> *Applicability*: The Iterator design pattern should be used
>
> - to access the contents of a collection without exposing its internal representation,
> - to support multiple traversals of collections (e.g., the nested traversal of the course list), and
> - to provide a uniform interface for traversing different collections (i.e., to support polymorphic iteration).

The structure of the Iterator pattern is illustrated in the following diagram.

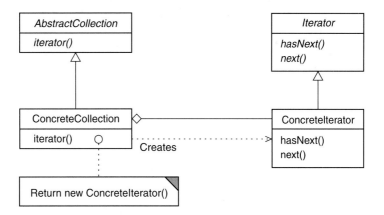

The participants of the Iterator pattern are

- *Iterator* (e.g., `Iterator`), which defines an interface for accessing and traversing the elements;
- *ConcreteIterator* (e.g., `LinkedListIterator`), which implements the iterator interface and keeps track of the current position in the traversal of the collection;
- *AbstractCollection* (e.g., `List`), which defines an interface for creating a concrete iterator (e.g., the `iterator()` method); and

- *ConcreteCollection* (e.g., `LinkedList`), which implements the `iterator()` method to return an instance of a proper concrete iterator.

The Iterator design pattern is used in the Java Collections Framework to provide a uniform way of iterating through a variety of collection classes. See Section 6.2.3 [p. 242] for discussion of the Java Collections Framework.

5.3 DESIGN CASE STUDY—ANIMATION OF SORTING ALGORITHMS

In this section, we develop an applet to animate different sorting algorithms. A screen shot of the animation is shown in Figure 5.8. We first develop a straightforward and monolithic implementation (i.e., the entire program is implemented as a single class). We then discuss the weakness of the initial implementation. Finally, we apply design patterns to address the weakness and accomplish greater flexibility and extensibility.

5.3.1 Initial Implementation

We would like to use the generic animation applet `DBAnimationApplet` that we developed in Example 5.2. Unfortunately, it isn't quite suited for animating sorting algorithms because it requires that the adjustment between two consecutive frames be done in the `paintFrame()` method, immediately before or after a frame is painted. Most sorting algorithms involve nested loops. Unwinding the loops so that each call to `paintFrame()` advances one iteration of the inner loop would be rather awkward. A better way to animate a complex algorithm is to let the algorithm control the progress of the animation and pause when a new frame needs to be painted. The algorithm animator class `AlgorithmAnimator` extends `DBAnimationApplet`. Again, the Template Method design pattern is used, defining the following three methods.

Figure 5.8

A screen shot of
`Sort`.

Method	Description
algorithm()	Hook method for subclasses to define the algorithm to be animated
run()	Template method, which simply calls the algorithm() method to start the animation
pause()	Method to be called inside method algorithm() of the subclasses when a frame needs to be painted, painting a frame and pausing for a duration specified by delay

The subclasses of AlgorithmAnimator are required to define the following methods.

Method	Description
algorithm()	Define the algorithm to be animated. It should call the pause() method when some progress is made and a new frame needs to be painted.
paintFrame()	Paint a frame.

Generic algorithm animation applet: `AlgorithmAnimator`

```
public abstract class AlgorithmAnimator
     extends DBAnimationApplet {

  // the hook method
  abstract protected void algorithm();

  // the template method
  public void run() {
    algorithm();
  }

  final protected void pause() {
    if (Thread.currentThread() == animationThread) {
      try {
        Thread.sleep(delay);
      } catch (InterruptedException e) {}
      repaint();
    }
  }
}
```

The Monolithic Sort

Now, we are ready to use the generic algorithm animator to animate sorting algorithms. The entire program is a single class `Sort`. In this animation, we sort an array of nonnegative integers. The array to be sorted is declared as a field of `Sort`: `protected int arr[];`. The methods of `Sort` are summarized in the following table.

Method	Description
scramble()	Initializes and scrambles the array to be sorted
paintFrame()	Paints a frame
bubbleSort()	Bubble sort algorithm
quickSort()	Quick sort algorithm
initAnimator()	Initializes the animation
algorithm()	Sorting algorithm to be animated
swap()	Auxiliary method used by sorting algorithms to swap two numbers in an array

The following is the overall structure of `Sort`.

Sorting animation `Sort`

```
import java.awt.*;

public class Sort extends AlgorithmAnimator {

    (Method scramble() on page 215)
    (Method paintFrame() on page 215)
    (Method bubbleSort() on page 216)
    (Method quickSort() on page 216)
    (Method initAnimator() on page 217)
    (Method algorithm() on page 217)
    (Method swap() on page 217)

    protected int     arr[];      // the array to be sorted
    protected String algName;  // the name of the algorithm to be animated
}
```

The scramble() method first determines the size of the array to be sorted. Then it initializes the array and scrambles the numbers in the array. The array size is determined by the height of the viewing area. Because each number in the array will represented by a horizontal line that is 1 pixel wide—and adjacent lines are separated by a 1 pixel wide gap—the size of the array is half the height of the viewing area in pixels. Suppose that n is the size of the array and that the array contains numbers from 0 to $n - 1$.

Method of class Sort: Scramble()
on page 214

```
protected void scramble() {
    arr = new int[getSize().height / 2];
    for (int i = arr.length; --i >= 0;) {
        arr[i] = i;
    }
    for (int i = arr.length; --i >= 0;) {
        int j = (int)(i * Math.random());
        swap(arr, i, j);
    }
}
```

The paintFrame() method paints a frame based on the current contents of the array arr. Each number in the array is represented by a horizontal line 1 pixel wide. The length of each line is proportional to the number it represents, with the longest line proportioned to occupy the entire width of the viewing area.

Method of class Sort: paintFrame() on page 214

```
protected void paintFrame(Graphics g) {
    Dimension d = getSize();
    g.setColor(Color.white);
    g.fillRect(0, 0, d.width, d.height);
    g.setColor(Color.black);
    int y = d.height - 1;
    double f = d.width / (double) arr.length;
    for (int i = arr.length; --i >= 0; y -= 2) {
        g.drawLine(0, y, (int)(arr[i] * f), y);
    }
}
```

The bubbleSort() and quickSort() methods are the two algorithms to be animated. Each time the program is invoked, one of them will be animated. The implementation of the algorithms is rather straightforward, except that method pause() is called whenever progress is made during the sorting process, to briefly pause the execution of the program and display the current state of the array.

Method of class Sort: bubbleSort() on page 214

```
protected void bubbleSort(int a[]) {
    for (int i = a.length; --i >= 0; )
        for (int j = 0; j < i; j++) {
            if (a[j] > a[j+1]) {
                swap(a, j, j + 1);
            }
            pause();
        }
}
```

Method of class Sort: quickSort() on page 214

```
protected void quickSort(int a[], int lo0, int hi0) {
    int lo = lo0, hi = hi0, mid;
    pause();
    if (hi0 > lo0) {
        mid = a[(lo0 + hi0) / 2];
        while(lo <= hi) {
            while ((lo < hi0) && (a[lo] < mid)) {
                ++lo;
            }
            while ((hi > lo0) && (a[hi] > mid)) {
                --hi;
            }
            if(lo <= hi) {
                swap(a, lo, hi);
                pause();
                ++lo;
                --hi;
            }
        }
        if(lo0 < hi) {
            quickSort(a, lo0, hi);
        }
        if(lo < hi0) {
            quickSort(a, lo, hi0);
        }
    }
}
```

Which of the two algorithms to be animated is determined by the parameter alg set in the applet tag. The initAnimator() method initializes the animation by first retrieving the parameter alg, storing it in the field algName, and then calling scramble() to set up the array to be sorted.

Method of class Sort:
initAnimator() on page 214

```
protected void initAnimator() {
   algName = "BubbleSort";
   String at = getParameter("alg");
   if (at != null) {
      algName = at;
   }
   setDelay(20);
   scramble();
}
```

The `algorithm()` method simply chooses one of the algorithms to animate, based on the value of the field `algName`.

Method of class Sort: algorithm()
on page 214

```
protected void algorithm() {
   if ("BubbleSort".equals(algName)) {
      bubbleSort(arr);
   } else if ("QuickSort".equals(algName)) {
      quickSort(arr, 0, arr.length - 1);
   } else {
      bubbleSort(arr);
   }
}
```

Finally, the auxiliary method `swap()` swaps two numbers in the array.

Method of class Sort: swap() on page 214

```
private void swap(int a[], int i, int j) {
   int temp = a[i]; a[i] = a[j]; a[j] = temp;
}
```

5.3.2 Separating Algorithms

The initial version of the sorting algorithm animation applet works, except that the design of the program is *not* object-oriented. It lumps everything into a single class, which for those who are accustomed to procedural programming is a natural thing to do. However, this approach usually results in huge classes that contain a wide variety of functionalities. The resulting programs are overly complex, inflexible, and difficult to maintain in the long run.

Large classes usually contain loosely coupled elements. Such elements in a class usually address different concerns in the problem to be solved. Separating these

Figure 5.9

Separating and
encapsulating
sorting algorithms,
using the Strategy
design pattern.

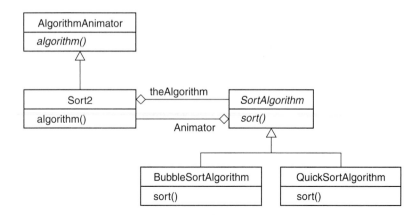

concerns into different classes can reduce the complexity of the design and enhance
its flexibility and maintainability.

Design Guideline   *Separate Functionalities That Address Different Concerns*

If a class contains components that address different concerns, these components are
candidates for separation from the original class.

By separating different concerns in a loosely coupled class, we end up with
classes that are smaller and tightly coupled (i.e., all their components are closely
related and highly interdependent). When separation is combined with the Template
Method and Strategy design patterns, the resulting design can offer great flexibility
in solving each aspect of the problem.

The initial version of the sorting algorithm animation Sort is rather loosely
coupled. The sorting algorithms are good candidates for separating because they are
largely independent of the animation mechanism. Thus adding or replacing sorting
algorithms will have little impact on the animation mechanism. The algorithms can
be separated from the animation class, and the Strategy design pattern can be used to
make the algorithms to be animated interchangeable. The structure of the new design
is shown in Figure 5.9.

The Abstract Sorting Algorithm

The abstract class sortAlgorithm is the *strategy* in the Strategy design pattern.
It represents an abstract sorting algorithm. The sort() method is the hook method.
The pause() and swap() methods are to be invoked by the subclasses of Sort-
Algorithm.

Abstract sorting algorithm: `SortAlgorithm`

```
public abstract class SortAlgorithm {
  abstract public void sort(int a[]);

  protected SortAlgorithm(AlgorithmAnimator animator) {
    this.animator = animator;
  }

  protected void pause() {
    if (animator != null) {
      animator.pause();
    }
  }

  protected static void swap(int a[], int i, int j) {
    int temp;
    temp = a[i]; a[i] = a[j]; a[j] = temp;
  }

  private AlgorithmAnimator animator;
}
```

The implementation of the `SortAlgorithm` class shows some interesting and common variations of the Strategy design pattern. The first variation is that the abstract strategy, `SortAlgorithm`, is an abstract class instead of an interface. Using an abstract class for the abstract strategy allows some utility methods needed by concrete strategy classes to be implemented in the abstract strategy class. In the `SortAlgorithm` class, two utility methods, `pause()` and `swap()`, are implemented. The second variation is that the abstract strategy class `SortAlgorithm` contains a reference to the client, the `Sort2` class. This reference allows the abstract and concrete strategy classes to access the client's interface. In this example, the reference to `Sort2` is used in the `pause()` method to delegate the invocation of `pause()`.

The Concrete Algorithms

The algorithms to be animated are represented as *concrete strategies*. The `Bubble-SortAlgorithm` and `QuickSortAlgorithm` classes both extend `Sort-Algorithm`. They define the bubble sort and the quick sort algorithms, respectively.

Concrete sorting algorithm: `BubbleSortAlgorithm`

```
public class BubbleSortAlgorithm extends SortAlgorithm {
  public void sort(int a[]) {
    for (int i = a.length; --i >= 0; ) {
      for (int j = 0; j < i; j++) {
        if (a[j] > a[j+1]) {
          swap(a, j, j+1);
        }
```

```
            pause();
        }
      }
  }

  public BubbleSortAlgorithm(AlgorithmAnimator animator) {
    super(animator);
  }
}
```

Concrete sorting algorithm: `QuickSortAlgorithm`

```
public class QuickSortAlgorithm extends SortAlgorithm {

  protected void qsort(int a[], int lo0, int hi0) {
    int lo = lo0;
    int hi = hi0;
    int mid;
    pause();
    if (hi0 > lo0) {
      mid = a[(lo0 + hi0) / 2];
      while (lo <= hi) {
        while ((lo < hi0) && (a[lo] < mid)) {
          lo++;
        }
        while ((hi > lo0) && (a[hi] > mid)) {
          hi--;
        }
        if (lo <= hi) {
          swap(a, lo, hi);
          pause();
          lo++;
          hi--;
        }
      }
      if (lo0 < hi) {
        qsort(a, lo0, hi);
      }
      if (lo < hi0) {
        qsort(a, lo, hi0);
      }
    }
  }

  public void sort(int a[]) {
    qsort(a, 0, a.length - 1);
  }

  public QuickSortAlgorithm(AlgorithmAnimator animator) {
    super(animator);
  }
}
```

Creating Instances of Concrete Algorithms

We utilize the concrete algorithms in a new version of sort animation—Sort2. The question is: Where are instances of these concrete algorithms to be created? One option is to create the instances in the initAnimator() method of Sort2.

```
public class Sort2 extends AlgorithmAnimator {

   protected SortAlgorithm theAlgorithm;

   protected void initAnimator() {
      algName = "BubbleSort";
      String at = getParameter("alg");
      if (at != null) {
         algName = at;
      }
      if ("BubbleSort".equals(algName)) {
         algorithm = new BubbleSortAlgorithm(this);
      } else if ("QuickSort".equals(algName)) {
         algorithm = new QuickSortAlgorithm(this);
      } else { // default algorithm
         algorithm = new BubbleSortAlgorithm(this);
      }
      setDelay(20);
      scramble();
   }

   // other methods and fields . . .
}
```

Although this solution works, it leaves the client (the Sort2 class) of the Strategy design pattern (the SortingAlgorithm class) to deal directly with the concrete strategies (the BubbleSortAlgorithm and QuickSortAlgorithm classes). This result negates one of the key advantages of using the Strategy design pattern; that is, to make concrete strategies interchangeable by decoupling the clients from the strategies. The client should be completely unaware of the concrete strategies.

A better alternative is to use a separate class whose sole responsibility is to create instances of concrete sorting algorithms. We call this class a *factory*. Using the factory, the client (the Sort2 class) can be completely decoupled from the concrete sorting algorithms.

The factory class can be implemented in several different ways. To allow the flexibility of using different factories and to insulate the client from future changes in them, the Strategy design pattern once again can be applied to make different factories interchangeable. The revised design of the sorting algorithm animation is shown in Figure 5.10. The abstract algorithm factory, AlgorithmFactory, is defined as an interface. The contract of the hook method makeSortAlgorithm() is:

Given the name of a sorting algorithm, return an instance of a subclass of Sort-Algorithm that implements the named sorting algorithm.

Figure 5.10

A revised design of
sort animation,
using factories.

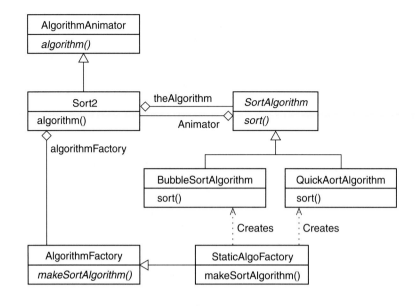

Abstract algorithm factory: `AlgorithmFactory`

```
public interface AlgorithmFactory {
   public SortAlgorithm makeSortAlgorithm(String algName);
}
```

A straightforward implementation of a concrete algorithm factory is the `Static-AlgoFactory` class.

Concrete algorithm factory: `StaticAlgoFactory`

```
public class StaticAlgoFactory implements AlgorithmFactory {

   public StaticAlgoFactory(AlgorithmAnimator animator) {
      this.animator = animator;
   }

   public SortAlgorithm makeSortAlgorithm(String algName) {
      if ("BubbleSort".equals(algName)) {
         return new BubbleSortAlgorithm(animator);
      } else if ("QuickSort".equals(algName)) {
         return new QuickSortAlgorithm(animator);
      } else {
         return new BubbleSortAlgorithm(animator);
      }
   }

   protected AlgorithmAnimator animator;

}
```

This static algorithm factory is tightly coupled with concrete sorting algorithms. Adding or changing concrete sorting algorithms requires changes to this factory. However, using Java's dynamic class loading capability, we can build a *dynamic* sorting algorithm factory that is completely decoupled from the concrete sorting algorithms; that is, adding or changing concrete sorting algorithms does not affect the dynamic factory![5]

The Revised Sort Animation

The revised sorting algorithm animation applet `Sort2` is now completely decoupled from the concrete sorting algorithms.

Revised sorting algorithm animation applet: `Sort2`

```
public class Sort2 extends AlgorithmAnimator {
    protected SortAlgorithm theAlgorithm;
    protected SortAlgorithmFactory algorithmFactory;

    protected void initAnimator() {
        algName = "BubbleSort";
        String at = getParameter("alg");
        if (at != null) {
            algName = at;
        }

        algorithmFactory = new StaticAlgoFactory(this);
        theAlgorithm = algorithmFactory.makeSortAlgorithm(algName);

        setDelay(20);
        scramble();
    }

    protected void algorithm() {
        if (theAlgorithm != null)
            theAlgorithm.sort(arr);

    }

    protected void scramble() {
        (The body is identical to that of scramble() in Sort on page 215)

    }

    protected void paintFrame(Graphics g) {
        (The body is identical to that of paintFrame() in Sort on page 215)

    }

    protected int    arr[];
    protected String algName;
}
```

---

[5] An implementation of a dynamic factory is included in the *Online Supplement* to this book.

Design Pattern: Factory

The use of factories to create concrete sorting algorithms illustrates another useful design pattern—Factory.

Design Pattern   *Factory*

Category: Creational design pattern.

Intent: Define an interface for creating objects but let subclasses decide which class to instantiate and how.

Applicability: The Factory design pattern should be used when a system should be independent of how its products are created.

The structure of the Factory design pattern is shown in the following diagram.

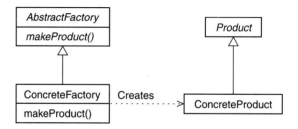

The participants in the Factory design pattern are

- *Product* (e.g., `SortAlgorithm`), which defines an interface of the objects that the factory will create;
- *ConcreteProduct* (e.g., `QuickSortAlgorithm`), which implements the `Product` interface;
- *AbstractFactory* (e.g., `AlgorithmFactory`), which defines a factory method (e.g., `makeSortAlgorithm()`) that returns an object of type `Product`; and
- *ConcreteFactory* (e.g., `StaticSortAlgorithmFactory`), which overrides the factory method to return an instance of `ConcreteProduct`.

5.3.3   Separating Display Strategies

If we examine the revised sorting algorithm animation applet `Sort3` closely, we find there is another loosely coupled component—the display strategy (i.e., the visual representation) of the array. The display strategy is independent of the algorithms being animated and the animation mechanism. Changing the display strategy should not affect the algorithms and the animation mechanism. The display strategy can be

Figure 5.11

Encapsulating the display strategies, using the Strategy design pattern.

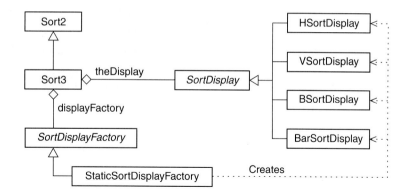

decoupled from the animation mechanism and the algorithms by using the Strategy and Factory design patterns so that different display strategies become interchangeable. The revised design is shown in Figure 5.11.

Three Design Options

The key issue here is the design of the interface of the display strategy—the `Sort-Display` interface, which represents an abstract display strategy. We start by designing the interface.

```
public interface SortDisplay {
   public void display(int a[], Graphics g, Dimension d);
}
```

The interface defines a single method for displaying the array. The parameters of the method are necessary for displaying the array. This solution is rather straightforward and the interface is small, which means low coupling. The change needed in the main class `Sort3` is for the `paintFrame()` method to delegate the painting responsibility to the display strategy.

```
public class Sort3 extends Sort2 {

   protected SortDisplay theDisplay;

   public void paintFrame(Graphics g) {
      theDisplay.display(arr, g, getSize());
   }
   // ...
}
```

This solution works, but it is inflexible because there is a subtle coupling between the display strategy and the display size. In the preceding implementation, the size of the array is determined in the `scramble()` method of the `Sort3` class based on the height of the viewing area. This condition means that the `scramble()` method is tightly coupled to the displaying scheme.

The second design option is to move the `scramble()` method to the `Sort-Display` interface so that tightly coupled functionalities are in the same class.

```
public interface SortDisplay {
   public void scramble(int a[], Dimension d);
   public void display(int a[], Graphics g, Dimension d);
}
```

The `scramble()` method of `Sort3` will also delegate the responsibility to the display strategy.

```
public class Sort3 extends Sort2 {

   protected SortDisplay theDisplay;

   public void scramble() {
      theDisplay.scramble(arr, getSize());
   }

   public void paintFrame(Graphics g) {
      theDisplay.display(arr, g, getSize());
   }
   // ...
}
```

Now, coupling between the display strategy and its client is reduced. However, `SortDisplay` is not very cohesive, as initializing the array and scrambling it have nothing to do with displaying it. These are basically independent functionalities, except that they all share the same array size. So, the third and best design option is to move `scramble()`'s functionality back into the `Sort3` class. We introduce a new method, `getArraySize()`, in the `SortDisplay` interface to capture the interdepency among these methods.

Abstract display strategy: `SortDisplay`

```
import java.awt.*;

public interface SortDisplay {
   public int getArraySize(Dimension d);
   public void display(int a[], Graphics g, Dimension d);
}
```

The design of the `SortDisplay` interface illustrates the following design guideline.

Design Guideline   *Minimize the Interface*

Design the smallest possible interface that provides the needed functionality of a class. Interface size is determined by the number of methods and their parameters. Large interfaces usually indicate high levels of coupling with collaborating classes and complexity.

Concrete Display Strategies

The original display strategy that uses 1-pixel horizontal lines can be reimplemented as a concrete strategy HSortDisplay that implements the SortDisplay interface.

Concrete display strategy: HSortDisplay

```java
import java.awt.*;
public class HSortDisplay implements SortDisplay {
   public int getArraySize(Dimension d) {
     return d.height / 2;
   }
   public void display(int a[], Graphics g, Dimension d) {
     double f = d.width / (double) a.length;
     g.setColor(Color.white);
     g.fillRect(0, 0, d.width, d.height);
     int y = d.height - 1;
     g.setColor(Color.black);
     y = d.height - 1;
     for (int i = a.length; --i >= 0; y -= 2)
       g.drawLine(0, y, (int)(a[i] * f), y);
   }
}
```

The revised design allows us to introduce new display strategies easily. Two variations of the original display strategy can be implemented easily.

- VSortDisplay: Use vertical lines, with all lines flush against the top edge and extending downward, as shown in Figure 5.12(a).
- BSortDisplay: Use vertical lines, with all lines flush against the bottom edge and extending upward, as shown in Figure 5.12(b).

The implementations follow.

Concrete display strategy: VSortDisplay

```java
import java.awt.*;
public class VSortDisplay implements SortDisplay {
   public int getArraySize(Dimension d) {
     return d.width / 2;
   }
   public void display(int a[], Graphics g, Dimension d) {
     g.setColor(Color.white);
     g.fillRect(0, 0, d.width, d.height);
     int x = d.width - 1;
     double f = d.height / (double) a.length;
     g.setColor(Color.black);
     for (int i = a.length; --i >= 0; x -= 2)
       g.drawLine(x, 0, x, (int)(a[i] * f));
   }
}
```

Figure 5.12

Screen shots of `Sort3` showing various display strategies.

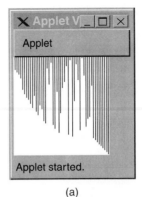

(a)

(b)

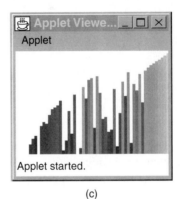

(c)

Concrete display strategy: `BSortDisplay`

```java
import java.awt.*;

public class BSortDisplay implements SortDisplay {

  public int getArraySize(Dimension d) {
    return d.width / 2;
  }

  public void display(int a[], Graphics g, Dimension d) {
    g.setColor(Color.white);
    g.fillRect(0, 0, d.width, d.height);
    double f = d.height / (double) a.length;
    int x = d.width - 1;
    g.setColor(Color.black);
    for (int i = a.length; --i >= 0; x -= 2)
      g.drawLine(x, d.height, x, d.height - (int)(a[i] * f));
  }
}
```

A more interesting display strategy is the `BarSortDisplay`, shown in Figure 5.12(c). The vertical lines are 3 pixels wide, the heights of the lines are proportional to the numbers they represent, and different colors are used to represent different numbers.

Concrete display strategy: `BarSortDisplay`

```java
public class BarSortDisplay implements SortDisplay {
  public int getArraySize(Dimension d) {
    return d.width / 3;
  }
  public void display(int a[], Graphics g, Dimension d) {
    g.setColor(Color.white);
    g.fillRect(0, 0, d.width, d.height);
    double f = d.height / (double) a.length;
    double cf = 255.0 / (double) a.length;
    int x = d.width - 3;
    for (int i = a.length; --i >= 0; x -= 3) {
      g.setColor(new Color((int)(a[i] * cf / 1.5), (int)(a[i] * cf), 0));
      g.fillRect(x, d.height - (int)(a[i] * f), 3, (int)(a[i] * f));
    }
  }
}
```

Display Factory

The instances of concrete display strategies are also created by a factory. The structure is similar to the algorithm factories. Implementation of a simple static factory is as follows.

Abstract display factory: `SortDisplayFactory`

```java
public interface SortDisplayFactory {
  SortDisplay makeSortDisplay(String name);
}
```

Concrete display factory: `StaticSortDisplayFactory`

```java
public class StaticSortDisplayFactory
    implements SortDisplayFactory {
  public SortDisplay makeSortDisplay(String name) {
    if ("horizontal".equals(name))
      return new HSortDisplay();
    else if ("vertical".equals(name))
      return new VSortDisplay();
    else if ("bottom".equals(name))
      return new BSortDisplay();
```

```
                        else if ("bar".equals(name))
                           return new BarSortDisplay();
                        else
                           return new HSortDisplay();
                }
        }
```

Putting All the Pieces Together

Sorting algorithm animation applet: Sort3

```
import java.awt.*;

public class Sort3 extends Sort2 {
    protected SortDisplay theDisplay;
    protected SortDisplayFactory displayFactory;

    protected void initAnimator() {

        String att = getParameter("dis");
        displayFactory = new StaticSortDisplayFactory();
        theDisplay = displayFactory.makeSortDisplay(att);
        super.initAnimator();

    }

    protected void scramble() {

        int n = theDisplay.getArraySize(getSize());

        arr = new int[n];
        for (int i = arr.length; --i >= 0;)
           arr[i] = i;
        for (int i = arr.length; --i >= 0;) {
           int j = (int)(i * Math.random());
           SortAlgorithm.swap(arr, i, j);
        }
    }

    protected void paintFrame(Graphics g) {

        theDisplay.display(arr, g, getSize());

    }
}
```

CHAPTER SUMMARY

■ Design patterns are schematic descriptions of solutions to recurring problems in software design. Each pattern represents a generic (i.e., reusable) solution to a recurring problem. Only a relatively small number of patterns are needed to capture the essence of the design process, and they can be adapted and combined in countless ways to generate endless possibilities.

- Generic components are program components, usually classes and packages, that can be adapted and used in many different contexts without modification of the source code. Generic components are also known as reusable components.

- Factorization is used to identify recurring, identical, or nearly identical code segments and to reorganize a program so that the recurring code segments are captured as a generic component that is defined once and is usable in many different contexts. Factorization can be accomplished by inheritance or delegation.

- Generalization is a process that takes a solution to a specific problem and reorganizes it so that it not only solves the original problem but also solves a category of problems that are similar to the original problem. Generalization is often accomplished by using abstract classes or interfaces and design patterns, such as Template Method and Strategy.

- An abstract method is a method whose implementation is deferred to its subclasses. Abstract methods are also known as deferred methods. An abstract class is a class that includes or inherits at least one abstract method.

- The Template Method design pattern defines the skeleton of an algorithm in a method, deferring some steps to subclasses and thus allowing the subclasses to redefine certain steps of the algorithm. The Template Method design pattern should be used to implement the invariant parts of an algorithm or to factorize and localize common behavior among subclasses.

- The Strategy design pattern defines a family of algorithms, encapsulates each one, and makes them interchangeable. The Strategy design pattern should be used when many related classes differ only in their behavior or when different variants of an algorithm are needed.

- Important design guidelines include the following.

    Maximize flexibility. Rarely can components be reused without adaptation. Flexibility allows components to be adapted to different contexts. The more flexible a component is, the better is the chance that it may be reused.

    Minimize the chance of misuse. Well-designed classes should minimize their possible misuse by clearly identifying any violation of the conventions of the classes, preferably at compile time.

    Program to an interface, not to an implementation. Separate interface from implementation. Clients of a class should access only the functionalities of the class via its interface. Implementation should be hidden and irrelevant to the client.

    Separate functionalities that address different concerns. If a class contains components that address different concerns, these components are candidates for separation from the original class.

    Minimize the interface. Design the smallest possible interface that provides the needed functionality of a class. Interface size is determined by the number of methods and their parameters. Large interfaces usually indicate high levels of coupling with collaborating classes and complexity.

EXERCISES

5.1. Extend the generic function plotter class
Plotter to plot the following functions.

(a) $y = \sqrt{x}$

(b) $y = \ln x$

(c) $y = \tan x$

(d) $y = x^3 - 3x^2 + 5x + 8$

5.2. Write a generic plotter applet that takes a
parameter func that represents a single-variable
polynomial function and plots the function. For
example, the input might be in the form

```
x^3 - 3 * x^2 + 5 * x + 8
```

5.3. Extend the generic multiple function plotter
MultiPlotter to plot the following functions
in the same two-dimensional canvas.

(a) $y = 5x$

(b) $y = 2x^2$

(c) $y = 0.5x^3$

(d) $y = 0.2e^x$

(e) $y = \ln x$

5.4. Write an applet that combines the applets in
Exercises 4.7 and 4.8. It should support two
display strategies: a bar chart or a pie chart. The
user should be able to choose either of the two
display strategies by setting a parameter. The
display strategies are to be implemented by
using the Strategy design pattern.

5.5. Write an animated applet with two bouncing
balls by extending the DBAnimationApplet
class. The balls should bounce off each other
when they collide. *Bonus:* Allow the user to add
more balls.

5.6. Enhance the latest version of the animation
applet Sort3 by adding the following
capabilities:

(a) new sorting algorithms, such as *insertion
sort*, and

(b) new display strategies.

5.7. Develop animation applets to animate graph
algorithms. Candidates include the following.

(a) Kruskal's and Prim's algorithms for
minimum spanning trees [Thomas Corman
and Rivest 1990]. Animate the process of
adding edges to the minimum spanning
tree.

(b) Dijkstra's algorithm for single-source
shortest path [Thomas Corman and Rivest
1990]. Animate the process of discovering
the edges on the shortest path.

6

Object-Oriented
Application Frameworks

CHAPTER OVERVIEW

In this chapter we discuss the design of application frameworks and the use of design patterns. We present three important frameworks in the Java Class Library—the collections framework, the input/output framework, and the graphical user interface (GUI) framework.

6.1 APPLICATION FRAMEWORKS

An *object-oriented application framework*, or *framework* for short, is a set of co-operating classes that represent reusable designs of software systems in a particular application domain. An application framework typically consists of a set of abstract classes and interfaces that are parts of semicomplete applications that can be specialized to produce custom applications. An application framework often prescribes a set of conventions for extending the abstract classes, implementing the interfaces, and allowing their instances to interact with one another. The main goal of application frameworks is to support the reuse of designs and implementations in particular application domains and thereby greatly simplify them.

The generic animation applet classes that we developed in Chapter 5 (`AnimationApplet` and `DBAnimationApplet`) can be considered as miniframeworks.

They exhibit some of the characteristics of application frameworks in that they are reusable and extendable, they are semicomplete programs, and the reusable design and implementation is captured in abstract classes with hook methods to be overridden by the subclasses.

Real application frameworks are of much larger scale. Some examples are graphical user interface (GUI) frameworks such as the Abstract Windows Toolkit (AWT) and Swing portion of the Java Foundation Classes (JFC), and the Microsoft Foundation Classes (MFC) for C++; and distributed computing frameworks such as the Java Remote Method Invocation (RMI), and the Common Object Request Broker Architecture (CORBA).

6.1.1   Characteristics

Key characteristics of application frameworks include the following.

Extendability

An application framework typically consists of a set of abstract classes and interfaces to be extended and specialized. Its changeable aspects, also known as the *hot spots* of the framework, are often represented as hook methods. Custom applications use the framework by extending or implementing the classes and interfaces in the framework and by overriding the hook methods to provide customized behaviors.

For example, a concrete animation applet, such as `BouncingBall3`, simply extends the `DBAnimationApplet` class and overrides the hook methods `paint-Frame()` and `initAnimator()`.

Inversion of Control

When we use a conventional library of routines and classes, the applications usually control the flow of execution. In other words, the applications are acting as the masters, whereas the routines and classes in the libraries are acting as servants to provide services. When we use an application framework, the control of the flow of execution often resides in the framework, not in the applications. In other words, the framework is acting as the master, whereas the applications are acting as servants to fill in the hot spots.

For example, with the `LinkedList` class, the applications are in control, and the `LinkedList` class simply provides services. That is quite different from using the `Applet` class, which can be considered a miniframework. The control resides in the `Applet` class and the applet context. A specific applet extends the `Applet` class and overrides the hook methods, `init()`, `start()`, and the like, which represent the hot spots of the applet framework.

Design Patterns as Building Blocks

Although both design patterns and frameworks are mechanisms used to capture reusable designs, they are quite different. On the one hand, design patterns are schematic descriptions of reusable designs that are not concrete programs and that are language indepedent. On the other hand, frameworks are compilable programs written in a specific programming language and often contain abstract classes and interfaces. Design patterns are the architectural building blocks of application frameworks. They help make application frameworks extendable and reusable.

For example, the design patterns Template Method and Strategy are used in almost all application frameworks.

6.1.2 Design Requirements

Designing application frameworks is more difficult than designing specific applications. A designer of application frameworks must foresee the potential changes and the variabilities required by potential applications that may use the frameworks. Booch [Booch 1994] has suggested the following design requirements of application frameworks.

Completeness

The framework must provide a family of classes, united by a shared interface but each employing a different representation. Developers can then select the classes having the time and space semantics most appropriate to their given application.

Adaptability

All platform-specific aspects of the framework must be clearly identified and isolated. That permits local substitutions to be made.

Efficiency

Components must be easily assembled (efficient in terms of compilation resources). They must impose minimal run-time and memory overhead (efficient in execution resources). And they must be more reliable than hand-built mechanisms (efficient in developer resources).

Safety

Each abstraction must be type-safe so that static assumptions about the behavior of a class may be enforced by the compilation system. Exceptions should be used to signify run-time violations of the contract concerning the dynamic semantics of the class. Raising an exception must not corrupt the state of the object that threw the exception.

Simplicity

The framework must have a clear and consistent organization that makes it easy to identify and select appropriate concrete classes.

Extendability

Developers must be able to add new classes independently. At the same time they must be able to preserve the architectural integrity of the framework.

6.1.3 Specific Frameworks Considered

To use application frameworks effectively, you must understand the interfaces, conventions, and restrictions of a framework. In return, using well-designed frameworks can significantly simplify the design and implementation of applications. The Java Class Library includes several well-designed and powerful application frameworks. In the remainder of this chapter, we discuss the interfaces, conventions, and designs of the following Java application frameworks.

> *The collections framework.* Collections are also known as containers.[1] The collections framework is a set of interfaces and classes that support storing and retrieving objects in collections of varying structures, algorithms, and time-space complexities.
>
> *The graphical user interfaces framework.* The graphical user interfaces framework consists of the Abstract Windows Toolkit (AWT) and the Swing portion of the Java Foundation Classes. It is a set of interfaces and classes that support the construction of graphical user interfaces with a great deal of versatility.
>
> *The input/output framework.* The input/output framework is a set of interfaces and classes that support the input and output of different types of objects to and from different media with varying capabilities.

6.2 THE COLLECTIONS FRAMEWORK

A *collection* is an object that contains other objects, which are called the *elements* of the collection. Based on their structures and capabilities, collections can be classified in a few major categories known as *abstract collections*.

6.2.1 Abstract Collections

There are four major types of collections: bags, sets, lists, and maps.

Bags

A *bag* is an unordered collection of elements that may contain duplicate elements. Bags are also known as *multisets*. Bags are the least restrictive and most general

---

[1] Not to be confused with the `Container` class in AWT. They are unrelated.

form of collections. In the Java collections framework, bags are represented by the `Collection` interface. Bags are rarely used directly. More restrictive forms of collections, such as sets and lists, are much more often used.

Sets

A *set* is an unordered collection of elements. No duplicate elements are allowed in sets. In other words, inserting the same elements in a set twice is the same as inserting the element just once. A set is denoted

$$\{e_1, e_2, \ldots, e_n\}$$

where $e_1, e_2, \ldots, e_n$ are the elements of the set. For example, the following is a set of languages:

```
{ "English", "Chinese", "German" }
```

A variation of sets is *sorted sets*, whose elements are automatically sorted according to a certain order. Sorted sets are also known as *ordered sets*. For example, the following is an ordered set of languages sorted in alphabetical order:

```
{ "Chinese", "English", "German" }
```

In the Java collections framework, sets are represented by the `Set` interface, and sorted sets are represented by the `SortedSet` interface.

Lists

A *list* is an ordered collection of elements. Lists are also known as *sequences*. Elements in a list are indexed sequentially starting from 0. Duplicate elements are allowed in lists. A list is denoted

$$\langle e_1, e_2, \ldots, e_n \rangle$$

where $e_1, e_2, \ldots, e_n$ are the elements of the set. For example, the following are three different lists:

```
⟨ "Chinese", "German",  "English" ⟩
⟨ "English", "Chinese", "German" ⟩
⟨ "English", "Chinese", "English", "German" ⟩
```

In the Java collections framework, lists are represented by the `List` interface.

Maps

A *map* is an unordered collection of key-value pairs, denoted *key* ↦ *value*. Maps are also known as *functions*, *dictionaries*, or *associative arrays*. The keys in a map must be unique (i.e., each key can map to at most one value). A map is denoted

$$\{k_1 \mapsto v_1, k_2 \mapsto v_2, \ldots, k_n \mapsto v_n\}$$

where $k_1, k_2, \ldots, k_n$ are the keys and $v_1, v_2, \ldots, v_n$ are the values of the map. For example, the following is a very small English-Chinese dictionary:

{ "welcome" ↦ "欢迎", "software" ↦ "软件", "coffee" ↦ "咖啡" }

A variation of maps is *sorted maps*, whose elements are automatically sorted by keys according to a certain order. Sorted maps are also known as *ordered maps*. In the Java collections framework, maps are represented by the Map interface, and sorted maps are represented by the SortedMap interface.

6.2.2   Interfaces of Collections

The abstract collections are represented by a set interfaces, as shown in Figure 6.1. The implementations of these collections are defined as classes that implement the abstract collection interfaces. The following design guideline is important to the design of the Java collections framework.

Design Guideline   *Maximize the Uniformity of Common Aspects of Related Classes/Interfaces*

The common aspects of related classes should be handled in a uniform way. These common aspects are usually captured as interfaces or abstract classes. The greater the uniformity, the simpler and more useful is the design.

Although each kind of abstract collection has its unique characteristics, together they have a lot in common. For example, all collections support insertion and deletion of elements. It is simpler if the insertion and deletion of different collections can be expressed by using the same methods and following the same conventions. More important, different implementations of an abstract collection will all implement the same interface. Thus, knowing the interface of an abstract collection is adequate for use of all the implementations of an abstract collection. For example, the Set interface can be implemented by using an array, a linked list, a tree, and so on. A user

Figure 6.1

The abstract collections.

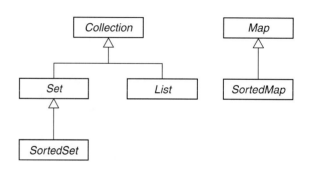

TABLE 6.1

Method	Description
add(o)	Adds a new element o to this collection
addAll(c)	Adds all of the elements in the collection c to this collection
clear()	Removes all of the elements from this collection
contains(o)	Returns true if this collection contains an element that equals o
containsAll(c)	Returns true if this collection contains all the elements in the collection c
isEmpty()	Returns true if this collection contains no elements
iterator()	Returns an iterator over the elements in this collection (see Section 6.2.4 [p. 245])
remove(o)	Removes an element that equals o from this collection if such an element exists
removeAll(c)	Removes from this collection all the elements that are contained in the collection c
retainAll(c)	Retains only the elements in this collection that are contained in the collection c
size()	Returns the number of elements in this collection

needs to study only the Set interface in order to use all its implementations, and switching from one implementation to another is easy.

The Collection Interface

The Collection interface represents a bag. The methods of the Collection interface are summarized in Table 6.1. In these methods, parameter o is of type Object and parameter c is of type Collection.

The elements of a collection can be of any reference type. To be stored, values of primitive types in a collection must be wrapped in an object of a suitable wrapper class (see Section 3.4.9 [p. 94]). In the methods contains(), containsAll(c), remove(o), removeAll(c), and retainAll(c), the notion of equality between two elements is defined by the equals() method of the class of the elements.

The Set Interface

The Set interface represents a set and extends the Collection interface. All the methods of the Collection interface are inherited, so the Set interface introduces no new methods. However, some of the methods have different semantics, or contracts, than those in the `Collection` interface, owing to the restriction of sets. The methods with altered semantics in the `Set` interface are summarized in the following table. In these methods, parameter o is of type `Object` and parameter c is of type `Collection`.

Method	Description
add(o)	Adds the element o to this set if it is not already present
addAll(c)	Adds all the elements in the collection c to this set if they are not already present

Here is an example of using sets.

```
Set set = new HashSet();    // HashSet is the class that implements Set
set.add("foo");             // the set is { foo }
set.add("bar");             // the set is { foo, bar }
int n = set.size();         // n is 2
if (set.contains("foo"))    // is true
    System.out.println("foo is in");
```

The `SortedSet` interface further extends the `Set` interface. We discuss it in Section 6.2.5 [p. 250].

The List Interface

The `List` interface represents a list, and it also extends the `Collection` interface. The `List` interface introduces some new methods and also alters the semantics of many methods inherited from the `Collection` interface because of the orders imposed by lists. The new methods and the methods with altered semantics in the `List` interface are summarized in Table 6.2. In these methods, parameter o is of type `Object`, parameter c is of type `Collection`, and parameters i and j are integers representing indices.

The Map Interface

The `Map` interface represents a map. Although maps are conceptually sets of key-value pairs and are often implemented as sets, the `Map` interface does not extend the `Collection` interface; nor does it extend the `Set` interface. Maps are more restrictive than sets because maps contains only key-value pairs and do not allow duplicate keys. Therefore some of the methods in the `Set` and `Collection` interfaces cannot be supported by maps. Maps are not sets, but they can be viewed as sets if so desired. The `Map` interface provides the following views of maps.

TABLE 6.2

Method	Description
add(i, o)	Inserts the element o at the ith position in this list
add(o)	Appends the element o to the end of this list
addAll(c)	Appends all the elements in the collection c to the end of this list, in the order that they are returned by the iterator of c
addAll(i, c)	Inserts all the elements in the collection c into this list, starting at the ith position
get(i)	Returns the element at the ith position in this list
indexOf(o)	Returns the index in this list of the first occurrence of the element o, or −1 if the element is not present in this list
lastIndexOf(o)	Returns the index in this list of the last occurrence of the element o, or −1 if the element is not present in this list
listIterator()	Returns a ListIterator of the elements in this list (see Section 6.2.4 [p. 245])
listIterator(i)	Returns a ListIterator of the elements in this list, starting at the ith position (see Section 6.2.4 [p. 245])
remove(i)	Removes the element at the ith position in this list and returns the removed element
remove(o)	Removes the first occurrence of the element o in this list
set(i, o)	Replaces the element at the ith position in this list with the element o, and returns the element that was replaced
subList(i, j)	Returns a sublist of this list from the ith position, inclusive, to the jth position, exclusive

- *The entry set view*: The set of all the entries (i.e., key-value pairs) of the map.
- *The key set view*: The set of all the keys contained in the map. It is a set because keys are unique.
- *The value collection view*: The collection of all the values contained in the map. It is a collection rather than a set because different keys can be mapped to the same value, in which case the value occurs multiple times in the value collection.

The methods of the Map interface are summarized in Table 6.3. In these methods, parameter k is of type Object and represents a key, parameter v is also of type Object and represents a value, and parameter m is of type Map.

TABLE 6.3

Method	Description
clear()	Removes all mappings from this map
containsKey(k)	Returns true if this map contains a mapping for the key k
containsValue(v)	Returns true if this map maps one or more keys to the value v
entrySet()	Returns a Set view of the mappings contained in this map
get(k)	Returns the value to which this map maps the key k
isEmpty()	Returns true if this map contains no key-value mappings
keySet()	Returns a Set view of the keys contained in this map
put(k, v)	Associates the value v with the key k in this map
putAll(m)	Copies all of the mappings from the map m to this map
remove(k)	Removes the mapping for the key k from this map if present
size()	Returns the number of key-value mappings in this map
values()	Returns a Collection view of the values contained in this map

The keys and values of a map can be of any reference type. The equals() and hashCode() methods must be defined in the class of the keys. Here is an example of using maps.

```
Map map = new HashMap();        // HashMap is class that implements Map
map.put("a", "X");              // the map is { a -> X }
map.put("b", "Y");              // the map is { a -> X, b -> Y }
map.put("c", "X");              // the map is { a -> X, b -> Y, c -> X }
map.put("a", "Z");              // the map is { a -> Z, b -> Y, c -> X }
Object val = map.get("a");      // val is "Z"
map.remove("a");                // the map is { b -> Y, c -> X }
```

The SortedMap interface extends the Map interface. We discuss it in Section 6.2.5 [p. 250].

6.2.3 Implementations of Collections

Each of the abstract collections can be implemented with various data structures and algorithms. An implementation of the abstract collections is called a *concrete collection.* The implementations may vary in many respects, including

- whether the collection is *bounded* (i.e., it has a fixed maximum size) or is *unbounded* (i.e., it may grow and shrink dynamically as needed); and
- the time and space complexity of various operations, such as searching, insertion, deletion, and iteration.

Common data structures used to implement the abstract collections include arrays, linked lists, trees, and hash tables.

Each concrete collection is a class that implements the interface of an abstract collection. This characteristic makes different implementations of the same abstract collection interchangeable. For example, an array implementation of a list can be switched to a linked-list implementation without affecting the clients. The concrete collections supported by the collections framework are summarized in Table 6.4. All these concrete collections support unbounded collections. The collections can grow and shrink dynamically as needed.

Choosing Implementations of Collections

The `TreeSet` can order the elements based on their natural order or a user-defined comparator (see Section 6.2.5 [p. 250]). The `HashSet` stores the elements in the

TABLE 6.4

Concrete Collection	Implementation	Description
HashSet	Set	Hash table implementation of sets
TreeSet	SortedSet	Balanced binary tree implementation of sorted sets
ArrayList	List	Resizable-array implementation of lists
LinkedList	List	Doubly linked list implementation of lists
Vector	List	Resizable-array implementation of lists that supports legacy methods that are available since JDK 1.0
HashMap	Map	Hash table implementation of maps
TreeMap	SortedMap	Balanced binary tree implementation of ordered maps
Hashtable	Map	Hash table implementation of maps that supports legacy methods that are available since JDK 1.0

order determined by the hash function. The `HashSet` is more efficient than the `TreeSet` in insertion (`add()`) and membership checking (`contains()`). The time complexity of these operations is $O(1)$ for `HashSet` and $O(\log n)$ for `TreeSet`, where n is the size of the set. When choosing a concrete set implementation, if the elements should maintain a certain order, then you should use the `TreeSet`. Otherwise, you should use `HashSet`.

The `ArrayList` uses an array to store the elements, whereas `LinkedList` uses a linked list to store the elements. The main differences are as follows.

- The `ArrayList` uses an array that is large enough to store all the elements. Often, a large portion of the array is unused. The `LinkedList` wastes no space.

- The `ArrayList` incurs a significant penalty of performance when the size of the list exceeds the size of the array, in which case a new larger array must be allocated and all the elements copied to the new array. The `LinkedList` incurs no extra penalty on performance when the list grows.

- The `ArrayList` is more efficient than the `LinkedList` for methods involving indices, such as `get()` and `set()`. The time complexity of these operations is $O(1)$ for `ArrayList` and $O(n)$ for `LinkedList`, where n is the size of the list.

The `Vector` class is implemented the same way as the `ArrayList` class. The main difference is that the `Vector` class supports additional "legacy methods" that predate the collection framework. When you are choosing a concrete list implementation, the volatility of the list is the main factor. The `LinkedList` is more suitable for volatile lists (i.e., lists that grow and shrink a lot). The `ArrayList` is more efficient for relatively stable lists.

The `TreeMap` can order the entries based on the natural order of the key or a user-defined comparator on keys. The `HashMap` stores the entries in the order determined by the hash function. The `HashMap` is more efficient than the `TreeMap` in insertion (`put()`) and mapping (`get()`). The time complexity of these operations is $O(1)$ for `HashMap` and $O(\log n)$ for `TreeMap`, where n is the size of the set. When choosing a concrete map implementation, if the entries should maintain a certain order according to their keys, then you should use the `TreeMap`. Otherwise, you should use HashMap. The `Hashtable` class is implemented the same way as the `HashMap` class. The main difference is that the `Hashtable` class supports additional legacy methods that predate the collection framework.

EXAMPLE 6.1   Count the Number of Different Words in a Text Input

PURPOSE

This example demonstrates the use of sets.

DESCRIPTION

This example is an extension of the program `Words` in Example 3.7 [p. 93]. In `Words`, we break the text input into words. In this example, we first add a simple counter to count the total number of words in the text input. If a word occurs multiple times, it will be counted multiple times. To count the number of different words in the text input, we must remember that the words that have already occurred. A set serves this purpose well. We use a `HashSet` to store the different words in the text input. Each word occurs only once in the set even if it occurs multiple times in the input text.

SOLUTION

Class `CountWords`

```java
import java.util.*;
import java.io.*;

public class CountWords {
    static public void main(String[] args) {
        Set words = new HashSet();
        BufferedReader in = new BufferedReader(
                        new InputStreamReader(System.in));
        String delim = " \t\n.,:;?!-/()[]\"\'";
        String line;
        int count = 0;
        try {
            while ((line = in.readLine()) != null) {
                StringTokenizer st = new StringTokenizer(line, delim);
                while (st.hasMoreTokens()) {
                    count++;
                    words.add(st.nextToken().toLowerCase());
                }
            }
        } catch (IOException e) {}
        System.out.println("Total number of words: " + count);
        System.out.println("Number of different words: " +
                        words.size());
    }
}
```

Using President Lincoln's *The Gettysburg Address* as the input, we obtain the output:

```
Total number of words: 270
Number of different words: 140
```

6.2.4   Iteration

The Iterator pattern is used to provide a uniform way to iterate through different concrete collections (i.e., polymorphic iteration). Two iterator interfaces are defined: `Iterator` and `ListIterator`. Instances of `Iterator` support traversal of collections in one direction (forward), and instances of `ListIterator` support traversal of lists in forward and backward directions. The methods of the `Iterator` interface are summarized in the following table.

Method	Description
hasNext()	Returns true if the iteration has more elements
next()	Returns the next element in the iteration
remove()	Removes from the underlying collection the last element returned by the iterator

The return type of next() is Object. Usually, the elements returned by the iterator must be downcast to their actual classes before they can manipulated. Here is an example of iterating through a set.

```
Iterator iter = set.iterator();
while (iter.hasNext()) {
    // assume the elments are strings
    String s = (String) iter.next();
    // ...
}
```

TABLE 6.5

Method	Description
add(o)	Inserts the element o into the list
hasNext()	Returns true if this list iterator has more elements when traversing the list in the forward direction
hasPrevious()	Returns true if this list iterator has more elements when traversing the list in the reverse direction
next()	Returns the next element in the list
nextIndex()	Returns the index of the element that would be returned by a subsequent call to next()
previous()	Returns the previous element in the list
previousIndex()	Returns the index of the element that would be returned by a subsequent call to previous()
remove()	Removes from the list the last element that was returned by next() or previous()
set(o)	Replaces the last element returned by next() or previous() with the element o

The `ListIterator` interface extends the `Iterator` interface. The methods of the `ListIterator` interface are summarized in Table 6.5. In these methods, parameter o is of type `Object`.

Iterations on all collections are done uniformly using these two abstract iterator interfaces. Each concrete collection provides a concrete iterator that implements the `Iterator` interface. Furthermore, each concrete collection that implements the `List` interface provides a concrete list iterator that implements the `ListIterator` interface. Instances of concrete iterators are obtained through one of the following methods defined in the `Collection` and `List` interfaces, respectively.

■ Defined in the Collection interface:

```
Iterator iterator()
```

■ Defined in the List interface:

```
ListIterator listIterator()
```

Iterate Through the Views of Maps

Usually, figuring out the classes of the elements in a collection is straightforward. In the case of views created by maps, the classes of the elements in these views are the following.

View	Type of Elements
key set	The class of keys
value collection	The class of values
entry set	`Map.Entry`

Here is an example of iterating through the key set view of a map.

```
Set keys = map.keySet();
Iterator iter = keys.iterator();
while (iter.hasNext()) {
    // assume the keys are strings
    String key = (String) iter.next();
    // ...
}
```

`Map.Entry` is an inner interface defined in the `Map` interface. The elements in the entry set view of maps are instances of `Map.Entry`. The `Map.Entry` interface is summarized in the following table. In these methods, parameter v is of type `Object` and represents a value in a key-value pair.

Method	Description
getKey()	Returns the key corresponding to this entry
getValue()	Returns the value corresponding to this entry
setValue(v)	Replaces the value corresponding to this entry with the value v

Here is an example of iterating through the entry set view of a map.

```
Set entries = map.entrySet();
Iterator iter = entries.iterator();
while (iter.hasNext()) {
   Map.Entry entry = (Map.Entry) iter.next();
   // assume the keys and values are strings
   String key = (String) entry.getKey();
   String value = (String) entry.getValue();
   // ...
}
```

EXAMPLE 6.2 Count the Number of Occurences of Each Word in a Text Input

PURPOSE

This example demonstrates iterating through the entry set of a map.

DESCRIPTION

In order to count the number of occurrences of each word, we need a map that maps each word to the number of its occurrences. To print out the result, we first obtain the entry set view of the map. We then iterate through the entry set and print out each entry.

SOLUTION

The values in the map are instances of the following classes.

Class Count

```
public class Count {
   public Count(String word, int i) {
      this.word = word;
      this.i = i;
   }

   public String word;
   public int i;
}
```

Class **WordFrequency**

```java
import java.util.*;
import java.io.*;

public class WordFrequency {
   static public void main(String[] args) {
      Map words = new HashMap();
      String delim = " \t\n.,:;?!-/()[]\"\'";
      BufferedReader in = new BufferedReader(
                          new InputStreamReader(System.in));
      String line, word;
      Count count;
      try {
         while ((line = in.readLine()) != null) {
            StringTokenizer st = new StringTokenizer(line, delim);
            while (st.hasMoreTokens()) {
               word = st.nextToken().toLowerCase();
               count = (Count) words.get(word);
               if (count == null) {
                  words.put(word, new Count(word, 1));
               } else {
                  count.i++;
               }
            }
         }
      } catch (IOException e) {}

      Set set = words.entrySet();
      Iterator iter = set.iterator();
      while (iter.hasNext()) {
        Map.Entry entry = (Map.Entry) iter.next();
        word = (String) entry.getKey();
        count = (Count) entry.getValue();
        System.out.println(word +
                           (word.length() < 8 ? "\t\t" : "\t") +
                           count.i);
      }
   }
}
```

Using President Lincoln's *The Gettysburg Address* as the input, we obtain the output:

devotion	2	...	
years	1	men	2
civil	1	remember	1
place	1	who	3
gave	2	did	1
they	3	work	1
struggled	1	rather	2
...		fathers	1

Note that the words in the output are not ordered in any particular sequence. ■

6.2.5 Ordering and Sorting

An *order*, more precisely a *partial order*, is a binary relation between two objects that is transitive. Let ≺ denote a partial order; then, for any three objects *a*, *b* and *c*, *a* ≺ *b* and *b* ≺ *c* implies *a* ≺ *c*. If a partial order ensures that for any two objects *a* and *b*, *a* ≺ *b* and *b* ≺ *a* implies *a* = *b*, then it is called a *total order*. A partial order that is not a total order is called a *strictly partial order*. A *sorted collection* is one that orders its elements according to a certain order. *Sorting* arranges the elements of a collection so that they are ordered according to a certain order.

There are two ways to define orders on objects.

1. Each class can define a *natural order* among its instances by implementing the `Comparable` interface.

2. Arbitrary orders among different objects can be defined by *comparators*, or classes that implement the `Comparator` interface.

Defining Natural Orders

The natural order of a class can be defined by implementing the `Comparable` interface and providing an implementation for method `compareTo()`, which is declared as

```
public int compareTo(Object o)
```

It compares the receiving object `this` with the parameter `o`. The contract of the method is

result < 0,	if `this` precedes `o`;
result 0,	if neither `this` precedes `o`, nor `o` precedes `this`; or
result > 0,	if `o` precedes `this`.

The `compareTo()` method must properly define a total order. For any two objects *a* and *b*,

a.`compareTo` (*b*) > 0 implies that *b*.`compareTo` (*a*) < 0,
a.`compareTo` (*b*) < 0 implies that *b*.`compareTo` (*a*) > 0, and
a.`compareTo` (*b*) = 0 implies that *b*.`compareTo` (*a*) = 0.

Also, the definition of the `compareTo()` method must be consistent with the definition of the `equals()` method. For any two objects *a* and *b*,

a.`equals` (*b*) is `true` if and only if *a*.`compareTo` (*b*) is 0.

The natural order of many classes in JDK, such as `String`, is already defined.

Defining Comparators

Comparators are used to define arbitrary orders on any objects. Comparators can be used to sort collections with elements for which no natural order is defined, or to sort the elements in an order different from the natural order of the elements. A comparator implements the `Comparator` interface and provides an implementation for method `compare()`, which is declared as

$$\text{int compare(Object o1, Object o2)}$$

The contract of the method is

result < 0,   if o1 precedes o2;
result 0,   if neither o1 precedes o2, nor o2 precedes o1; or
result > 0,   if o2 precedes o1.

Similar to the preceding `compareTo()` method, the `compare()` method must properly define a total order. For any two objects a and b, and a comparator c,

c.`compare` $(a, b) > 0$ implies that c.`compareTo` $(b, a) < 0$,
c.`compareTo` $(a, b) < 0$ implies that c.`compareTo` $(b, a) > 0$, and
c.`compareTo` $(a, b) = 0$ implies that c.`compareTo` $(b, a) = 0$.

Also, the definition of the `compareTo()` method must be consistent with the definition of the `equals()` method in the class of objects being compared. For any two objects a and b, and a comparator c,

c.`compare` (a, b) is 0 if and only if both a.`equals` (b) and b.`equals` (a)
    are `true`;
a.`equals` (b) is `true` implies c.`compare` (a, b) is 0; and
c.`compareTo` $(a, b) > 0$ implies c.`compareTo` $(b, a) < 0$, and
    c.`compareTo` $(a, b) < 0$ implies c.`compareTo` $(b, a) > 0$.

Sorted Collections

There are two sorted abstract collections: `SortedSet` and `SortedMap`. The `SortedSet` interface extends the `Set` interface. All the methods of the `Set` interface are inherited. The new methods in the `SortedSet` interfaces are summarized in the following table. The parameters of the methods, o, o1, and o2, are all `Objects` representing elements.

Method	Description
comparator()	Returns the comparator associated with this sorted set, or `null` if the natural order is used
first()	Returns the first (lowest) element currently in this sorted set
headSet(o)	Returns a set view of the portion of this sorted set whose elements are strictly less than o
last()	Returns the last (highest) element currently in this sorted set
subSet(o1, o2)	Returns a set view of the portion of this sorted set whose elements range from o1, inclusive, to o2, exclusive
tailSet(o)	Returns a set view of the portion of this sorted set whose elements are greater than or equal to o

The `SortedMap` interface extends the `Map` interface. All the methods of the `Map` interface are inherited. The new methods in the `SortedMap` interfaces are summarized in the following table. The parameters of the methods, k, k1, and k2, are all of type `Object` representing keys.

Method	Description
comparator()	Returns the comparator associated with this sorted map, or null if the natural order is used
firstKey()	Returns the first (lowest) key currently in this sorted map
headMap(k)	Returns a map view of the portion of this sorted map whose keys are strictly less than k
lastKey()	Returns the last (highest) key currently in this sorted map
subMap(k1, k2)	Returns a map view of the portion of this sorted map whose keys range from k1, inclusive, to k2, exclusive
tailMap(k)	Returns a map view of the portion of this sorted map whose keys are greater than or equal to k

A concrete sorted collection *S* that implements the `SortedSet` or `SortedMap` interface provides at least two constructors:

■ `ConcreteSortedCollection()` creates a sorted collection that is sorted according to the natural order of the elements, and

■ `ConcreteSortedCollection(Comparator comparator)` creates a sorted collection that is sorted according to the order defined by the specified comparator.

EXAMPLE 6.3   Count the Number of Occurences of Each Word in a Text Input. Print Out the Results as a List Sorted According to the Alphabetical Order of the Words

PURPOSE

This example demonstrates the use of a sorted map ordered according to the natural order of its keys.

DESCRIPTION

This is a variation of Example 6.2. The words are the keys of the map, and the alphabetical order of words is the natural order of `String`. So we can simply use a `TreeMap`, which by default maintains its entries according to the natural order of its keys.

SOLUTION

Class `WordFrequency2`

```java
import java.util.*;
import java.io.*;

public class WordFrequency2 {
   static public void main(String[] args) {
      Map words = new TreeMap();

      String delim = " \t\n.,:;?!-/()[]\"\'";
      BufferedReader in = new BufferedReader(
                     new InputStreamReader(System.in));
      String line, word;
      Count count;
      try {
         while ((line = in.readLine()) != null) {
            StringTokenizer st = new StringTokenizer(line, delim);
            while (st.hasMoreTokens()) {
               word = st.nextToken().toLowerCase();
               if (words.containsKey(word)) {
                  count = (Count) words.get(word);
                  count.i++;
               } else {
                  words.put(word, new Count(word, 1));
               }
            }
         }
      } catch (IOException e) {}

      Set set = words.entrySet();
      Iterator iter = set.iterator();
      while (iter.hasNext()) {
         Map.Entry entry = (Map.Entry) iter.next();
         word = (String) entry.getKey();
         count = (Count) entry.getValue();
         System.out.println(word +
                     (word.length() < 8 ? "\t\t" : "\t") +
                     count.i);
      }
   }
}
```

Note that the class `WordFrequency2` is nearly identical to class `WordFrequency` in Example 6.2 [p. 248]; the exception is the line in boldface. Using President Lincoln's *The Gettysburg Address* as the input, we obtain the output:

a	7	...	
above	1	whether	1
add	1	which	2
address	1	who	3
advanced	1	will	1

ago	1	work	1
all	1	world	1
...		years	1

EXAMPLE 6.4 *Count the Number of Occurences of Each Word in a Text Input. Print Out the Results as a List Sorted According to the Reverse Alphabetical Order of the Words*

PURPOSE

This example demonstrates the use of a sorted map ordered according to a user-defined order on the keys.

DESCRIPTION

This is another variation of Example 6.2. To sort the entries according to an order other than the natural order of the keys, we need to provide a user-defined comparator. An instance of `TreeMap` can be instantiated by specifying the user-defined order in the constructor.

SOLUTION

The following program contains the comparator for the reverse alphabetical order of strings. To obtain the reverse alphabetical order, we simply negate the sign of the result of the `compareTo()` method of the `String` class.

Comparator for strings: `StringComparator`

```java
public class StringComparator implements Comparator {
    public int compare(Object o1, Object o2) {
        if (o1 != null &&
            o2 != null &&
            o1 instanceof String &&
            o2 instanceof String) {
          String s1 = (String) o1;
          String s2 = (String) o2;

          return - (s1.compareTo(s2));

        } else {
          return 0;
        }
    }
}
```

Class `WordFrequency3`

```java
import java.util.*;
import java.io.*;

public class WordFrequency3 {
    static public void main(String[] args) {

        Map words = new TreeMap(new StringComparator());

        String delim = " \t\n.,:;?!-/()[]\"\'";
```

```
BufferedReader in = new BufferedReader(
                       new InputStreamReader(System.in));
String line, word;
Count count;
try {
   while ((line = in.readLine()) != null) {
      StringTokenizer st = new StringTokenizer(line, delim);
      while (st.hasMoreTokens()) {
         word = st.nextToken().toLowerCase();
         if (words.containsKey(word)) {
           count = (Count) words.get(word);
           count.i++;
         } else {
           words.put(word, new Count(word, 1));
         }
      }
   }
} catch (IOException e) {}

Set set = words.entries();
Iterator iter = set.iterator();
while (iter.hasNext()) {
   Map.Entry entry = (Map.Entry) iter.next();
   word = (String) entry.getKey();
   count = (Count) entry.getValue();
   System.out.println(word +
                  (word.length() < 8 ? "\t\t" : "\t") +
                  count.i);
}
}
}
```

Again, note that the class `WordFrequency3` is also nearly identical to class `WordFrequency` in Example 6.2 [p. 248]; the exception is the line in boldface. Using President Lincoln's *The Gettysburg Address* as the input, we obtain the output:

years	1	...	
world	1	all	1
work	1	ago	1
will	1	advanced	1
who	3	address	1
which	2	add	1
whether	1	above	1
...		a	7

Algorithms

Besides the sorted collections, the collection framework also provide a set of useful algorithms related to ordering and sorting independent from the collections. They are provided as static methods of the `Collections` class. These methods are summarized in Table 6.6. Parameter `l` is of type `List`, parameter `c` is of type `Collection`, parameter `k` is of type `Object`, and parameter `comp` is of type `Comparator`.

TABLE 6.6

Method	Description
sort(l)	Sorts the list l according to the natural order of the elements
sort(l, comp)	Sorts the list l according to the order defined by the comparator comp
binarySearch(l, k)	Searches for the element k in the list l, using the binary search algorithm. The list l is sorted according to the natural order of the elements. The return value is the index of element k if it is present in the list, or – (*insertion point*) – 1. The insertion point is the index at which the element should be inserted
binarySearch(l, k, comp)	Same as preceding, except that the list l is sorted according to the order defined by the comparator comp
min(c)	Returns the minimum element in the collection c according to the natural order of the elements in the collection
min(c, comp)	Returns the minimum element in the collection c according to the order defined by the comparator comp
max(c)	Returns the maximum element in the collection c according to the natural order of the elements in the collection
max(c, comp)	Returns the maximum element in the collection c according to the order defined by the comparator comp

EXAMPLE 6.5   Count the Number of Occurences of Each Word in a Text File. Print Out the Results as a List Sorted by the Frequencies

PURPOSE

This example demonstrates the use of sorting utilities to sort collections according to user-defined orders.

DESCRIPTION

This is another variation of Example 6.2. In this case, the desired order is not based on keys but on values, so sorted maps offer no help. We use a HashMap to store the word counts. After all the words have been counted, we obtain a collection view of the values contained in the map, and then sort the value collection according to a user-defined comparator CountComparator.

SOLUTION

The comparator is used to sort the frequency list.

Comparator for word count: `CountComparator`

```java
public class CountComparator implements Comparator {
    public int compare(Object o1, Object o2) {
        if (o1 != null &&
            o2 != null &&
            o1 instanceof Count &&
            o2 instanceof Count) {
          Count c1 = (Count) o1;
          Count c2 = (Count) o2;
          return (c2.i - c1.i);
        } else {
            return 0;
        }
    }
}
```

Class `WordFrequency4`

```java
import java.util.*;
import java.io.*;

public class WordFrequency4 {
    static public void main(String[] args) {
      Map words = new HashMap();
      String delim = " \t\n.,:;?!-/()[]\"\'";
      BufferedReader in = new BufferedReader(
                      new InputStreamReader(System.in));
      String line, word;
      Count count;
      try {
         while ((line = in.readLine()) != null) {
            StringTokenizer st = new StringTokenizer(line, delim);
            while (st.hasMoreTokens()) {
               word = st.nextToken().toLowerCase();
               count = (Count) words.get(word);
               if (count == null) {
                  words.put(word, new Count(word, 1));
               } else {
                  count.i++;
               }
            }
         }
      } catch (IOException e) {}

      List list = new ArrayList(words.values());
      Collections.sort(list, new CountComparator());
      Iterator iter = list.iterator();

      while (iter.hasNext()) {
```

```
            count = (Count) iter.next();
            word = count.word;
            System.out.println(word +
                        (word.length() < 8 ? "\t\t" : "\t") +
                        count.i);
        }
    }
}
```

Using President Lincoln's *The Gettysburg Address* as the input, we obtain the output:

```
the     13          ...
that    12          consecrate     1
we      10          world          1
here    8           consecrated    1
to      8           remember       1
a       7           did            1
and     6           work           1
...                 fathers        1
```

THE GRAPHICAL USER INTERFACE FRAMEWORK

Java provides an extensive framework for building high-quality graphical user interfaces (GUI). The graphical user interface framework is part of the *Java Foundation Classes* (JFC). We focus on two important packages in the JFC: the *Abstract Windows Toolkit* (AWT) and *Swing*.

The Java GUI framework consists of several categories of classes. The main categories are the following.

GUI widgets. Widgets are the building blocks of the visual aspect of graphical user interfaces. Each widget class defines a particular type of widget by its visual characteristics, the *look*, and its behavior pattern in response to user input, the *feel*. Examples of the GUI widget classes include `Button`, `Label`, `Checkbox`, `Scrollbar`, `Frame`, and `Dialog`.

Layout managers. Layout managers define strategies for laying out widgets in windows. Commonly used layout managers include `FlowLayout`, and `BorderLayout`.

Events and event listeners. Events represent user input or actions. Each event class represents a particular type of user input, such as the `KeyEvent` class for keyboard input and the `MouseEvent` class for mouse actions. Each event class is associated with an event listener class responsible for handling this type of events. For example, the `KeyListener` class is associated with the `KeyEvent` class, and the `MouseListener` class is associated with the `MouseEvent` class.

Graphics and imaging classes. These classes allow widgets to draw their visual appearances and include graphics (`Color`, `Font`, `Graphics`, etc.), geometry (`Point`, `Rectangle`, `Dimension`, etc.), and imaging (`Image`, `Icon`, etc.).

The Abstract Windows Toolkit (AWT) package provides the basic support for building graphical user interfaces. The Swing package is an extension of AWT, which provides extensive support for building sophisticated-looking and high-quality graphical user interfaces.

6.3.1 The Widgets

The inheritance hierarchy of GUI widget classes in AWT is shown in Figure 6.2. All classes shown in the diagram belong to the package `java.awt`, except the `Applet` class, which belongs to package `java.applet`. All Java GUI widget classes are subclasses of the `Component` class. Hence, in Java terminology, GUI widgets are also known as *components*. The `Component` class is an abstract class that defines the characteristics and behaviors that are common to all the components. The subclasses of `Component` are divided into two groups: *primitive components*, which do not contain other components, and *containers*, which may contain other primitive components and containers.

The `Container` class is an abstract class that defines the characteristics and behaviors common to all the containers. In Figure 6.2, the left branch of the `Component`

Figure 6.2

The GUI widget classes in AWT.

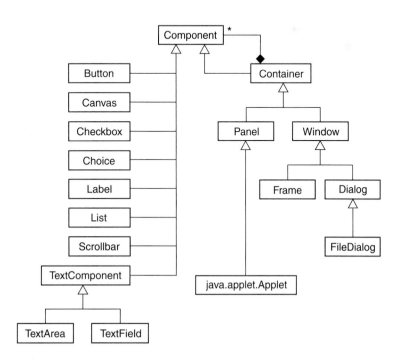

class consists of the primitive components, and the right branch of the `Component` class consists of the containers. Using containers, we can construct graphical user interfaces by organizing widgets into tree structures, in which the primitive components are the leaves and the containers are the interior nodes. Furthermore, as both primitive components and containers are subclasses of the `Component` class, they can be treated uniformly. The design pattern Composite covers design of the GUI components hierarchy.

Design Pattern: Composite

Design Pattern *Composite*

Category: Structural design pattern.

Intent: Compose objects into tree structures to represent a part or whole hierarchy. Composite lets clients treat individual objects and compositions of objects uniformly.

Applicability: Use the Composite pattern when

- you want to represent a part or whole hierarchy of objects; and

- you want clients to be able to ignore the difference between compositions of objects and individual objects (clients will treat all objects in the composite structure uniformly).

The structure of the Composite design pattern is shown in the following diagram.

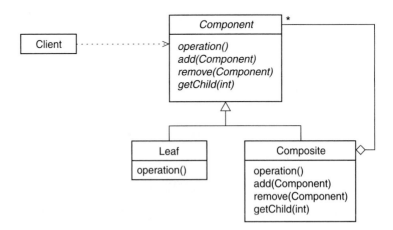

The participants of the Composite design pattern are

- *Component* (e.g., `Component`), which declares the interface for objects in the composition; implements default behavior for the interface common to all classes, as appropriate; and (optional) defines an interface for accessing a component's parent in the recursive structure and implements it if appropriate.

- *Leaf* (e.g., `Button`, `Label`, and `Checkbox`), which defines behavior for primitive objects in the composition.
- *Composite* (e.g., `Container` and `Panel`), which declares an interface for accessing and managing its child components, defines behavior for components having children, stores child components, and implements child-related operations in the `Component` interface.
- *Client*, which manipulates objects in the composition through the `Component` interface.

For a detailed discussion on the Composite design pattern see [Gamma et al. 1995].

The AWT Components

The primitive components and containers in AWT are summarized in Table 6.7.

The Swing Components

The Swing package supports building high-quality graphical user interfaces. It is an extension of AWT and provides many more varieties of more sophisticated components than AWT. A major difference between the AWT components and the Swing components is that most of the Swing components are *lightweight*, whereas all the components in AWT are *heavyweight*. Heavyweight components are associated with *native* components created by the underlying window system, such as Win32 or Motif. The native component associated with an AWT component is known as its *peer* component. The appearance of the AWT component is determined by its peer component and is thus platform dependent. In other words, a GUI application written in Java with AWT can run on different platforms with the same behavior but different looks. Lightweight components have no peers. Their looks are determined by the Java run-time environment, not the underlying window system. Lightweight components eliminate the overhead associated with peer components and ensure that GUI applications written in Java will not only run on different platforms with same behavior, but also will have the same look. Furthermore, lightweight components emulate the looks of various window systems regardless of the underlying window system. For example, a Java GUI application using Swing can have a Motif look even when it is running on a Win32 platform. This capability is known as the *pluggable* look and feel.

The Swing package consists of several hundred classes and numerous subpackages, of which we cover only a few. The most straightforward part of Swing consists of classes with counterparts in AWT. These classes are shown Figure 6.3, with the shaded boxes being classes in AWT. The names of Swing classes begin with a prefix `J` followed by the name of their counterparts in AWT. The subclasses of `JComponent` represent lightweight components. Note that `JWindow`, `JFrame`, and `JDialog` are not lightweight components. The differences between these Swing components and their AWT counterparts are summarized in Table 6.8 [p. 264].

TABLE 6.7

AWT Component	Description
Button	Text labeled "push" button that responds to mouse button clicks
Canvas	Blank rectangular area of the screen onto which the application can draw or from which the application can trap input events from the user
Checkbox	Component that can be in either the "on" (true) or "off" (false) state
Choice	Pop-up menu of text choices from which the user can choose
Label	Component with a text that does not respond to any user input
List	Scrolling list of text items from which the user can choose
Scrollbar	Scroll bar
TextComponent	Superclass of any component that allows the editing of some text
TextField	Text component that allows for the editing of a single line of text
TextArea	Multiline region that displays text and allows editing of multiline text

AWT Container	Description
Dialog	Window that takes input from the user
FileDialog	Dialog window from which the user can select a file
Frame	Top-level window with a title and a border
Panel	Borderless, titleless, and transparent container
Window	Borderless and titleless top-level window

6.3.2 Layout Managers

Each container has a *layout manager*, which handles the layout of the components contained in the container. Several layout managers are provided in the JDK, as illustrated in Figure 6.4. Each layout manager defines a layout strategy. One of the advantages of using layout managers is that we do not have to specify the absolute coordinates and dimensions of each component. The components in the container are displayed based on their *relative positions*. The relative positions of components can be specified explicitly with *positional constraints* or implicitly by the order in which they are inserted in the container. The positions and sizes of the components

Figure 6.3

Swing countparts of AWT components.

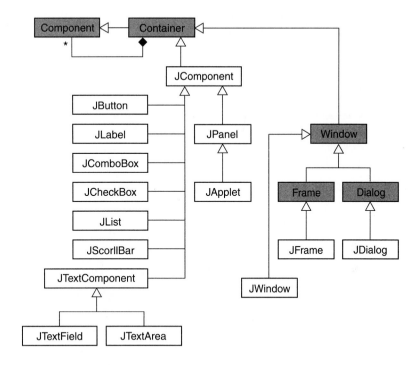

are computed by the layout manager based on the dimensions of the container and automatically adjusted whenever the dimensions of the container change, which is usually caused by resizing the top-level window.

We discuss and illustrate the use of several commonly used layout managers: `FlowLayout`, `GridLayout`, and `BorderLayout`. We also demonstrate how to do customized layout without using the layout managers.

Using Layout Managers

The design of layout managers uses the Strategy design pattern, with each layout manager implemented as a strategy. Different layout managers can be used uniformly and interchangeably. The following methods of the `Container` class deal

Figure 6.4

The layout managers.

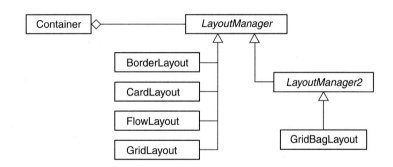

TABLE 6.8

Swing Component	Description
JButton	Allows an image icon and a text label; supports keyboard accelerators
JCheckbox	Allows user-defined icons for the on and off states
JComboBox	An extension of `Choice`. The items are not limited to text. They can be icons or components. The choices can be editable.
JLabel	Allows an image icon and a text label
JList	The items are not limited to text. They can be icons or components.
JScrollbar	Lightweight scroll bar
JTextComponent	Superclass of lightweight components for text editing
JTextField	Lightweight single-line text component; supports multilingual text displaying and editing
JTextArea	Lightweight multiline text component; supports multilingual text displaying and editing
JPanel	Lightweight container
JDialog	Dialog tailored for lightweight components
JFrame	Frame tailored for lightweight components
JWindow	Window tailored for lightweight components

with the use of layout managers. In the parameters of the methods, `lm` represents a layout manager, `comp` represents a component, and `cst` represents a positional constraint.

Method	Description
setLayout(lm)	Sets `lm` as the layout manager of this container
add(comp)	Adds component `comp` to this container
add(comp, cst)	Adds component `comp` to this container with a positional constraint `cst` (e.g., the position key in `BorderLayout`)

Flow Layout

The flow layout is the most straightforward layout strategy. It arranges the components in a left-to-right flow, in the order in which they were inserted in the container. If the container is not wide enough for all the components, it breaks the flow into several lines, and all lines are centered by default. Each component is sized to its *natural size*. A flow layout manager can be created by using one of the following constructors of the `FlowLayout` class.

Constructor	Description
`FlowLayout(align, hGap, vGap)`	Creates a flow layout manager with the alignment set to `align` and the horizontal and vertical gaps set to `hGap` and `vGap`, respectively
`FlowLayout(align)`	Creates a flow layout manager with the alignment set to `align` and the horizontal and vertical gaps set to the default value
`FlowLayout()`	Creates a flow layout manager with the alignment and the horizontal and vertical gaps all set to their respective default values

The alignment of the flow layout can be one of the following:

`FlowLayout.LEFT`	The components are flush left.
`FlowLayout.CENTER`	The components are centered.
`FlowLayout.RIGHT`	The components are flush right.

The default alignment is centered. The horizontal and vertical gaps are the gaps between the adjacent components, specified in pixels. The defaults are 5 pixels for both the horizontal and vertical gaps.

EXAMPLE 6.6   Using Flow Layout

PURPOSE

This example demonstrates use of the flow layout and the creation of buttons.

DESCRIPTION

The `Applet` class is a subclass of `Panel`, so the drawing area of an applet is actually a container. We can add any component to the panel. Here, we simply create and add six buttons to the panel. The results are shown in Figure 6.5. The layout shown in Figure 6.5(a) is the result of using the flow layout in a panel that is 400 pixels wide and 50 pixels high. The layout shown in Figure 6.5(b) is the result of using

Figure 6.5

Flow layouts.

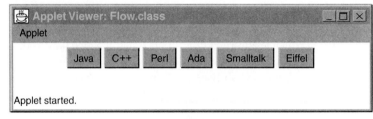

(a)

(b)

the same flow layout in a panel that is 100 pixels wide and 120 pixels high. Note the correspondence between the order of insertion and order of buttons in the layouts.

SOLUTION

A button can be created as follows:

new Button(*label*)

where *label* is the label of the button.

Flow layout applet: `Flow`

```
import java.awt.*;
import java.applet.Applet;

public class Flow extends Applet {
  public Flow () {
    setLayout(new FlowLayout());
    add(new Button("Java"));
    add(new Button("C++"));
    add(new Button("Perl"));
    add(new Button("Ada"));
    add(new Button("Smalltalk"));
    add(new Button("Eiffel"));
  }
}
```

Grid Layout

The grid layout arranges components in a rectangular grid, and all components are given the same size. The components can be stretched vertically and horizontally, if necessary, to fill the entire space of the container. A grid layout manager can be created by using one of the following constructors of the `GridLayout` class.

Constructor	Description
`GridLayout(r, c, hGap, vGap)`	Creates a grid layout manager with `r` rows and `c` columns and with the horizontal and vertical gaps set to `hGap` and `vGap`, respectively
`GridLayout(r, c)`	Creates a grid layout manager with `r` rows and `c` columns and with the horizontal and vertical gaps set to 0
`GridLayout()`	Creates a grid layout manager with a single row and with the horizontal gap set to 0

When the first two constructors are used, `r` and `c` must be nonnegative integers. One of them, but not both, can be 0. If `r` is 0, the grid may have any number of rows, depending on the number of components in the container. Similarly, if `c` is 0, the grid may have any number of columns, also depending on the number of components in the container.

EXAMPLE 6.7   Using Grid Layout

PURPOSE

This example demonstrates use of the grid layout.

DESCRIPTION

This program is similar to the one in Example 6.6. The main difference is that a grid layout manager is used here. The number of rows and columns of the grid are specified as the parameters of the applet.

Figure 6.6 shows the effects of grid layout in a panel with six buttons. The layout shown in Figure 6.6(a) is the result of specifying 1 row and 0 column, or (1, 0). The layout shown in Figure 6.6(b) is the result of specifying 3 rows and 2 columns, or (3, 2). The layout shown in Figure 6.6(c) is the result of specifying 0 row and 1 column, or (0, 1).

Figure 6.6

Grid layouts.

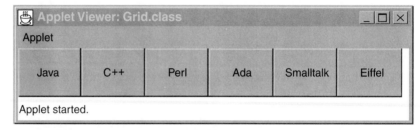

(a)

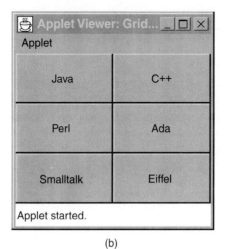

(b)

(c)

SOLUTION

Grid layout applet: `Grid`

```
import java.awt.*;
import java.applet.Applet;
public class Grid extends Applet {
  public void init () {
    int row = 0, col = 0;
    String att = getParameter("row");
    if (att != null)
      row = Integer.parseInt(att);
    att = getParameter("col");
```

```
              if (att != null)
                 col = Integer.parseInt(att);
              if (row == 0 && col == 0) {
                 row = 3; col = 2;
              }
              setLayout(new GridLayout(row, col));
              add(new Button("Java"));
              add(new Button("C++"));
              add(new Button("Perl"));
              add(new Button("Ada"));
              add(new Button("Smalltalk"));
              add(new Button("Eiffel"));
         }
     }
```

Border Layout

The border layout is one of the most versatile layout managers. It arranges as many as five components in five regions identified as *North*, *South*, *East*, *West*, and *Center*, as illustrated in Figure 6.7. The North and South components are placed at the top and bottom of the container, respectively. They are set to their natural heights and may be stretched horizontally to fill the entire width of the container. The East and West components are placed at the right and left sides of the container, respectively. They are set to their natural widths and may be stretched vertically to fill the space between the North and South components. The Center component may be stretched horizontally and vertically to fill the space left in the center. If one or more of the five components are absent, the remaining components will be stretched vertically and/or horizontally to fill the space left by the missing components. A border layout manager can be created by using one of the following constructors of the `BorderLayout` class.

Method	Description
BorderLayout(hGap, vGap)	Creates a border layout manager with the horizontal and vertical gaps set to hGap and vGap, respectively
BorderLayout()	Creates a border layout manager with the horizontal and vertical gaps set to 0

The components managed by a border layout manager should be inserted with one of the following positional constraints, which are symbolic constants defined in the `BorderLayout` class:

BorderLayout.NORTH	Places the component in the North region
BorderLayout.SOUTH	Places the component in the South region
BorderLayout.EAST	Places the component in the East region
BorderLayout.WEST	Places the component in the West region
BorderLayout.CENTER	Places the component in the Center region

Figure 6.7

Border layout.

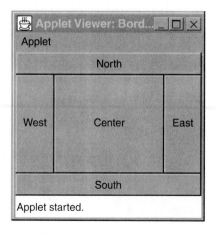

EXAMPLE 6.8   Using Border Layout

PURPOSE

This example demonstrates use of the border layout.

DESCRIPTION

This applet uses a border layout manager and simply inserts a button in each of the five regions.

SOLUTION

Border layout applet `Border`

```
import java.awt.*;
import java.applet.Applet;

public class Border extends Applet {
  public Border () {
    setLayout(new BorderLayout());
    add(new Button("North"),   BorderLayout.NORTH);
    add(new Button("South"),   BorderLayout.SOUTH);
    add(new Button("East"),    BorderLayout.EAST);
    add(new Button("West"),    BorderLayout.WEST);
    add(new Button("Center"), BorderLayout.CENTER);
  }
}
```

EXAMPLE 6.9   Nested Border Layouts

PURPOSE

This example demonstrates the nesting of containers and creation of choices and labels.

DESCRIPTION

See Figure 6.8. The outer panel contains two nested panels and uses a border layout manager. Three buttons are inserted in the North, East, and West regions of the outer panel. The center region contains another panel, which also uses a border layout manager. A button is inserted in each of the five regions of the panel at the center. The South region of the outer panel contains yet another panel, which uses a flow layout manager. A button, a choice, and a label are inserted in the panel in the South region.

SOLUTION

Nested panel applet: `NestedPanels`

```java
import java.awt.*;
import java.applet.Applet;

public class NestedPanels extends Applet {
    public NestedPanels () {
        // set up the center panel
        Panel center = new Panel();
        center.setLayout(new BorderLayout());
        center.add(new Button("south"),  BorderLayout.SOUTH);
        center.add(new Button("north"),  BorderLayout.NORTH);
        center.add(new Button("east"),   BorderLayout.EAST);
        center.add(new Button("west"),   BorderLayout.WEST);
        center.add(new Button("center"), BorderLayout.CENTER);

        // set up the south panel
        Panel south = new Panel();
        south.setLayout(new FlowLayout());
        south.add(new Button("Help"));
        choice = new Choice();
        choice.addItem("one");
        choice.addItem("two");
        choice.addItem("three");
        choice.addItem("four");
        choice.addItem("five");
        south.add(choice);
        messageBar = new Label("This is a message bar.");
        south.add(messageBar);

        // set up the outer panel
        setLayout(new BorderLayout());
        add(new Button("North"), BorderLayout.NORTH);
        add(new Button("East"),  BorderLayout.EAST);
        add(new Button("West"),  BorderLayout.WEST);
        add(south, BorderLayout.SOUTH);
        add(center, BorderLayout.CENTER);
    }

    protected Label messageBar;
    protected Choice choice;
}
```

Figure 6.8

Nested border layout.

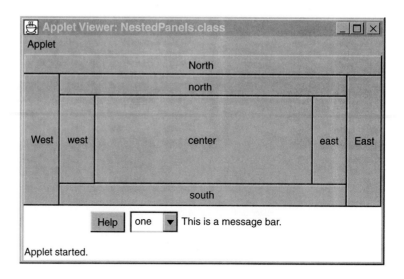

Other layout managers in JDK include the `GridBagLayout` and `CardLayout` in AWT and the `BoxLayout` in Swing. For details about the use of these layout managers see [Chan and Lee 1998] and [Walrath and Campione 1999].

6.3.3 Handling Events

GUI components communicate with the rest of the applications through *events*, which represent user inputs or actions. The *source* of an event is the component from which the event originated. A *listener* of an event is an object that receives and processes the event. Events are classified as different types, each of which is represented by an event class, which is a subclass of `AWTEvent`. The class hierarchy of event classes is shown in Figure 6.9. Each type of event is also associated with a listener interface, which the listeners of this type of events must implement. The listener interfaces and their associations with event classes are also shown in Figure 6.9. Listeners must be registered to their respective sources before they can receive events from their sources.

Handling events in Java programs involves the following steps.

- Determine the types of events to be handled and their associated listener interfaces. For example, to handle button clicks, the event class is the `ActionEvent` and the associated listener interface is `ActionListener`.

- Declare listener classes that implement the listener interfaces and all the methods of the interfaces. For example, to handle button clicks, the listener class must implement the interface `ActionListener`.

```
class MyButtonHandler implements ActionListener {
    public void actionPerformed(ActionEvent event) {
        //... handle button click
    }
}
```

Figure 6.9

The event classes
and listeners.

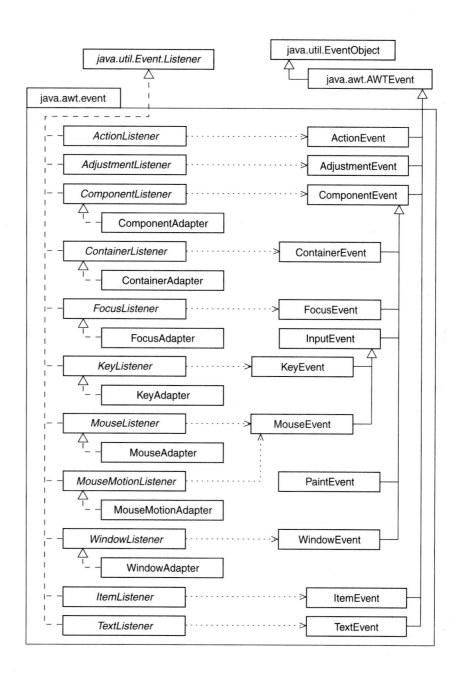

- Create instances of the components, which are the sources of the events. For example,

```
Button button1 = new Button("One");
```

- Create instances of the listeners and register the listeners to their sources. For example, to handle button clicks using `MyButtonHandler` use

```
MyButtonHandler handler = new MyButtonHandler();
button1.addActionListener(handler);
```

A listener may listen to several sources. Continuing with the preceding example, we can create another button, `button2`, and let the listener `handler` handle clicks on both buttons:

```
Button button2 = new Button("Two");
button2.addActionListener(handler);
```

A listener may also listen to different types of events by simply implementing multiple listener interfaces. Event *adapters* are classes that implement listener interfaces and provide null implementations for all the methods. They are provided for listener interfaces with more than one method.

The event handling process can roughly be described as follows.

1. When an event is triggered, the Java virtual machine (JVM) first determines its source and type.

2. If a listener is registered to the source that listens to this type of events, then an event object is created.

3. For each listener that listens to this type of events, the JVM invokes the appropriate event handling method of the listener and passes the event object as the parameter.

Naming Convention   *Events and Listeners*

The following conventions are used throughout AWT and Swing.

- The names of event classes end with the suffix `Event`.
- For event class *Xyz*`Event`, the associated listener interface is usually named *Xyz*`Listener`. If there is also an associated adapter class, it will be named *Xyz*`Adapter`.
- For a listener that implements interface *Xyz*`Listener`, the name of the method to register the listener to its source is `add`*Xyz*`Listener`.

EXAMPLE 6.10   Handling Button Clicks and Choice Item Selections

PURPOSE

This example demonstrates event handling.

DESCRIPTION

This program extends the NestedPanel class presented in Example 6.9 by adding event handling. When one of the buttons is clicked or one of the items in the choice is selected, a message is displayed in the message bar, which is a label. The class NestedPanels2 is the listener of both types of events and listens to all the buttons and the choice contained in the nested panel.

SOLUTION

The event class for button click is ActionEvent and the associated listener interface is ActionListener. The event class for choice item selection is ItemEvent, and the associated listener interface is ItemListener.

Nested panels applet with event handling: NestedPanels2

```java
import java.awt.*;
import java.awt.event.*;

public class NestedPanels2 extends NestedPanels
      implements ActionListener, ItemListener {
   public NestedPanels2() {
      super(); // create all the components
      choice.addItemListener(this); // register item listener
      registerButtonHandler(this);   // register action listener
   }

   (Event handling methods on page 275)

   (Method registerButtonHandler on page 276)

}
```

The method itemStateChanged is declared in the ItemListener interface for handling choice item selections. The method actionPerformed is declared in the ActionListener interface for handling button clicks.

Method of class NestedPanels2: event handling methods on page 275

```java
public void itemStateChanged(ItemEvent event) {
   if (event.getStateChange() == ItemEvent.SELECTED) {
      messageBar.setText("Choice selected: " + event.getItem());
   }
}

public void actionPerformed(ActionEvent event) {
   Button source = (Button) event.getSource();
   messageBar.setText("Button pushed: " + source.getLabel());
}
```

This method registers this object to all the buttons contained in the component comp. If comp is a container, it recursively registers this object to all the components contained in the container.

Method of class `NestedPanels2`:
`registerButtonHandler` on page 275

```
protected void registerButtonHandler(Component comp) {
   if (comp != null) {
      if (comp instanceof Button) {
         Button button = (Button) comp;
         button.addActionListener(this);
      } else if (comp instanceof Container) {
         Container container = (Container) comp;
         int n = container.getComponentCount();
         for (int i = 0; i < n; i++)
            registerButtonHandler(container.getComponent(i));
      }
   }
}
```

Event listeners are usually very small. Listeners are commonly declared as inner classes.

EXAMPLE 6.11   Event Handlers as Inner Classes

PURPOSE

This example demonstrates the use of inner classes as event listeners.

DESCRIPTION

This program behaves the same as the program in Example 6.10. It uses two inner classes: one handles the button clicks and the other handles the choice item selections.

SOLUTION

Nested panels applet using inner class event listeners:
`NestedPanels3`

```
import java.awt.*;
import java.awt.event.*;

public class NestedPanels3
      extends NestedPanels {
   public NestedPanels3() {
      super();
      ChoiceEventHandler cHandler = new ChoiceEventHandler();
      choice.addItemListener(cHandler);
      ButtonEventHandler bHandler = new ButtonEventHandler();
      bHandler.registerButtonHandler(this);
   }

   (Inner class ChoiceEventHandler on page 277)

   (Inner class ButtonEventHandler on page 277)

}
```

Inner class of class NestedPanels3:
ChoiceEventHandler on page 276

```
class ChoiceEventHandler implements ItemListener {
  public void itemStateChanged(ItemEvent event) {
    if (event.getStateChange() == ItemEvent.SELECTED) {
      messageBar.setText("Choice selected: " + event.getItem());
    }
  }
}
```

Inner class of class NestedPanels3:
ButtonEventHandler on page 276

```
class ButtonEventHandler implements ActionListener {
  public void actionPerformed(ActionEvent event) {
    Button source = (Button) event.getSource();
    messageBar.setText("Button pushed: " + source.getLabel());
  }

  protected void registerButtonHandler(Component comp) {
    if (comp != null) {
      if (comp instanceof Button) {
        Button button = (Button) comp;
        button.addActionListener(this);
      } else if (comp instanceof Container) {
        Container container = (Container) comp;
        int n = container.getComponentCount();
        for (int i = 0; i < n; i++)
          registerButtonHandler(container.getComponent(i));
      }
    }
  }
}
```

EXAMPLE 6.12   Bouncing Ball Applet with Controls

PURPOSE

This example demonstrates factorization by delegation and the use of buttons and choices to control animations.

DESCRIPTION

This is an enhancement of the bouncing ball applets in Example 4.4. The layout of the applet is shown in Figure 6.10. Three GUI components are added to the original applet to control the animation:

- a *start* button to start the animation,
- a *stop* button to stop the animation, and
- a *choice* to choose the color of the ball.

Figure 6.10

The bouncing ball applet with controls.

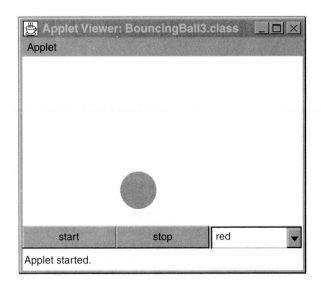

SOLUTION

In the original bouncing ball applet, the animation occupies the entire viewing area. The program consists of only one GUI component, the top-level panel. All methods dealing with animation belong to the applet class. In the reusable animation applet class `AnimationApplet` in Example 5.1 [p. 183], we also assumed that the animation occupies the entire viewing area. However, in the present case the animation occupies only a portion of the viewing area. We need a reusable animation component that is not tied to the top-level panel of an applet but that can be associated with any GUI component. In this case, it is better to use delegation to factorize the animation component so that the concrete animation class does not have to be the subclass of the reusable animation class. This approach permits multiple instances of the reusable animation class in a single program. The structure of the delegation-based reusable animation class is shown in Figure 6.11. The implementation is shown in the following program.

Figure 6.11

The delegation-based reusable animation class.

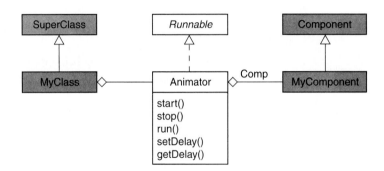

Delegation-based generic animator: `Animator`

```java
import java.awt.*;

public class Animator implements Runnable {
    public Animator(Component comp) {
        this.comp = comp;
    }

    final public void setDelay(int delay) {
        this.delay = delay;
    }

    final public int getDelay() {
        return delay;
    }
    public void start() {
        animationThread = new Thread(this);
        animationThread.start();
    }

    public void stop() {
        animationThread = null;
    }

    public void run() {
        while (Thread.currentThread() == animationThread) {
            try {
                Thread.sleep(delay);
            } catch (InterruptedException e) {}
            comp.repaint();
        }
    }

    protected Component comp; // the component to be animated
    protected int delay = 100;
    protected Thread animationThread;
}
```

Similarly, delegation can be used to factorize double-buffering. The structure of the delegation-based reusable double-buffering class is shown in Figure 6.12. The implementations are shown in the following programs.

Interface for defining the double-buffered component, `DoubleBufferedComponent`

```java
import java.awt.*;

public interface DoubleBufferedComponent {
    void paintFrame(Graphics g);
    Dimension getSize();
    Image createImage(int width, int height);
}
```

Figure 6.12

The
delegation-based
reusable
double-buffering
class.

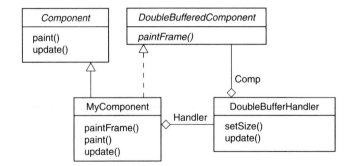

**Delegation-based generic double-buffering handler,
`DoubleBufferHandler`**

```java
import java.awt.*;

public class DoubleBufferHandler {
   public DoubleBufferHandler(DoubleBufferedComponent comp) {
      this.comp = comp;
   }

   final public void setSize(Dimension dim) {
      d = dim;
      im = comp.createImage(d.width, d.height);
      offScreen = im.getGraphics();
   }

   final public void update(Graphics g) {
      if (im == null) {
         setSize(comp.getSize());
      }
      comp.paintFrame(offScreen);
      g.drawImage(im, 0, 0, null);
   }

   protected DoubleBufferedComponent comp;
   protected Dimension d;
   protected Image im;
   protected Graphics offScreen;
}
```

A component that uses the double-buffer handler should be in the following form.

```java
class MyComponent extends AComponent {
   DoubleBufferHandler handler;

   public MyComponent() {
      handler = new DoubleBufferHandler(this);
   }

   public void paintFrame() {
      // paint a frame
   }

   public void update(Graphics g) {
      handler.update(g); // delegation
   }
```

```
      public void paint(Graphics g) {
         update(g);
      }
```
      // other methods and fields
```
   }
```

In the bouncing ball applet with controls, the animation component is the BouncingBallCanvas; it is also double-buffered. The top-level applet is the BouncingBall3 class. The structure of the entire program is shown in Figure 6.13.

Double-buffered canvas: `BouncingBallCanvas`

```java
import java.awt.*;

public class BouncingBallCanvas
      extends Canvas implements DoubleBufferedComponent {
   public void initCanvas() {
      dbHandler = new DoubleBufferHandler(this);
      d = getSize();
      x = d.width * 2 / 3 ;
      y = d.height - radius;
   }

   public void update(Graphics g) {
      dbHandler.update(g);
   }

   public void paint(Graphics g) {
      update(g);
   }

   public void paintFrame(Graphics g) {
      g.setColor(Color.white);
      g.fillRect(0, 0, d.width, d.height);
      if (x < radius || x > d.width - radius)
         dx = -dx;
      if (y < radius || y > d.height - radius)
         dy = -dy;
      x += dx; y += dy;
      g.setColor(ballColor);
      g.fillOval(x - radius, y - radius, radius * 2, radius * 2);
   }

   public void setBallColor(Color c) {
      ballColor = c;
   }

   public void setBallPosition(int x, int y) {
      this.x = x; this.y = y;
   }

   protected int x, y, dx = -2, dy = -4, radius = 20;
   protected Color ballColor = Color.red;
   protected Dimension d;
   protected DoubleBufferHandler dbHandler;
}
```

Figure 6.13

The structure of
the bouncing ball
applet with
controls.

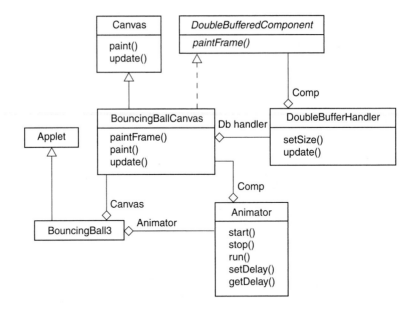

Concrete double-buffered applet with controls: `BouncingBall3`

```java
import java.awt.*;
import java.awt.event.*;

public class BouncingBall3
        extends java.applet.Applet {

    public BouncingBall3() {
        setLayout(new BorderLayout());
        canvas = new BouncingBallCanvas();
        add(canvas, BorderLayout.CENTER);
        animator = new Animator(canvas);

        controlPanel = new Panel();
        controlPanel.setLayout(new GridLayout(1,0));
        Button startButton = new Button("start");
        controlPanel.add(startButton);
        Button stopButton = new Button("stop");
        controlPanel.add(stopButton);
        Choice choice = new Choice();
        choice.addItem("red");
        choice.addItem("green");
        choice.addItem("blue");
        controlPanel.add(choice);
        add(controlPanel, BorderLayout.SOUTH);

        startButton.addActionListener(new ButtonHandler());
        stopButton.addActionListener(new ButtonHandler());
        choice.addItemListener(new ColorChoiceHandler());
    }
```

```
      public void init() {
         String att = getParameter("delay");
         if (att != null) {
            int delay = Integer.parseInt(att);
            animator.setDelay(delay);
         }
         doLayout();
         canvas.initCanvas();
      }

      public void start() {
         animator.start();
      }

      public void stop() {
         animator.stop();
      }

      protected BouncingBallCanvas canvas;
      protected Animator animator;
      protected Panel controlPanel;

      protected class ButtonHandler implements ActionListener {
         public void actionPerformed(ActionEvent event) {
            Button b = (Button) event.getSource();
            if ("start".equals(b.getLabel())) {
               animator.start();
            } else if ("stop".equals(b.getLabel())) {
               animator.stop();
            }
         }
      }

      protected class ColorChoiceHandler implements ItemListener {
         public void itemStateChanged(ItemEvent event) {
            if (event.getStateChange() == ItemEvent.SELECTED) {
               if ("red".equals(event.getItem())) {
                  canvas.setBallColor(Color.red);
               } else if ("green".equals(event.getItem())) {
                  canvas.setBallColor(Color.green);
               } else if ("blue".equals(event.getItem())) {
                  canvas.setBallColor(Color.blue);
               }
               canvas.repaint();
            }
         }
      }
   }
```

6.3.4   Frames and Dialogs

A *frame* is a top-level window with a border, a title bar, and control buttons located at the upper corners of the frame. A GUI app starts with a frame. The main work area of a GUI app is usually contained in a frame. A *dialog* is a pop-up window that usually requires immediate attention of the user, and it appears for only a short period of time. Dialog windows are used for displaying messages or getting input.

EXAMPLE 6.13 A Simple Online Ordering GUI App, Using Swing

PURPOSE

This example demonstrates building GUI apps with frames and dialogs; the use of Swing components, including image labels, borders, and button groups; and customized layout.

DESCRIPTION

The frame of the online ordering app contains two components: an image label, which consists of an image and a text, and the Order button. When the Order button

Figure 6.14

The online ordering form.

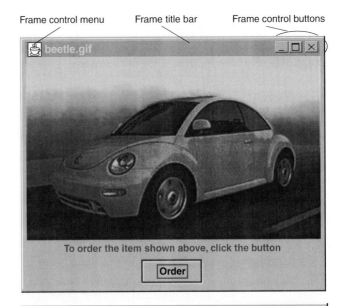

is pushed, a dialog box pops up. The dialog box has three compartments, as shown in Figure 6.14.

- The top compartment contains text labels and text fields. The layout of the labels and the fields are not handled by a layout manager. Rather a customized layout is specified, using the absolute position and dimension of each component.
- The middle compartment has a titled border with the title Credit Card. It contains three check boxes that are exclusive.
- The bottom compartment has an etched border. It contains the Ok and Cancel buttons. An order is completed when the Ok button is pushed, and the order information will be printed to the standard output.

The structure of the online ordering app is shown in Figure 6.15.

SOLUTION

The top-level class for the online shopping app `Order`

```
import java.awt.*;
import java.awt.event.*;
import javax.swing.*;

public class Order extends JFrame {
    public Order(String imageFile) {
        setTitle(imageFile);
        getContentPane().setLayout(new BorderLayout());
        Icon image = new ImageIcon(imageFile);
        JLabel center =
            new JLabel("To order the item shown above, click the button",
                       image,
                       SwingConstants.CENTER);
        center.setHorizontalTextPosition(SwingConstants.CENTER);
        center.setVerticalTextPosition(SwingConstants.BOTTOM);
        JPanel bottom = new JPanel();
        JButton orderButton = new JButton("Order");
        bottom.add(orderButton);
        orderButton.addActionListener(makeOrderHandler());
        getContentPane().add(center, BorderLayout.CENTER);
        getContentPane().add(bottom, BorderLayout.SOUTH);
        addWindowListener(new AppCloser());
    }

    ActionListener makeOrderHandler() {
        return new OrderHandler();
    }

    (Inner class AppCloser on page 286)

    (Inner class OrderHandler on page 286)

    (The main() method on page 287)

}
```

Figure 6.15

The structure of the online shopping app.

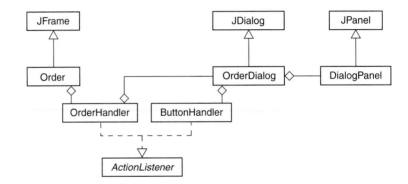

The AppCloser is an event listener that listens to the *window events*—the events triggered by the frame menus and control buttons that usually are located at the upper left and upper right corners of the window frame, respectively (see Figure 6.14). The AppCloser simply terminates the program when the close window (X) button is pushed. Without the AppCloser, pushing the close window button will get no response. The implementation of AppCloser here is simplistic. In real applications, before terminating the program the user should be prompted to confirm the action, and any unsaved data should be saved to disk to prevent data loss.

Inner class of class Order: AppCloser on page 285

```
static class AppCloser extends Window Adapter {
   public void window Closing(WindowEvent e) {
      System.exit(0);
   }
}
```

The OrderHandler is the listener class of the Order button. The first time the Order button is pushed, an instance of OrderDialog, which represents the order dialog box, is created with the invocation of new OrderDialog(Order.this). The order dialog box becomes visible when dialog.show() is invoked. The order dialog box is created only once. After that, pushing the Order button causes the order dialog box to reappear by invoking dialog.show().

Inner class of class Order: OrderHandler on page 285

```
class OrderHandler implements ActionListener {
   JDialog dialog;
   public void actionPerformed(ActionEvent evt) {
      if (dialog == null) {
         dialog = new OrderDialog(Order.this);
      }
      dialog.show();
   }
}
```

The `main()` method creates an instance of the order frame. The order frame becomes visible when `frame.show()` is invoked.

Method of class `Order`: `main()` on page 285

```
public static void main(String[] args) {
    if (args.length > 0) {
        Order frame = new Order(args[0]);
        frame.show();
    }
}
```

The `OrderDialog` is a dialog box that pops up when the Order button in the order frame is pushed. It contains the Ok and Cancel buttons and the order panel.

A dialog with Ok and Cancel buttons: `OrderDialog`

```
import java.awt.*;
import java.awt.event.*;
import javax.swing.*;

public class OrderDialog extends JDialog {
    JPanel bottom;
    JButton okButton, cancelButton;
    DialogPanel dialogPanel;

    public OrderDialog(JFrame owner) {
        super(owner, true);
        setTitle("Order");
        okButton = new JButton("Ok");
        cancelButton = new JButton("Cancel");
        ButtonHandler bHandler = new ButtonHandler();
        okButton.addActionListener(bHandler);
        cancelButton.addActionListener(bHandler);
        bottom = new JPanel();
        bottom.add(okButton);
        bottom.add(cancelButton);
        bottom.setBorder(BorderFactory.createEtchedBorder());
        dialogPanel = new DialogPanel();
        getContentPane().setLayout(new BorderLayout());
        getContentPane().add(bottom, BorderLayout.SOUTH);
        getContentPane().add(dialogPanel, BorderLayout.CENTER);
    }

    (Inner class ButtonHandler on page 290)

}
```

The `DialogPanel` contains text fields for the customer's name, address, and e-mail. Each text field is accompanied by a text label. It also has three check boxes for choosing a credit card. The check boxes are contained in another panel.

Class `DialogPanel`

```
class DialogPanel extends JPanel {
    JLabel nameLabel;
    JTextField nameField;
    JLabel addressLabel;
    JTextField addressField;
    JLabel cityLabel;
    JTextField cityField;
    JLabel stateLabel;
    JTextField stateField;
    JLabel zipLabel;
    JTextField zipField;
    JLabel emailLabel;
    JTextField emailField;
    JCheckBox visaBox, mcBox, discoverBox;
    JPanel creditCard;
    ButtonGroup group;

    (The constructor on page 288)

    (The layout methods on page 289)

    (Method reset on page 290)

}
```

The constructor creates instances of the text fields and labels. The Swing components can be bordered. The panel for check boxes has a titled border. The three check boxes are added to the same button group, so they are exclusive.

The constructor of class `DialogPanel` on page 288

```
DialogPanel() {
    nameLabel = new JLabel("Name");
    nameField = new JTextField();
    addressLabel = new JLabel("Address");
    addressField = new JTextField();
    cityLabel = new JLabel("City");
    cityField = new JTextField();
    stateLabel = new JLabel("State");
    stateField = new JTextField();
    zipLabel = new JLabel("ZIP");
    zipField = new JTextField();
    emailLabel = new JLabel("E-Mail");
    emailField = new JTextField();

    creditCard = new JPanel();
    visaBox = new JCheckBox("Visa", true);
    mcBox = new JCheckBox("MasterCard");
    discoverBox = new JCheckBox("Discover");
    creditCard.add(visaBox);
    creditCard.add(mcBox);
    creditCard.add(discoverBox);
    creditCard.setBorder(BorderFactory.createTitledBorder("Credit Card"));
    group = new ButtonGroup();
```

```
group.add(visaBox);
group.add(mcBox);
group.add(discoverBox);

add(nameLabel);
add(nameField);
add(addressLabel);
add(addressField);
add(cityLabel);
add(cityField);
add(stateLabel);
add(stateField);
add(zipLabel);
add(zipField);
add(emailLabel);
add(emailField);
add(creditCard);
}
```

The layout of the components contained in a container is handled by the doLayout() method. By default, the doLayout() method delegates the responsibility to the layout manager associated with the container. To create a customized layout, you need to override the doLayout() method. Furthermore, you should also override the methods getPreferredSize() and getMinimumSize() to return the preferred and minimum sizes of the container, respectively. The actual layout is done in the doLayout() method. The position and dimension of each component are set with the setBounds() methods defined in the Component class.

The layout methods of class DialogPanel on page 288

```
public Dimension getPreferredSize() {
   return new Dimension(350, 200);
}

public Dimension getMinimumSize() {
   return new Dimension(350, 200);
}

public void doLayout() {
   nameLabel.setBounds(10, 10, 60, 30);
   nameField.setBounds(70, 15, 270, 20);
   addressLabel.setBounds(10, 40, 60, 30);
   addressField.setBounds(70, 45, 270, 20);
   cityLabel.setBounds(10, 70, 60, 30);
   cityField.setBounds(70, 75, 100, 20);
   stateLabel.setBounds(180, 70, 40, 30);
   stateField.setBounds(220, 75, 30, 20);
   zipLabel.setBounds(260, 70, 30, 30);
   zipField.setBounds(290, 75, 50, 20);
   emailLabel.setBounds(10, 100, 60, 30);
   emailField.setBounds(70, 105, 270, 20);
   creditCard.setBounds(10, 140, 330, 50);
}
```

The reset() method clears the text fields so the same dialog panel can be used by the next customer.

Method of class `DialogPanel`:
`reset` on page 288

```
public void reset() {
    nameField.setText("");
    addressField.setText("");
    cityField.setText("");
    stateField.setText("");
    zipField.setText("");
    emailField.setText("");
    visaBox.setSelected(true);
}
```

The `ButtonHandler` is the event listener class for the buttons in the order dialog box. If the Ok button is pushed the order information is printed to the standard output. When either the Ok or the Cancel button is pushed, the text fields are cleared, and the dialog box is closed.

Inner class of class `OrderDialog`: `ButtonHandler` on page 287

```
class ButtonHandler implements ActionListener {
    public void actionPerformed(ActionEvent evt) {
        JButton button = (JButton) evt.getSource();
        String label = button.getText();
        if ("Ok".equals(label)) {
            System.out.println("An order is received:");
            System.out.println("\tName:    " + dialogPanel.nameField.getText());
            System.out.println("\tAddress: " + dialogPanel.addressField.getText());
            System.out.println("\tCity:    " + dialogPanel.cityField.getText());
            System.out.println("\tState:   " + dialogPanel.stateField.getText());
            System.out.println("\tZIP:     " + dialogPanel.zipField.getText());
            System.out.println("\tE-Mail:  " + dialogPanel.emailField.getText());
            System.out.print("\tCredit card: ");
            if (dialogPanel.visaBox.isSelected()) {
                System.out.println("Visa");
            } else if (dialogPanel.mcBox.isSelected()) {
                System.out.println("MasterCard");
            } else if (dialogPanel.discoverBox.isSelected()) {
                System.out.println("Discover");
            }
        }
        dialogPanel.reset();
        setVisible(false); // close the dialog box
    }
}
```

6.4 THE INPUT/OUTPUT FRAMEWORK

The Java input/output framework is designed to be flexible and easily configurable. Java supports two types of input/output (I/O).

1. *Stream I/O*. A stream is a sequence of bytes. Stream-based I/O supports reading or writing data *sequentially*, that is, reading or writing data successively in one direction. A stream may be opened for reading *or* writing, but not reading *and* writing.

2. *Random Access I/O*. Random access I/O supports reading and writing data at any position of a file. A random access file may be opened for both reading and writing.

There are two kinds of streams: *byte streams* and *character streams*. Byte streams support reading and writing data of any type, including strings, in the binary format. Character streams support reading and writing of text, using locale-dependent character encodings.

6.4.1 Byte Streams

The most primitive stream I/O capabilities are declared in two abstract classes: `InputStream` and `OutputStream`. They support reading and writing of a single byte and a byte array. The methods are summarized in the following table. In these methods, b is a byte, ba is a byte array, and `off` and `len` are integers that specify a segment of an array; `off` represents the offset (i.e., the starting index of the segment), and `len` represents the length (i.e., the number of elements in the segment).

Input Method	Output Method	Description
read()	write(b)	Reads/writes a single byte
read(ba)	write(ba)	Reads/writes an entire byte array
read(ba,off,len)	write(ba,off,len)	Reads/writes a segment of the byte array
close()	close()	Closes the stream

Two concrete I/O streams that implement the two interfaces are `FileInputStream` and `FileOutputStream`, as shown in Figure 6.16. Instances of the two classes can be constructed by specifying the filename.

Figure 6.16

The file input
stream and the file
output stream.

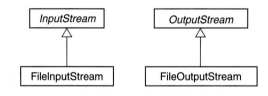

Constructor	Description
FileInputStream(filename)	Create, an input stream reading from the file named filename. An IOException is thrown if the file does not exist.
FileOutputStream(filename)	Create, an output stream writing to the file named filename. If the file does not exist a new file is created. If the file already exists, the original file is overwritten.
FileOutputStream(filename, append)	Create, an output stream writing to the file named filename. If the file does not exist a new file is created. If the file already exists, the new data will be appended to the end of the original file if the boolean flag append is true; otherwise, the the original file is overwritten.

The primitive I/O capabilities provided in these classes make reading and writing data of any types possible, but hardly convenient.

EXAMPLE 6.14 Reading and Writing a Two-Dimensional Matrix, Using Byte I/O

PURPOSE

This example demonstrates reading and writing data, using the primitive I/O capabilities provided in the FileInputStream and FileOutputStream.

DESCRIPTION

WriteMatrix1 writes a 2 × 3 matrix to a file. It first writes the number of rows and columns of the matrix, followed by the numbers in the matrix. ReadMatrix1 reads the file written by WriteMatrix1 and restores the matrix.

SOLUTION

The data to be written to file are defined in the following interface.

Matrix data

```
public interface MatrixData {
   double[][] data = {
      { Math.exp(2.0), Math.exp(3.0), Math.exp(4.0) },
      { Math.exp(-2.0), Math.exp(-3.0), Math.exp(-4.0) },
   };
}
```

In the following WriteMatrix1 class program, the writeInt() method converts an integer value to a byte array and writes the byte array to the output stream. Similarly, the writeDouble() method converts a double value to a byte array and writes the byte array to the output stream.

Class WriteMatrix1

```
import java.io.*;

public class WriteMatrix1 implements MatrixData {
   public static void main(String[] args) {
      int row = data.length;
      int col = data[0].length;
      int i, j;
      for (i = 0; i < row; i++) {
         for (j = 0; j < col; j++) {
            System.out.println("data[" + i + "][" + j + "] = " + data[i][j]);
         }
      }

      if (args.length > 0) {
         try {
            FileOutputStream out = new FileOutputStream(args[0]);
            writeInt(row, out);
            writeInt(col, out);
            for (i = 0; i < row; i++) {
               for (j = 0; j < col; j++) {
                  writeDouble(data[i][j], out);
               }
            }
            out.close();
         } catch (IOException e) {}
      }
   }

   public static void writeInt(int i, OutputStream out)
         throws IOException {
      byte[] buf = new byte[4];
      for (int k = 3; k >= 0; k--) {
         buf[k] = (byte)(i & 0xFF);
         i >>>= 8;
      }
      out.write(buf);
   }
```

```
    public static void writeDouble(double d, OutputStream out)
        throws IOException {
      byte[] buf = new byte[8];
      long l = Double.doubleToLongBits(d);
      for (int k = 7; k >= 0; k--) {
        buf[k] = (byte)(l & 0xFF);
        l >>>= 8;
      }
      out.write(buf);
    }

  }
```

The output is:

```
            venus% java WriteMatrix1 data1.out
            data[0][0] = 7.38905609893065
            data[0][1] = 20.085536923187668
            data[0][2] = 54.598150033144236
            data[1][0] = 0.1353352832366127
            data[1][1] = 0.049787068367863944
            data[1][2] = 0.01831563888873418
```

In the following ReadMatrix1 class program, the readInt() method reads 4 bytes from the input stream into a byte array and converts the byte array to an integer value. Similarly, the readDouble() method reads 8 bytes from the input stream into a byte array and converts the byte array to a double value.

Class **ReadMatrix1**

```
import java.io.*;

public class ReadMatrix1 {
  static double[][] data;
  public static void main(String[] args) {
    if (args.length > 0) {
      try {
        FileInputStream in = new FileInputStream(args[0]);
        int row = readInt(in);
        System.out.println("row = " + row);
        int col = readInt(in);
        System.out.println("col = " + col);
        data = new double[row][col];
        for (int i = 0; i < row; i++) {
          for (int j = 0; j < col; j++) {
            data[i][j] = readDouble(in);
            System.out.println("data[" + i + "][" + j + "] = " + data[i][j]);
          }
        }
      } catch (IOException e) {}
    }
  }
  public static int readInt(InputStream in)
      throws IOException {
    byte[] buf = new byte[4];
    in.read(buf);
    int i = 0;
```

```
        for (int k = 0; k < 4; k++) {
          i <<= 8;
          i += (((int) buf[k]) & 0xFF);
        }
        return i;
    }
    public static double readDouble(InputStream in)
            throws IOException {
        byte[] buf = new byte[8];
        in.read(buf);
        long l = 0;
        for (int k = 0; k < 8; k++) {
          l <<= 8;
          l += (((int) buf[k]) & 0xFF);
        }
        return Double.longBitsToDouble(l);
    }
}
```

The output is:

```
venus% java ReadMatrix1 data1.out
row = 2
col = 3
data[0][0] = 7.38905609893065
data[0][1] = 20.085536923187668
data[0][2] = 54.598150033144236
data[1][0] = 0.1353352832366127
data[1][1] = 0.049787068367863944
data[1][2] = 0.01831563888873418
```

Data Input And Data Output

Such laboring of reading and writing data by using bytes is rarely necessary. The methods for reading and writing data of various types are declared in two interfaces, DataInput and DataOutput, respectively. These methods are summarized in the following table.

Input Method	Output Method	Description
readBoolean()	writeBoolean(b)	Reads/writes a boolean value
readByte()	writeByte(b)	Reads/writes a byte value
readChar()	writeChar(c)	Reads/writes a char value
readDouble()	writeDouble(d)	Reads/writes a double value
readFloat()	writeFloat(f)	Reads/writes a float value
readInt()	writeInt(i)	Reads/writes an int value
readLong()	writeLong(l)	Reads/writes a long value
readShort()	writeShort(s)	Reads/writes a short value
readUTF()	writeUTF(s)	Reads/writes a String value

Figure 6.17

The data input
stream and the
data output stream.

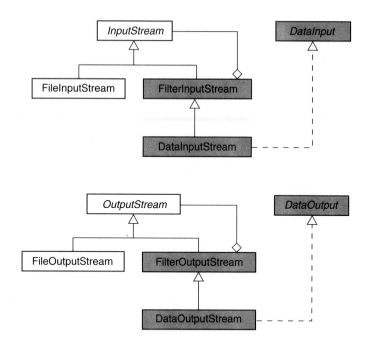

Two concrete streams, DataInputStream and DataOutputStream, implement the DataInput and DataOutput interfaces, respectively, as illustrated in Figure 6.17. The DataInputStream and DataOutputStream are defined as filters, or decorators; that is, they take I/O streams with primitive I/O capabilities and transform them into I/O streams with data input and output capabilities.

Constructor	Description
DataInputStream(in)	Creates a data input stream that reads data from the specified input stream in
DataOutputStream(out)	Creates a data output stream that writes data to the specified output stream out

EXAMPLE 6.15   Reading and Writing a Two-Dimensional Matrix, Using DataInput and DataOutput

PURPOSE

This example demonstrates use of the I/O decorators DataInputStream and DataOutputStream.

DESCRIPTION

The WriteMatrix2 and ReadMatrix2 classes perform the same tasks as the WriteMatrix1 and ReadMatrix1 classes in Example 6.14. The main differences are the construction of the data input and output streams, which are shown in boldface in the following programs. The writeInt(), writeDouble(), readInt(), and readDouble() methods in the previous examples are no longer needed.

SOLUTION

Class **WriteMatrix2**

```java
import java.io.*;

public class WriteMatrix2 implements MatrixData {

    public static void main(String[] args) {
        int row = data.length;
        int col = data[0].length;
        int i, j;
        for (i = 0; i < row; i++) {
            for (j = 0; j < col; j++) {
                System.out.println("data[" + i + "][" + j + "] = " + data[i][j]);
            }
        }

        if (args.length > 0) {
            try {

                DataOutputStream out =
                    new DataOutputStream(new FileOutputStream(args[0]));

                out.writeInt(row);
                out.writeInt(col);
                for (i = 0; i < row; i++) {
                    for (j = 0; j < col; j++) {
                        out.writeDouble(data[i][j]);
                    }
                }
                out.close();
            } catch (IOException e) {}
        }
    }
}
```

Class **ReadMatrix2**

```java
import java.io.*;

public class ReadMatrix2 {

    static double[][] data;

    public static void main(String[] args) {
        if (args.length > 0) {
            try {
```

```
DataInputStream in =
    new DataInputStream(new FileInputStream(args[0]));

int row = in.readInt();
System.out.println("row = " + row);
int col = in.readInt();
System.out.println("col = " + col);
data = new double[row][col];
for (int i = 0; i < row; i++) {
  for (int j = 0; j < col; j++) {
    data[i][j] = in.readDouble();
    System.out.println("data[" + i + "][" + j + "] = " + data[i][j]);
  }
}
} catch (IOException e) {}
}
}
}
```

This example produces the same output as Example 6.14.

Buffered Input and Output Streams

The `BufferedInputStream` and `BufferedOutputStream` are filter streams
that support buffered I/O, as indicated in Figure 6.18. They take I/O streams and
transform them into buffered I/O streams, as shown in the table on the next page.

Figure 6.18

The buffered input
stream and the
buffered output
stream.

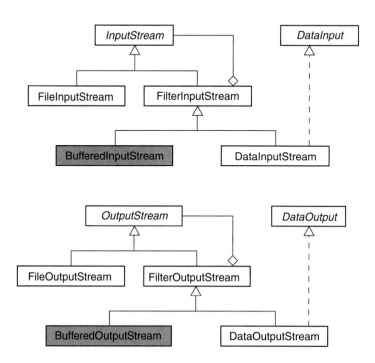

Constructor	Description
BufferedInputStream(in)	Creates a buffered input stream that reads data from the specified input stream in
BufferedOutputStream(out)	Creates a buffered output stream that writes data to the specified output stream out

EXAMPLE 6.16   Reading and Writing a Two-Dimensional Matrix, Using Buffered I/O

PURPOSE

This example demonstrates the use of buffered input and output streams.

DESCRIPTION

The WriteMatrix3 and ReadMatrix3 classes perform the same tasks as in Examples 6.14 and 6.15. The main differences are the construction of the buffered input and output streams, which are shown in boldface in the following programs.

SOLUTION

Class WriteMatrix3

```
import java.io.*;

public class WriteMatrix3 implements MatrixData {
   public static void main(String[] args) {
      int row = data.length;
      int col = data[0].length;
      int i, j;
      for (i = 0; i < row; i++) {
         for (j = 0; j < col; j++) {
            System.out.println("data[" + i + "][" + j + "] = " + data[i][j]);
         }
      }

      if (args.length > 0) {
         try {
            DataOutputStream out =
               new DataOutputStream(
               new BufferedOutputStream(
               new FileOutputStream(args[0])));

            out.writeInt(row);
            out.writeInt(col);
```

```
              for (i = 0; i < row; i++){
                for (j = 0; j < col; j++){
                   out.writeDouble(data[i][j]);
                }
              }
              out.close();
            } catch (IOException e) {}
        }
      }
    }
```

Class **ReadMatrix3**

```
import java.io.*;

public class ReadMatrix3 {

  static double[][] data;

  public static void main(String[] args) {
    if (args.length > 0) {
      try {
        DataInputStream in =
            new DataInputStream(
            new BufferedInputStream(
            new FileInputStream(args[0])));

        int row = in.readInt();
        System.out.println("row = " + row);
        int col = in.readInt();
        System.out.println("col = " + col);
        data = new double[row][col];
        for (int i = 0; i < row; i++) {
          for (int j = 0; j < col; j++) {
            data[i][j] = in.readDouble();
            System.out.println("data[" + i + "][" + j + "] = " + data[i][j]);
          }
        }
      } catch (IOException e) {}
    }
  }
}
```

Object Streams

Java supports object serialization. It involves two processes.

1. *Serializing*. To write an object and all the objects that are directly or indirectly referenced by the object to a stream.
2. *Deserializing*. To restore an object and all the objects that are directly or indirectly referenced by the object that have been serialized.

Figure 6.19

The object input stream and the object output stream.

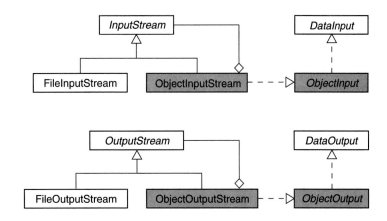

Instances of classes that implement the `Serializable` interface can be serialized. Most classes in the Java Class Libraries can be serialized, as can arrays.

The methods for serializing and deserializing are declared in the `ObjectInput` and `ObjectOutput` interfaces, which extend `DataInput` and `DataOutput`, respectively. The input method is `readObject()`, the output method is `writeObject()`, and the data type is `Object`.

The `ObjectInputStream` and `ObjectOutputStream` are two I/O filter classes that implement the `ObjectInput` and `ObjectOutput` interfaces, respectively, as shown in Figure 6.19. The constructors are described in the following table.

Constructor	Description
`ObjectInputStream(in)`	Creates an object input stream that reads data from the specified input stream `in`
`ObjectOutputStream(out)`	Creates an object output stream that writes data to the specified output stream `out`

EXAMPLE 6.17 Reading and Writing a Two-Dimensional Matrix, Using Object Serialization

PURPOSE

This example demonstrates the use of object serialization.

DESCRIPTION

Using object serialization, we can easily read and write the entire array with a single method invocation.

SOLUTION

Class WriteMatrix4

```java
import java.io.*;

public class WriteMatrix4 implements MatrixData {

   public static void main(String[] args) {
      int row = data.length;
      int col = data[0].length;
      int i, j;
      for (i = 0; i < row; i++) {
        for (j = 0; j < col; j++) {
           System.out.println("data[" + i + "][" + j + "] = " + data[i][j]);
        }
      }

      if (args.length > 0) {
        try {

           ObjectOutputStream out =
               new ObjectOutputStream(new FileOutputStream(args[0]));

           out.writeObject(data);
           out.close();
        } catch (IOException e) {}
      }
   }
}
```

Class ReadMatrix4

```java
import java.io.*;

public class ReadMatrix4 {

  static double[][] data;

  public static void main(String[] args) {
    if (args.length > 0) {
      try {

         ObjectInputStream in =
             new ObjectInputStream(new FileInputStream(args[0]));
         data = (double[][]) in.readObject();

         int row = data.length;
         int col = data[0].length;
         for (int i = 0; i < row; i++){
           for (int j = 0; j < col; j++){
              System.out.println("data[" + i + "][" + j + "] = " + data[i][j]);
           }
         }
      } catch (Exception e) {}
    }
  }
}
```

Design Pattern: Decorator

The design of the Java input/output framework illustrates the Decorator design pattern. The basic byte-based I/O capability is provided by the `InputStream` and `OutputStream` classes. Also, there are many *add-on* features that enhance the basic I/O capability, such as reading and writing data of primitive types, read and write objects, buffered read and write, compression and decompression of data, encryption and decryption of data and, so on. These add-on features can be combined in many different ways, and in different contexts we may need to use different combinations of them. One approach to satisfying all the potential needs is to extend the `InputStream` and `OutputStream` classes to add these features. A large number of classes is necessary to cover every possible combination of these add-on features, such as `BufferedDataInputStream`, `EncryptedDataInputStream`, `CompressedInputStream`, `EncryptedCompressedDataInputStream` and so on. An alternative approach is to define each add-on feature as a separate class known as a *decorator*, or *filter*,[2] that adds a feature to the basic I/O capability through object composition. A particular combination of the add-on features is composed by adding the corresponding decorators of these add-on features to the basic I/O capability, as in:

```
new Decorator2(new Decorator1(inputStream))
```

This approach avoids an explosion of the number classes and provides flexibility through object composition.

Design Pattern *Decorator*

Category: Structural design pattern.

Intent: Attach additional responsibilities to an object dynamically. Decorators provide a flexible alternative to subclassing for extending functionality.

Applicability: The Decorator design pattern should be used

- to add responsibilities to individual objects dynamically without affecting other objects in the same class,

- for responsibilities that can be withdrawn, and

- when extension by subclassing is impractical owing to a large number of possible independent extensions, which would produce an explosion of subclasses to support every combination.

The structure of the Decorator design pattern is shown in the following diagram.

[2] *Decorator* seems to be a better name than *filter* because *decorate* connotes adding, whereas *filter* connotes removing.

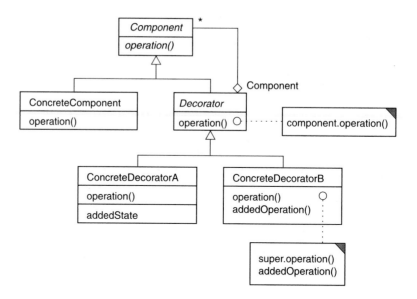

The participants of the Decorator design pattern are

Component (e.g., `InputStream`), which defines the interface for objects that can have responsibilities added to them dynamically;

ConcreteComponent (e.g., `FileInputStream`), which defines an object to which additional responsibilities can be added;

Decorator (e.g., `FilterInputStream`), which maintains a reference to a component object and defines an interface that conforms to the component's interface; and

ConcreteDecorator (e.g., `DataInputStream` and `BufferedOutputStream`), which adds responsibilities to the component.

For a detailed discussion of the Decorator design pattern see [Gamma et al. 1995].

6.4.2 Character Streams

In Java programs, strings are represented internally in Unicode, in which all characters are encoded in two bytes. Externally, text files are stored in the default character encoding of the machine on which the programs are running. The default character encoding of a machine is often determined by the machine's locale. A *locale* is a geographic or political region that shares the same language and customs. For example, in the United States, the default character encoding is ISO-8859-1, commonly known as the ASCII code, in which all characters are encoded in a single byte. In the People's Republic of China, the default character encoding is GB-2312, in which all Latin characters are encoded in a single byte, and all Chinese ideographs are encoded in two bytes.

Figure 6.20

The character-based readers and writers.

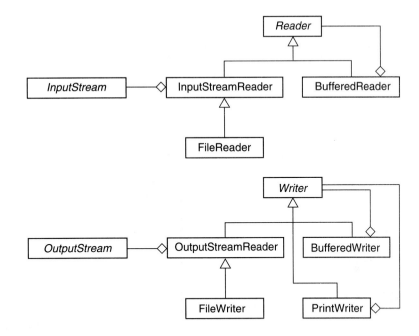

The character-based I/O streams perform conversions between the Unicode and the locale-sensitive character encodings when reading and writing strings. In other words, character streams are locale sensitive, but byte streams are not.

Reader and Writer are two abstract classes that are the roots of inheritance hierarchies of the character-based input and output streams, respectively. The relationships among the key character I/O streams are shown in Figure 6.20. The Reader and Writer classes provide the basic capabilities for reading and writing characters. Their methods are summarized in the following table. The parameter c represents a character, ca represents a character array, and off and len are integers that specify a segment of an array; off represents the offset (i.e., the starting index of the segment), and len represents the length (i.e., the number of elements in the segment).

Input Method	Output Method	Description
read()	write(c)	Reads/writes a single character
read(ca)	write(ca)	Reads/writes an entire character array
read(ca,off,len)	write(ca,off,len)	Reads/writes a segment of the character array
close()	close()	Closes the stream

TABLE 6.9

Constructor	Description
InputStreamReader(in)	Creates an input stream reader that reads data from the specified input stream in and uses the default character encoding
InputStreamReader(in, encoding)	Creates an input stream reader that reads data from the specified input stream in and uses the specified character encoding
OutputStreamWriter(out)	Creates an output stream writer that writes data to the specified output stream out and uses the default character encoding
OutputStreamWriter(out, encoding)	Creates an output stream writer that writes data to the specified output stream out and uses the specified character encoding

The InputStreamReader and OutputStreamWriter are two filters that serve as bridges between byte-based I/O and character-based I/O (Table 6.9).

The parameter encoding is a string that denotes the character encoding used by the reader/writer. For example, the ISO-8859-1 encoding for English is denoted "8859_1", and the GB-2312 encoding for simplified Chinese is denoted "GB2312".

The FileReader and FileWriter are two concrete character streams that provide the basic character based I/O capabilities (Table 6.10).

The BufferedReader and BufferedWriter are two filters that support buffered character-based I/O.

Constructor	Description
BufferedReader(reader)	Creates a buffered reader that reads data from the specified reader
BufferedWriter(writer)	Creates a buffered writer that writes data to the specified writer

TABLE 6.10

Constructor	Description
FileReader(filename)	Creates a file reader reading from the file named filename. An IOException is thrown if the file does not exist.
FileWriter(filename)	Creates a file writer writing to the file named filename. If the file does not exist a new file is created. If the file already exists, the original file is overwritten.
FileWriter(filename, append)	Creates a file writer writing to the file named filename. If the file does not exist a new file is created. If the file already exists, the new data will be appended to the end of the original file if the boolean flag append is true; otherwise, the original file is overwritten.

The BufferedReader class adds the method readLine(), which reads a line of text.

PrintWriter is a useful filter class that supports writing values of various data types by converting them to their string representations. The PrintWriter class has the constructor PrintWriter(writer), which creates a print writer that writes data to the specified writer. PrintWriter also supports the following two methods that are overloaded on all data types. The parameter v can be of any type.

Method	Description
print(v)	Prints the string representation of v
println(v)	Prints the string representation of v followed by a new line

The string representations of values of primitive types are formatted according to the usual and customary conventions. The string representations of objects are defined by the toString() method of their classes.

EXAMPLE 6.18 Reading and Writing a Two-Dimensional Matrix, Using Strings

PURPOSE

This example demonstrates character-based I/O.

DESCRIPTION

To read and write data using strings, all data must be converted to and from their string representations. To write data, we must insert delimiters between consecutive values. `WriteMatrix5` writes the two-dimensional array to a text file. Each line contains a single value. The first two lines contain the number of rows and columns followed by the numbers in the matrix. `ReadMatrix5` reads the text file written by `WriteMatrix5` and restores the array.

SOLUTION

Class **WriteMatrix5**

```java
import java.io.*;

public class WriteMatrix5 implements MatrixData {

  public static void main(String[] args) {
    int row = data.length;
    int col = data[0].length;
    int i, j;
    for (i = 0; i < row; i++) {
      for (j = 0; j < col; j++) {
        System.out.println("data[" + i + "][" + j + "] = " + data[i][j]);
      }
    }

    if (args.length > 0) {
      try {
        PrintWriter out =
            new PrintWriter(
            new BufferedWriter(
            new FileWriter(args[0])));
        out.println(row);
        out.println(col);
        for (i = 0; i < row; i++) {
          for (j = 0; j < col; j++) {
            out.println(data[i][j]);
          }
        }
        out.close();
      } catch (IOException e) {}
    }
  }
}
```

Class ReadMatrix5

```
import java.io.*;

public class ReadMatrix5 {

   static double[][] data;

   public static void main(String[] args) {
      if (args.length > 0) {
         try {
            BufferedReader in =
                new BufferedReader(
                new FileReader(args[0]));
            String line;
            line = in.readLine();
            int row = Integer.parseInt(line);
            System.out.println("row = " + row);
            line = in.readLine();
            int col = Integer.parseInt(line);
            System.out.println("col = " + col);
            data = new double[row][col];
            for (int i = 0; i < row; i++){
               for (int j = 0; j < col; j++){
                  line = in.readLine();
                  data[i][j] = Double.valueOf(line).doubleValue();
                  System.out.println("data[" + i + "][" + j + "] = " + data[i][j]);
               }
            }
         } catch (IOException e) {}
      }
   }
}
```

Character streams are also able to use character encodings that are different from the default character encoding.

EXAMPLE 6.19   A Universal Text Viewer

PURPOSE

This example demonstrates the use of character-based readers to view text files in any character encoding.

DESCRIPTION

This GUI application makes use of Swing components. It consist of an instance of JTextArea inside an instance of JScrollPane, which allows the text area to be scrolled both vertically and horizontally. The program expects two arguments: the text file name, and the character encoding.

SOLUTION

Class `UniversalTextViewer`

```java
import java.awt.*;
import java.awt.event.*;
import java.io.*;
import javax.swing.*;

public class UniversalTextViewer extends JPanel {

    public UniversalTextViewer(String filename, String enc) {
        setLayout(new BorderLayout());
        JTextArea textArea = new JTextArea(40, 80);
        textArea.setEditable(false);
        textArea.setFont(new Font("Monospaced", Font.BOLD, 16));
        add(new JScrollPane(textArea), BorderLayout.CENTER);
        try {
            BufferedReader in =
                    new BufferedReader(
                    new InputStreamReader(new FileInputStream(filename),
                                          enc));
            String line;
            while ((line = in.readLine()) != null) {
                textArea.append(line + "\n");
            }
        } catch (IOException e) {}
    }

    public static void main(String args[]) {
        if (args.length >= 2) {
            JFrame frame = new JFrame();
            frame.setTitle("Universal Text Viewer: " +
                        args[0] + " [" + args[1] + "]");
            frame.getContentPane().setLayout(new BorderLayout());
            frame.getContentPane().add(new UniversalTextViewer(args[0], args[1]),
                              BorderLayout.CENTER);
            frame.addWindowListener(new AppCloser());
            frame.setSize(600, 400);
            frame.show();
        }
    }

    protected static final class AppCloser extends WindowAdapter {
        public void windowClosing(WindowEvent e) {
            System.exit(0);
        }
    }
}
```

The universal text viewer can be invoked as

```
venus% java UniversalTextViewer filename encoding
```

Figure 6.21

The universal text viewer.

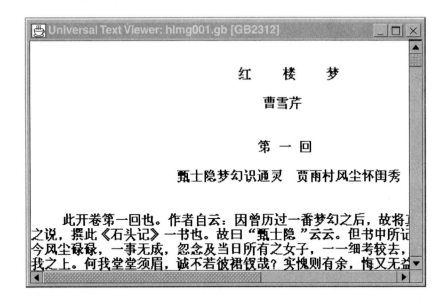

Figure 6.21 shows a screen shot of the universal text viewer presenting a text file in simplified Chinese (GB2312 encoding).[3]

6.4.3 Random Access Files

Random access files support reading and writing data at any position in the files and can support reading and writing at the same time. The `RandomAccessFile` class provides the basic capabilities of random access I/O. The constructor of the `RandomAccessFile` class is the following.

Constructor	Description
`RandomAccessFile(filename, mode)`	Creates a random access file that reads from, and optionally writes to, the file named `filename`. The mode argument is a string whose value must be either `"r"`, for read-only, or `"rw"`, for read–write.

---

[3] For the Chinese characters to be displayed properly, Chinese fonts must be installed and the `font.properties` file of the JDK or JRE must be configured to use the appropriate fonts. See the online supplement of the book for details of setting up the fonts.

The RandomAccessFile class implements both DataInput and DataOutput interfaces. Moreover, it supports the following methods for moving the read/write position. The read/write position is where the next read or write will occur. In the parameters of the methods, i is an integer, and l is a long integer.

Method	Description
seek(l)	Moves the read/write position to the lth byte counting from the beginning of the file
skipBytes(i)	Moves the read/write position i bytes relative to the current position; moves forward if i > 0 and moves backward if i < 0

EXAMPLE 6.20 Store Serialized Objects in Random Access Files

PURPOSE

This example demonstrates the use of a random access file.

DESCRIPTION

The RandomAccessFile does not implement the ObjectInput and the ObjectOutput interfaces. So serialized objects cannot be directly written to random access files. In this example, we extend the RandomAccessFile to support reading and writing serialized objects in random access files. Because serialized objects vary in size, for each object we first store its size as an integer (4-byte) and then store the serialized object itself. The writeObject() method first serializes the object in a byte array, copies the array to the file, and then the total number of bytes written to the file (including the size count) is returned. The readObject() method reads a serialized object at the current read/write position. It first reads the size count and then reads the serialized object into a byte array and deserializes the object.

SOLUTION

Class ObjectRandomAccessFile

```java
import java.io.*;

public class ObjectRandomAccessFile extends RandomAccessFile {

  protected ByteArrayOutputStream bOut;
  protected byte[] buf;

  public ObjectRandomAccessFile(String name, String mode) throws IOException {
    super(name, mode);
    bOut = new ByteArrayOutputStream();
  }

  public int writeObject(Object obj) throws IOException {
```

```
        if (obj != null &&
              obj instanceof Serializable) {
          ObjectOutputStream objOut = new ObjectOutputStream(bOut);
          objOut.writeObject(obj);
          int count = bOut.size();
          byte[] buf = bOut.toByteArray();
          writeInt(count);
          write(buf, 0, count);
          bOut.reset();
          return count + 4;
        } else {
          return 0;
        }
    }

    public Object readObject() throws IOException, ClassNotFoundException {
        int count = readInt();
        if (buf == null ||
              count > buf.length) {
          buf = new byte[count];
        }
        read(buf, 0, count);
        ObjectInputStream objIn =
              new ObjectInputStream(new ByteArrayInputStream(buf, 0, count));
        Object obj = objIn.readObject();
        objIn.close();
        return obj;
    }
}
```

The following simple test writes three serialized strings into a random access file.

Test of the `writeObject()` method of `ObjectRandomAccessFile`

```
import java.io.*;

public class TestWrite {
   public static void main(String[] args) {
      if (args.length > 0) {
        try {
          ObjectRandomAccessFile out = new ObjectRandomAccessFile(args[0], "rw");
          Object[] obj = {"Tic", "Tac", "Toe" };
          long offset = 0;
          int count;
          for (int i = 0; i < obj.length; i++) {
            count = out.writeObject(obj[i]);
            System.out.println(obj[i] + " written at offset " + offset +
                              " size = " + count);
            offset += count;
          }
        } catch (IOException e) {}
      }
   }
}
```

The output is:

```
venus% java TestWrite obj.out
Tic written at offset 0 size = 14
Tac written at offset 14 size = 14
Toe written at offset 28 size = 14
```

The following is a simple test that reads the random access file created by `Test-Write`. It expects the first argument to be the file name and the following arguments to be integers specifying the offsets at which the objects are to be read.

Test of the `readObject()` method of `ObjectRandomAccessFile`

```java
import java.io.*;

public class TestRead {
   public static void main(String[] args) {
      if (args.length > 0) {
         try {
            ObjectRandomAccessFile in = new ObjectRandomAccessFile(args[0], "r");
            Object obj;
            long offset;
            for (int i = 1; i < args.length; i++) {
               offset = Long.parseLong(args[i]);
               in.seek(offset);
               obj = in.readObject();
               System.out.println(obj + " read at offset " + offset);
            }
         } catch (Exception e) {}
      }
   }
}
```

The output is:

```
venus% java TestRead obj.out 28 14 0
Toe read at offset 28
Tac read at offset 14
Tic read at offset 0
```

CHAPTER SUMMARY

- An object-oriented application framework is a set of cooperating classes that represent reusable designs of software systems in a particular application domain. It typically consists of a set of abstract classes and interfaces that are parts of semi-complete applications that can be specialized to produce custom applications. The key characteristics of application frameworks are extendability, inversion of control, and use of design patterns.

- Although both design patterns and frameworks are mechanisms used to capture reusable designs, they are quite different. Design patterns are schematic descriptions of reusable designs that are not concrete programs and are language independent. In contrast, frameworks are semicomplete applications that are written in a specific programming language.

■ A collection is an object that contains other objects, which are called the elements of the collection. The collections framework is a set of interfaces and classes that support storing and retrieving objects in collections of varying structures, algorithms, and time–space complexities. The collections can be grouped in the following abstract collection categories.

> A bag is an unordered collection of elements that may contain duplicate elements. Bags are also known as multisets.
> A set is an unordered collection of elements with no duplicate elements.
> A sorted set is a set whose elements are automatically sorted according to a certain sequence.
> A list is an ordered collection of elements that allows duplicate elements. Lists are also known as sequences.
> A map is an unordered collection of key-value pairs. The keys in a map must be unique. Maps are also known as functions, dictionaries, or associative arrays.

Each of the abstract collections can be implemented by using different data structures and algorithms.

■ The Iterator design pattern is used to provide a uniform way to iterate through different concrete collections (i.e., polymorphic iteration). Two iterator interfaces are defined: `Iterator` and `ListIterator`.

■ The graphical user interface (GUI) framework consists of the Abstract Windows Toolkit (AWT) and the Swing portion of the Java Foundation Classes. It is a set of interfaces and classees that support the construction of graphical user interfaces with a great deal of versatility.

■ GUI widgets are the building blocks of the visual aspect of graphical user interfaces. All Java GUI widget classes are subclasses of the `Component` class. These subclasses are divided into two groups: primitive components, which do not contain other components, and containers, which may contain other primitive components and containers.

■ Each container has a layout manager, which handles the layout of the components contained in the container. Each layout manager defines a layout strategy. Commonly used layout managers include `FlowLayout`, `BorderLayout`, and `GridLayout`.

■ GUI components communicate with other applications through events, which represent user input or actions. The source of an event is the component from which the event originated. A listener of an event is an object that receives and processes the event. Events are classified as different types, with each type of event represented by an event class. Each type of event is also associated with a listener interface, which the listeners of this type of events must implement. Listeners must be registered to their respective sources before they can receive events from their sources.

- The input/output framework is a set of interfaces and classes that support the input and output of different types of objects to and from different media with varying capabilities.

- Java supports two types of I/O: stream I/O and random access I/O. A stream is a sequence of bytes. Stream-based I/O supports reading or writing data sequentially. A stream may be opened for reading or writing, but not reading and writing. There are two kinds of streams: byte streams and character streams. Byte streams support reading and writing data of any type, including strings, in the binary format. Character streams support reading and writing of text using locale dependent character encodings. Random access I/O supports reading and writing data at any position of a file. A random access file may be opened for both reading and writing.

- Serialization is the process of writing an object and all the objects that are directly or indirectly referenced by the object to a stream. Deserialization is the process of restoring an object and all the objects that are directly or indirectly referenced by the object that have been serialized.

- The Composite design pattern composes objects into tree structures to represent a part–whole hierarchy. The Composite design pattern lets clients treat individual objects and compositions of objects uniformly. The Composite design pattern should be used to represent a part–whole hierarchy of objects or to allow clients to treat all objects in the composite structure uniformly.

- The Decorator design pattern attaches additional responsibilities to an object dynamically. Decorators provide a flexible alternative to subclassing for extending functionality. The Decorator design pattern should be used to add responsibilities to individual objects dynamically without affecting other objects in the same class, or to avoid an explosion of subclasses caused by an extension by subclassing.

- The common aspects of related classes should be handled uniformly. These common aspects are usually interfaces or abstract classes. The greater the uniformity, the simpler and more useful is the design.

EXERCISES

6.1 The $\texttt{Set}$ interface defines only the most primitive operations on sets. Some of the common operations on sets that are not included in the $\texttt{Set}$ interface and their definitions are the following.

- The union of two sets:

$$S_1 \cup S_2 \equiv \{x \mid x \in S_1 \vee x \in S_2\}$$

- The intersection of two sets:

$$S_1 \cap S_2 \equiv \{x \mid x \in S_1 \wedge x \in S_2\}$$

- The nonsymmetric difference of two sets:

$$S_1 \setminus S_2 \equiv \{x \mid x \in S_1 \wedge x \notin S_2\}$$

Define and implement a class that supports these operations on sets as algorithms that can be applied to any concrete classes that implement the $\texttt{Set}$ interface.

6.2 Write a simple calculator applet. It should contain buttons for the digits, the operators

(+, −, *, and /), and the equals sign (=). The results can be displayed by using a text field.

6.3 Enhance the digital clock applet so that it can display the time of any time zone around the world. Use a choice for choosing the time zone.

6.4 Enhance the applet developed in Exercise 5.4 Use a button to dynamically switch between the pie chart display and the bar chart display. Flip the button labels as well.

6.5 Enhance the bouncing ball applet in Example 6.12 so that there can be several balls. Use a pair of buttons to increase or decrease the number of balls. If two balls collide, change the direction of their movement.

7

Design Case Study:
A Drawing Pad

CHAPTER OVERVIEW

In this chapter we present a case study in developing graphical user interfaces (GUI), using the Java Foundation class (JFC). We also demonstrate the iterative development process by designing and implementing a graphical drawing pad in successive increments. We introduce two new design patterns: Factory Method and State.

7.1   ITERATIVE DEVELOPMENT

The *iterative development process* is used to develop large-scale software systems in a succession of iterations. Each iteration builds on the result of the preceding iteration and enhances functionality in small increments. Each iteration involves a complete development cycle, including conceptualization, analysis and modeling, design, and implementation. Each iteration results in a completely functional intermediate product.

The use of design patterns plays a crucial role in the iterative development process because each increment must be designed to be flexible and extendable to accommodate changes and additions in future iterations.

We develop a graphical drawing pad in four successive iterations to demonstrate the iterative development process.

Iteration 1: Creates a simple scribble pad, which consists of only a drawing canvas.

Iteration 2: Adds a control panel that contains a Clear button to clear the canvas and a choice control to select the pen color.

Iteration 3: Enhances the scribble pad to a drawing pad by adding tools for drawing lines, rectangles, and ovals and a tool for erasing.

Iteration 4: Adds tools for typing text and drawing filled rectangles and ovals.

We use the lightweight components in the Swing package of the Java Foundation class. The drawing pad program is both an application and an applet.

7.2   ITERATION 1—A SIMPLE SCRIBBLING PAD

A screen shot of the simple scribble pad, `Scribble pad`, is shown in Figure 7.1. The key issues addressed in this iteration are developing a double-buffered canvas for drawing, handling mouse events, and making the program a dual app and applet.

The structure of the simple scribble pad is shown in Figure 7.2. The shaded classes are the ones to be developed; the rest are classes and interfaces of the Java Class Library. The classes to be developed are summarized in the following table.

Class	Description
Scribble	The top class
ScribbleCanvas	The double-buffered drawing canvas
ScribbleCanvasListener	The event listener that listens to mouse events in the drawing canvas

Figure 7.1

The simple scribble pad.

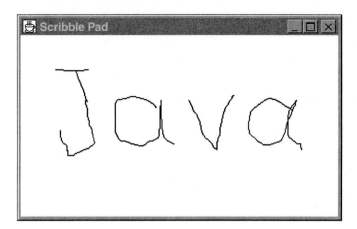

Figure 7.2

The structure of the simple scribble pad.

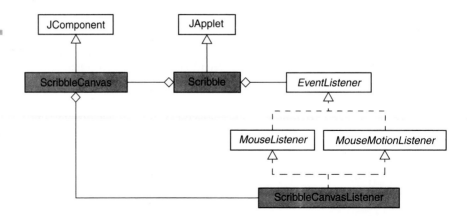

7.2.1 The Drawing Canvas

There is no Swing counterpart of the Canvas class in AWT. To have a blank space for drawing, we simply extend the JComponent class. To make the drawing smoother, we use double-buffering. The fields and methods of the ScribbleCanvas class are summarized in Table 7.1.

TABLE 7.1

Member	Description
width, height	Width and height of the canvas
im	Off-screen image
offScreen	Graphics context associated with the off-screen image
penColor	Color used for drawing
mouseButtonDown	Whether one of the mouse buttons is being pressed down
x, y	Current mouse position in the canvas
paint(), update()	Copies the off-screen image to the screen
getOffScreenGraphics()	Returns the off-screen graphics context
setPenColor()	Sets the pen color
clearCanvas()	Clears the canvas
setBounds()	Sets up the off-screen image whenever the canvas is resized

The fields mouseButtonDown, x, and y are used by the mouse event listener ScribbleCanvasListener [p. 323] for tracking the mouse position and the state of the mouse buttons.

The drawing canvas for the simple drawing pad:
ScribbleCanvas

```java
import java.awt.*;
import java.awt.event.*;
import javax.swing.*;

public class ScribbleCanvas extends JComponent {

    protected Image im;
    protected int width, height;
    protected Graphics offScreen;
    protected Color penColor = Color.black;
    protected boolean mouseButtonDown = false;
    protected int x, y;

    public ScribbleCanvas() {
        setBackground(Color.white);
    }

    public void update(Graphics g) {
        g.drawImage(im, 0, 0, this);
    }

    public void paint(Graphics g) {
        update(g);
    }

    (Method getOffScreenGraphics() on page 321)

    (Method setPenColor() on page 322)

    (Method clearCanvas() on page 322)

    (Method setBounds() on page 322)

}
```

The getOffScreenGraphics() method simply returns the off-screen graphics context for other objects to draw on the canvas.

Method of class ScribbleCanvas:
getOffScreenGraphics() on page 321

```java
public Graphics getOffScreenGraphics() {
    return offScreen;
}
```

The setPenColor() method sets the pen color used for drawing. In the current iteration, this method is not used and the pen color remains unchanged.

**Method of class `ScribbleCanvas`:
`setPenColor()` on page 321**

```
public void setPenColor(Color c) {
   penColor = c;
   offScreen.setColor(penColor);
}
```

The `clearCanvas()` method simply clears the canvas by filling the entire canvas with white color, the background color of the canvas.

**Method of class `ScribbleCanvas`:
`clearCanvas()` on page 321**

```
public void clearCanvas() {
   offScreen.setColor(Color.white);
   offScreen.fillRect(0, 0, width, height);
   offScreen.setColor(penColor);
}
```

The `setBounds()` method is declared in the `Component` class. It is invoked by the Java GUI framework before the component first becomes visible and whenever the component is resized. In the `ScribbleCanvas` class, the `setBounds()` method is overridden to set up the off-screen image of the drawing canvas. The original image is copied to the new image whenever the canvas is resized so that the drawings can be preserved.[1] The `super.setBounds()` method is invoked at the end to preserve the default behavior defined in the `Component` class.

**Method of class `ScribbleCanvas`: `SetBounds()`
on page 321**

```
public void setBounds(int x, int y,
                      int width, int height) {
   this.width = width;
   this.height = height;
   Image newIm = createImage(width, height);
   offScreen = newIm.getGraphics();
   clearCanvas();
   if (im != null) {
      offScreen.drawImage(im, 0, 0, this);
   }
   im = newIm;
   super.setBounds(x, y, width, height);
   repaint();
}
```

---

[1] This implementation preserves the drawings only when the size of the canvas is enlarged. The drawings are cropped when the canvas is shrunk. Try shrinking, then enlarging, the canvas.

7.2.2 The Mouse Event Listener

The `ScribbleCanvasListener` class handles the mouse events that occur in the drawing canvas. The desired behavior of scribbling involves the following actions.

- A stroke begins when any mouse button is pressed.
- The stroke continues when the mouse is dragged.
- The stroke finishes when the mouse button is released.

Two event listener interfaces are associated with mouse events:

1. `MouseListener`, for events related to the actions of the buttons on the mouse, such as button press and release; and
2. `MouseMotionListener`, for events related to the movement of the mouse, such as mouse move or drag.

The `ScribbleCanvasListener` class must handle button press, button release, and mouse drag actions, so it must implement both the `MouseListener` and `MouseMotionListener` interfaces. The relevant methods of the `Scribble-CanvasListener` class are summarized in the following table.

Methods	Description
`mousePressed()`	Handles the mouse button pressed event
`mouseReleased()`	Handles the mouse button released event
`mouseDragged()`	Handles the mouse dragged event

The other methods declared in the `MouseListener` and `MouseMotion-Listener` interfaces are of no interest here, so empty implementations are provided for them.

The mouse event listener for the drawing canvas:
`ScribbleCanvasListener`

```
import java.awt.*;
import java.awt.event.*;

public class ScribbleCanvasListener
    implements MouseListener, MouseMotionListener {

  public ScribbleCanvasListener(ScribbleCanvas canvas) {
    this.canvas = canvas;
  }

  protected ScribbleCanvas canvas;
```

⟨Method mousePressed() on page 324⟩
⟨Method mouseDragged() on page 324⟩
⟨Method mouseReleased() on page 325⟩

```
// The following methods are of no concern in this program.
public void mouseClicked(MouseEvent e) {}
public void mouseEntered(MouseEvent e) {}
public void mouseExited(MouseEvent e) {}
public void mouseMoved(MouseEvent e) {}
}
```

The mousePressed() method handles the beginning of a stroke. It sets the boolean flag mouseButtonDown of the ScribbleCanvas to true and stores the current mouse position. The current mouse position is obtained by invoking e.getPoint(). The position is relative to the upper-left corner of the source component (i.e., the canvas).

Method of class ScribbleCanvas:
mousePressed() on page 324

```
public void mousePressed(MouseEvent e) {
    Point p = e.getPoint();
    canvas.mouseButtonDown = true;
    canvas.x = p.x;
    canvas.y = p.y;
}
```

While the mouse is being dragged, a series of mouse drag events are posted by the Java virtual machine (JVM). Each event indicates the current mouse position. The mouseDragged() method handles the continuation of a stroke. It draws a line from the previous mouse position to the current position and updates the current mouse position in ScribbleCanvas. This method also repaints the canvas. Usually, the distance between two consecutive mouse drag events is fairly short, and the area affected by each mouse drag is fairly small. Therefore repainting the entire canvas each time the mouse is dragged is unnecessary and inefficient. In the following implementation, canvas.repaint(x0, y0, dx, dy) will repaint only the rectangle area that is located at (x0, y0) with the width and height of dx and dy, respectively.

Method of class ScribbleCanvas:
mouseDragged() on page 324

```
public void mouseDragged(MouseEvent e) {
    Point p = e.getPoint();
    if (canvas.mouseButtonDown) {
        canvas.getOffScreenGraphics().
            drawLine(canvas.x, canvas.y, p.x, p.y);
        int x0 = Math.min(canvas.x, p.x);
        int y0 = Math.min(canvas.y, p.y);
        int dx = Math.abs(p.x - canvas.x) + 1;
```

```
            int dy = Math.abs(p.y - canvas.y) + 1;
            canvas.repaint(x0, y0, dx, dy);
            canvas.x = p.x;
            canvas.y = p.y;
        }
    }
```

The `mouseReleased()` method handles the end of a drawing stroke. It sets the boolean flag `mouseButtonDown` of the canvas to `false`.

Method of class `ScribbleCanvas`: `mouseReleased()` on page 324

```
public void mouseReleased(MouseEvent e) {
    canvas.mouseButtonDown = false;
}
```

7.2.3   The `Scribble` Class

`Scribble` is the top class of the simple scribble pad. The fields and methods of the `Scribble` class are summarized in the following table.

Member	Description
`canvas`	Drawing canvas
`listener`	Mouse event listener of the drawing canvas
`isApplet`	Whether the scribble pad is invoked as an applet (It could be an app)
`makeCanvas()`	Factory method that creates the drawing canvas
`makeCanvasListener()`	Factory method that creates the mouse event listener
`main()`	Method for the scribble pad to be invoked as an app

The `Scribble` class also contains an inner `class AppCloser` for closing the top-level frame when the scribble pad is invoked as an app.

The top class of the simple scribble pad: `Scribble`

```
import java.awt.*;
import java.awt.event.*;
import java.util.EventListener;
import javax.swing.*;

public class Scribble extends JApplet {
```

```
          protected ScribbleCanvas canvas;
          protected EventListener listener;
          protected boolean isApplet = false;


          (Constructors of Scribble on page 326)

          (Method makeCanvas() on page 327)

          (Method makeCanvasListener() on page 327)

          (Method main() on page 327)

          (Inner class AppCloser)



     }
```

The `Scribble` class has two constructors. The first is the main constructor. It takes a boolean argument that indicates whether the program is invoked as an applet or application. The second is the no-arg constructor, which allows the scribble pad to be invoked as an applet. Applets are always created by the applet context, usually a Java-enabled browser, using the no-arg constructor.

The main contructor of the `Scribble` class creates an instance of the canvas and an instance of the listener. It then registers the listener to the canvas as the `MouseListener` and `MouseMotionListener`. Note that the canvas and the listener are not created directly by using the `new operator`; rather they are created indirectly by using two *factory methods*—`makeCanvas()` and `makeCanvasListener()`. When factory methods are used, creation of the canvas and the listener can be deferred to the subclasses.

The advantage of using factory methods here instead of the `new operator` is that the canvas and the listener classes can be enhanced in subsequent iterations. To use the enhanced canvas and listeners, subclasses of the `Scribble` class can override the factory methods to create instances of the enhanced canvas and listeners. No change in the `Scribble` class would be necessary. The advantages of using factory methods will become clear in Iteration 3 (see Section 7.4 [p. 332]).

Constructors of class `Scribble` on page 326

```
public Scribble(boolean isApplet) {
   this.isApplet = isApplet;
   getContentPane().setLayout(new BorderLayout());
   getContentPane().add(makeCanvas(), BorderLayout.CENTER);
   listener = makeCanvasListener(canvas);
   canvas.addMouseListener((MouseListener) listener);
   canvas.addMouseMotionListener((MouseMotionListener) listener);
}

public Scribble() {
   // invoked as an applet
   this(true);
}
```

The makeCanvas() method is the factory method for creating an instance of the drawing canvas.

Method of class Scribble:
makeCanvass() on page 326

```
protected Component makeCanvas() {
    canvas = new ScribbleCanvas();
    return canvas;
}
```

The makeCanvasListener() method is the factory method for creating an instance of the mouse event listener of the drawing canvas.

Method of class Scribble: makeCanvassListener() on page 326

```
protected EventListener makeCanvasListener(ScribbleCanvas canvas) {
    return new ScribbleCanvasListener(canvas);
}
```

The main() method creates a frame and places an instance of the Scribble class at the center.

Method of class Scribble: main() on page 326

```
public static void main(String[] args) {
    JFrame frame = new JFrame();
    frame.setTitle("Scribble Pad");
    frame.getContentPane().setLayout(new BorderLayout());
    frame.getContentPane().add(new Scribble(false),
                            BorderLayout.CENTER);
    frame.addWindowListener(new AppCloser());
    frame.pack();
    frame.setSize(600, 400);
    frame.show();
}
```

AppCloser is an inner class whose purpose is to terminate the application when the Close Window button on the frame is clicked.

Inner class of class Scribble: AppCloser
on page 326

```
static class AppCloser extends WindowAdapter {
    public void windowClosing(WindowEvent e) {
        System.exit(0);
    }
}
```

This completes the first iteration. The result is a simple but completely functional program.

7.2.4   Idiom: Dual Applet/Application

The `Scribble` class illustrates the dual applet/application idiom that makes a program both an applet and an application.

Idiom   *Dual Applet/Application*

Category: Structural implementation idiom.
Intent: Makes a Java program both an applet and an application.
Applicability: When a program needs to be invoked as an applet or an app, with identical behavior.

Implementation of a dual applet/app, using Swing, is as follows.

```java
public class DualAppletApp extends JApplet {

protected boolean isApplet;

public DualAppletApp(boolean isApplet) {
   this.isApplet = isApplet;
   // ...
   if (!isApplet) {
      init();
      start();
   }

}

public DualAppletApp() {
   // invoked as an applet
   this(true);
}

public static void main(String[] args) {
   // invoked as an app
   JFrame frame = new JFrame();
   frame.setTitle(title);
   frame.getContentPane().setLayout(new BorderLayout());
```

```
        frame.getContentPane().add(new DualAppletApp(false),
                                    BorderLayout.CENTER);
        frame.addWindowListener(new FrameListener());
        frame.pack();
        frame.setSize(width, height);
        frame.show();
    }
}
```

The first constructor is called the *main* constructor, and the second is called the *applet* constructor. Invocations of the `init()` and `start()` methods in the main constructor are optional. They are necessary when the `init()` or `start()` methods of `Applet` are overriden in `DualAppletApp` with nonempty implementations. In the main constructor of `Scribble`, neither method is invoked. In the main constructor of `DrawingPad` in Iteration 3 [p. 356], the `init()` method is invoked. Implementation of this idiom with AWT is quite similar: The `JApplet` and `JFrame` classes are replaced by `Applet` and `Frame`, respectively.

7.3 ITERATION 2—THE CONTROL PANEL

In this iteration, we enhance the simple scribble pad in Iteration 1 by adding a control panel that contains a Clear button to clear the canvas and a choice control to choose the pen color. A screen shot of the enhanced scribble pad, `Scribble Pad 2`, is shown in Figure 7.3, and the structure of the enhanced scribble pad is shown in Figure 7.4. This iteration involves one new class—`Scribble2` (the shaded class in Figure 7.4), which extends the `Scribble` class from Iteration 1.

Figure 7.3

The enhanced scribble pad.

Figure 7.4

The structure of
the enhanced
scribble pad.

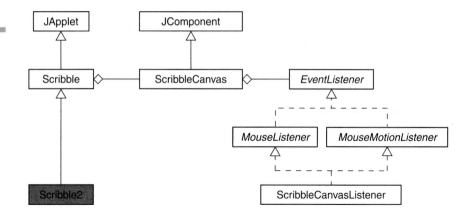

The `Scribble2` class contains a control panel created by the factory method `makeControlPanel()`. The `Scribble2` class has two inner classes, `Clear-ButtonListener` and `ColorChoiceListener`, which are event listeners for the button and the choice on the control panel.

The top class of the enhanced scribble pad: `Scribble2`

```
import java.awt.*;
import java.awt.event.*;
import java.util.EventListener;
import javax.swing.*;

public class Scribble2 extends Scribble {

   public Scribble2(boolean isApplet) {
      super(isApplet);
      getContentPane().add(makeControlPanel(), BorderLayout.SOUTH);
   }

   public Scribble2() {
      // invoked as an applet
      this(true);
   }

   (Method makeControlPanel() on page 331)

   (Method main() on page 332)

   (Inner class ClearButtonListener on page 331)

   (Inner class ColorChoiceListener on page 331)

}
```

The first constructor of the `Scribble2` class is the main constructor. The no-arg constructor invokes the scribble pad as an applet. The main constructor of `Scribble2` invokes the constructor of its superclass `Scribble`. After the drawing canvas and the mouse event listener have been created by the constructor of the

Scribble class, a new control panel is created and inserted to the south position of the border layout.

The makeControlPanel() method is a factory method for creating the control panel, which is an instance of the JPanel class. It contains a button labeled Clear, a text label Pen color, and a choice control that contains the names of commonly used colors.

Method of class Scribble2: makeControlPanel()
on page 330

```
protected Component makeControlPanel() {
    JPanel controlPanel = new JPanel();
    JButton button = new JButton("Clear");
    controlPanel.add(button);
    button.addActionListener(new ClearButtonListener());

    controlPanel.add(new JLabel("Pen color"));
    JComboBox choice = new JComboBox();
    choice.addItem("black");
    choice.addItem("blue");
    choice.addItem("green");
    choice.addItem("red");
    choice.addItemListener(new ColorChoiceListener());
    controlPanel.add(choice);
    return controlPanel;
}
```

The inner class ClearButtonListener is the listener for the Clear button and clears the canvas.

Inner class of class Scribble2: ClearButtonListener
on page 330

```
class ClearButtonListener implements ActionListener {
    public void actionPerformed(ActionEvent event) {
        canvas.clearCanvas();
        canvas.repaint();
    }
}
```

The inner class ColorChoiceListener is the listener for the color choice control.

Inner class of class Scribble2: ColorChoiceListener
on page 330

```
class ColorChoiceListener implements ItemListener {
    public void itemStateChanged(ItemEvent event) {
        if (event.getStateChange() == ItemEvent.SELECTED) {
```

```
                    if ("black".equals(event.getItem())) {
                      canvas.setPenColor(Color.black);
                    } else if ("blue".equals(event.getItem())) {
                      canvas.setPenColor(Color.blue);
                    } else if ("green".equals(event.getItem())) {
                      canvas.setPenColor(Color.green);
                    } else if ("red".equals(event.getItem())) {
                      canvas.setPenColor(Color.red);
                    }
                  }
                }
              }
```

The main() method of the Scribble2 class is identical to the main() method of the Scribble class, except that it places an instance of Scribble2 instead of Scribble at the center.

Method of class Scribble2: main() on page 330

```
public static void main(String[] args) {
  JFrame frame = new JFrame();
  frame.setTitle("Scribble Pad 2");
  frame.getContentPane().setLayout(new BorderLayout());
  frame.getContentPane().add(new Scribble2(false),
                             BorderLayout.CENTER);
  frame.addWindowListener(new AppCloser());
  frame.pack();
  frame.setSize(600, 400);
  frame.show();
}
```

This completes the second iteration.

7.4   ITERATION 3—THE DRAWING TOOLS

In this iteration, we further enhance the scribble pad to create a drawing pad. A screen shot of the drawing pad, Drawing Pad, is shown in Figure 7.5. The drawing pad has a tool bar at the left, with each tool button representing a different tool. The tools supported by this drawing pad are the scribbling tool, the line drawing tool, the rectangle drawing tool, the oval drawing tool, and the eraser tool.

The key issues addressed in this iteration are use of the State design pattern to support the different behaviors associated with different tools and to switch dynamically among different tools; use of the Factory Method design pattern to allow some flexibility in the constructors of a class; and use of the advanced GUI components in Swing to build image buttons, a tool bar, a menu bar, tool tips, and a dialog box (see Figure 7.5).

Figure 7.5

The drawing pad.

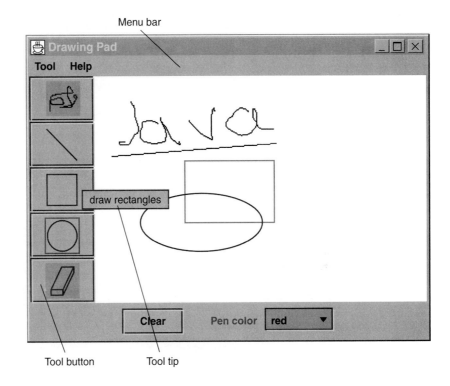

Menu bar

Tool button   Tool tip

The structure of the drawing pad is shown in Figure 7.6. The shaded classes are the new classes to be developed.

7.4.1 Support for Multiple Tools

The drawing pad supports multiple tools, so the responses to a mouse button press or release and mouse dragging on the drawing canvas depend on which tool is currently selected. In the `DrawingPad` class, an integer field is used to indicate which tool is currently selected.

```
public class DrawingPad {

    // constants representing tools
    public static final int SCRIBBLE_TOOL = 0;
    public static final int LINE_TOOL = 1;
    public static final int RECTANGLE_TOOL = 2;
    public static final int OVAL_TOOL = 3;
    public static final int ERASER_TOOL = 4;

    // the currently selected tool
    protected int currentTool = SCRIBBLE_TOOL;
```

Figure 7.6

The structure of
the drawing pad.

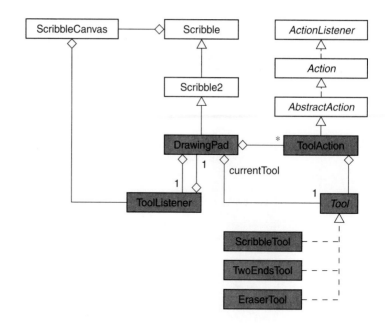

```
// set the current tool
public void setCurrentToo(int toolId) {
    currentTool = toolId;
}

// get the current tool
public int getCurrentTool() {
    return currentTool;
}

// other fields and methods
}
```

In the `listener` class of the canvas, the methods handling mouse button press
and release and mouse dragging are somewhat like the following.

```
public class DrawingPadListener
    implements MouseListener, MouseMotionListener {

    protected ScribbleCanvas canvas;
    protected DrawingPad     drawingPad;

    public ScribbleCanvasListener(ScribbleCanvas canvas,
                                  DrawingPad drawingPad) {
        this.canvas = canvas;
        this.drawingPad = drawingPad;
    }

    public void mousePressed(MouseEvent e) {
        Point p = e.getPoint();
        switch (drawingPad.getCurrentTool()) {
```

```
      case DrawingPad.SCRIBBLE_TOOL:
         // handle mouse pressed for the scribble tool
         break;
      case DrawingPad.LINE_TOOL:
         // handle mouse pressed for the line tool
         break;
      case DrawingPad.RECTANGLE_TOOL:
         // handle mouse pressed for the rectangle tool
         break;
      case DrawingPad.OVAL_TOOL:
         // handle mouse pressed for the oval tool
         break;
      case DrawingPad.ERASER_TOOL:
         // handle mouse pressed for the eraser tool
         break;
      }
}

public void mouseReleased(MouseEvent e) {
   Point p = e.getPoint();
   switch (drawingPad.getcCurrentTool()) {
   case DrawingPad.SCRIBBLE_TOOL:
      // handle mouse released for the scribble tool
      break;
   case DrawingPad.LINE_TOOL:
      // handle mouse released for the line tool
      break;
   case DrawingPad.RECTANGLE_TOOL:
      // handle mouse released for the rectangle tool
      break;
   case DrawingPad.OVAL_TOOL:
      // handle mouse released for the oval tool
      break;
   case DrawingPad.ERASER_TOOL:
      // handle mouse released for the eraser tool
      break;
   }
}

public void mouseDragged(MouseEvent e) {
   Point p = e.getPoint();
   switch (drawingPad.getCurrentTool()) {
   case DrawingPad.SCRIBBLE_TOOL:
      // handle mouse dragged for the scribble tool
      break;
   case DrawingPad.LINE_TOOL:
      // handle mouse dragged for the line tool
      break;
   case DrawingPad.RECTANGLE_TOOL:
      // handle mouse dragged for the rectangle tool
      break;
```

```
        case DrawingPad.OVAL_TOOL:
            // handle mouse dragged for the oval tool
            break;
        case DrawingPad.ERASER_TOOL:
            // handle mouse dragged for the eraser tool
            break;
        }
    }

    //...
}
```

This implementation works. However, it is not very flexible and rather inelegant, for the following reasons. First, the coupling between the DrawingPad and DrawingPadListener classes is high. The labels of the switch statements in the DrawingPadListener class must exactly match the constants defined in the DrawingPad class. Adding new tools or removing existing tools requires coordinating changes in both classes. Second, the behavior of each tool is defined in three separate methods—mousePressed(), mouseReleased(), and mouseDragged()—intermixed with the behaviors of all other tools. Thus any change to the behavior of a tool requires coordinated changes in three methods. This requirement is a severe hindrance to the readability of the code and makes changes to the code error-prone.

A better implementation is to encapsulate the behavior of each tool in a separate class. The behavior of each tool is defined by its response to the following events: mouse button pressed, mouse button released, and mouse dragged. The following interface Tool represents an abstraction of the tools. Here a tool is an instance of a class that implements the Tool interface.

Interface Tool

```
import java.awt.*;

public interface Tool {
    void mousePressed(Point p, ScribbleCanvas canvas);
    void mouseReleased(Point p, ScribbleCanvas canvas);
    void mouseDragged(Point p, ScribbleCanvas canvas);
}
```

In this iteration, we define three concrete tools: ScribbleTool [p. 340], EraserTool [p. 340], and TwoEndsTool [p. 341].

7.4.2   The Current Tool of the Drawing Pad

The DrawingPad class is the top-level class of the drawing pad. The members of the DrawingPad class are summarized in Table 7.2.

TABLE 7.2

Member	Description
`currentTool`	Current tool being selected
`getCurrentTool()`	Gets the current tool
`setCurrentTool()`	Sets the current tool
`init()`	Initializes the program
`makeToolBar()`	Auxiliary method that creates the tool bar
`makeMenuBar()`	Auxiliary method that creates the menu bar
`makeCanvasListener()`	Factory method that creates the listener of the canvas
`initActions()`	Auxiliary method that initializes the actions associated with the tools
`getImageIcon()`	Auxiliary method that creates the icons on the tool buttons
`AboutAction`	Inner class that pops up a dialog box when the About menu is selected

The top class of the drawing pad: `DrawingPad`

```java
import java.awt.*;
import java.awt.event.*;
import java.net.*;
import java.util.*;
import javax.swing.*;

public class DrawingPad extends Scribble2 {

    protected Tool currentTool;

    public void setCurrentTool(Tool tool) {
        currentTool = tool;
    }

    public Tool getCurrentTool() {
        return currentTool;
    }

    〈Constructors of DrawingPad on page 356〉

    〈Method init() on page 350〉

    〈Method makeToolBar() on page 351〉

    〈Method makeMenuBar() on page 351〉

    〈Method makeCanvasListener() on page 354〉
```

(Method initActions() on page 352)

(Method getImageIcon() on page 353)

(Method main() on page 356)

(Inner class AboutAction on page 352)

```
        }
```

7.4.3   The Mouse Event Listener of the Canvas

The mouse event listener associated with the drawing canvas simply delegates the handling of mouse button presses and releases and mouse dragging to the current tool.

The mouse event listener for the drawing pad

```java
import java.awt.*;
import java.awt.event.*;
import java.util.EventListener;

public class ToolListener extends ScribbleCanvasListener {

    protected DrawingPad drawingPad;

    public ToolListener(DrawingPad drawingPad,
                        ScribbleCanvas canvas) {
        super(canvas);
        this.drawingPad = drawingPad;
    }

    public void mousePressed(MouseEvent e) {
        Tool tool = drawingPad.getCurrentTool();
        if (tool != null) {
            tool.mousePressed(e.getPoint(), canvas);
        }
    }

    public void mouseReleased(MouseEvent e) {
        Tool tool = drawingPad.getCurrentTool();
        if (tool != null) {
            tool.mouseReleased(e.getPoint(), canvas);
        }
    }

    public void mouseDragged(MouseEvent e) {
        Tool tool = drawingPad.getCurrentTool();
        if (tool != null) {
            tool.mouseDragged(e.getPoint(), canvas);
        }
    }
}
```

7.4.4 Design Pattern: State

The mouse event listener design illustrates the use of the State design pattern. With it we are able to encapsulate the behavior of each tool in a separate class and decouple tools from the `DrawingPad` class. As we show in the next iteration, this allows much easier addition of tools.

Design Pattern *State*

Category: Behavioral design pattern.
Intent: Allow an object to alter its behavior when its internal state changes.
Also Known As: Objects for states.
Applicability: Use the State design pattern when

- an object's behavior depends on its state and it must change its behavior at run time, depending on that state (e.g., selecting among several tools), and

- methods have large, multipart conditional statements that depend on the object's state (e.g., the switch statements in the `DrawingPadListener` class [p. 334]).

The structure of the State design pattern is shown in the following diagram.

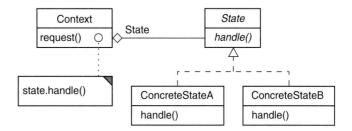

The participants of the State design pattern are

- *Context* (e.g., `DrawingPad`), which maintains an instance of a `Concrete-State` that defines the current state (e.g., the `currentTool` field in the `DrawingPad` class);

- *State* (e.g., `Tool`), which defines an interface for encapsulating the behavior associated with a particular state of the `Context`; and

- *ConcreteState* (e.g., `ScribbleTool`, `TwoEndsTool`, and `EraserTool`), in which each subclass implements a behavior associated with a state of `Context`.

7.4.5 The Scribble Tool

The `ScribbleTool` class is a concrete tool for scribbling. When the scribble tool is selected, the behavior of the drawing pad is identical to that of the scribble pad in the previous two iterations. Implementation of the methods in `ScribbleTool` is essentially the same as implementation of the corresponding methods in `ScribbleCanvasListener` [p. 323].

A tool for scribbling: `ScribbleTool`

```java
import java.awt.*;

public class ScribbleTool implements Tool {

    public void mousePressed(Point p, ScribbleCanvas canvas) {
        canvas.mouseButtonDown = true;
        canvas.x = p.x;
        canvas.y = p.y;
    }

    public void mouseDragged(Point p, ScribbleCanvas canvas) {
        if (canvas.mouseButtonDown) {
            int x0, y0, dx, dy;
            x0 = Math.min(canvas.x, p.x);
            y0 = Math.min(canvas.y, p.y);
            dx = Math.abs(p.x - canvas.x) + 1;
            dy = Math.abs(p.y - canvas.y) + 1;
            canvas.getOffScreenGraphics().
                drawLine(canvas.x, canvas.y, p.x, p.y);
            canvas.repaint(x0, y0, dx, dy);
            canvas.x = p.x;
            canvas.y = p.y;
        }
    }

    public void mouseReleased(Point p, ScribbleCanvas canvas) {
        canvas.mouseButtonDown = false;
    }

}
```

7.4.6 The Eraser Tool

The eraser tool erases the drawing under the mouse pointer. It fills a 5 × 5 (pixels) square centered on the mouse pointer with the background color—white.

A tool for erasing drawings: `EraserTool`

```java
import java.awt.*;

public class EraserTool implements Tool {

    Graphics offScreen;

    public void mousePressed(Point p, ScribbleCanvas canvas) {
        canvas.mouseButtonDown = true;
        canvas.x = p.x;
        canvas.y = p.y;
        offScreen = canvas.getOffScreenGraphics();
        offScreen.setColor(Color.white);
    }

    public void mouseDragged(Point p, ScribbleCanvas canvas) {
        if (canvas.mouseButtonDown) {
            int x0, y0, dx, dy;
            x0 = Math.min(canvas.x, p.x) - 2;
            y0 = Math.min(canvas.y, p.y) - 2;
            dx = Math.abs(p.x - canvas.x) + 5;
            dy = Math.abs(p.y - canvas.y) + 5;
            offScreen.fillRect(x0, y0, dx, dy);
            canvas.repaint(x0, y0, dx, dy);
            canvas.x = p.x;
            canvas.y = p.y;
        }
    }

    public void mouseReleased(Point p, ScribbleCanvas canvas) {
        canvas.mouseButtonDown = false;
        canvas.setPenColor(canvas.penColor);
    }

}
```

7.4.7 The Two-Ends Tool

When we select the line-drawing, rectangle-drawing, or oval-drawing tool, we can use the mouse to draw a line, a rectangle, or a circle. Although these shapes have little in common, the ways in which they are drawn are quite similar. Each shape can be defined by two points: the two endpoints for lines and the two diagonally opposite corners for rectangles and ovals. We call these two points the *endpoints*. These shapes are drawn as follows.

■　When the mouse button is pressed, the current mouse position is the first endpoint of the selected shape.

■　When the mouse is dragged, temporary frames of the selected shape are drawn. These temporary frames follow the mouse as it is being dragged. This process is commonly known as *rubber banding* because dragging the mouse is like stretching a rubber band.

■ When the mouse button is released, the current mouse position is the second endpoint of the selected shape. The selected shape defined by the two endpoints is drawn.

Because of the similarities in drawing lines, rectangles, and ovals, we design a single tool, the `TwoEndsTool`, to handle all three shapes. Each shape is identified by an integer constant: `LINE`, `OVAL`, or `RECT`. The fields of the `TwoEndsTool` are summarized in the following table.

Field	Description
shape	Shape to be drawn
xStart, yStart	Coordinates of the first endpoint
onScreen	On-screen graphics context for drawing the temporary frames during rubber banding

A tool for drawing lines, rectangle, and ovals: **`TwoEndsTool`**

```
import java.awt.*;

public class TwoEndsTool implements Tool {
   public static final int LINE = 0;  // constant for the line shape
   public static final int OVAL = 1;  // constant for the oval shape
   public static final int RECT = 2;  // constant for the rectangle shape
   protected int shape = LINE;        // the default shape is line
   protected int xStart, yStart;
   protected Graphics onScreen;

   public TwoEndsTool(int shape) {
      this.shape = shape;
   }

   (Method mousePressed() on page 343)

   (Method mouseDragged() on page 343)

   (Method mouseReleased() on page 344)

   Auxiliary methods drawLine(), drawRect(), and drawOval() on page 344)
}
```

The `mousePressed()` method records the coordinates of the first endpoint and prepares for rubber banding. Rubber banding is accomplished by using the *exclusive-or* (XOR) mode of the graphics context. When the XOR mode is used in a graphics context and a figure is drawn once, the figure is visible. However, the color of the figure depends not only on the current pen color but also on the colors of the pixels that the figure covers. When the same figure is drawn twice in the same position, the figure disappears.

Method of class `TwoEndsTool`: `mousePressed()` on page 342

```
public void mousePressed(Point p, ScribbleCanvas canvas) {
   canvas.mouseButtonDown = true;
   xStart = canvas.x = p.x;
   yStart = canvas.y = p.y;
   onScreen = canvas.getGraphics();
   onScreen.setXORMode(Color.darkGray);
   onScreen.setColor(Color.lightGray);

   switch (shape) {
   case LINE:
      drawLine(onScreen, xStart, yStart, xStart, yStart);
      break;
   case OVAL:
      drawOval(onScreen, xStart, yStart, 1, 1);
      break;
   case RECT:
      drawRect(onScreen, xStart, yStart, 1, 1);
      break;
   }
}
```

The `mouseDragged()` method performs the rubber banding. The fields `canvas.x` and `canvas.y` are the coordinates of the preceding intermediate endpoint. Two frames are drawn: one at the preceding endpoint to erase the previous frame and the other one at the current endpoint. Rubber banding is done directly in the on-screen graphics. The `repaint()` method is not invoked.

Method of class `TwoEndsTool`: `mouseDragged()` on page 342

```
public void mouseDragged(Point p, ScribbleCanvas canvas) {
   if (canvas.mouseButtonDown) {
      switch (shape) {
      case LINE:
         drawLine(onScreen, xStart, yStart, canvas.x, canvas.y);
         drawLine(onScreen, xStart, yStart, p.x, p.y);
         break;
      case OVAL:
         drawOval(onScreen, xStart, yStart,
                  canvas.x - xStart + 1, canvas.y - yStart + 1);
         drawOval(onScreen, xStart, yStart,
                  p.x - xStart + 1, p.y - yStart + 1);
         break;
      case RECT:
         drawRect(onScreen, xStart, yStart,
                  canvas.x - xStart + 1, canvas.y - yStart + 1);
         drawRect(onScreen, xStart, yStart,
                  p.x - xStart + 1, p.y - yStart + 1);
         break;
```

```
      }
      canvas.x = p.x;
      canvas.y = p.y;
    }
  }
```

The `mouseReleased()` method sets the second endpoint of the shape. It sets the mode of the on-screen graphics context to the default paint mode. The selected shape is drawn in the off-screen graphics, and the `canvas.repaint()` method is invoked to copy the off-screen image to the screen.

Method of class `TwoEndsTool`: `mouseReleased()` on page 342

```
public void mouseReleased(Point p, ScribbleCanvas canvas) {
    canvas.mouseButtonDown = false;
    onScreen.setPaintMode();
    Graphics offScreen = canvas.getOffScreenGraphics();
    switch (shape) {
    case LINE:
        drawLine(offScreen, xStart, yStart, p.x, p.y);
        break;
    case OVAL:
        drawOval(offScreen, xStart, yStart,
                 p.x - xStart + 1, p.y - yStart + 1);
        break;
    case RECT:
        drawRect(offScreen, xStart, yStart,
                 p.x - xStart + 1, p.y - yStart + 1);
        break;
    }
    canvas.repaint();
}
```

The following auxiliary methods simply draw lines, rectangles, and ovals, respectively. The `drawRect()` and `drawOval()` methods remove the restriction of the corresponding methods in the `Graphics` class—that the width and the height must be nonnegative.

Auxiliary static methods of class `TwoEndsTool`: `drawLine()`, `drawRect()`, and `drawOval()` on page 342

```
public static void drawLine(Graphics g, int x1, int y1, int x2, int y2) {
    g.drawLine(x1, y1, x2, y2);
}

public static void drawRect(Graphics g, int x, int y, int w, int h) {
    if (w < 0) {
        x = x + w; w = -w;
    }
    if (h < 0) {
        y = y + h; h = -h;
    }
```

```
      g.drawRect(x, y, w, h);
   }

public static void drawOval(Graphics g, int x, int y, int w, int h) {
   if (w < 0) {
      x = x + w; w = -w;
   }
   if (h < 0) {
      y = y + h; h = -h;
   }
   g.drawOval(x, y, w, h);
}
```

7.4.8   Icons

Icons are small pictures of fixed size and typically are used to decorate components, such as buttons and menu items. Icons are represented by the `Icon` interface in Swing.

```
public interface Icon {
   void paintIcon(Component c, Graphics g, int x, int y);
   int getIconWidth();
   int getIconHeight();
}
```

The `ImageIcon` class in Swing implements the `Icon` interface. An image icon can be created by giving a file name or a URL that contains an image in GIF or JPEG format. Image icons can be created as follows.

```
Icon icon1 = new ImageIcon("java.gif");
Icon icon2 = new ImageIcon("http://venus.cs.depaul.edu/se/java.jpg");
```

In the drawing pad, the icons for the scribbling and erasing tools are created from image files (see Figure 7.5). Icons can also be created by drawing the picture desired. The icons of the line, rectangle, and oval drawing tools in the drawing pad are created by drawing. To draw icons, we implement the `Icon` interface and draw the pictures of the icons with the `paintIcon()` method. The methods of the `Icon` interface are summarized in the following table.

Methods	Description
paintIcon()	Draws the picture of the icon
getIconWidth()	Returns the width of the icon
getIconHeight()	Returns the height of the icon

The `ToolIcon` class draws the tool icons used in the current and the next iteration of the drawing pad (see Figures 7.5 and 7.9).

Class ToolIcon

```java
import java.awt.*;
import java.awt.event.*;
import javax.swing.*;
public class ToolIcon implements Icon {
   public static final int LINE = 1;
   public static final int RECT = 2;
   public static final int OVAL = 3;
   public static final int FILLRECT = 4;
   public static final int FILLOVAL = 5;
   public static final int TEXT = 6;

   protected Dimension dim = new Dimension(36, 36);
   protected int id;

   public ToolIcon(int id) {
      this.id = id;
   }

   public void paintIcon(Component c, Graphics g, int x, int y) {
      Color oldColor = g.getColor();
      g.setColor(c.getBackground());
      g.fillRect(x, y, dim.width, dim.height);
      g.setColor(Color.black);
      int x0 = x + 2;
      int y0 = y + 2;
      int w0 = dim.width - 4;
      int h0 = dim.height - 4;
      switch (id) {
      case LINE:
         g.drawLine(x0, y0, x0 + w0, y0 + h0);
         break;
      case RECT:
         g.drawRect(x0, y0, w0, h0);
         break;
      case OVAL:
         g.drawOval(x0, y0, w0, h0);
         break;
      case FILLRECT:
         g.fillRect(x0, y0, w0, h0);
         break;
      case FILLOVAL:
         g.fillOval(x0, y0, w0, h0);
         break;
      case TEXT:
         g.setFont(new Font("Serif", Font.BOLD, h0));
         FontMetrics fm = g.getFontMetrics();
         g.drawString("T", x0, y0 + fm.getAscent());
         break;
      }
      g.setColor(oldColor);
   }

   public int getIconWidth() { return dim.width; }
   public int getIconHeight() { return dim.height; }
}
```

Figure 7.7

The buttons in
Swing.

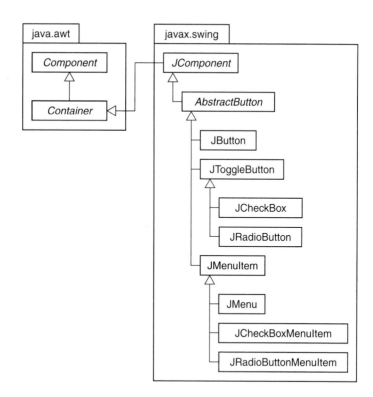

7.4.9 Buttons

The `Button` class in AWT can have only a text label. The `JButton` class in Swing can have a text label, an icon, or both. For example, instances of the `JButton` class can be created as follows.

```
JButton button1 = new JButton("A Label");
JButton button2 = new JButton(icon1);
JButton button3 = new JButton("A Label", icon1);
```

Swing provides a variety of buttons (see Figure 7.7). The `AbstractButton` class is the common superclass of all button classes. Most of the methods of the button classes are defined in the `AbstractButton` class. Hence instances of different button classes can be manipulated in rather similar ways. The methods of the `AbstractButton` class are summarized in Table 7.3.

7.4.10 Tool Selection

In the drawing pad, each tool is represented by a button on the tool bar and a menu item, which is also a button, on the menu bar. Tools can be selected from either the

TABLE 7.3

Method	Description
setText (*text*)	Set the text label
getText()	Get the text label
setIcon(*icon*)	Set the icon
getIcon()	Get the icon
setVerticalAlignment(*align*)	Set the vertical alignment to one of:
	TOP, CENTER, BOTTOM
getVerticalAlignment()	Get the vertical alignment setting
setHorizontalAlignment(*align*)	Set the horizontal alignment to one of:
	LEFT, CENTER, RIGHT
getHorizontalAlignment()	Get the horizontal alignment setting
setVerticalTextPosition(*pos*)	Set the vertical text position relative to the Icon to one of:
	TOP, CENTER, BOTTOM
getVerticalTextPosition()	Get the vertical text position relative to the Icon
setHorizontalTextPosition(*pos*)	Set the horizontal text position relative to the icon to one of:
	LEFT, CENTER, RIGHT
getHorizontalTextPosition()	Get the horizontal text position relative to the icon

tool bar or the menu bar. The action of a button on the tool bar or a menu item in the menu bar is to set its corresponding tool as the current tool of the drawing pad.

The Action interface in Swing provides a useful extension to the Action-Listener interface in cases where the same functionality may be accessed by several controls, such as from the tool buttons or menu items. In addition to the actionPerformed() method defined by the ActionListener interface, the Action interface allows the application to define, in a single place,

▪ one or more text strings that describe the function, which can be used, for example, to display the *flyover* text for a button (i.e., the tool tip) or to set the text in a menu item;

- one or more icons that depict the function, which can be used for the images in a tool button or menu item; and
- the enabled/disabled state of the functionality.

Containers in Swing, such as menu bars and tool bars, can add an `Action` object and other components, using a version of the `add()` method. When an `Action` object is added to such a container, the container

- creates a component that is appropriate for that container (e.g., a tool bar creates a button component),
- retrieves the appropriate attributes from the `Action` object to customize the component (e.g., the icon image and tool tip text), and
- sets the initial enabled or disabled state of the `Action` object and renders the component in the appropriate fashion.

The following constants are defined in the `Action` interface as keys for setting or getting the various attributes (text or icon).

```
NAME       DEFAULT       LONG_DESCRIPTION
SHORT_DESCRIPTION     SMALL_ICON
```

The methods of the `Action` interface are summarized in the following table.

Methods	Description
`putValue(key, value)`	Set an attribute using the associated key
`getValue(key)`	Retrieve an attribute using the associated key
`setEnabled(b)`	Set the enabled state
`isEnabled()`	Test the enabled state

The `AbstractAction` class is an abstract class that implements all the methods in the `Action` interface, except the `actionPerformed()` method. Concrete action classes often subclass the `AbstractAction` class.

We declare the `ToolAction` class for the drawing pad by subclassing the `AbstractAction` class. Each instance of the `ToolAction` class contains an instance of a concrete tool class; a name, which is used as the text label of the menu item; an icon that is keyed by the constant `Action.DEFAULT`; and a tool tip text that is keyed by the constant `Action.SHORT_DESCRIPTION`.

Class `ToolAction`

```
import java.awt.*;
import java.awt.event.*;
import java.util.EventListener;
import javax.swing.*;

public class ToolAction extends AbstractAction {

    public ToolAction(String name, Icon icon, String tip,
                        DrawingPad drawingPad, Tool tool) {
        super(name);
        putValue(Action.DEFAULT, icon);
        putValue(Action.SHORT_DESCRIPTION, tip);
        setEnabled(tool != null);
        this.drawingPad = drawingPad;
        this.tool = tool;
    }

    public void actionPerformed(ActionEvent event) {
        drawingPad.setCurrentTool(tool);
    }

    protected DrawingPad drawingPad;
    protected Tool tool;
}
```

The action objects for tools, the tool bar, and the menu bar are initialized in the init() method. First, a list of action objects for the tools are created by the initActions() method. Then the action list is used to create the tool bar in method makeToolBar(). Finally, the action list is used to create the menu bar in method makeMenuBar().

Method of class `DrawingPad`: `init()` on page 337

```
public void init() {
    List actions = initActions();
    getContentPane().add(makeToolBar(actions), BorderLayout.WEST);
    getContentPane().add(makeMenuBar(actions), BorderLayout.NORTH);
}
```

7.4.11   Tool Bar Construction

The tool bar is a container that contains buttons for the tools. The lightweight container class Box in Swing is suitable for the tool bar. It uses a BoxLayout object as its layout manager, which allows multiple components to be laid out either vertically (from left to right) or horizontally (from top to bottom). The components will not wrap when the container is resized. When we create a BoxLayout, we specify whether its major axis is the *x* axis or *y* axis. Components are arranged in the same order as they were added to the container.

The method makeToolBar() retrieves the actions from the action list actions. It creates an image button for each tool and attaches a tool tip to each tool button. It returns the tool bar.

Method of class DrawingPad: makeToolBar() on page 337

```
protected Component makeToolBar(List actions) {
   Box toolBar = new Box(BoxLayout.Y_AXIS);
   Iterator iter = actions.iterator();
   while (iter.hasNext()) {
     Action a = (Action) iter.next();
     JButton button =
        new JButton((Icon) a.getValue(Action.DEFAULT));
     button.setToolTipText(
        (String) a.getValue(Action.SHORT_DESCRIPTION));
     button.addActionListener(a);
     toolBar.add(button);
   }
   toolBar.add(Box.createVerticalGlue());
   return toolBar;
}
```

7.4.12 Menu Bar Construction

The method makeMenuBar() creates a menu bar that consists of two menus: *Tool* and *About*. The makeToolBar() method retrieves the actions in the action list actions and adds a menu item to the *Tool* menu for each tool. The add() method of the JMenu class used here takes an action object. It adds a menu item to the menu. The name of the action is the label of the menu item and the action object is registered as the action listener of the menu item.

Method of class DrawingPad: makeMenuBar() on page 337

```
protected Component makeMenuBar(List actions) {
   JMenuBar menuBar = new JMenuBar();
   JMenu tools = new JMenu("Tool");
   Iterator iter = actions.iterator();
   while (iter.hasNext()) {
     Action a = (Action) iter.next();
     tools.add(a);
   }
   menuBar.add(tools);
   JMenu help = new JMenu("Help");
   help.add(new AboutAction());
   menuBar.add(help);
   return menuBar;
}
```

7.4.13 Pop-Up Dialog

The AboutAction class is an inner class that defines the action associated with the *About* menu item. It pops up an information dialog box with the version and copyright information, using the JOptionPane class in Swing. The JOptionPane class provides various static methods to display the most commonly used dialog boxes with a single method invocation.

Inner class of class DrawingPad: AboutAction on page 338

```java
class AboutAction extends AbstractAction {

  public AboutAction() {
    super("About"); // the name of the action
  }

  public void actionPerformed(ActionEvent event) {
    JOptionPane.showMessageDialog(null,
                         "DrawingPad version 1.0" +
                         "Copyright (c) Xiaoping Jia 1999",
                         "About",
                         JOptionPane.INFORMATION_MESSAGE);
  }

}
```

7.4.14 Action List Construction

The initActions() method creates an action for each tool and inserts the actions in a list.

Method of class DrawingPad: initActions() on page 338

```java
protected List initActions() {
  List actions = new ArrayList();
  actions.add(
    new ToolAction("Scribble",                          // name
                   getImageIcon("scribble.gif"),        // icon
                   "scribble tool",                     // tip
                   this,
                   currentTool = new ScribbleTool()));
  actions.add(
    new ToolAction("Line",                              // name
                   new ToolIcon(ToolIcon.LINE),         // icon
                   "draw line segments",                // tip
                   this,
                   new TwoEndsTool(TwoEndsTool.LINE)));
```

```
actions.add(
   new ToolAction("Rectangle",                                    // name
                  new ToolIcon(ToolIcon.RECT),                    // icon
                  "draw rectangles",                              // tip
                  this,
                  new TwoEndsTool(TwoEndsTool.RECT)));
actions.add(
   new ToolAction("Oval",                                         // name
                  new ToolIcon(ToolIcon.OVAL),                    // icon
                  "draw ovals",                                   // tip
                  this,
                  new TwoEndsTool(TwoEndsTool.OVAL)));
actions.add(
   new ToolAction("Eraser",                                       // name
                  getImageIcon("eraser.gif"),                     // icon
                  "eraser tool",                                  // tip
                  this,
                  new EraserTool()));
   return actions;
}
```

This method uses an auxiliary method getImageIcon() to create image icons for the tool buttons. How the image icons are created depends on whether the drawing pad is invoked as an applet or app. If the drawing pad is invoked as an app, image icons can be created by reading files on the local host. If the drawing pad is invoked as an applet, it is prohibited from reading files on the local host. The image icons can be created by reading files on the server.

**Method of class DrawingPad: getImageIcon()
on page 338**

```
protected ImageIcon getImageIcon(String fileName) {
   if (isApplet) {
      try {
         URL url = new URL(getCodeBase(), fileName);
         return new ImageIcon(url);
      } catch (MalformedURLException e) {
         return null;
      }
   } else {
      return new ImageIcon(fileName);
   }
}
```

7.4.15   The Drawing Canvas Listener

We have built all the components we need in this iteration. The only task left is to register an instance of the ToolListener class as the mouse event listener of the drawing canvas. We can accomplish this task in the main constructor of the DrawingPad class.

```
public DrawingPad(boolean isApplet) {
  super(isApplet);
  listener = new ToolListener(this, canvas);
  canvas.addMouseListener((MouseListener) listener);
  canvas.addMouseMotionListener((MouseMotionListener) listener);
  // ...
}
```

In this implementation, before the `ToolListener` object is created and registered, the constructors of all the superclasses (i.e., `Scribble` and `Scribble2`) are invoked. In the constructor of the superclass `Scribble`, an instance of the `ScribbleCanvasListener` class is created and registered as the mouse listener of the drawing canvas. Actually, creation and registration of this object is totally unnecessary, as it is immediately replaced by a `ToolListener` object in the constructor of the `DrawingPad`.

To avoid the unnecessary creation and registration of the `ScribbleCanvasListener` object and to allow subclasses to create and register the appropriate listener objects, a factory method `makeCanvasListener()` is used to create indirectly the listener object. In the `DrawingPad` class, the factory method `makeCanvasListener()` is overridden to create the `ToolListener` object.

Method of class `DrawingPad`:
`makeCanvasListener()` on page 337

```
protected EventListener makeCanvasListener(
        ScribbleCanvas canvas) {
  return new ToolListener(this, canvas);
}
```

The sequence of invocations involved in using the factory method is illustrated in Figure. 7.8. The three instances in the diagram are actually the same object being treated as instances of three different classes.

Figure 7.8

The invocation sequence of **`DrawingPad()`**.

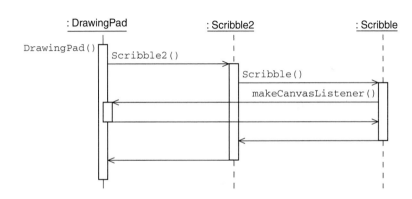

7.4.16 Design Pattern: Factory Method

Factory methods comprise another design pattern.

Design Pattern   *Factory Method*

    Category: Creational design pattern.
    Intent: Define an interface for creating an object but let subclasses decide
        which class to instantiate.
    Also Known As: Virtual constructor.
    Applicability: Use the Factory Method design pattern when

      ▪   a class cannot anticipate the class of objects it must create, and

      ▪   a class wants its subclass to specify the objects it creates.

The structure of the Factory Method design pattern is shown in the following diagram.

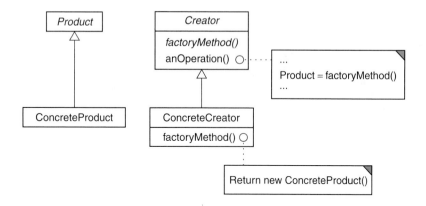

The participants of the Factory Method design pattern are

- *Product* (e.g., `EventListener`), which defines the interface of the objects the factory method creates;
- *ConcreteProduct* (e.g., `ScribbleCanvasListener` and `ToolListener`), which implements the `Product` interface;
- *Creator* (e.g., `Scribble`), which declares the factory method (e.g., `makeCanvasListener()`) that returns an object of type `Product`, may also define a default implementation of the factory method that returns a default `Concrete-Product` object (e.g., implementation of the `makeCanvasListener()`

method in the `Scribble class`), and may call factory method to create a `Product` object (e.g., invocation of the `makeCanvasListener()` method in the Scribble constructor); and

■ *ConcreteCreator* (e.g., `DrawingPad`), which overrides the factory method to return an instance of a `ConcreteProduct` (e.g., implementation of the `makeCanvasListener()` method in the `DrawingPad` class).

Factory Method and Factory (see Section 5.3.2) are different design patterns. The Factory design pattern involves a factory class whose sole responsibility is to create objects. The Factory Method is for a class to defer the creation of certain objects to its subclasses.

7.4.17 The Constructors and the `main()` Method

The constructors and the `main()` method of the `DrawingPad` class use the dual applet/app idiom. In the main constructor, the `init()` method should be explicitly invoked when the drawing pad is invoked as an application.

Constructors of class `DrawingPad`
on page 337

```
public DrawingPad() {
   // invoked as an applet
   this(true);
}

public DrawingPad(boolean isApplet) {
   super(isApplet);
   if (!isApplet) {
      init();
   }
}
```

Method of class `DrawingPad`: `main()` on page 338

```
public static void main(String[] args) {
   JFrame frame = new JFrame();
   frame.setTitle("Drawing Pad");
   frame.getContentPane().setLayout(new BorderLayout());
   frame.getContentPane().add(new DrawingPad(false), BorderLayout.CENTER);
   frame.addWindowListener(new AppCloser());
   frame.pack();
   frame.setSize(600, 400);
   frame.show();
}
```

This completes the third iteration.

7.5   ITERATION 4—MORE TOOLS

In this iteration, we further enhance the drawing pad by adding tools to support using the keyboard to type text and drawing filled ovals and rectangles. A screen shot of the enhanced drawing pad, `Drawing Pad 2`, is shown in Figure 7.9, and the structure of the enhanced drawing pad is shown in Figure 7.10. The shaded classes in the diagram are the new classes to be developed in this iteration. The key issues addressed in this iteration are handling keyboard input and keyboard focus and using the Strategy design pattern to eliminate switch statements for the sake of flexibility.

7.5.1   Handling Keyboard Input

The `Tool` interface defined earlier is intended to handle the input from a mouse. It is inadequate to handle input from a keyboard. The following is an extended interface for handling key presses on a keyboard.

Figure 7.9

The enhanced drawing pad.

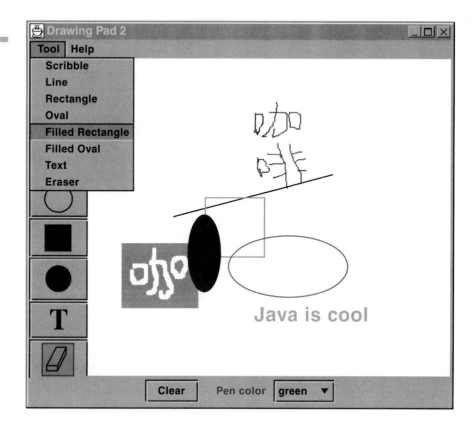

Figure 7.10

The enhanced
drawing pad.

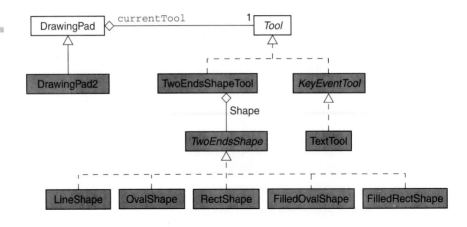

Extended tool interface: `KeyEventTool`

```
public interface KeyEventTool extends Tool {
    void keyPressed(char c, ScribbleCanvas canvas);
}
```

The event listener of the canvas must also be extended to receive and handle the events originating from the keyboard. The listener interface for keyboard events is `KeyListener`. The extended event listener of the canvas is presented in the following program.

Extended tool listener: `KeyToolListener`

```
import java.awt.*;
import java.awt.event.*;
import java.util.EventListener;

public class KeyToolListener extends ToolListener
        implements KeyListener {
    public KeyToolListener(DrawingPad drawingPad,
                           ScribbleCanvas canvas) {
        super(drawingPad, canvas);
    }

    (Method keyPressed() on page 359)
    (Method mouseClicked() on page 359)

    // the following methods are of no concern here
    public void keyReleased(KeyEvent e) {}
    public void keyTyped(KeyEvent e) {}
}
```

The method `keyPressed()` of a key listener is invoked when one or more keys on the keyboard is pressed. In the following implementation, if the current tool is an instance of `KeyEventTool`, the `keyPressed()` method of the current tool is invoked; otherwise, the key press is ignored.

Method of class `KeyToolListener: keyPressed()`
on page 358

```
public void keyPressed(KeyEvent e) {
   Tool tool = drawingPad.getCurrentTool();
   if (tool != null &&
       tool instanceof KeyEventTool) {
     KeyEventTool keyTool = (KeyEventTool) tool;
     keyTool.keyPressed((char) e.getKeyChar(), canvas);
   }
}
```

When dealing with input from the keyboard, we face another complication: keyboard focus. Often several windows are open on the screen, and multiple components could accept input from the keyboard. However, only one component will receive the input at any moment: the component that currently has the *keyboard focus*. The component having the keyboard focus is determined by a focus manager, which provides a set of conventions for navigating the focus. In our drawing pad, we specify that whenever the mouse is clicked on a component, that component will have the keyboard focus. Therefore clicking the mouse on the canvas ensures that the canvas has the keyboard focus. The method `mouseClicked()` of the event listener of the canvas implements this specification by requesting keyboard focus when a mouse click event occurs on the canvas.

Method of class `KeyToolListener:`
`mouseClicked()` on page 358

```
public void mouseClicked(MouseEvent e) {
   canvas.requestFocus();
}
```

The Text Input Tool

The `TextTool` class handles input from the keyboard. The `text` field stores the characters that have been typed. Because the `text` field needs to be updated whenever a key is pressed, we use `StringBuffer` instead of `String` for the sake of efficiency.

Text input tool: `TextTool`

```
import java.awt.*;
import java.awt.event.*;

class TextTool implements KeyEventTool {
  protected StringBuffer text;
```

```
protected Font font =
  new Font("Serif", Font.BOLD, 24);
protected FontMetrics fm =
  Toolkit.getDefaultToolkit().getFontMetrics(font);
protected int ascent = fm.getAscent();
protected int descent = fm.getDescent();
protected Graphics offScreen;

⟨Methods mousePressed(), mouseDragged(), and mouseReleased() on page 360⟩

⟨Method keyPressed() on page 360⟩
}
```

A mouse press indicates the position in the canvas where the text will be displayed.

**Methods of class `TextTool`: `mousePressed()`,
`mouseDragged()`, and `mouseReleased()` on page 360**

```
public void mousePressed(Point p, ScribbleCanvas canvas) {
   canvas.mouseButtonDown = true;
   canvas.x = p.x;
   canvas.y = p.y;
   offScreen = canvas.getOffScreenGraphics();
   offScreen.setFont(font);
   text = new StringBuffer();
}

public void mouseDragged(Point p, ScribbleCanvas canvas) {}

public void mouseReleased(Point p, ScribbleCanvas canvas) {
   canvas.mouseButtonDown = false;
}
```

Whenever a key is pressed, the corresponding character is appended to `text`, and it is drawn in the canvas. This way of handling keyboad input is rather primitive. It does not support editing capabilities, such as deleting characters and moving the cursor.

Method of class `TextTool`: `keyPressed()` on page 360

```
public void keyPressed(char c, ScribbleCanvas canvas) {
   text.append(c);
   offScreen.drawString(text.toString(), canvas.x, canvas.y);
   canvas.repaint(canvas.x, canvas.y - ascent - 1,
                  fm.stringWidth(text.toString()) + 1,
                  ascent + descent + 2);
}
```

7.5.2 Drawing Filled Shapes

Drawing filled rectangles and ovals is similar to drawing unfilled rectangles and ovals. They can be handled by modifying the `TwoEndsTool` as follows.

```
public class TwoEndsTool implements Tool {
public static final int FILLED_OVAL = ... ;
public static final int FILLED_RECT = ... ;
public void mousePressed(Point p, ScribbleCanvas canvas) {
   // ...
   switch (shape) {
   case LINE: // ...
   case OVAL: // ...
   case RECT: // ...
      case FILLED_OVAL: // ...
      case FILLED_RECT: // ...
      }
   }

   public void mouseDragged(Point p, ScribbleCanvas canvas) {
      // ...
      switch (shape) {
      case LINE: // ...
      case OVAL: // ...
      case RECT: // ...
      case FILLED_OVAL: // ...
      case FILLED_RECT: // ...
      }
   }

   public void mouseReleased(Point p, ScribbleCanvas canvas) {
      // ...
      switch (shape) {
      case LINE: // ...
      case OVAL: // ...
      case RECT: // ...
      case FILLED_OVAL: // ...
      case FILLED_RECT: // ...
      }
   }
}
```

Modification is required for each new shape. The relevant code segments for each shape are scattered in three different methods: mousePressed(), mouseDragged(), and mouseReleased(). Modifications to these methods must be carefully coordinated because the shapes to be drawn are tightly coupled with the two-ends tool. Adding new shapes would be much simpler if the shapes to be drawn were decoupled from the two-ends tool.

Using the Strategy Design Pattern

Another situation in which the Strategy design pattern is useful is when the shapes to be drawn by the two-ends tool are captured as the abstract strategy defined in the TwoEndsShape interface. The specific two-ends shapes are the concrete strategies, and each two-ends shape is completely determined by its two endpoints. The drawShape() method draws the shape when the two endpoints are given. The drawOutline() method draws a temporary frame of the shape for rubber banding.

Interface TwoEndsShape

```java
import java.awt.*;

public interface TwoEndsShape {
    void drawShape(Graphics g, int x1, int y1, int x2, int y2);
    void drawOutline(Graphics g, int x1, int y1, int x2, int y2);
}
```

The refined two-ends tool, the TwoEndsShapeTool class, is the context of the Strategy design pattern that refers to the abstract strategy but not to the concrete strategies (i.e., the specific shapes). Adding new shapes requires no modification to the context, the TwoEndsShapeTool class.

Class TwoEndsShapeTool

```java
import java.awt.*;

public class TwoEndsShapeTool implements Tool {
    protected int xStart, yStart;
    protected TwoEndsShape shape;
    protected Graphics onScreen;

    public TwoEndsShapeTool(TwoEndsShape shape) {
        this.shape = shape;
    }

    ⟨Method mousePressed() on page 363⟩

    ⟨Method mouseDragged() on page 363⟩

    ⟨Method mouseReleased() on page 363⟩

}
```

The mousePressed(), mouseDragged(), and mouseReleased() methods delegate the call to the concrete strategy.

Method of class TwoEndsShapeTool: mousePressed on page 362

```java
public void mousePressed(Point p, ScribbleCanvas canvas) {
    canvas.mouseButtonDown = true;
    xStart = canvas.x = p.x;
    yStart = canvas.y = p.y;
    onScreen = canvas.getGraphics();
    onScreen.setXORMode(Color.darkGray);
    onScreen.setColor(Color.lightGray);
    if (shape != null) {
        shape.drawOutline(onScreen, xStart, yStart, xStart, yStart);
    }
}
```

Method of class `TwoEndsShapeTool`: mouseDragged on page 362

```java
public void mouseDragged(Point p, ScribbleCanvas canvas) {
  if (canvas.mouseButtonDown &&
      shape != null) {
    shape.drawOutline(onScreen, xStart, yStart, canvas.x, canvas.y);
    shape.drawOutline(onScreen, xStart, yStart, p.x, p.y);
    canvas.x = p.x;
    canvas.y = p.y;
  }
}
```

**Method of class `TwoEndsShapeTool`: mouseReleased
on page 362**

```java
public void mouseReleased(Point p, ScribbleCanvas canvas) {
  canvas.mouseButtonDown = false;
  onScreen.setPaintMode();
  if (shape != null) {
    Graphics offScreen = canvas.getOffScreenGraphics();
    shape.drawShape(offScreen, xStart, yStart, p.x, p.y);
    canvas.repaint();
  }
}
```

Concrete Two-Ends Shapes

The following are two concrete two-ends shapes. The LineShape class represents
line segments.

Class `LineShape`

```java
import java.awt.*;

public class LineShape implements TwoEndsShape {
  public void drawShape(Graphics g, int x1, int y1, int x2, int y2) {
    g.drawLine(x1, y1, x2, y2);
  }

  public void drawOutline(Graphics g, int x1, int y1, int x2, int y2) {
    g.drawLine(x1, y1, x2, y2);
  }
}
```

The FilledRectShape class represents filled rectangles.

Class `FilledRectShape`

```java
public class FilledRectShape implements TwoEndsShape {
  public void drawShape(Graphics g, int x1, int y1, int x2, int y2) {
    int x = Math.min(x1, x2);
```

```
      int y = Math.min(y1, y2);
      int w = Math.abs(x1 - x2) + 1;
      int h = Math.abs(y1 - y2) + 1;
      g.fillRect(x, y, w, h);
   }

  public void drawOutline(Graphics g, int x1, int y1, int x2, int y2) {
      int x = Math.min(x1, x2);
      int y = Math.min(y1, y2);
      int w = Math.abs(x1 - x2) + 1;
      int h = Math.abs(y1 - y2) + 1;
      g.drawRect(x, y, w, h);
   }
}
```

The DrawingPad2 Class

The enhanced drawing pad, DrawingPad2, extends DrawingPad. Implementation of the factory method makeCanvasListener() is again overridden, as a new event listener that listens for keyboard events must be created. The new event listener must also be registered to the canvas as a key listener.

The top class of the enhanced drawing pad DrawingPad2

```
import java.awt.*;
import java.awt.event.*;
import java.util.*;
import javax.swing.*;

public class DrawingPad2 extends DrawingPad {

   public DrawingPad2() {
      // invoked as an applet
      this(true);
   }

   public DrawingPad2(boolean isApplet) {
      super(isApplet);
      canvas.addKeyListener((KeyListener) listener);
   }

   protected EventListener makeCanvasListener(ScribbleCanvas canvas) {
      return new KeyToolListener(this, canvas);
   }

   (Method initActions() on page 365)

   (Method main() on page 366)

}
```

The initActions() method is overridden to create tools. The scribble and eraser tools are identical to those in DrawingPad. The behaviors of the tools for drawing lines, rectangles, and ovals are identical to those of the corresponding tools in DrawingPad. However, the tools are instances of TwoEndsShapeTool instead of TwoEndsTool. The tools for drawing filled rectangles and filled ovals and the tool for typing text are the new tools added in this iteration.

Method of class DrawingPad2: initActions on page 365

```
protected List initActions() {
  List actions = new ArrayList();
  actions.add(
    new ToolAction("Scribble",                          // name
                   getImageIcon("scribble.gif"),        // icon
                   "scribble tool",                     // tip
                   this,
                   currentTool = new ScribbleTool()));
  actions.add(
    new ToolAction("Line",                              // name
                   new ToolIcon(ToolIcon.LINE),         // icon
                   "draw line segments",                // tip
                   this,
                   new TwoEndsShapeTool(new LineShape())));
  actions.add(
    new ToolAction("Rectangle",                         // name
                   new ToolIcon(ToolIcon.RECT),         // icon
                   "draw rectangles",                   // tip
                   this,
                   new TwoEndsShapeTool(new RectShape())));
  actions.add(
    new ToolAction("Oval",                              // name
                   new ToolIcon(ToolIcon.OVAL),         // icon
                   "draw ovals",                        // tip
                   this,
                   new TwoEndsShapeTool(new OvalShape())));
  actions.add(
    new ToolAction("Filled Rectangle",                  // name
                   new ToolIcon(ToolIcon.FILLRECT),     // icon
                   "draw filled rectangles",            // tip
                   this,
                   new TwoEndsShapeTool(new FilledRectShape())));
  actions.add(
    new ToolAction("Filled Oval",                       // name
                   new ToolIcon(ToolIcon.FILLOVAL),     // icon
                   "draw filled ovals",                 // tip
                   this,
                   new TwoEndsShapeTool(new FilledOvalShape())));
  actions.add(
    new ToolAction("Text",                              // name
                   new ToolIcon(ToolIcon.TEXT),         // icon
                   "type text",                         // tip
                   this,
                   new TextTool()));
```

```
            actions.add(
              new ToolAction("Eraser",                           // name
                             getImageIcon("eraser.gif"),         // icon
                             "eraser tool",                      // tip
                             this,
                             new EraserTool()));
            return actions;
          }
```

The `main()` method is similar to those in the previous iterations.

Method of class `DrawingPad2: main()` on page 365

```
public static void main(String[] args) {
  JFrame frame = new JFrame();
  frame.setTitle("Drawing Pad 2");
  frame.setBackground(Color.lightGray);
  frame.getContentPane().setLayout(new BorderLayout());
  frame.getContentPane().add(new DrawingPad2(false), BorderLayout.CENTER);
  frame.addWindowListener(new AppCloser());
  frame.pack();
  frame.setSize(700, 500);
  frame.show();
}
```

This completes the fourth iteration.

CHAPTER SUMMARY

- The iterative process is used to develop large-scale software systems in a succession of iterations. Each iteration builds on the result of the preceding iteration and enhances functionality in small increments. Each iteration involves a complete development cycle, including conceptualization, analysis and modeling, design, and implementation. Each iteration results in a completely functional intermediate product.

- Design patterns, such as Strategy, Templetate Method, Factory Method, and State, are often used in the iterative development process to allow the functionality of systems to be enhanced incrementally and changed dynamically.

- The State design pattern allows an object to alter its behavior when its internal state changes. The State design pattern should be used when an object's behavior depends on its state and it must change its behavior at run time, depending on that state, or when methods have large, multipart conditional statements that depend on the object's state.

- The Factory Method design pattern defines an interface for creating an object but lets subclasses decide which class to instantiate. The Factory Method design pattern should be used when a class cannot anticipate the class of objects it must create or when a class wants its subclass to specify the objects it creates.

- A dual applet/application is a Java program that can be invoked as either an applet or an application. In both cases, program behavior will be identical.

EXERCISES

7.1. Use the iterative development approach to add some of the following enhancements to the drawing pad program.

   (a) Add a new choice control to the control panel of the drawing pad to allow the user to set a different background color.

   (b) Add new drawing tools to draw diamonds and polygons.

   (c) Add a menu item to the drawing pad for changing the font used in drawing text.

   (d) In the current version of the drawing pad, the drawings are cropped when the canvas is shrunk. Enhance the drawing pad so that the drawings remain intact when the canvas is enlarged or shrunk. (*Hint:* Define classes to represent the drawings in the canvas (e.g., *scribble*, *rectangle*, *text*, etc.) and store the drawings as a set of objects.)

   (e) Use object serialization to save the drawings in a file and to load the drawings from a file.

8

Concurrent Programming

CHAPTER OVERVIEW

In this chapter we introduce concurrent, or multithreaded, programming. We discuss the mechanisms that Java provides to support concurrent programming. We also address the issues of synchronization and cooperation among threads.

8.1 THREADS

Concurrent programming is also known as *multithreaded programming*. A *thread* is a single sequential flow of control within a program. Most conventional programming languages are single-threaded, or sequential. A single-threaded program can handle only one task at any given moment during its execution. In contrast, a *multithreaded*, or *concurrent*, program has multiple threads running simultaneously and so may handle multiple tasks at the same time during its execution. It is not necessary to have multiprocessor systems to run multithreaded programs. Most modern operating systems support *multitasking*, which allows multithreaded programs to run on single-processor systems on a time-sharing basis.

Multithreaded programming offers some important advantages over single-threaded programming.

- It is suitable for developing *reactive systems*, which continuously monitor arrays of sensors and react to control systems according to the sensor readings.

Examples of reactive systems include autopilot systems, which control modern aircraft from takeoff to landing, and patient monitoring systems, which monitor patients' vital signs.

- It makes applications more responsive to user input. For example, it allows a GUI application to respond to user input immediately even if the application is engaged in a time-consuming computation task.

- It allows a server to handle multiple clients simultaneously.

- It may take advantage of the availability of multiple processors by executing the threads on different processors in parallel.

However, multithreaded programming is more difficult than single-threaded programming because each thread proceeds independently from the others. The exact order of execution of different threads is nondeterministic. Interaction and cooperation among different threads often become complicated. Such complications may lead to *safety* and *liveness* problems, which are unique to multithreaded programs. Multithreaded programs also involve significant overhead, owing to the cost of thread creation, context switching, and synchronization.

Threads are different from *processes*. A process is a heavyweight flow that executes concurrently with other processes. A thread is a lightweight flow that executes concurrently with other threads within the same process.

8.1.1 Creation of Threads

A thread is an instance of the `java.lang.Thread` class. A `Thread` object is also known as an *active object*. The graphical notation for active objects is shown in Figure 8.1.

Threads can be created and declared in one of two ways: by directly extending the `java.lang.Thread` class or by implementing the `java.lang.Runnable` interface.

Extending the `Thread` Class

All threads are instances of the `Thread` class. Therefore the most straightforward way of defining a new thread is by directly extending the `Thread` class. The `run()` method of the `Thread` class is a hook method, which must be overridden in the subclass. The `run()` method defines the body of the thread and is similar to the `main()` method of a sequential program. The `run()` method of a thread is invoked

Figure 8.1

Graphical notation for active objects (i.e., threads).

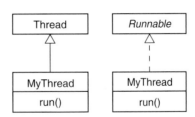

when execution starts. Execution of a thread ends when the `run()` method returns. A template for defining a new thread class is presented in the following program segment.

```
public class MyThread extends Thread {
    public void run() {
        // the thread body
    }

    // other methods and fields
}
```

To start a new thread defined by `MyThread`, we have to create an instance of the `MyThread` class and invoke the `start()` method, which indirectly invokes the `run()` method: `new MyThread().start();`.

Conversely, the `run()` method should not be invoked directly. Doing so would cause the method to be executed in the thread of the caller, not in a new thread.

EXAMPLE 8.1   A Simple Counter

PURPOSE

This example demonstrates thread creation by extending the `Thread` class.

DESCRIPTION

This class defines a thread whose body consists of an infinite loop. It maintains a counter, which is incremented by the amount of `inc` in each iteration. Each iteration of the loop sleeps a duration specified by the field `delay` in milliseconds.

A simple thread class: `Counter1`

```
public class Counter1 extends Thread {

    protected int count;
    protected int inc;
    protected int delay;

    public Counter1(int init, int inc, int delay) {
        this.count = init;
        this.inc = inc;
        this.delay = delay;
    }

    public void run() {
        try {
            for (;;) {
                System.out.print(count + " ");
                count += inc;
                sleep(delay);
            }
        } catch (InterruptedException e) {}
    }
```

```
public static void main(String[] args) {
  new Counter1(0, 1, 33).start();
  new Counter1(0, -1, 100).start();
}

}
```

SOLUTION

Two threads are started in the `main()` method. Both start counting from 0, but in different directions. The second thread, the one with a negative increment, receives a longer delay. Note in the following output that the output from the two threads is interleaved.

```
venus% java Counter1
0 0 1 2 -1 3 4 5 -2 6 7 8 -3 9 10 -4 11 12 13 -5 14 15 16 -6 17 18
-7 19 20 21 -8 22 23 24 -9 25 26 -10 27 28 -11 29 30 31 -12 32 33
34 -13 35 36 37 -14 38 39 -15 40 41 42 -16 43 44 45 -17 46 47 -18
48 49 50 -19 51 52 -20 53 54 55 -21 56 57 -22 58 59 60 -23 61 62 63
-24 64 65 -25 66 67 68 -26 69 70 -27 71 72 73 -28 74 75 -29 76 77
-30 78 79 80 -31 81 82 83 -32 84 85 -33 86 87 88 -34 89 90 91 -35
92 93 -36 94 95 96 -37 97 98 -38 99 100 -39 101 102 103 -40 104 105
106 -41 107 108 -42 109 -43 110 111 -44 112 113 114 -45 115 116 -46
...
```

Execution of this program actually involves three threads: the thread that executes the `main()` method and the two `Counter1` threads created inside the `main()` method. The thread that executes the `main()` method terminates when the `main()` method returns from creating the two `Counter1` threads. The two `Counter1` threads will run concurrently and indefinitely until they are explicitly killed. ▪

EXAMPLE 8.2   Stock Quote Generator

PURPOSE

This is another example that demonstrates thread creation by extending the `Thread` class.

DESCRIPTION

The random number generation function `Math.random()` is used to simulate the fluctuation of stock prices.

Stock quote generator: `Quote`

```
public class Quote extends Thread {

  protected int value;

  public Quote(int init) {
    value = init;
  }
```

```
public void run() {
    try {
        for (;;) {
            System.out.println(value);
            value += (Math.random() - 0.4) * (10.0 * Math.random());
            sleep(100);
        }
    } catch (InterruptedException e) {}
}

public static void main(String[] args) {
    new Quote(100).start();
}

}
```

SOLUTION

The following is the output.

```
venus% java Quote
100
99
97
98
99
99
100
100
100
101
104
103
102
101
...
```

Implementing the `Runnable` Interface

Defining threads by directly extending the `Thread` class is one solution. Sometimes, however, using it is not possible because Java supports only single inheritance among classes. For example, applets are required to extend the class `java.applet.Applet`. Thus applets cannot also extend the `Thread` class. Java provides an alternative for defining threads—by means of the `Runnable` interface.

The `Runnable` interface is rather simple. It consists of a single method, `run()`.

```
public interface Runnable {
    public abstract void run();
}
```

A template for defining a new thread class by implementing the `Runnable` interface is shown in the following code fragment. As in the first approach, the `run()` method defines the body of the thread.

```
public class MyThread extends AnotherClass implements Runnable {
   public void run() {
      // the thread body
   }

   // other methods and fields
}
```

To start a new thread defined in this way, we must first create an instance of MyThread. We use the instance to create an instance of Thread and then invoke the start() method: `new Thread(new MyThread()).start();`.

EXAMPLE 8.3   *Another Implementation of the Simple Counter*

PURPOSE

This example demonstrates thread creation by implementation of the Runnable interface.

DESCRIPTION

This class defines a thread that behaves the same as the one in Example 8.1.

SOLUTION

A simple thread class: `Counter2`

```
public class Counter2 implements Runnable {

   protected int count;
   protected int inc;
   protected int delay;

   public Counter2(int init, int inc, int delay) {
      this.count = init;
      this.inc = inc;
      this.delay = delay;
   }

   public void run() {
      try {
         for (;;) {
            System.out.print(count + " ");
            count += inc;
            Thread.sleep(delay);
         }
      } catch (InterruptedException e) {}
   }

   public static void main(String[] args) {
      new Thread(new Counter2(0, 1, 33)).start();
      new Thread(new Counter2(0, -1, 100)).start();
   }

}
```

The following is the output.

```
venus% java Counter2
0 0 1 2 -1 3 4 5 -2 6 7 8 -3 9 10 -4 11 12 13 -5 14 15 16 -6 17 18
-7 19 20 21 -8 22 23 24 -9 25 26 -10 27 28 -11 29 30 31 -12 32 33
34 -13 35 36 -14 37 38 39 -15 40 41 42 -16 43 44 45 -17 46 47 -18
48 49 50 -19 51 52 -20 53 54 55 -21 56 57 -22 58 59 60 -23 61 62 63
-24 64 65 -25 66 67 68 -26 69 70 -27 71 72 -28 73 74 -29 75 76 77
-30 78 79 -31 80 81 82 -32 83 84 -33 85 86 87 -34 88 89 90 -35 91
92 -36 93 94 95 -37 96 97 -38 98 99 -39 100 101 102 -40 103 104 105
-41 106 107 -42 108 109 110 -43 111 112 -44 113 114 115 -45 116 117
...
```

8.1.2   Controlling Threads

Programmers have only high level control of thread execution by controlling the states of the life cycle of threads. The execution of threads are ultimately controlled by the JVM and the underlying operating system. Programmers may also influence the execution of threads by manipulating the priorities of threads.

The Life Cycle of a Thread

The life cycle of a thread is shown in Figure 8.2 on a state chart. A thread can be in one of the following states.

Figure 8.2

The life cycle of threads.

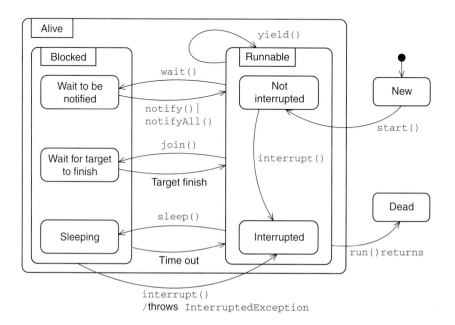

New   A thread is in the New state after its creation (i.e., new MyThread())
    and before the start() method is invoked.
Alive   When the start() method is invoked on a thread, it enters the Alive
    state. The run() method is invoked implicitly, and the execution of the
    thread begins. The Alive state has two substates.
    Runnable Threads in the Runnable state are ready to run. Threads in this
        state may be running or waiting for their turn to run.
    Blocked   A thread in the Blocked state is not ready to run. It is blocked
        until certain events happen, at which time it may become runnable.
Dead   A thread enters the Dead state, when the run() method returns. A
    dead thread cannot be restarted.

The methods of the Thread class for controlling threads are summarized in
Table 8.1.

TABLE 8.1

Method	Description
start()	The thread should be in the New state. The start() method causes the thread to enter the Alive state and start execution.
sleep()	The thread should be in the Runnable state. The sleep() method causes the thread to enter the Blocked state and sleep a given amount of time. It will be awakened when the specified duration of time expires and returned to the Runnable state.
join()	The thread should be in the Runnable state. The join() method causes the thread to enter the Blocked state and wait for another thread to finish, at which time it will be returned to the Runnable state.
yield()	The thread should be in the Runnable state and will remain in the Runnable state. The yield() method gives other runnable threads an opportunity to run.
interrupt()	If the thread is in the Runnable state, the interrupted flag will be set. If the thread is in the Blocked state, it is awakened, enters the Runnable state, and an InterruptedException is thrown.
isAlive()	Returns true if the thread is in the Alive state.
isInterrupted()	Returns true if the interrupted flag is set.

The `wait()`, `notify()`, and `notifyAll()` methods defined in the `Object` class also affect the states of threads. Invoking the `wait()` method on an object will cause the thread to be blocked until either the `notify()` or `notifyAll()` method is invoked on the same object, at which time the thread will be returned to the Runnable state. The `wait()`, `notify()`, and `notifyAll()` methods are discussed in more detail in Section 8.2.2 [p. 385].

Thread Priority and Scheduling

The Java virtual machine implements a rather simple scheduling strategy to determine which of the runnable threads should be running. It is based on the *priority* of each runnable thread. Each thread contains a priority attribute, which is an integer value assigned when the thread is created. By default, a new thread has the same priority as the one that creates it. The priority of a thread may be changed during its lifetime.

The JVM will select the runnable thread with the highest priority for execution. If more than one runnable thread have the same priority, the highest one will be selected *arbitrarily*. In other words, the JVM is not required to guarantee *fairness*. A thread of higher priority will preempt a thread of lower priority.

A thread that is currently running will relinquish control when it yields (i.e., `yield()` is invoked), it is blocked, (i.e., `sleep()`, `join()`, or `wait()` is invoked), a thread with a higher priority becomes runnable, and its time-slice has expired. The following guideline is an important constraint on the use of priorities.

Design Guideline   *Thread Priority*

Use priorities only to tune the performance of programs. The correctness of programs should not depend on the priorities of the threads involved.

8.2   THREAD SAFETY AND LIVENESS

Safety properties are conditions that should hold throughout the lifetime of a program. They stipulate that nothing bad will ever happen. An important safety property is the consistency of object states. While an object is being modified, it may go through a series of intermediate states that are *inconsistent* or *invalid*. If the thread that is modifying the object is interrupted, it may leave the object in an inconsistent state. When another thread tries to access an object in an inconsistent state, this action may lead to incorrect, perhaps disastrous, behavior. Let's consider an example of a simplified bank account class. The `withdraw()` method attempts to withdraw a specified amount of money from an account. It succeeds when the withdraw amount is less than or equal to the balance in the account.

```
public class Account {
    // ...
    public boolean withdraw(long amount) {
        if (amount <= balance) {
            long newBalance = balance - amount;
            balance = newBalance;
            return true;
        } else {
            return false;
        }
    }
    private long balance;
}
```

This implementation is valid when used in single-thread programs. However, this class cannot safely be used with multithreaded programs. Consider the following scenario:

Assume that the initial balance is $1,000,000. Two withdrawal requests of $1,000,000 each are issued almost simultaneously, and they are executed on separate threads.

The following is a possible, although highly unlikely, sequence of events, which would lead to both withdrawal requests being successful, albeit incorrect.

Balance	Withdrawal 1	Withdrawal 2
1000000	amount <= balance	
1000000		amount <= balance
1000000	newBalance = ...;	
1000000		newBalance = ...;
0	balance = ...;	
0		balance = ...;
0	return true;	
0		return true;

This problem, which is common in multithreaded programs, is known as a *race hazard*. A class is said to be *thread safe* if it ensures the consistency of the states of the objects and the results of method invocations upon these objects in the presence of multiple threads. As we have demonstrated, the `Account` class is not thread safe.

To maintain the consistency of object states and the results of method invocations, more than one thread must be prevented from simultaneously entering certain program regions, known as *critical regions*, which are segments of code that should be executed by only one thread at a time. Java provides a *synchronization* mechanism to ensure that, while a thread is executing the statements in a critical region, no other threads can execute statements in the same critical region at the same time.

8.2.1 Synchronization

An operation that cannot be interrupted is known as an *atomic operation*. In Java the reading and assignment of variables of primitive types, except `long` and `double`, are atomic. All other operations should be explicitly *synchronized* to ensure atomicity.

Synchronization can be applied to methods or a block of statements. A synchronized instance method can be declared as in the following code segment.

```
class MyClass {

    synchronized void aMethod() {

        ⟨do something⟩

    }

}
```

In this case, the entire body of the method is the critical region. A synchronized statement takes the following form.

```
synchronized(exp) {

    ⟨do something⟩

}
```

The expression *exp* must be of reference type. The statements enclosed in the synchronized block comprise the critical region.

The synchronization mechanism is implemented by associating each object with a *lock*. A thread must obtain *exclusive possession* of the appropriate lock before entering the critical region.

- For a synchronized instance method, the lock associated with the receiving object `this` is used.
- For a synchronized statement, the lock associated with the result of the expression *exp* is used.

The lock is released when the thread leaves the critical region. The lock may also be released temporarily before leaving the critical region, when the `wait()` method is invoked (see Section 8.2.2 [p. 385]).

The synchronized method

```
class MyClass {
    synchronized void aMethod() {
        (do something)
    }
}
```

is equivalent to the synchronized statement

```
class MyClass {
    void aMethod() {
        synchronized(this) {
            (do something)
        }
    }
}
```

As only one thread can have exclusive possession of the lock of a critical region, only one thread at a time can execute the statements in the critical region. Moreover, different critical regions may share the same lock. For example, all the synchronized instance methods use the lock associated with the receiving object. Consider the following example.

```
public class A {
    synchronized void m1() { ... }
    synchronized void m2() { ... }
    void m3() { ... } // unsynchronized
}
```

Given an instance a of class A, when one thread is executing a.m1(), another thread will be prohibited from executing a.m1() or a.m2(). A synchronized method is allowed to invoke another synchronized method of the same class because the invocation will be on the same thread. In the preceding example, m2() may be invoked inside the body of method m1().

A synchronized method may execute concurrently with unsynchronized methods on the same object. In the preceding example, when one thread is executing a.m1(), another thread may execute a.m3() concurrently.

EXAMPLE 8.4　　Bounded Queue (Sequential Version)

PURPOSE

This example shows a simple bounded queue implementation that is not thread safe.

DESCRIPTION

A bounded queue is a first-in, first-out queue with a fixed capacity. The following program for the BoundedQueue class is implemented with a circular array. The capacity of the queue is specified by the argument to the constructor. The capacity of the queue may not be changed. The methods of the BoundedQueue class are summarized in the following table.

Method	Description
isEmpty()	Returns true if the queue is empty
isFull()	Returns true if the queue is full
getCount()	Returns the number of elements in the queue
put()	Inserts an element at the end of the queue
get()	Removes the element at the head of the queue and returns the element

SOLUTION

Bounded queue (sequential version)

```java
public class BoundedQueue {

    protected Object rep[];
    protected int front = 0;
    protected int back = -1;
    protected int size = 0;
    protected int count = 0;

    public BoundedQueue(int size) {
        if (size > 0) {
            this.size = size;
            rep = new Object[size];
            back = size - 1;
        }
    }

    public boolean isEmpty() {
        return (count == 0);
    }

    public boolean isFull() {
        return (count == size);
    }

    public int getCount() {
        return count;
    }

    public void put(Object e) {
        if (e != null && !isFull()) {
```

```
        back++;
        if (back >= size)
          back = 0;
        rep[back] = e;
        count++;
      }
    }
    public Object get() {
      Object result = null;
      if (!isEmpty()) {
        result = rep[front];
        rep[front] = null;
        front++;
        if (front >= size)
          front = 0;
        count--;
      }
      return result;
    }
    public static void main(String args[]) {
      BoundedQueue queue = new BoundedQueue(10);
      for (int i = 0; !queue.isFull(); i++) {
        queue.put(new Integer(i));
        System.out.println("put: "+i);
      }
      while (!queue.isEmpty()) {
        System.out.println("get: "+queue.get());
      }
    }
  }
```

This implementation of the bounded queue has two shortcomings. The put() method ignores the new element when the queue is full, and the get() method returns null when the queue is empty. When used with sequential programs, however, this implementation is reasonable.

The main() method carries out a simple test of the BoundedQueue class, giving the following output.

```
                    put: 0
                    put: 1
                    put: 2
                    put: 3
                    put: 4
                    put: 5
                    put: 6
                    put: 7
                    put: 8
                    put: 9
                    get: 0
                    get: 1
                    get: 2
                    get: 3
```

```
get:  4
get:  5
get:  6
get:  7
get:  8
get:  9
```

The result in Example 8.4 is exactly what we expected. However, the sequential version of the `BoundedQueue` class is not thread safe. An easy way to make a class thread safe is to synchronize all the methods in the class.

EXAMPLE 8.5   Bounded Queue (Fully Synchronized Version)

PURPOSE

This example demonstrates the use of synchronization to ensure thread safety.

DESCRIPTION

The `SyncBoundedQueue` class is identical to the the `BoundedQueue` in Example 8.4, except that it is fully synchronized and thread safe.

Bounded queue (fully synchronized version)

```java
public class SyncBoundedQueue extends BoundedQueue {

    public SyncBoundedQueue(int size) {
        super(size);
    }

    synchronized public boolean isEmpty() {
        return super.isEmpty();
    }

    synchronized public boolean isFull() {
        return super.isFull();
    }

    synchronized public int getCount() {
        return super.getCount();
    }

    synchronized public void put(Object e) {
        super.put(e);
    }

    synchronized public Object get() {
        return super.get();
    }

    (Method main() for testing on page 384)

}
```

Figure 8.3

The producer, consumer, and bounded queue.

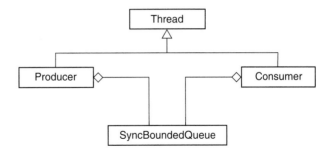

A typical use of the `SyncBoundedQueue` class is to serve as a buffer between a producer and a consumer, both of which are threads. The producer produces items and puts them in the bounded queue, and the consumer retrieves items from the bounded queue and consumes them. The relationships among the producer, consumer, and the bounded queue are shown in Figure 8.3.

The **Producer** class

```java
public class Producer extends Thread {

    protected BoundedQueue queue;
    protected int n;

    public Producer(BoundedQueue queue, int n) {
        this.queue = queue;
        this.n = n;
    }

    public void run() {
        for (int i = 0; i < n; i++) {
            queue.put(new Integer(i));
            System.out.println("produce: " + i);
            try {
                sleep((int)(Math.random() * 100));
            } catch (InterruptedException e) {}
        }
    }

}
```

The **Consumer** class

```java
public class Consumer extends Thread {

    protected BoundedQueue queue;
    protected int n;

    public Consumer(BoundedQueue queue, int n) {
        this.queue = queue;
        this.n = n;
    }
```

```
      public void run() {
        for (int i = 0; i < n; i++) {
          Object obj = queue.get();
          if (obj != null)
            System.out.println("\tconsume: "+obj);
          try {
            sleep((int)(Math.random() * 400));
          } catch (InterruptedException e) {}
        }
      }

  }
```

**Method of class `SyncBoundedQueue`: `main()`
for testing on page 382**

```
public static void main(String args[]) {
  SyncBoundedQueue queue = new SyncBoundedQueue(5);
  new Producer(queue, 15).start();
  new Consumer(queue, 10).start();
}
```

The following is the output.

```
          produce: 0
                  consume: 0
          produce: 1
          produce: 2
          produce: 3
          produce: 4
          produce: 5
                  consume: 1
          produce: 6
          produce: 7
                  consume: 2
          produce: 8
          produce: 9
          produce: 10
          produce: 11
                  consume: 3
          produce: 12
          produce: 13
          produce: 14
                  consume: 4
                  consume: 5
                  consume: 6
                  consume: 8
                  consume: 12
```

Note that the producer produces items faster than the consumer consumes the items. Hence some of the items are lost.

8.2.2 Cooperation Among Threads

Synchronization addresses the mutual exclusion of two or more threads in the critical regions, but it does not address cooperation among threads. The SyncBoundedQueue in the preceding example is thread safe. However, the producer and the consumer threads are not cooperating very well, which leads to a loss of items in the queue. The producer and the consumer should cooperate in the following ways.

- When the producer attempts to put a new item into the queue while the queue is full, it should wait for the consumer to consume some of the items in the queue, making room for the new item.
- When the consumer attempts to retrieve an item from the queue while the queue is empty, it should wait for the producer to produce items and put them in the queue.

Thread cooperation is a requirement in many applications and can be accomplished with guarded suspension. A *guard* is the precondition for a certain action to complete successfully. *Guarded suspension* is a requirement for threads to cooperate in the following way.

- Before a method is executed, the guard is tested.
- Execution continues only when the guard is true, which ensures the successful completion of the method invocation.
- Execution is temporarily suspended until the guard becomes true, at which time execution may continue.

Guarded suspension can be implemented by using the wait(), notify(), and notifyAll() methods of the Object class. The wait() method should be invoked when a thread is temporarily unable to continue and we want to let other threads proceed. The notify() or notifyAll() methods should be invoked when we want a thread to notify other threads that they may proceed. These three methods can be invoked only by a thread that currently owns the lock of the receiving object. The methods are summarized in Table 8.2.

EXAMPLE 8.6   Bounded Queue with Guarded Suspension

PURPOSE

This example demonstrates use of the wait() and notify() methods to implement guarded suspension and ensure cooperation among threads.

DESCRIPTION

The BoundedQueueWithGuard class extends the BoundedQueue class. It is fully synchronized. The put() and get() methods are overridden to support cooperation between the producer and the consumer.

TABLE 8.2

Method	Description
wait()	The current thread is temporarily blocked and is placed in the *wait* queue associated with the receiving object. The lock associated with the receiving object is temporarily released. The thread will resume execution when it is awakened by notify() or notifyAll().
notify()	One of the threads in the wait queue associated with the receiving object will be awakened and removed from the wait queue. The awakened thread must reobtain the lock before it can resume at the point immediately following the invocation of the wait() method.
notifyAll()	This method is the same as the notify() method, except that all threads that are in the wait queue associated with the receiving object will be awakened and removed from the wait queue.

SOLUTION

Bounded queue with guarded suspension

```java
public class BoundedQueueWithGuard extends BoundedQueue {

  public BoundedQueueWithGuard(int size) {
    super(size);
  }

  synchronized public boolean isEmpty() {
    return super.isEmpty();
  }

  synchronized public boolean isFull() {
    return super.isFull();
  }

  synchronized public int getCount() {
    return super.getCount();
  }

  (Method put() on page 387)

  (Method get() on page 387)

  (Method main() for testing on page 388)

}
```

The guard of the put() method ensures that *the queue is not full*, and the guard of the get() method ensures that *the queue is not empty*. The put() method invokes the wait() method to suspend temporarily the producer thread when the queue is full. Similarly, the get() method invokes the wait() method to suspend temporarily the consumer thread when the queue is empty. Both methods invoke the notify() method at the end to wake up a suspended threaded, if any.

Method of class BoundedQueueWith-Guard: put() on page 386

```
synchronized void put(Object obj) {
    try {
        while (isFull()) {
            wait();
        }
    } catch (InterruptedException e) {}
    super.put(obj);
    notify();
}
```

Method of class BoundedQueueWith-Guard: get() on page 386

```
synchronized Object get() {
    try {
        while (isEmpty()) {
            wait();
        }
    } catch (InterruptedException e) {}
    Object result = super.get();
    notify();
    return result;
}
```

The interaction between the put() and get() methods, which are invoked by the producer and consumer threads respectively, is best illustrated by two scenarios.

SCENARIO A:

The producer produces items faster than the consumer consumes them.

1. The producer thread accquires the lock associated with the queue and invokes the put() method, but the queue is full.

2. The wait() method is invoked and the producer thread is suspended. The lock associated with queue is temporarily released by the producer thread.

3. The consumer thread accquires the lock associated with the queue and invokes the get() method. The queue must not be empty; indeed, it is full. So the guard of the get() method returns true, and one item is removed from the queue.

4. The notify() method is invoked to awaken the suspended producer thread. The consumer thread completes the invocation of the get() method and releases the lock associated with the queue.

5. The producer thread is awakened in the put () method and reacquires the lock associated with the queue. The guard of the put () method is true this time, and execution resumes where it left off.

SCENARIO B:

The producer produces items more slowly than the consumer consumes them.

1. The consumer thread accquires the lock associated with the queue and invokes the get () method when the queue is empty.
2. The wait () method is invoked, and the consumer thread is suspended. The lock associated with queue is temporarily released by the consumer thread.
3. The producer thread accquires the lock associated with the queue and invokes the put () method. The queue is not full; indeed, it is empty. So the guard of the put () method returns true, and one item is inserted into the queue.
4. The notify () method is invoked to awaken the suspended consumer thread. The producer thread completes the invocation of the put () method and releases the lock associated with the queue.
5. The consumer thread is awakened in the get () method and reacquires the lock associated with the queue. The guard of the get () method returns true this time, and execution resumes where it left off.

The main () method performs a simple test of the bounded queue, with the producer and the consumer running on separate threads.

Method of class `BoundedQueueWith-Guard`: `main()` for testing on page 386

```
public static void main(String args[]) {
    BoundedQueueWithGuard queue =
        new BoundedQueueWithGuard(5);
    new Producer(queue, 15).start();
    new Consumer(queue, 15).start();
}
```

The following is the output.

```
produce: 0
            consume: 0
produce: 1
produce: 2
            consume: 1
produce: 3
            consume: 2
produce: 4
produce: 5
            consume: 3
produce: 6
produce: 7
```

```
produce: 8
        consume: 4
produce: 9
        consume: 5
produce: 10
        consume: 6
produce: 11
        consume: 7
produce: 12
        consume: 8
produce: 13
        consume: 9
produce: 14
        consume: 10
        consume: 11
        consume: 12
        consume: 13
        consume: 14
```

8.2.3   Liveness Failures

Liveness refers to desirable conditions that will come about during the lifetime of a program. In other words, liveness properties stipulate that something positive will eventually happen. For example, common liveness properties include: (a) A certain task will be completed eventually; (b) a thread should always respond to user input until the thread is terminated; and the status of certain systems must be displayed and updated constantly.

Safety properties can be ensured locally, but liveness properties are context dependent. Ensuring liveness properties is a much more difficult task than ensuring safety properties. Some common types of liveness failures are contention, dormancy, deadlock, and premature termination.

Contention

Contention (also called *starvation* or *indefinite postponement*) occurs when a runnable thread never gets a chance to run. This can occur when there is always one or more runnable threads with higher priorities or when there is a runnable thread with the same priority but it never yields.

Let's consider the run() method of a typical animation applet.

```java
public class AnAnimation {
    protected Thread animationThread;

    public void run() {
        while (Thread.currentThread() == animationThread) {
            repaint();
            try {
                Thread.currentThread().sleep(delay);
```

```
                    } catch (InterruptedException e){}

              }

        }

        // other fields and methods . . .

   }
```

The `repaint()` method draws the current frame on a separate thread having the same priority as the animation thread. If the `sleep()` method were not invoked, the repaint thread would never get a chance to run and the animation would appear as a blank area.

To avoid contention, the thread with the highest priority must periodically invoke the `sleep()` or `yield()` method to provide other cooperating threads having the same or lower priorities a chance to run.

Dormancy

Dormancy occurs when a thread that is blocked never becomes runnable. A common cause of dormancy is that a thread blocked by an invocation of the `wait()` method is never awakened by `notify()` or `notifyAll()`. For example, in the BoundedQueueWithGuard class [p. 385], if the invocation of the `notify()` method in either the `put()` or `get()` methods were omitted, the consumer and the producer threads could both become dormant. If the invocation of `notify()` in the `put()` method were omitted, the following scenario could occur.

1. The queue becomes empty. The consumer thread invokes the `wait()` method inside the `get()` method and becomes blocked.
2. The producer thread puts items into the queue, but the consumer thread is not awakened because the invocation of the `notify()` method is omitted. The comsumer thread remains blocked.
3. The queue becomes full. The producer thread invokes the `wait()` method inside the `put()` method and becomes blocked.

At this point, both the consumer and producer threads are blocked. If there are no other threads to awaken them, they become dormant.

To avoid dormancy caused by waiting, be sure that each thread that can be blocked by the `wait()` method will be awakened by another thread that invokes the `notify()` or `notifyAll()` methods. When in doubt, use the `notifyAll()` method, which awakens all the waiting threads and makes the system less dormancy-prone.

Deadlock

Deadlock occurs when two or more threads block each other and none can make progress. It is usually caused by two or more threads competing for multiple shared resources and each thread requiring exclusive possession of those resources simultaneously. Consider the following oversimplified example. The `DiskDrive` class represents a disk drive, and the copy() method copies a file from this disk drive to another drive.

```
public class DiskDrive {

    public synchronized void copy(DiskDrive destination, String filename) {
        InputStream in = openFile(filename);
        destination.writeFile(filename, in);
    }

    public synchronized InputStream openFile(String filename) {
        // ...
    }

    public synchronized void writeFile(String filename, InputStream in) {
        // copy the contents read from the parameter in to a file
    }
}
```

To maintain the integrity of the file being copied, all the methods are synchronized. The copy() method needs to acquire the locks associated with both the source and destination disk drives. Let's assume that we have two disk drives, c and d. On one thread we do c.copy(d, file1), and on another thread we do d.copy(c, file2). The following is a possible scenario.

Thread 1: c.copy(d, file1)	Thread 2: d.copy(c, file2)
Invoke c.copy(...)	
Obtain lock of c	
	Invoke d.copy(...)
	Obtain lock of d
Invoke c.openFile(...)	
	Invoke d.openFile(...)
Invoke d.writeFile(...)	
Unable to obtain lock of d	
	Invoke c.writeFile(...)
	Unable to obtain lock of c

Neither thread is able to obtain the lock needed to proceed, so they are in a "deadlock."

In general, detecting and preventing deadlock is difficult. An extensive body of work on deadlock detection and prevention is available. A more detailed discussion on this topic is presented in [Lea 1997].

Premature Termination

Premature termination occurs when a thread is terminated before it should be, impeding the progress of other threads. For example, in the BoundedQueueWithGuard class [p. 385], premature termination of either the producer or the consumer thread causes the other thread to be blocked forever (i.e., to become dormant).

8.3 DESIGN CASE STUDY—TIC-TAC-TOE GAME

In this section, we will develop a simple game: tic-tac-toe. Here we implement it as a two-player game on a 3 × 3 board, but it is designed so that it can be extended to a k-player ($k \geq 2$) game on an $m \times n$ board. The program is multi-threaded, and each player is a thread. Two types of players are implemented:

- a human player, which waits for a human to make moves by clicking the mouse on the game board; and
- a machine player, which automatically generates moves (not necessarily good ones).

The game can be played by two human players, two machine players, or a human and a machine player. The structure of the program is shown in Figure 8.4.

8.3.1 The Game Board

The class `Board` represents the game board.

Class Board

```
import java.awt.*;
import java.awt.event.*;
public class Board extends Canvas {
    protected Game game;
    protected int row, col;
    protected int rowHeight, colWidth;
    protected int board[][];
    protected int maxMoves;
    protected int moves;
    protected boolean over = false;
    protected int winner = 0;

    (Constructor Board() on page 393)

    (Accessors of fields on page 394)

    (Method paint() on page 395)

    (Method recordMove() on page 396)

    (Method isLegalMove() on page 396)

    (Method checkGame() on page 396)

    (Auxiliary methods checkRow(), checkCol(), and checkDiagonal() on page 397)

    (Inner class MouseHandler on page 398)

}
```

The fields of the `Board` class are described in Table 8.3.

Figure 8.4

Structure of the
tic-tac-toe game.

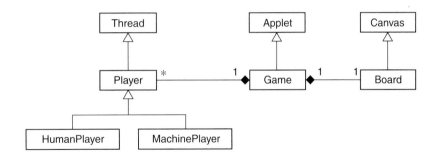

The constructor of the `Board` class simply initializes the fields.

Constructor of class Board on page 392

```
public Board(Game game, int row, int col) {
    this.game = game;
    this.row = row;
    this.col = col;
    maxMoves = row * col;
    moves = 0;
    board = new int[row][col];
    addMouseListener(new MouseHandler());
}
```

TABLE 8.3

Methods	Description
game	Game object with which this game board is associated
row, col	Number of rows and columns on the game board
rowHeight	Height of each row
colWidth	Width of each column
board	Two-dimensional array that records the state of the game board, each cell containing the ID of the player who occupies the cell and the player ID starting at 1
moves	Number of moves that have been made
maxMoves	Maximum number of moves allowed in the game
over	Boolean flag that is set to true if the game is over
winner	ID of the player who won the game, which is 0 while the game is in progress

The following accessors return the values of the corresponding fields.

**Methods of class `Board`:
Accessors of fields on
page 392**

```
public int getRow() {
    return row;
}

public int getCol() {
    return col;
}

public boolean isOver() {
    return over;
}

public int getWinner() {
    return winner;
}
```

The `paint()` method paints the game board. A screen shot of the game board is shown in Figure 8.5. The `paint()` method first draws the grid. It then draws

Figure 8.5

The tic-tac-toe
game board.

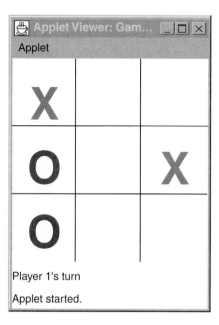

an X for each cell occupied by player 1 and an O for each cell occupied by player 2.

Method of class `Board`: `paint()` on page 392

```
public void paint(Graphics g) {
   Dimension d = getSize();
   rowHeight = d.height / row;
   colWidth = d.width / col;
   int i, j;
   for (i = 1; i < row; i++)
      g.drawLine(0, i * rowHeight, d.width, i * rowHeight);
   for (j = 1; j < col; j++)
      g.drawLine(j * colWidth, 0, j * colWidth, d.height);

   Font font = new Font("Sans-serif", Font.BOLD, 48);
   g.setFont(font);
   for (i = 0; i < row; i++) {
      for (j = 0; j < col; j++) {
         if (board[i][j] != 0) {
            int x = i * colWidth + 12;
            int y = j * rowHeight + 60;
            switch (board[i][j]) {
            case 1:
               g.setColor(Color.red);
               g.drawString("X", x, y);
               break;
            case 2:
               g.setColor(Color.blue);
               g.drawString("O", x, y);
               break;
            }
         }
      }
   }
}
```

The `recordMove()` method records a move made by the specified player. A move is an instance of the following `Move` class, which indicates the cell the player intends to occupy.

Class `Move`

```
public class Move {
   public int row, col;
}
```

Before the move is recorded, the `recordMove()` method checks to determine whether the move is a legal move. It returns `true` if the move is legal and `false` if the move is illegal.

Method of class `Board`: `recordMove()` on page 392

```
public boolean recordMove(Move move, int playerId) {
  if (isLegalMove(move)) {
    moves++;
    board[move.row][move.col] = playerId;
    repaint();
    return true;
  } else {
    return false;
  }
}
```

The `isLegalMove()` method returns `true` if the specified move is legal. A move is legal if the cell is unoccupied.

Method of class `Board`: `isLegalMove()` on page 392

```
public boolean isLegalMove(Move move) {
  return (board[move.row][move.col] == 0);
}
```

The `checkGame()` method checks to determine whether the game is over. The game is over if all the cells on the game board are occupied or one of the players has won. It depends on three auxiliary methods—`checkRow()`, `checkCol()`, and `checkDiagonal()`, to determine whether one of the players has won.

Method of class `Board`: `checkGame()` on page 392

```
protected void checkGame(int playerId) {
  if (moves >= maxMoves) {
    over = true;
    return;
  }
  boolean win = false;
  for (int i = 0; i < row; i++) {
    if (checkRow(playerId, i)) {
      win = true;
      break;
    }
  }
  if (!win) {
    for (int i = 0; i < col; i++) {
      if (checkCol(playerId, i)) {
        win = true;
        break;
      }
    }
  }
}
```

```
        if (!win) {
           win = checkDiagonal(playerId);
        }

        if (win) {
           winner = playerId;
           over = true;
        }
     }
}
```

The auxiliary methods checkRow(), checkCol(), and checkDiagonal() check on whether the specified player occupied an entire row, an entire column, or an entire diagonal.

Methods of class Board: checkRow(), checkCol(), and checkDiagonal() on page 392

```
protected boolean checkRow(int playerId, int row) {
   for (int i = 0; i < col; i++) {
      if (board[row][i] != playerId) {
         return false;
      }
   }
   return true;
}

protected boolean checkCol(int playerId, int col) {
   for (int i = 0; i < row; i++) {
      if (board[i][col] != playerId) {
         return false;
      }
   }
   return true;
}

protected boolean checkDiagonal(int playerId) {
   boolean result = true;
   for (int i = 0; i < row; i++) {
      if (board[i][i] != playerId) {
         result = false;
         break;
      }
   }
   if (result) {
      return true;
   }
   result = true;
   for (int i = 0; i < row; i++) {
      if (board[i][col - i - 1] != playerId) {
         result = false;
         break;
      }
   }
   return result;
}
```

The inner class `MouseHandler` receives mouse clicks on the game board, which indicate moves made by a human player.

Inner class of class `Board`: `MouseHandler` on page 392

```
class MouseHandler extends MouseAdapter {
  public void mouseClicked(MouseEvent event) {
    Point p = event.getPoint();
    game.getPlayer().selectCell(p.x / colWidth, p.y / rowHeight);
  }
}
```

8.3.2   The Game

The `Game` class extends the `Applet` class. It contains a game board and a message bar. The field `player` is an array of players in the game. In this implementation the number of players is fixed at 2. The field `turn` refers to the player who currently has the turn (i.e., the player who is supposed to make the next move).

Class `Game`

```
import java.awt.*;
import java.applet.Applet;

public class Game extends Applet {
    protected Board board;
    protected Label messageBar;
    protected Player players[];
    protected Player turn;

    ⟨Constructor Game() on page 398⟩

    ⟨Method init() on page 403⟩

    ⟨Method getPlayer() on page 399⟩

    ⟨Method getBoard() on page 399⟩

    ⟨Method isOver() on page 399⟩

    ⟨Method displayMessage() on page 399⟩

    ⟨Method recordMove() on page 399⟩
}
```

The constructor initializes the fields by creating the board and the message bar.

Constructor of class `Game` on page 398

```
public Game() {
  players = new Player[2];
  board = new Board(this, 3, 3);
```

```
        messageBar = new Label("Game begin.");
        setLayout(new BorderLayout());
        add(board, BorderLayout.CENTER);
        add(messageBar, BorderLayout.SOUTH);
    }
```

The getPlayer() method returns the player who has the turn.

Method of class Game:
getPlayer() on page 398

```
public Player getPlayer() {
    return turn;
}
```

The getBoard() method returns the game board.

Method of class Game:
getBoard() on page 398

```
public Board getBoard() {
    return board;
}
```

The isOver() method returns true if the game is over.

Method of class Game:
isOver() on page 398

```
public boolean isOver() {
    return board.isOver();
}
```

The displayMessage() method displays a message on the message bar.

Method of class Game: displayMessage()
on page 398

```
public void displayMessage(String msg) {
    messageBar.setText(msg);
}
```

The recordMove() method records a move made by a player. It returns true if the move is illegal and returns false otherwise. It also displays messages regarding the outcome of the game.

Method of class Game: recordMove() on page 398

```
public boolean recordMove(Move move) {
    if (board.recordMove(move, turn.getId())) {
        board.checkGame(turn.getId());
```

```
                          if (isOver()) {
                            int winner = board.getWinner();
                            if (winner >= 1) {
                              displayMessage("Player " + winner + " won.");
                            } else {
                              displayMessage("It's a draw");
                            }
                            for (int n = 0; n < players.length; n++) {
                              players[n].stop();
                            }
                          }
                          return true;
                        } else {
                          return false;
                        }
                      }
```

8.3.3   The Players

The Player class is an abstract class that represents players in the game. Different types of players are represented by different subclasses of this class. The field game refers to the game the players are in. The field id is the ID of the first player. The field next refers to the player whose turn follows that of the preceding player. In two-player games, next refers to the second player. The field turn refers to the player who currently has the turn. It is this player's turn if turn == this. The turn and next fields of the player objects are initialized in the init() method of the Game class.

Class **Player**

```
abstract public class Player extends Thread {
    protected Game game;
    protected int id;
    protected Player next;
    protected Player turn;

    public Player(Game game, int id) {
        this.game = game;
        this.id = id;
    }

    ⟨Method getId() on page 401⟩

    ⟨Method setNext() on page 401⟩

    ⟨Method hasTurn() on page 401⟩

    ⟨Method makeMove() on page 401⟩

    ⟨Method selectCell() on page 401⟩

    ⟨Method run() on page 402⟩

}
```

The getId() method returns the ID of this player.

Method of class
Player: getId() on
page 400

```
public int getId() {
    return id;
}
```

The setNext() method sets which player is after this player.

Method of class Player: setNext()
on page 400

```
public synchronized void setNext(Player p){
    next = p;
}
```

The hasTurn() method is invoked when this player should have the turn. This method is invoked by the preceding player and it awakens this player (see the run() method).

Method of class Player: hasTurn()
on page 400

```
public synchronized void hasTurn() {
    turn = this;
    game.turn = this;
    notify();
}
```

The makeMove() method is a hook method for the subclasses to override. This method should return the next move to be made by the player.

Method of class Player:
makeMove() on page 400

```
abstract public Move makeMove();
```

The selectCell() method is invoked by the MouseHandler of the Board class. It informs the player that a mouse click has been received and a cell position given. This method is ignored by the MachinePlayer class, but it is used by the HumanPlayer class to get the move made by a human.

Method of class Player: selectCell()
on page 400

```
public void selectCell(int x, int y) {}
```

The run() method is the body of the player thread and is also a template method. First, it waits until this player gets the turn. Then it invokes the hook method makeMove() to make a move.

Method of class `Player`: `run()` on page 400

```
public synchronized void run() {
   while (!game.isOver()) {
      while (turn != this) {
         try {
            wait();
         }
         catch (InterruptedException ex) { return; }
      }
      game.displayMessage("Player " + id + "'s turn");
      while (true) {
         Move move = makeMove();
         if (game.recordMove(move)) {
            break;
         } else {
            game.displayMessage("Illegal move!");
         }
      }
      turn = null;
      next.hasTurn();
   }
}
```

The HumanPlayer class implements the makeMove() method. It simply waits for a mouse click on the game board.

Class `HumanPlayer`

```
public class HumanPlayer extends Player {
   protected Move move;

   public HumanPlayer(Game game, int id) {
      super(game, id);
      move = new Move();
   }

   synchronized public Move makeMove() {
      try {
         wait();
      } catch (InterruptedException e) {}
      return move;
   }

   synchronized public void selectCell(int x, int y) {
      move.row = x;
      move.col = y;
      notify();
   }
}
```

The MachinePlayer also implements the makeMove() method. It randomly generates a move.

Class **MachinePlayer**

```
public class MachinePlayer extends Player {

   protected int nCells;

   public MachinePlayer(Game game, int id) {
      super(game, id);
      Board board = game.getBoard();
      nCells = board.getRow() * board.getCol();
   }

   public Move makeMove() {
      try {
         Thread.currentThread().sleep(1000);
      } catch (InterruptedException e) {}

      Move move = new Move();
      Board board = game.getBoard();
      int row = game.getBoard().getRow();
      int i = (int)(Math.random() * nCells);
      move.row = i / row;
      move.col = i % row;
      while (!board.isLegalMove(move)) {
         i++;
         if (i >= nCells) {
            i = i % nCells;
         }
         move.row = i / row;
         move.col = i % row;
      }
      return move;
   }
}
```

The init() method of the Game class initializes the players according to the parameter type.

Method of class **Game: init()** on page 398

```
public void init() {
   String gameType = getParameter("type");
   if (gameType.equals("human-human")) {
      players[0] = new HumanPlayer(this, 1);
      players[1] = new HumanPlayer(this, 2);
   } else if (gameType.equals("machine-machine")) {
      players[0] = new MachinePlayer(this, 1);
      players[1] = new MachinePlayer(this, 2);
   } else {
      players[0] = new HumanPlayer(this, 1);
      players[1] = new MachinePlayer(this, 2);
```

```
        }
        players[0].start();
        players[1].start();
        players[0].setNext(players[1]);
        players[1].setNext(players[0]);
        players[0].hasTurn();
    }
```

8.3.4　Idiom: Taking Turns

The `Player` class implements a behavior that allows each player to make a move. This behavior can be generalized by the following idiom that extends to more than two objects, or players, and applies to nongame applications.

Idiom　*Taking Turns*

Category: Behavioral implementation idiom.

Intent: For each participant in a group of objects to take turns in a fixed order and performs certain task.

Applicability: This idiom can be used to implement k-player games ($k \geq 2$), or other applications that require the participants to take turns.

Each participant is a thread. The following code comprises the implementation.

```
class Participant extends Thread {

    protected Participant next;

    protected Participant turn;

    public synchronized void run() {

        while (!isDone()) {

            while (turn != this) {

                try {

                    wait();

                }

                catch (InterruptedException ex) {return; }

            }

            // perform an action or make a move

            turn = null;

            next.hasTurn();
```

```
        }

    }

    public synchronized void hasTurn() {

        turn = this;

        notify();

    }

    // other fields and methods

}
```

If there are n participants and they take turns in the order, $p_0, p_1, \ldots, p_{n-1}$, they must be initialized as

$$p_0.\text{next} == p_1$$
$$p_1.\text{next} == p_2$$
$$\ldots$$
$$p_{n-2}.\text{next} == p_{n-1}$$
$$p_{n-1}.\text{next} == p_0$$

To start the process, we do the following.

```
p0.start();
p1.start();
    ...
pn-1.start();
p0.hasTurn();
```

Using the taking turn idiom, we can extend the two-player game shown here to multiplayer games. Doing so is left as an excercie (Exercise 8.4).

CHAPTER SUMMARY

- Concurrent programs, also known as multithreaded programs, are capable of running several threads simultaneaously.
- A thread is a single sequential flow of control within a program. Threads are different from processes. A process is a heavyweight flow that executes concurrently with other processes. A thread is a lightweight flow that executes concurrently with other threads within the same process.
- Threads can be defined by extending the `Thread` class or by implementing the `Runnable` interface.

- The life cycle of a thread includes three main states: new, alive, and dead. Threads in the alive state can be either runnable or blocked.

- The Java virtual machine assigns and maintains a priority for each thread. This priority, which is an integer value, should be manipulated only by the programmer for performance tuning.

- Critical regions are segments of code that should be executed by only one thread at a time. Race hazards occur when more than one thread execute the statements in a critical region at the same time. Race hazards could leave objects in inconsistent or invalid states. Java provides a synchronization mechanism to ensure that, while a thread is executing the statements in a critcal region, no other threads can execute statements in that same critical region at the same time.

- A guard is the precondition for a certain action to complete successfully. Guarded suspension is a policy for threads to cooperate in the following way.

  1. Before executing a method, the guard is tested.

  2. Execution continues only when the guard is true, which ensures successful completion of the method invocation.

  3. Execution is temporarily suspended until the guard becomes true, at which time execution may continue.

- Liveness refers to desirable conditions that will come about during the lifetime of a program. Some common types of liveness failures are

  contention, (also called *Starvation* or *Indefinite postponement*) when a runnable thread never gets a chance to run;

  dormancy, when a thread that is blocked never becomes runnable;

  deadlock, when two or more threads block each other and none can progress; and

  premature termination, when a thread is terminated before it should be, impeding the progress of other threads.

EXERCISES

8.1. Complete the `Account` class on page 377 and be sure that it is thread safe. It should contain methods such as `deposit()` and `getBalance()`. All critical regions of the class should be protected with synchronization as needed.

8.2. Implement a thread safe linked list class based on the `LinkedList` class in Chapters 4 and 5. All critical regions of the class should be protected with synchronization as needed.

8.3. Using the `BoundedQueueWithGuard` class as a model, implement a thread safe `Stack`

class with guarded suspension. The `Stack` class should contain the methods `pop()`, `push()`, `isFull()`, and `isEmpty()`. Test the `Stack` class by using classes similar to the `Producer` and `Consumer` classes presented in this chapter.

8.4. Design and implement a multiplayer tic-tac-toe game. (*Hint:* Use a larger board and design a new scoring system.)

8.5. Develop a Java program that simulates a traffic control system for a four-way intersection. The system controls four sets of traffic lights, facing north, east, south, and west. Each set of lights can be in one of the following states: *green*, *yellow*, and *red*. The goals of the traffic control system are

- never to give green lights simultaneously to traffic flows that may collide,

- to avoid unnecessary blocking of the traffic flows, and

- to give green lights to emergency vehicles.

For testing purposes, use independent threads to generate simulated traffic flows, which have emergency vehicles occassionally, in different directions. Develop a GUI program to animate trafic lights and traffic flows. (*Note:* Take precautions so that your program does not deadlock.) *Bonus:* Add a left-turn signal to each set of traffic lights.

8.6. Develop a Java program that simulates an elevator control system for a bank of *m* elevators of an *n*-story buiding. Each floor, except the top and bottom, has an *Up* and a *Down* button. The top floor has only the *Down* button, and the bottom floor has only the *Up* button. Inside each elevator is a button for each floor. The goal of the system is to ensure that

(a) one of the elevators moving upward will stop at the floor for which the *Up* button is pushed,

(b) one of the elevators moving downward will stop at the floor for which the *Down* button is pushed, and

(c) each elevator must stop at the ith floor if the button i in this elevator is pushed.

Develop a GUI program to animate the status of all the buttons and the movement of the elevators. Two testing modes of the system should be supported.

(a) Use independent threads to simulate the requests of the passengers.

(b) Manually push the buttons on each floor and inside each elevator.

9

Distributed Computing

CHAPTER OVERVIEW

In this chapter we discuss two pure Java mechanisms for distributed computing: socket-based communication and remote method invocation (RMI). We illustrate the design and implementation of distributed applications, using a stock ticker application. We also discuss two mechanisms for interfacing Java applications with non-Java applications in distributed computing environments: Java database connectivity (JDBC) and the Common Object Request Broker Architecture (CORBA). This chapter serves as an introduction to developing distributed applications in Java.

Today's computing environments are inherently distributed and heterogeneous. Internet and intranet applications often run on different operating systems in different locations. *Distributed applications* consist of collaborating components that reside and execute on different network hosts. The components residing on different hosts do not share storage space (i.e., memory and disc). Exchange of information among these components can take place only via communication connections, or links, among the hosts. Furthermore, the hosts can be running different operating systems, forming a heterogeneous network computing environment.

In this chapter we discuss two pure Java mechanisms provided by Java for distributed computing.

> *Socket-based communication.* Sockets are the endpoints of two-way
> connections between two distributed components that communicate

with each other. A connection must be explicitly established by both parties.

Remote method invocation. RMI makes the network "transparent." It allows distributed components to be manipulated (almost) as if they were all on the same host. Programmers need not to deal with interhost communications at all. All are handled implicitly by the run-time environment supporting the remote method invocation.

We also briefly discuss two mechanisms for interfacing Java applications with non-Java applications in distributed computing environments.

Java database connectivity. JDBC allows Java applications to interface with relational databases, which are widely used today. A wealth of information is stored in relational databases. Through JDBC, Java applications can access information stored in existing databases and share information with applications written in other languages.

The Common Object Request Broker Architecture. CORBA is an object-oriented framework that supports interoperability among objects written in different languages and running on different platforms. CORBA support is available for most programming languages, including Java, and platforms used for industrial applications. CORBA is especially useful in interfacing applications developed with modern languages, such as Java and C++, with legacy systems.

This chapter serves only as an introduction to developing distributed applications in Java.

9.1 SOCKET-BASED COMMUNICATION

Sockets are the endpoints of logical connections between hosts and can be used to send and receive data. At the application programming level, it is assumed that the socket connections are reliable; that is, the data sent from one end of the connection will be received at the other end in the same order and with no loss. Sockets are supported by most programming languages and platforms in use today. Java applications can use sockets to communicate with applications written in other languages.

9.1.1 Server and Client Sockets

There are two kinds of sockets: server sockets and client sockets. A server socket waits for requests for connections from clients. A client socket can be used to send and receive data.

Server Sockets

Each server socket listens at a specific *port*. The port number is necessary to distinguish different servers running on the same host, so each server must have a unique port number.

A server socket must be running on the server host before its clients initiate contacts. After the server socket is contacted by a client, a connection can be established, and a client socket is created for the application running on the server host to communicate with the client that initiated the contact.

A server socket is an instance of the `ServerSocket` class and can be created with one of these constructors:

```
ServerSocket(int port)
ServerSocket(int port, int backlog)
```

The parameter `port` specifies the port number at which the server socket will be listening to requests from clients. When multiple clients are contacting the same server socket at the same time, they will be put in a waiting queue and will be processed in the order they are received. The optional parameter `backlog` specifies the maximum length of the waiting queue. Server sockets can be created only with Java apps, not applets. The commonly used methods of the `ServerSocket` class are summarized in the following table.

Method	Description
`accept()`	Waits for a connection request. The thread that executes the method will be blocked until a request is received, at which time the method returns a client socket
`close()`	Stops waiting for requests from clients

The following program segment is a typical use of server sockets.

```
try {
   ServerSocket s = new ServerSocket(port);
   for (;;) {
      Socket incoming = s.accept(); // obtain a client socket
      (Handle a client)
   }
} catch (IOException e) {

   (Handle exception: fail to create a server socket)

}
```

Client Sockets

A client socket is an instance of the `Socket` class and can be obtained in two ways.

1. On the client side, client sockets can be created by using the constructor `Socket (String host, int port)`. The parameter `host` specifies the address of

the host, and the parameter `port` specifies the port number. Client sockets can be created and used by both Java apps and applets.

2. On the server side, client sockets are returned by the `accept()` method of the `ServerSocket` class, after requests for connection have been reveived from clients.

Communication between the server and the client is handled by client sockets at both ends. Each client socket has an `InputStream` object for receiving data and an `OutputStream` object for sending data. When the `InputStream` and `OutputStream` objects are used, sending and receiving data between a client and a server is essentially no different from reading data from and writing data to files. The commonly used methods of the `Socket` class are summarized in the following table.

Method	Description
getInputStream()	Returns an `InputStream` object for receiving data
getOutputStream()	Returns an `OutputStream` object for sending data
close()	Closes the socket connection

The following program segment illustrates the typical use of client sockets for sending and receiving text data.

```
try {
    Socket s = new Socket(host, port); // create a client socket
    PrintWriter out = new PrintWriter(
      new OutputStreamWriter(s.getOutputStream()));
    BufferedReader in = new BufferedReader(
      new InputStreamReader(s.getInputStream()));

    ⟨Send and receive data⟩

    in.close();
    out.close();
    s.close();
} catch (IOException e) {

    ⟨Handle exception: connection fails⟩

}
```

9.1.2 Servers and Clients Using Sockets

In this section, we illustrate client–server programming, using sockets, through a series of examples. Let's start with a simple server that only echoes the messages it receives from its client.

EXAMPLE 9.1   A Simple Echo Server

PURPOSE

This example illustrates the basic elements of a server application.

DESCRIPTION

This server echoes each line of text that it receives from its client. The client can terminate the connection by sending a line that says "BYE."

SOLUTION

Typically, a server is supposed to run for a long time. So a server usually contains an infinite loop of some kind. In this case, each iteration of the loop handles one client. Thus this server can handle multiple clients sequentially (i.e., only one client at a time), not simultaneously.

A simple echo server

```java
import java.io.*;
import java.net.*;

public class EchoServer {

   public static void main(String[] args) {
      try {
         ServerSocket s = new ServerSocket(8008);
         while (true) {
            Socket incoming = s.accept();
            BufferedReader in
               = new BufferedReader(new InputStreamReader(
                                          incoming.getInputStream()));
            PrintWriter out
               = new PrintWriter(new OutputStreamWriter(
                                       incoming.getOutputStream()));
            out.println("Hello! This is the Java EchoServer.");
            out.println("Enter BYE to exit.");
            out.flush();

            while (true) {
               String str = in.readLine();
               if (str == null) {
                  break; // client closed connection
               } else {
                  out.println("Echo: " + str);
                  out.flush();
                  if (str.trim().equals("BYE")) {
                     break;
                  }
               }
            }
            incoming.close();
         }
      } catch (Exception e) {}
   }
}
```

The echo server will listen on port 8008. The method invocation `in.read-Line()` attempts to receive a line of text from the client. If the connection is alive but the client does not send anything, the method invocation will be blocked. If the client sends a line of text, the method invocation will return with that line of text. If the client closes the connection, the method invocation will return with `null`. The `flush()` call on the output stream forces the messages to be sent to the client right away.

The server application can be compiled as usual. Let's say that we compile and start the echo server on a host called `saturn`: `saturn% java EchoServer`. Now, the server is ready and is waiting for clients. We can test the echo server with the `telnet` program, which is available on almost all platforms. Let's say that we run `telnet` on a host called `venus`.[1]

```
venus% telnet saturn 8008
Trying 140.192.34.63 ...
Connected to saturn.
Escape character is '^]'.
Hello! This is the Java EchoServer.
Enter BYE to exit.
Hi, this is from venus
Echo: Hi, this is from venus
BYE
Echo: BYE
Connection closed by foreign host.
```

We can also write a Java client that communicates with the echo server.

EXAMPLE 9.2   A Simple Client Talks to the Echo Server

PURPOSE

This example illustrates the basic elements of a client application.

DESCRIPTION

This client contacts the echo server, and sends 10 lines of text to the echo server and prints out the data it receives from the server.

SOLUTION

A simple client for the echo server

```java
import java.io.*;
import java.net.*;

public class EchoClient {

    public static void main(String[] args) {
        try {
            String host;
            if (args.length > 0) {
                host = args[0];
```

---

[1] Although here we run the server and the client on different hosts, it should be okay to test the server and client on the same host. In this case, the host name is `localhost` or `127.0.0.1`.

```
        } else {
          host = "localhost";
        }
        Socket socket = new Socket(host, 8008);
        BufferedReader in
            = new BufferedReader(new InputStreamReader(
                                   socket.getInputStream()));
        PrintWriter out
            = new PrintWriter(new OutputStreamWriter(
                                   socket.getOutputStream()));
        // send data to the server
        for (int i = 1; i <= 10; i++) {
          System.out.println("Sending: line " + i);
          out.println("line " + i);
          out.flush();
        }
        out.println("BYE");
        out.flush();

        // receive data from the server
        while (true) {
          String str = in.readLine();
          if (str == null) {
            break;
          } else {
            System.out.println(str);
          }
        }
      } catch (Exception e) {}
    }
}
```

The first argument of the program is the name of the host on which the server is running. If the host name is absent, localhost is assumed. This client contacts the server on the given host at port 8008. The method invocation in.readLine() behaves the same on the client side as on the server side. To test this client, we first need to run the echo server on the host saturn: saturn% java EchoServer. Then we compile and run EchoClient on the host called venus. The output is:

```
venus% java EchoClient saturn
Sending: line 1
...
Sending: line 10
Hello! This is Java EchoServer.
Enter BYE to exit.
Echo: line 1
...
Echo: line 10
Echo: BYE
```

This echo server handles one client at a time. This behavior is not acceptable in some situations. It is more desirable, if the server can serve multiple clients simultaneously. To accomplish that, each client should be handled by a separate thread.

EXAMPLE 9.3   An Echo Server that Handles Multiple Clients Simultaneously

PURPOSE

This example illustrates a server that handles multiple clients simultaneously with the use of threads.

DESCRIPTION

The behavior of this echo server is similar to that of the simple echo server; the difference is that each client is handled by a separate thread.

SOLUTION

The `ClientHandler` class defines the threads that handle the clients. Note that the body of the `run()` method is essentially the same as the body of the loop of the echo server.

Thread that handles a client: `ClientHandler`

```java
import java.io.*;
import java.net.*;

public class ClientHandler extends Thread {

  protected Socket incoming;

  public ClientHandler(Socket incoming) {
    this.incoming = incoming;
  }

  public void run() {
    try {
      BufferedReader in
        = new BufferedReader(new InputStreamReader(
                                  incoming.getInputStream()));
      PrintWriter out
        = new PrintWriter(new OutputStreamWriter(
                               incoming.getOutputStream()));
      out.println("Hello! This is the Java MultiEchoServer.");
      out.println("Enter BYE to exit.");
      out.flush();

      while (true) {
        String str = in.readLine();
        if (str == null) {
          break;
        } else {
          out.println("Echo: " + str);
          out.flush();
          if (str.trim().equals("BYE"))
            break;
        }
      }
      incoming.close();
    } catch (Exception e) {}
  }
}
```

The `MultiEchoServer` class is the server, which creates a server socket. Whenever a client request is received, a new `ClientHandler` object, which is a thread, is created and started.

Echo server that handles multiple clients simultaneously

```
public class MultiEchoServer {

    public static void main(String[] args) {
        try {
            ServerSocket s = new ServerSocket(8009);
            while (true) {
                Socket incoming = s.accept();
                new ClientHandler(incoming).start();
            }
        } catch (Exception e) {}
    }

}
```

So far, we have developed two servers and a client that are all Java apps. Although only a Java app can be a server in socket-based client–server applcations, a client can be written as either an app or an applet. Example 9.4 shows a client that is written as an applet.

EXAMPLE 9.4 Visitor Counter Applet and Server

PURPOSE

This example illustrates a client implemented as an applet.

DESCRIPTION

This applet shows the number of visits, or hits, of the Web page that contains the applet. A screen shot of the applet is shown in Figure 9.1.

SOLUTION

The `CounterServer` class is the visitor counter server. It must be running on the host where the Web server (i.e., the HTTP server) is running.

Figure 9.1

The visitor counter applet.

Applet Viewer: Counter.class

Applet

You are visitor: 17

Applet started.

The visitor counter server: `CounterServer`

```java
import java.io.*;
import java.net.*;

public class CounterServer {

  public static void main(String[] args) {
    System.out.println("CounterServer started.");
    int i = 1;
    try {
      // read count from the file
      InputStream fin = new FileInputStream("Counter.dat");
      DataInputStream din = new DataInputStream(fin);
      i = din.readInt() + 1;
      din.close();
    } catch (IOException e) {}

    try {
      ServerSocket s = new ServerSocket(8190);
      while (true) {
        Socket incoming = s.accept();
        DataOutputStream out
          = new DataOutputStream(incoming.getOutputStream());
        System.out.println("Count: " + i);
        out.writeInt(i);
        incoming.close();
        OutputStream fout = new FileOutputStream("Counter.dat");
        DataOutputStream dout = new DataOutputStream(fout);
        dout.writeInt(i);
        dout.close();
        out.close();
        i++;
      }
    } catch (Exception e) {}
    System.out.println("CounterServer stopped.");
  }

}
```

When the server starts up, it attempts to open data file named `Counter.dat` to retrieve the last count. If the file `Counter.dat` does not exist, an `IOException` will be thrown. The exception will be caught and the count set to 1, the initial value of `i`. The current count is saved to the file every time the count changes so that the count can be restored and continue after the server is shut down and restarted. The data file is written with a `DataOutputStream` object, so it is in binary form. Similarly, the count is sent to the client in binary form.

The `Counter` class is the visitor counter applet. The applet communicates with the server to retrieve the count. In the `init()` method, a client socket is created. Recall that an applet can communicate only with a server that resides on the same host as the Web server. The host name of the client socket can only be the host of the document base.

Visitor counter applet: `Counter`

```java
import java.io.*;
import java.net.*;
import java.awt.*;
import java.applet.Applet;

public class Counter extends Applet {

    protected int count = 0;
    protected Font font = new Font("Serif", Font.BOLD, 24);

    public void init() {
        URL url = getDocumentBase();
        try {
            Socket t = new Socket(url.getHost(), 8190);
            DataInputStream in
                = new DataInputStream(t.getInputStream());
            count = in.readInt();
        } catch (Exception e) {}
    }

    public void paint(Graphics g) {
        int x = 0, y = font.getSize();
        g.setColor(Color.green);
        g.setFont(font);
        g.drawString("You are visitor: " + count, x, y);
    }
}
```

The servers in all the examples so far deal with each client independently from other clients. No client-to-client communication is supported. Example 9.5 illustrates how clients can communicate with each other via the server.

EXAMPLE 9.5   An Echo Server that Handles Multiple Clients Simultaneously and Broadcasts Messages to All Active Clients

PURPOSE

This example illustrates how clients can interact with one another through the server.

DESCRIPTION

The behavior of this echo server is similar to that of the echo server in Example 9.1; the difference is that this server will broadcast messages received from a client to all other active clients. This capability allows its clients to "chat" online.

SOLUTION

The `BroadcastClientHandler` class defines a thread that handles the clients. The `BroadcastEchoServer` class is the server. It contains a set of active clients, which will be used while the server is broadcasting messages.

The broadcast echo server

```
public class BroadcastEchoServer {
   static protected Set activeClients = new HashSet();

   public static void main(String[] args) {
      int i = 1;
      try {
         ServerSocket s = new ServerSocket(8010);
         while (true) {
            Socket incoming = s.accept();
            BroadcastClientHandler newClient =
               new BroadcastClientHandler(incoming, i++);
            activeClients.add(newClient);
            newClient.start();
         }
      } catch (Exception e) {}
   }
}
```

The `BroadcastClientHandler` class defines a thread that handles a client. The `sendMessage()` method sends a message to the client. The key feature in this client handling thread is the loop that iterates through the active clients set `BroadcastEchoServer.activeClient`. The message received from this client is also broadcast to all other active clients. Thus the `sendMessage()` method needs to synchronized because it will be invoked by all the threads that are handling clients.

Thread that handles a client

```
public class BroadcastClientHandler extends Thread {
   protected Socket incoming;
   protected int id;
   protected BufferedReader in;
   protected PrintWriter out;
   public BroadcastClientHandler(Socket incoming, int id) {
      this.incoming = incoming;
      this.id = id;
      try {
         if (incoming != null) {
            in = new BufferedReader(new InputStreamReader(
                                 incoming.getInputStream()));
            out = new PrintWriter(new OutputStreamWriter(
                                 incoming.getOutputStream()));
         }
      } catch (Exception e) {}
   }

   public synchronized void sendMessage(String msg) {
      if (out != null) {
         out.println(msg);
         out.flush();
      }
   }
}
```

```
public void run() {
   if (in != null &&
      out != null) {
     sendMessage("Hello! This is Java BroadcastEchoServer.");
     sendMessage("Enter BYE to exit.");
     try {
       while (true) {
         String str = in.readLine();
         if (str == null) {
           break;
         } else {
           // echo back to this client
           sendMessage("Echo: " + str );
           if (str.trim().equals("BYE")) {
             break;
           } else {
             // broadcast to other active clients
             Iterator iter = BroadcastEchoServer.activeClients.iterator();
             while (iter.hasNext()) {
               BroadcastClientHandler t =
                   (BroadcastClientHandler) iter.next();
               if (t != this) {
                 t.sendMessage("Broadcast(" + id + "): " + str);
               }
             }
           }
         }
       }
     }
     incoming.close();
     // this client is no longer active
     BroadcastEchoServer.activeClients.remove(this);
   } catch (IOException e) {}
  }
 }
}
```

To test this braodcast server, we first start the server on a host called `neptune`: `neptune% java BroadcastEchoServer`. Then we start two `telnet` clients on hosts `venus` and `saturn`, respectively.

Client 1 on venus

```
venus% telnet neptune 8010
Hello! This is Java BroadcastEchoServer.
Enter BYE to exit.
Echo: Hi there!
Broadcast(2): Hello!
Echo: I'm on venus. Where are you?
Broadcast(2): I'm on saturn.
...
```

Client 2 on saturn

```
saturn% telnet neptune 8010
Hello! This is Java BroadcastEchoServer.
Enter BYE to exit.
Broadcast(1): Hi there!
Echo: Hello!
Broadcast(1): I'm on venus. Where are you?
Echo: I'm on saturn.
...
```

The broadcast echo server is a prototype of many useful applications, including multiplayer games, and distributed online collaboration.

9.1.3 Design Case Study—Stock Market Quotes (1)

In this section, we develop a stock quote server and stock ticker client applet. The stock quote server maintains the current quotes of the stocks of various companies. A random number generator is used to simulate the fluctuation of the quotes (see Example 8.2 [p. 371]). The stock ticker client applet displays the quotes of a selected list of companies that are of interest. The ticker symbols and quotes scroll across the ticker banner continuously. A screen shot of the stock ticker client applet is shown in Figure 9.2.

This application involves real-time updates of stock quotes. There are generally two strategies for handling real-time updates.

Client pull: The client periodically contacts the server to receive the current quotes from the server.

Server push: The server notifies clients whenever the quote of one of stocks watched by the clients has changed.

The strategy chosen depends on many factors, including acceptable latency of updates, frequency of changes, and the like. We implement the stock ticker application by using both strategies.

The Client Pull Implementation

The information flow of the client pull implementation is as follows: (a) Periodically, the ticker client connects to the quote server; and (b) the quote server sends the quotes of all the companies in the following format and then disconnects:

$$name_1 \ quote_1$$
$$name_2 \ quote_2$$
$$...$$
$$name_n \ quote_n$$

The structure of the design is shown in Figure 9.3. The three shaded classes are the new classes to be implemented here. The `Ticker` class handles the display and animation of the quotes. The display and animation portion of the client is implemented similarly to the `ScrollingBanner` applet in Example 4.3 [p. 164]. The

Figure 9.2

The stock ticker client applet.

Figure 9.3

The client pull design of stock ticker applet and the quote server.

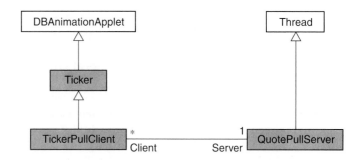

update strategy of the stock quote is separate from the display and animation of the stock quotes and is implemented in the class `TickerPullClient`. The separation allows the `Ticker` class to be reused in different implementations of the stock ticker client with different update strategies and communication mechanisms.

The Stock Ticker Animator

The `Ticker` class extends the double-buffered generic animation applet class `DBAnimationApplet` in Example 5.2 [p. 186]. The fields are summarized in the following table.

Field	Description
watch	Watch list—a string that consists of a list of the names of the companies to be watched by this client
symbol	Array of names of the companies in the watch list
quote	Array of current quotes of the corresponding companies in the `symbol` array
prevQuotes	String containing the quotes of the previous cycle
curQuotes	String containing the quotes of the current cycle
url	URL of the quote server

In order to create the appearance of continuously scrolling stock quotes, we use two strings: `prevQuotes` and `curQuotes`. For example, at any given moment, the two strings may have the following values.

```
prevQuotes:  "IBM 91 Sun 105 Intel 99"
curQuotes:   "IBM 89 Sun 106 Intel 99"
```

The methods of the `Ticker` class are summarized in the following table.

Method	Description
initAnimator()	Initializes the ticker client
initQuotes()	Hook method for retrieving the initial quotes from the quote server
updateQuotes()	Hook method for updating quotes. The prevQuotes and curQuotes strings will be updated and properly formated after calling this method
paintFrame()	Paints the current frame

The generic ticker banner class `Ticker`

```
import java.awt.*;
import java.util.*;
import java.net.*;
import java.io.*;

public class Ticker extends DBAnimationApplet {

    protected Font font = new Font("Sans-serif", Font.BOLD, 24);
    protected int offset = 1;
    protected int x, y;

    protected String watch;
    protected String symbol[], quote[];
    protected String prevQuotes, curQuotes;
    protected URL url;

    〈Method initAnimator() on page 423〉

    〈Method paintFrame() on page 424〉

    〈Methods initQuotes() and updateQuotes() on page 425〉

}
```

The initAnimator() method initializes the fields of the ticker client. The watch list is obtained from the applet parameter watch. The watch list is broken down into single names and then stored in the array symbol.

Method of class `Ticker`: `initAnimator` on page 423

```
public void initAnimator() {
    String att = getParameter("delay");
    if (att != null) {
        setDelay(Integer.parseInt(att));
    }
```

```
            watch = getParameter("watch");
            if (att != null) {
               StringTokenizer tk = new StringTokenizer(watch);
               List list = new ArrayList();
               while (tk.hasMoreTokens()) {
                  list.add(tk.nextToken());
               }
               int n = list.size();
               symbol = new String[n];
               quote = new String[n];
               for (int i = 0; i < n; i++) {
                  symbol[i] = (String) list.get(i);
                  quote[i] = "0";
               }
            }
            url = getDocumentBase();
            initQuotes();
            updateQuotes();
            prevQuotes = curQuotes;
            x = d.width;
            y = font.getSize();
         }
```

The paintFrame() method implements a behavior similar to that of the scrolling banner. The drawing of the ticker strings is done by concatenating two strings: prevQuotes and curQuotes, as illustrated in Figure 9.4. When the string prevQuote moves completely off the left end of the viewing area, the updateQuotes() method is invoked to retrieve the new quotes of the companies and form a new curQuotes strings. The current curQuotes becomes the prevQuotes.

Method of class `Ticker`: `paintFrame` on page 423

```
public void paintFrame(Graphics g) {
   g.setColor(Color.black);
   g.fillRect(0,0,d.width,d.height);

   // set the font and color, and draw the text
   g.setFont(font);
   g.setColor(Color.green);
   g.drawString(prevQuotes + curQuotes, x, y);

   // get the font metrics to determine the length of the text
   FontMetrics fm = g.getFontMetrics();
   int length = fm.stringWidth(prevQuotes);
```

Figure 9.4

The drawing of stock ticker string.

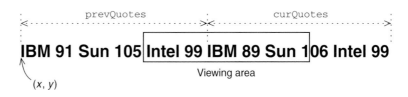

```
// adjust the position of ticker string for the next frame
x -= offset;

// if the prevQuotes string is completely off to the left end
// update the quotes and adjust the position.
if (x < -length) {
    x = 0;
    prevQuotes = curQuotes;
    updateQuotes();
}
}
```

The methods initQuotes() and updateQuotes() are hook methods that can be overridden in the subclasses. A null implementation is provided for init-Quotes(). The implementation of updateQuotes() simply forms the cur-Quotes string by concatenating all the symbols and quotes.

Methods of class Ticker: initQuotes and updateQuotes on page 423

```
public void initQuotes() {}

protected synchronized void updateQuotes() {
    StringBuffer sb = new StringBuffer();
    for (int i = 0; i < quote.length; i++) {
        sb.append(symbol[i] + " " + quote[i] + " ");
    }
    curQuotes = sb.toString();
}
```

The Stock Ticker Pull Client

The TickerPullClient class is the client applet. It extends the Ticker class and overrides the updateQuotes() method. In the updateQuotes() method, a socket connection is established with the quote server to retrieve the current quotes of all the companies in the format

$$name_1 \ quote_1$$
$$name_2 \ quote_2$$
$$...$$
$$name_n \ quote_n$$

The client picks out the companies on its watch list and updates the quote array. Then a new curQuotes string is formed, using the new quotes.

Ticker pull client

```
import java.awt.*;
import java.util.*;
import java.net.*;
import java.io.*;
public class TickerPullClient extends Ticker {
```

```
protected void updateQuotes() {
   int i;
   try {
      Socket t = new Socket(url.getHost(), 8001);
      BufferedReader in =
         new BufferedReader(new InputStreamReader(t.getInputStream()));
      String line;
      while ((line = in.readLine()) != null) {
         StringTokenizer tk = new StringTokenizer(line);
         String name = tk.nextToken();
         for (i = 0; i < quote.length; i++) {
            if (symbol[i].equals(name)) {
               String newQuote = tk.nextToken();
               quote[i] = newQuote;
            }
         }
      }
      t.close();
   } catch (IOException e) {}
   super.updateQuotes(); // form the curQuotes string
 }
}
```

This completes the implementation of the stock ticker client with the client pull strategy.

The Stock Quote Pull Server

The quote server involves two threads: (a) The main thread listens to incoming clients; and (b) another thread monitors changes in the quotes. In this example, changes are simulated with a random number generator. The array symbol contains the names of all the companies and the array quote contains the current quotes of the corresponding companies in the array symbol.

The stock quote pull server

```
import java.io.*;
import java.net.*;

public class QuotePullServer extends Thread {
   static protected String symbol[] =
      { "IBM", "Sun", "Intel", "Apple", "Compaq" };
   static protected int quote[] =
      { 100, 100, 100, 100, 100 };

   (Method main() on page 427)

   (Method run() on page 427)

}
```

The main() method listens to incoming ticker clients. It sends the quotes of all companies to any client that contacts the quote server.

Method of class QuotePullServer: main() on page 426

```
public static void main(String[] args) {
  new QuotePullServer().start();
  try {
    ServerSocket s = new ServerSocket(8001);
    while (true) {
      Socket incoming = s.accept();
      PrintWriter out =
          new PrintWriter(new OutputStreamWriter(
                incoming.getOutputStream()));
      for (int i = 0; i < quote.length; i++) {
        out.println(symbol[i] + " " + quote[i]);
      }
      out.flush();
      out.close();
      incoming.close();
    }
  } catch (Exception e) {}
}
```

The run() method simulates the changes of the quotes with a random number generator and updates the quote array.

Method of class QuotePullServer: run() on page 426

```
public void run() {
  while (true) {
    try {
      Thread.currentThread().sleep(10000);
      for (int i = 0; i < quote.length; i++) {
        quote[i] += (Math.random() - 0.4) * (10.0 * Math.random());
      }
    } catch (Exception e) {}
  }
}
```

This completes the stock quote server implementation using the client pull strategy.

The Server Push Implementation

The information flow of the server push implementation is as follows.

■ The ticker client contacts the quote server initially and provides a watch list in the format WATCH name$_1$ name$_2$ ... name$_n$.

Figure 9.5

The server push
design of the stock
ticker applet and
the quote server.

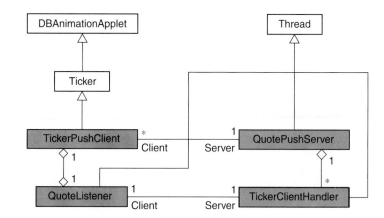

- The quote server registers the client and sends the quotes of only the companies on the watch list to the client in the format

$$name_1 \ quote_1$$
$$name_2 \ quote_2$$
$$...$$
$$name_n \ quote_n$$
$$DONE$$

- The connection between the ticker client and the quote server is maintained until the client decides to close it.

- Whenever the quote of a company is changed, the quote server sends the quote to those clients who are watching the company, in the format

$$name \ quote$$

- The client closes the connection by sending the message CLOSE.

The structure of the design is shown in Figure 9.5. The shaded boxes contain the new classes to be implemented here.

The Stock Ticker Push Client

The client involves two classes.

1. The TickerPushClient class extends the Ticker class. It make the initial contact with the quote server, retrieves the initial quotes, and handles the display of the quotes.

2. The QuoteListener class is a thread that listens to the quote server for updates on the quote. Each client has a QuoteListener object that maintains a connection with the quote server and updates the quotes displayed by the ticker client when changes occur.

The TickerPushClient overrides the initQuotes() method of the Ticker class. In the initQuotes() method, the quote server is contacted to retrieve the initial quotes of the companies on the watch list. Then a Quote-Listener object, which is a thread, is created and started to listen to the changes in the quotes.

The stock ticker push client

```java
import java.awt.*;
import java.util.*;
import java.net.*;
import java.io.*;

public class TickerPushClient extends Ticker {

    protected Socket socket;
    protected PrintWriter out;
    protected QuoteListener quoteListener;

    public void initQuotes() {
        try {
            socket = new Socket(url.getHost(), 8002);

            // send the watch list
            out = new PrintWriter(new OutputStreamWriter(
                                socket.getOutputStream()));
            out.println("WATCH " + watch);
            out.flush();

            // receive the initial quotes
            BufferedReader in =
                new BufferedReader(new InputStreamReader(
                                socket.getInputStream()));
            String line;
            while ((line = in.readLine()) != null) {
                if (line.trim().equals("DONE")) {
                    break;
                }
                StringTokenizer tk = new StringTokenizer(line);
                String name = tk.nextToken();
                for (int i = 0; i < quote.length; i++) {
                    if (symbol[i].equals(name)) {
                        String newQuote = tk.nextToken();
                        quote[i] = newQuote;
                    }
                }
            }

            quoteListener = new QuoteListener(this, in);
            quoteListener.start();
        } catch (IOException e) {}
    }

    public void destroy() {
        out.println("CLOSE");
        quoteListener.interrupt();
    }
}
```

The Quote Listener

A QuoteListener object is a thread that listens to the quote server for changes of the quotes. In contrast to the client pull strategy, a QuoteListener object does not actively contact the quote server but passively waits for the server to send any changes.

Class **QuoteListener**

```
class QuoteListener extends Thread {

   public QuoteListener(TickerPushClient ticker, BufferedReader in) {
      this.ticker = ticker;
      this.in = in;
   }

   public void run() {
      String line;
      try {
         while ((line = in.readLine()) != null) {
            StringTokenizer tk = new StringTokenizer(line);
            String name = tk.nextToken();
            for (int i = 0; i < ticker.n; i++) {
               if (ticker.symbol[i].equals(name)) {
                  String newQuote = tk.nextToken();
                  ticker.quote[i] = newQuote;
               }
            }
            if (isInterrupted()) {
               break;
            }
         }
         in.close();
      } catch (IOException e) {}
   }

   protected TickerPushClient ticker;
   protected BufferedReader in;
}
```

This completes the implementation of the stock ticker client using the server push strategy.

The Stock Quote Push Server

The quote server implementation consists of two classes.

1. The QuotePushServer class involves two threads: one listens to incoming clients, and the other monitors the changes in the quotes.

2. The TickerClientHandler class defines a thread that handles a ticker client. A TickerClientHandler object maintains a connection with a Quote-Listener object of a ticker client and pushes the changes of quotes to that client.

The field clients is a set that holds handlers for active ticker clients.

The stock quote push server

```
import java.io.*;
import java.util.*;
import java.net.*;

public class QuotePushServer extends Thread {

    static protected String symbol[] =
        { "IBM", "Sun", "Intel", "Apple", "Compaq" };
    static protected int quote[] =
        { 100, 100, 100, 100, 100 };
    static protected Set clients = new HashSet();

    (Method main() on page 431)

    (Method run() on page 431)

    (Static method getQuote() on page 432)

}
```

The main() method listens to incoming ticker clients, and creates a Ticker-ClientHandler object, which is a thread, for each ticker client, adds the client handler to the active clients set clients, and starts the thread.

Method of class QuotePushServer: main() on page 431

```
public static void main(String[] args) {
    new QuotePushServer().start();
    try {
        ServerSocket s = new ServerSocket(8002);
        while (true) {
            Socket incoming = s.accept();
            TickerClientHandler newClient = new TickerClientHandler(incoming);
            clients.add(newClient);
            newClient.start();
        }
    } catch (Exception e) {}
}
```

The run() method simulates the changes of the quotes with a random number generator and updates the quote array. Furthermore, if the quote of a stock is changed, it iterates through the set of handlers of active ticker clients and invokes the newQuote() method of the TickerClientHandler class to request that the handlers push the change to their respective clients.

Method of class QuotePushServer: run() on page 431

```
public void run() {
    while (true) {
        try {
            Thread.currentThread().sleep(10000);
```

```
      for (int i = 0; i < quote.length; i++) {
        int dq = 0;
        if (Math.random() < 0.5) {
          dq = (int) ((Math.random() - 0.4) * (10.0 * Math.random()));
        }
        if (dq != 0) {
          // quote is changed
          quote[i] += dq;
          // push to ticker clients
          Iterator iter = clients.iterator();
          while (iter.hasNext()) {
            TickerClientHandler t = (TickerClientHandler) iter.next();
            t.newQuote(symbol[i], quote[i]);
          }
        }
      }
    }
  } catch (Exception e) {}
}
```

The getQuote() method retrieves the current quote of a company by its name. It is used by the TickerClientHandler class when sending the initial quotes of companies to the clients on its watch list.

Static method of class QuotePushServer: getQuote on page 431

```
static public int getQuote(String name) {
  for (int i = 0; i < n; i++) {
    if (symbol[i].equals(name)) {
      return quote[i];
    }
  }
  return 0;
}
```

The Client Handler for the Stock Quote Push Server

The TickerClientHandler class defines a thread that handles a ticker client.

Class ClientHandler

```
class TickerClientHandler extends Thread {

  protected PrintWriter out;
  protected BufferedReader in;
  protected Socket socket;
  protected String symbol[];

  public TickerClientHandler (Socket socket) {
    this.socket = socket;
    try {
      out = new PrintWriter(new OutputStreamWriter(
              socket.getOutputStream()));
```

```
        in = new BufferedReader(new InputStreamReader(
                socket.getInputStream())));
    } catch (IOException e) {}
}

(Method run() on page 433)

(Method newQuote() on page 434)

}
```

The run() method defines the body of the thread that handles a ticker client. It waits for messages sent by its client and responds to two messages.

1. WATCH: This watch list is sent by the client at the beginning of the session. The client handler responds by sending to the client the initial quotes of companies on the watch list.

2. CLOSE: This message should be the last one received from the client. The client handler responds by removing itself from the active clients set QuotePush-Server.clients and terminates itself.

The handler thread is blocked during the session.

Method of class `TickerClientHandler`: `run()` on page 433

```
public void run() {
   try {
      String line;
      while ((line = in.readLine()) != null) {
         if (line.startsWith("WATCH")) {
            StringTokenizer tk = new StringTokenizer(line);
            tk.nextToken();
            Vector v = new Vector();
            while (tk.hasMoreTokens()) {
               v.addElement(tk.nextToken());
            }
            int n = v.size();
            String symbol[] = new String[n];
            int i;
            for (i = 0; i < n; i++) {
               symbol[i] = (String) v.elementAt(i);
            }
            this.symbol = symbol;
            for (i = 0; i < n; i++) {
               out.println(symbol[i] + " " +
                     QuotePushServer.getQuote(symbol[i]));
            }
            out.println("DONE");
            out.flush();
         } else if (line.trim().equals("CLOSE")) {
            break;
         }
      }
   }
   socket.close();
```

```
            in.close();
            out.close();
        } catch (IOException e) {}
        QuotePushServer.clients.remove(this);
    }
```

The newQuote() method pushes a new quote to the ticker client. This method is not invoked by the client handler thread but by the quote monitoring thread defined in the run() method of the QuotePushServer class [p. 433].

Method of class `TickerClientHandler`: `newQuote` on page 433

```
public void newQuote(String name, int quote) {
    boolean needToSend = false;
    if (symbol != null) {
        for (int i = 0; i < symbol.length; i++)
            if (symbol[i].equals(name)) {
                needToSend = true;
                break;
            }
    } else {
        needToSend = true;
    }
    if (needToSend) {
        out.println(name + " " + quote);
        out.flush();
    }
}
```

This completes the stock quote server implementation using the server push strategy.

9.2   REMOTE METHOD INVOCATION

Developing distributed applications using socket-based communications requires explicit connections between clients and servers and transmission of data through the connections. Java *remote method invocation* (RMI) is a mechanism that simplifies the programming model of distributed applications. It does not require explicit connections and data transmission. Objects residing on different hosts can be manipulated as if they were all on the same host. Interaction and communication among objects residing on different hosts can be accomplished similarly to regular method invocation in Java. The connections among different hosts and the transmission of data are handled implicitly by JVM.

9.2.1   The Architecture

The key participants of the RMI architecture are the following.

Figure 9.6

The architecture of remote method invocation (RMI).

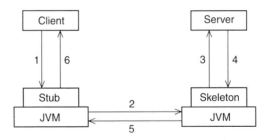

Server: An object that provides services to objects residing on remote hosts.

Service contract: An interface that defines the services provided by the server.

Client: An object that uses the services provided by objects residing on remote hosts.

Stub: An object that resides on the same host as the client and serves as a proxy, or surrogate, of the remote server.

Skeleton: An object that resides on the same host as the server, receiving requests from the stubs and dispatching the requests to the server.

The clients and servers are written by programmers. Stubs and skeletons are automatically generated by the RMI compiler from the server code.

A remote method invocation is simply an invocation of a method of a remote object. Remote method invocation uses the same syntax as regular method invocations. Figure 9.6 is a high-level view of the RMI invocation process.

1. The remote method invocation `server.m()` by the client is carried out as an invocation of a method of the stub: `stub.m()`.

2. The stub marshals[2] the arguments and sends the arguments and call information to the skeleton on the server host.

3. The skeleton unmarshals the call information and the arguments and invokes the method of the server: `server.m()`.

4. The server object executes the method and returns the result to the skeleton.

5. The skeleton marshals the result and sends the result back to the stub.

6. The stub unmarshals the result and returns the result to the client.

Key Issues

In Java, there are actually two types of objects: (a) Objects that are accessible only within the local host are called *local objects* or nonremote objects (by default, objects are local); and (b) objects that are accessible from a remote host are called *remote objects*, and are instances of classes that implement a marker interface called `java.rmi.Remote`.

Remote objects and local objects are similar in the following respects. References to local or remote objects can be passed as arguments and returned as results of method invocation (local or remote). References to local or remote objects can be

---

[2] *Marshal* in this context means to arrange the information in a linear stream.

cast, using the same syntax. The `instanceof` operator can be applied to local or remote objects.

One difference between remote and local objects is that the clients of remote objects interact with the stubs representing the remote object, not the actual objects. Another difference between remote and local objects is in the passing of arguments and return values of remote method invocations. If an argument or return value of a remote method invocation is a local object, the object is serialized, sent to the remote host, and deserialized (i.e., a copy of the local object is passed to the remote host). If an argument or return value of a remote method invocation is a remote object, a remote object reference is passed. A remote object reference can uniquely identify and locate a remote object in the network. In short, in remote method invocation, local objects are passed by value and remote objects are passed by reference.

An important question is: How does a client locate the server that will provide the service? This question is resolved by use of a naming scheme coupled with the RMI *registry*. Each RMI server is identified by a URL with the protocol `rmi`. An RMI registry is like a telephone directory. It contains a mapping between the RMI servers and their names. Each RMI server must be registered to an RMI registry to make it available to remote clients, a process known as *binding*. A client can locate an RMI server by contacting an RMI registry running on a remote host and looking up the server by name. The following URL identifies an RMI server:

$$\text{rmi://}host{:}port/name$$

Host is the name or IP address of the host on which the RMI registry is running. `Port` is the port number of the RMI registry. Name is the name bound to the RMI server.

9.2.2 Using RMI

The classes and interfaces related to RMI are contained in the `java.rmi` package. The programming interface of the RMI registry is provided in the class `Naming`. All the methods of the `Naming` class are static. They are summarized in the following table.

Method	Description
bind(name, obj)	Binds the remote object `obj` to the specified name
rebind(name, obj)	Binds the remote object `obj` to the specified name, even if the name is already bound. The old binding is discarded
unbind(name)	Removes the binding of the specified name
lookup(url)	Returns the remote object bound to the specified URL
list(url)	Returns a list of the bindings registered in the RMI registry at the specified URL

Using remote method invocation involves the following steps.

1. Define an interface of the remote object. This is the contract between the server and its clients.

```
public interface Contract extends Remote {
    public void aService(...) throws RemoteException;
    // other services . . .
}
```

The Contract interface must extend the Remote interface. The methods in this interface must declare that they may throw the RemoteException exception. The types of the arguments and return values must be serializable.

2. Define a service implementation class that implements the Contract interface.

```
public class ServiceProvider extends UnicastRemoteObject,
    implements Contract {

    public String aService(...) throws RemoteException {
        // implementation . . .
    }
    // implementation of other services . . .
}
```

The service implementation class must extend the UnicastRemoteObject class.

3. Create an instance of the server and register the server to a RMI registry:

```
Contract server = new ServiceProvider(...);
Naming.rebind(name, server);
```

4. Generate the stub and skeleton classes, using the RMI compiler. The stub class is named ServiceProvider_Stub, and the skeleton class is named ServiceProvider_Skel. The stub class also implements the Contract interface.

5. Develop a client that uses the service provided by the Contract interface. The client can be a local or remote object. It must first locate the remote object that provides the service before remote methods can be invoked:

```
Remote remoteObj = Naming.lookup(name);
Contract serverObj = (Contract) remoteObj;
// . . .
serverObj.aService(...); // remote method invocation
// . . .
```

The remoteObj is actually an instance of the stub class, which also implements the Contract interface. It should be downcast to Contract by invoking its methods.

The typical structure of RMI applications is shown in Figure 9.7.

Design Pattern: Proxy

The structure of RMI applications illustrates the Proxy design pattern.

Figure 9.7

The typical structure of RMI applications.

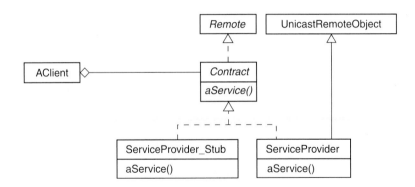

Design Pattern *Proxy*

Category: Structural design pattern.

Intent: Provide a surrogate or placeholder that represents another object.

Applicability: The Proxy design pattern is applicable when there is a need for a more versatile or sophisticated reference to an object than a simple reference (or pointer). Common situations in which the Proxy design pattern is applicable include

- a *remote proxy*, such as the stub in RMI, providing a local representative for an object residing on a remote host;

- a *virtual proxy*, creating space or time-consuming objects on demand; and

- a *protection proxy*, controlling access to the original object to provide different levels of access rights.

The structure of the Proxy design patterns is shown in the following diagram.

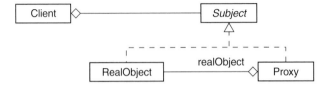

The participants of the Template Method patterns are:

- *Proxy* (e.g., `ServiceProvider_Stub`), which maintains a reference that lets the proxy access the real object and implements the Subject interface so that a proxy can be substituted for a real object;

- *Subject* (e.g., `Contract`), which defines the common interface for RealObject and Proxy so that a Proxy can be used anywhere a RealObject is expected; and
- *RealObject* (e.g., `ServiceProvider`), which defines the real object that the proxy represents.

For a detailed discussion of the Proxy design pattern see [Gamma et al. 1995].

EXAMPLE 9.6   A Simple RMI Program—Hello from Venus!

PURPOSE

This example shows the basic elements and steps involved in building an RMI application.

DESCRIPTION

We develop an RMI server and an RMI client. The server sends a string `"Hello from Venus!"` to its clients. The client, which is an applet, displays the string it receives from the server.

SOLUTION

The `Hello` interface defines the service to be provided by the server. The `HelloImpl` class is the server that implements the `Hello` interface. The `HelloApplet` class is the client.

The contract interface for RMI pull server

```
public interface Hello extends java.rmi.Remote {
   String sayHello() throws java.rmi.RemoteException;
}
```

The `main()` method of the `HelloImpl` class creates an instance of the server and binds it to the name `HelloServer` in the RMI registry.

The RMI server implementation

```
import java.rmi.*;
import java.rmi.server.UnicastRemoteObject;
public class HelloImpl
    extends UnicastRemoteObject
    implements Hello {
  private String name;
  public HelloImpl(String s)
      throws java.rmi.RemoteException {
    super();
    name = s;
  }
  public String sayHello() throws RemoteException {
    return "Hello from Venus!";
  }

  public static void main(String args[]) {
    System.setSecurityManager(new RMISecurityManager());
```

```
        try {
           HelloImpl obj = new HelloImpl("HelloServer");
           Naming.rebind("HelloServer", obj);
        } catch (Exception e) {}
     }
  }
```

Running the RMI server involves the following steps.

1. Compile the server implementation class `HelloImpl.java`.

2. Generate the stubs and skeletons, using the RMI compiler `rmic`:

```
                venus% rmic HelloImpl
```

The compiler `rmic` generates two files: `HelloImpl_Stub.class` (the stub) and `HelloImpl_Skel.cla` (the skeleton).

3. Start the RMI registry on the server host:

```
                venus% rmiregistry &
```

4. Run the server:

```
                venus% java HelloImpl &
```

The `init()` of the client applet looks up the server through the RMI registry on the server host. It downcasts the server to `Hello`, the contract interface, and makes remote method invocation `obj.sayHello()`.

The RMI client

```
import java.awt.*;
import java.rmi.*;
public class HelloApplet
     extends java.applet.Applet {
  String message = "";
  public void init() {
     try {
        Hello obj = (Hello)
           Naming.lookup("rmi: //" + getCodeBase().getHost() +
                         "/HelloServer");
        message = obj.sayHello();
     } catch (Exception e) {}
  }
  public void paint(Graphics g) {
     g.drawString(message, 25, 50);
  }
}
```

The client can be compiled and executed as usual on any host.

9.2.3   Design Case Study—Stock Market Quotes (2)

In this section we implement the stock sticker application by using RMI. We implement both the client pull and server push strategies.

Figure 9.8

The client pull
design of stock
ticker applet and
the quote server,
using RMI.

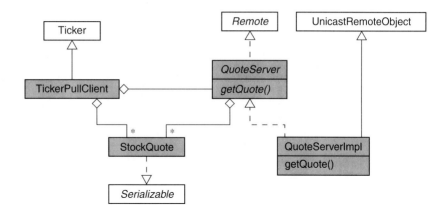

The RMI Client Pull Implementation

In the client pull implementation, the clients periodically contact the server for current quotes. Therefore only the server needs to be a remote object; the clients are local objects. The structure of the design is shown in Figure 9.8.

The RMI Pull Server Contract Interface

The service provided by the server simply returns an array of quotes, so the service contract interface is quite simple.

Remote interface `QuoteServer`

```
public interface QuoteServer extends java.rmi.Remote {
   StockQuote[] getQuote()
      throws java.rmi.RemoteException;
}
```

The `StockQuote` class is a simple class that represents the quote of a stock. Its instances are passed as the results of the `getQuote()` method, so it must be serializable.

Class `StockQuote`

```
import java.io.*;
public class StockQuote implements Serializable {

   public String name;
   public int quote;

   public StockQuote(String name, int quote) {
      this.name = name;
      this.quote = quote;
   }
}
```

The RMI Stock Quote Pull Server

The RMI server implementation class QuoteServerImpl provides an implementation for the getQuote() method defined in the QuoteServer interface.

The RMI server implementation QuoteServerImpl

```
import java.rmi.*;
import java.rmi.server.UnicastRemoteObject;

public class QuoteServerImpl extends UnicastRemoteObject
      implements QuoteServer {

  public QuoteServerImpl() throws java.rmi.RemoteException {}

  protected StockQuote quote[] = {
     new StockQuote("IBM", 100),
     new StockQuote("Sun", 100),
     new StockQuote("Intel", 100),
     new StockQuote("Apple", 100),
     new StockQuote("Compaq", 100) };

  public StockQuote[] getQuote() throws java.rmi.RemoteException {
     return quote;
  }

  (Method main() on page 442)

  (Method monitorQuotes() on page 443)

}
```

The main() method creates an instance of QuoteServerImpl and binds it to the name QuoteServer. At the end, the monitorQuotes() method is invoked, which continuously monitors the changes to the stock quotes. Unlike a socket server, an RMI server does not need to wait for a client to contact the server. An RMI client will contact the RMI registry first, and a remote reference of the RMI server will be passed to the client.

Method of class QuoteServerImpl: main() on page 442

```
public static void main(String[] args) {
   System.setSecurityManager(new RMISecurityManager());
   try {
      QuoteServerImpl obj = new QuoteServerImpl();
      Naming.rebind("QuoteServer", obj);
      obj.monitorQuotes();
   } catch (Exception e) {}
}
```

The monitorQuotes() method contains an infinite loop that simulates the changes to the quotes with a random number generator.

Method of class `QuoteServerImpl`: `monitorQuotes()` on page 442

```
public void monitorQuotes() {
  while (true) {
    try {
      Thread.currentThread().sleep(10000);
      for (int i = 0; i < quote.length; i++) {
        quote[i].quote += (Math.random() - 0.4) * (10.0 * Math.random());
      }
    } catch (Exception e) {}
  }
}
```

This completes the RMI stock quote server implementation using the client pull strategy.

The RMI Stock Ticker Pull Client

The RMI client `TickerPullClient` class extends the class `Ticker`, which handles the display of the quotes. It contains a reference to the remote server and overrides the `initQuotes()` and the `updateQuotes()` methods.

RMI client `TickerPullClient`

```
import java.awt.*;
import java.util.*;
import java.io.*;
import java.rmi.*;

public class TickerPullClient extends Ticker {
  protected QuoteServer server;

  ⟨Method initQuotes() on page 443⟩

  ⟨Method updateQuotes() on page 444⟩

}
```

In the `initQuotes()` method, the client looks up the quote server.

Method of class `TickerPullClient`: `initQuotes()` on page 443

```
public void initQuotes() {
  try {
    server = (QuoteServer)
      Naming.lookup("rmi://" + getCodeBase().getHost() +
                    "/QuoteServer");
  } catch (Exception e) {}
}
```

In the `updateQuotes()` method, the client invokes a remote method, `server.getQuote()`, and updates the `quote` array with the new quotes.

Method of class `TickerPullClient`: `updatesQuotes()` on page 443

```
protected void updateQuotes() {
   int i, j;
   try {
      StockQuote newQuote[] = server.getQuote();
      for (j = 0; j < newQuote.length; j ++) {
         for (i = 0; i < quote.length; i++) {
            if (newQuote[j].name.equals(symbol[i])) {
               quote[i] = Integer.toString(newQuote[j].quote);
            }
         }
      }
   } catch (Exception e) {}
   super.updateQuotes();
}
```

This completes the implementation of the RMI stock ticker client using the client pull strategy.

The RMI Server Push Implementation

In the server push implementation, a client contacts the server and provides a watch list. The client also retrieves the current quotes of the companies that it watches. The server keeps track of all the active clients. When the quote of a company changes, it contacts (also known as a *call-back*) all the clients that are watching the company. Thus the server and the clients are all remote objects. Each client has a reference to the server, and the server maintains references to all the active clients. We have two remote interfaces: one for the server and one for the clients. The structure of the design is shown in Figure 9.9.

Figure 9.9

The server push design of the stock ticker applet and the quote server, using RMI.

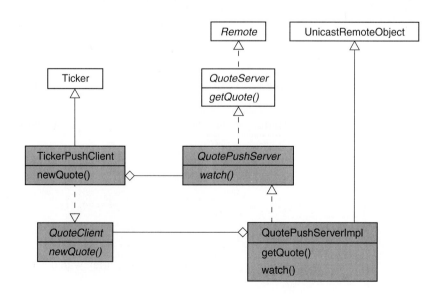

The RMI Push Server and Client Contract Interfaces

The contract interface for the push server extends the `QuoteServer` interface. The `watch()` method lets the clients provide their watch lists to the server.

The contract interface for RMI push server

```
import java.rmi.*;

public interface QuotePushServer extends QuoteServer {
   void watch(QuoteClient client, String[] list)
      throws RemoteException;
}
```

The `QuoteClient` interface defines a call-back method supported by the clients. The `newQuote()` method allows the push server to inform the clients of new quotes of the stocks that they are watching.

The contract interface for RMI push client

```
import java.rmi.*;

public interface QuoteClient extends Remote {
   void newQuote(StockQuote newQuote)
      throws RemoteException;
}
```

The RMI Stock Quote Push Server

The `QuotePushServerImpl` class implements the `QuotePushServer` interface. The field `clients` is a set of active clients. Each element in the `clients` set is an instance of the inner class `ClientInfo`, which contains a remote reference to the client and the client's watch list. The `getQuote()` method returns the array of current quotes. The `watch()` method creates a `ClientInfo` object and adds it to the `clients` set.

The push server `QuotePushServerImpl`

```
import java.util.*;
import java.rmi.*;
import java.rmi.server.UnicastRemoteObject;

public class QuotePushServerImpl extends UnicastRemoteObject
      implements QuotePushServer {

  public QuotePushServerImpl() throws java.rmi.RemoteException {}

  protected StockQuote quote[] = {
     new StockQuote("IBM", 100),
     new StockQuote("Sun", 100),
     new StockQuote("Intel", 100),
     new StockQuote("Apple", 100),
     new StockQuote("Compaq", 100) };
```

```
protected Set clients = new HashSet();

class ClientInfo {
  ClientInfo(QuoteClient client, String[] watch) {
    this.client = client;
    this.watch = watch;
  }
  QuoteClient client;  // remote reference to a client
  String watch[];
}

public StockQuote[] getQuote() throws java.rmi.RemoteException {
  return quote;
}

public void watch(QuoteClient client, String[] list)
    throws java.rmi.RemoteException {
  clients.add(new ClientInfo(client, list));
}

(Method main() on page 446)

(Method monitorQuotes() on page 446)

}
```

The main() method creates an instance of QuotePushServerImpl and binds it to the name QuotePushServer. At the end, the monitorQuotes() method is invoked, which continuously monitors changes in the stock quotes.

Method of class QuotePushServerImpl: main() on page 446

```
public static void main(String[] args) {
  System.setSecurityManager(new RMISecurityManager());
  try {
    QuotePushServerImpl obj = new QuotePushServerImpl();
    Naming.rebind("QuotePushServer", obj);
    monitorQuotes();
  } catch (Exception e) {}
}
```

The monitorQuotes() method simulates the changes to the quotes with a random number generator. When the quote of a stock is changed, it iterates through the clients set. For each client that is watching the stock, the newQuote() method is invoked through the remote reference to the client.

Method of class QuotePushServerImpl: monitorQuotes() on page 446

```
public void monitorQuotes() {
  while (true) {
    try {
      Thread.currentThread().sleep(10000);
      for (int i = 0; i < quote.length; i++) {
```

```
                      int dq = 0;
                      if (Math.random() < 0.5) {
                         dq = (int) ((Math.random() - 0.4) * (10.0 * Math.random()));
                      }
                      if (dq > 0) {
                         quote[i].quote += dq;
                         Iterator iter = clients.iterator();
                         while (iter.hasNext()) {
                            ClientInfo ci = (ClientInfo) iter.next();
                            for (int k = 0; k < ci.watch.length; k++) {
                               if (ci.watch[k].equals(quote[i].name)) {
                                  ci.client.newQuote(quote[i]);
                                  break;
                               }
                            }
                         }
                      }
                   }
               } catch (Exception e) {}
          }
     }
```

This completes the RMI stock quote server implementation using the server push strategy.

The RMI Stock Ticker Push Client

The `TickerPushClient` class implements the remote client interface `Quote-Client`. The `newQuote()` method is remotely invoked by the quote server. It updates the `quote` array, which is local to each client. The `initQuotes()` method locates the quote server and sends the server the watch list by invoking the `watch()` method of the server. Note that it passes itself, `this`, as the argument to the remote method invocation. The object reference to a remote object is automatically converted to a remote object reference when it is passed as an argument to a remote method invocation. Furthermore, to allow the server to invoke the client's call-back method `newQuote()`, the client must be exported as a remote object by calling the static method `exportObject()` of the `UnicastRemoteObject` class.

The ticker push client

```
import java.awt.*;
import java.util.*;
import java.io.*;
import java.rmi.*;
import java.rmi.server.*;

public class TickerPushClient extends Ticker
      implements QuoteClient {

   public void initQuotes() {
```

```
    try {
      UnicastRemoteObject.exportObject(this);

      QuotePushServer obj = (QuotePushServer)
          Naming.lookup("//" + getCodeBase().getHost() + "/QuotePushServer");
      obj.watch(this, symbol);
      StockQuote newQuote[] = obj.getQuote();
      for (int j = 0; j < newQuote.length; j ++) {
        for (int i = 0; i < n; i++) {
          if (newQuote[j].name.equals(symbol[i])) {
            quote[i] = Integer.toString(newQuote[j].quote);
          }
        }
      }
    } catch (Exception e) {}
  }

  public void newQuote(StockQuote newQuote) throws java.rmi.RemoteException {
    for (int i = 0; i < n; i++) {
      if (newQuote.name.equals(symbol[i])) {
        quote[i] = Integer.toString(newQuote.quote);
      }
    }
  }
}
```

This completes the implementation of the RMI stock ticker client using the server push strategy.

9.3   DISTRIBUTED COMPUTING WITH NON-JAVA APPLICATIONS

Socket-based communication and remote method invocation are adequate and effective mechanisms for distributed Java applications. However, the reality of today's computing environment is that the majority of existing applcations are written in languages other than Java. In this section we discuss two important mechanisms for interfacing Java applications with non-Java applications in distributed computing environments: Java database connectivity (JDBC) and Common Object Request Broker Architecture (CORBA).

9.3.1   Java Database Connectivity

Java database connectivity is a mechanism that allows Java programs to access relational databases. It is a simple Java interface for Structured Query Language (SQL), the standard language for accessing relational databases. The JDBC interface supports full access to relational databases, including creating new tables, modifying existing tables, inserting and updating data in existing tables, querying a database, and retrieving meta data (information about a database and its contents).

A key component in the implementation of JDBC is the *JDBC driver*, which communicates between Java applications and the databases. The following table summarizes the main characteristics of the four types of JDBC drivers.[3]

Driver	Description
1. JDBC-ODBC bridge	Provides JDBC access via most ODBC drivers
2. Native-API (partially Java)	Converts JDBC calls to DBMS calls
3. Net-protocol (pure Java)	Translates JDBC calls into a DBMS independent net protocol, which is then translated to a DBMS protocol by a net server. The net server can connect all its Java clients to several different databases
4. Native-protocol (pure Java)	Converts JDBC calls to the network protcol used by the DBMS directly

An Overview of the Structured Query Language

The SQL is a programming language for accessing relational databases. Most industrial-strength relational databases support SQL. Some of the commonly used SQL commands are summrized in the following table.

Command	Description
INSERT	Inserts new row(s) in a table
DELETE	Removes row(s) from a table
UPDATE	Modifies the values of existing table row(s)
SELECT	Retrieves database information based on a condition
CREATE	Creates a new database object
DROP	Removes an existing database object
ALTER	Alters the format of an existing database object

Assume that we want to create the following table in a relational database.

---

[3] For more information about JDBC drivers and their availability, capabilities, and limitations, see http://java.sun.com/.

name	address	city	state	zip	email	creditCard	orderno
M. Jordan	549 E. Surf	Chicago	IL	60657	mjordan@nba.com	Visa	102219985502
S. Pippen	11 S. 59th	Oakbrook	IL	60606	spippen@nba.com	Discover	103119983212
D. Rodman	234 N. 3rd	Chicago	IL	60030	drodman@nba.com	MasterCard	103119983223
S. Kerr	4010 Pine	Los Angeles	CA	90507	skerr@nba.com	Visa	010219991201
R. Harper	234 N. 3rd	New York	NY	20304	rharper@nba.com	MasterCard	012019992013

The following SQL statement creates a new table called `Beetles`. It specifies the columns that the table must have and declares a datatype for each. For example, the column specification name VARCHAR(35) defines a 35-character column called name.

```
CREATE TABLE Beetles (name VARCHAR(35),
                      address VARCHAR(35),
                      city VARCHAR(20),
                      state VARCHAR(2),
                      zip VARCHAR(5),
                      email VARCHAR(30),
                      creditCard VARCHAR(15));
```

Note that the `orderno` column is missing from the `Beetles` table. We can add the column to the table by using the SQL statement

```
ALTER TABLE Beetles ADD orderno VARCHAR(12);
```

After the table is built, rows are added to it with the INSERT command. The following SQL statement adds a row to the Beetles table.

```
INSERT INTO Beetles VALUES('Michael Owen',
                           '123 Elmwood Street',
                           'Lake Forest',
                           'IL', '65431',
                           'mowen@aol.com',
                           'MasterCard',
                           '112819981304');
```

The SELECT statement retrieves data from a database, based on a specified criterion. When no criterion is supplied, as in the following example, all the rows will be returned from the specified table.

```
SELECT * from Beetles;
```

The following example would *select* every row from the Beetles table *where* the name column contained the value 'Michael OWEN.'

```
SELECT * from Beetles WHERE name = 'Michael Owen';
```

For the remainder of this section, familiarity with SQL and relational databases is assumed. For detailed discussions of SQL and relational databases see [Bowman et al. 1996] and [Darwen and Date 1997].

An Overview of JDBC

The interfaces and classes of JDBC are contained in the `java.sql` package. The commonly used JDBC interfaces and classes are summarized in the following table.

Interface/Class	Description
DriverManager	Manages the loading of JDBC drivers and supports new database connections
Connection	Represents database connections
Statement	Represents SQL statements to be passed to the DBMS via an already established connection
ResultSet	Provides access to the results of a query, as well as information about the database
ResultSetMetaData	Provides information about the columns in a ResultSet

Using JDBC involves establishing a connection with a database, using the `DriverManager` and `Connection` classes; using `Statement` objects to pass SQL commands to a DBMS; and processing the results of an SQL query, which are captured as `ResultSet` objects.

Establishing a Connection with a Database

The `DriverManager` class is used for loading and managing JDBC drivers. A JDBC driver must be loaded before any other activities can take place. The JDBC drivers are loaded, using *dynamic class loading*, as follows:

$$Class.forName(JDBCDriverName);$$

For example, the following statement loads the *JDBC–ODBC Bridge driver* provided by Sun Microsystems:

$$Class.forName("sun.jdbc.odbc.JdbcOdbcDriver");$$

JDBC uses URLs to locate databases. JDBC URLs are presented in one of two formats.

■ For a database on the local machine:

$$jdbc:subprotocol:subname$$

■ For a database on a network host:

jdbc:*subprotocol*: //*host*[:*port*] /*subname*

The components of a JDBC URL are summarized in the following table.

Component	Description
subprotocol	Specifies a driver or a database connectivity mechanism that may be supported by one or more drivers. A common example of a subprotocol name is odbc.
subname	Identifies a database

Instances of the Connection class represent open database connections. Connection objects are created by using a static method getConnection() of the DriverManager class. The getConnection() method takes a JDBC URL, a user ID, and a password as parameters. In the following example the ODBC subprotocol is used to access a database named myDatabase:

```
String url = "jdbc:odbc:myDatabase";
Connection conn = DriverManager.getConnection(url, "myID", "myPassword");
```

Once the connection to a database has been established successfully, a Connection object is returned. It can be used to query the database. The most commonly used methods of the Connection interface are summarized in the following table.

Method	Description
createStatement()	Returns a new Statement object for executing SQL statements
commit()	Commits (makes permanent) any database changes that have been made since the last call to *commit*. A call to commit also releases any database locks held by this Connection object
close()	Releases the DBMS and any other JDBC resourses currently being used by this Connection object

Querying the Database

Instances of the `Statement` class are used to compose SQL commands and send them to a DBMS. `Statement` objects can be obtained from an opened database connection:

```
Statement stmt = conn.createStatement();
```

The commonly used methods of the `Statement` interface are summarized in the following table. The parameter `sql` is a string that represents a SQL statement.

Method	Description
executeQuery(sql)	Executes the statement `sql` that retrieves data from the database and returns a `ResultSet` object
executeUpdate(sql)	Executes the statement `sql` that updates the database (i.e., one of `INSERT`, `UPDATE`, or `DELETE` statements) and returns an integer indicating the number of rows affected by the statement
close()	Releases the DBMS and any other JDBC resources currently being used by this Statement object, immediately rather than relying on automatic closure by the garbage collector

Using the `Beetles` table example, the following statements create the table, using JDBC.

```
String createString =
   "CREATE TABLE Beetles (name VARCHAR(35), " +
                         "address VARCHAR(35), " +
                         "city VARCHAR(20), " +
                         "state VARCHAR(2), " +
                         "zip VARCHAR(5), " +
                         "email VARCHAR(30), " +
                         "creditCard VARCHAR(15))";
stmt.executeUpdate(createString);
```

A query on the Beetles table can be made as

```
ResultSet rset = stmt.executeQuery("SELECT name, email FROM Beetles");
```

It retrieves the `name` and `email` columns of the `Beetles` table.

Processing the Results

The results of a query are stored as a set of rows and columns in a `ResultSet` object. The methods of the `ResultSet` interface are summarized in Table 9.1.

TABLE 9.1

Methods of the `ResultSet` interface.

Method	Description
next()	Advances to the next row of the result set; returns `true` if successful or `false` when there are no more rows in the result set
get*Type*(i)	Returns the value of the `i`th column. *Type* is the data type of the column, and it can be one of Byte, Boolean, Double, Float, Int, Long, or String among others. The return value is of the corresponding type.
get*Type*(name)	Same as the preceding method, except that it retrieves the values of a column by its name
void close()	Releases the DBMS and any other JDBC resourses currently being used by this `ResultSet` object

The rows of the `ResultSet` object can be accessed by using a combination of the `next()` method and the get*Type*() method. The `next()` method moves the cursor to the next row of a `ResultSet` object and makes that the current row (i.e., the row that is currently available for processing). Initially, the cursor is positioned just above the first row of a `ResultSet` object. Invoking `next()` moves the cursor to the first row and makes it the current row. Subsequent calls to `next()` cause the cursor to be moved down through the result set, one row at a time, from top to bottom. The `next()` method will return `false` when there are no more rows. There are two ways to identify the columns in the current row: by the column name or by the column index. For example, `getString(1)` returns the first column of the result set as a `String` object, and `getString("name")` returns the name column as a `String` object. The following `while` loop iterates through the rows of the `ResultSet` object, displaying the name and email fields as it goes.

```
while (rset.next()) {
    String name = rset.getString("name");
    String email = rset.getString("email");
    System.out.println(name + ", " + email);
}
```

The following is an example of what the output might look like.

```
Michael Jordan, mjordan@nba.com
Scotty Pippen, spippen@nba.com
Dennis Rodman, drodman@nba.com
Steve Kerr, skerr@nba.com
```

EXAMPLE 9.7   Building a Table with JDBC

PURPOSE

Illustrate the basic concepts of JDBC.

DESCRIPTION

This program builds a new Beetles table, inserts a test record into the table, and queries the table.

SOLUTION

Build JDBC Table

```
import java.sql.*;
import java.io.*;
import java.util.Date;

public class BuildBeetlesTable {
   public static void main(String args[])
                 throws SQLException, IOException {

     System.out.print("\nLoading JDBC-ODBC driver...\n\n");
     try {
       Class.forName("sun.jdbc.odbc.JdbcOdbcDriver");
     } catch(ClassNotFoundException e) {
       System.exit( 1 );
     }
     System.out.print("Connecting to Orders database...\n\n");
     String url = "jdbc:odbc:OrdersDriver";
     Connection conn =
             DriverManager.getConnection(url,"rPasenko","mpf98eub");
     System.out.print("Building new Beetles table...\n\n");
     String createString =
             "CREATE TABLE Beetles (name VARCHAR(35), " +
                             "address VARCHAR(35), " +
                             "city VARCHAR(20), " +
                             "state VARCHAR(2), " +
                             "zip VARCHAR(5), " +
                             "email VARCHAR(30), " +
                             "creditCard VARCHAR(15))";
     stmt.executeUpdate(createString);
     System.out.print("Inserting test row in Beetles table...\n\n");
     String insertString =
             "INSERT INTO Beetles VALUES ('Michael Owen', " +
                             "'123 Elmwood Street', " +
                             "'Lake Forest', " +
                             "'IL', " +
                             "'65431', " +
                             "'mowen@aol.com', " +
                             "'MasterCard')";
     stmt.executeUpdate(insertString);
     ResultSet rset = stmt.executeQuery("SELECT * FROM Beetles");
```

```
        while( rset.next() ) {
          System.out.print("     " + rset.getString( "name" ) + ", ");
          System.out.print(rset.getString( 2 ) + ", " );
          System.out.print(rset.getString( 3 ) + ", " );
          System.out.print(rset.getString( 4 ) + ",\n     " );
          System.out.print(rset.getString( 5 ) + ", ");
          System.out.print(rset.getString( 6 ) + ", ");
          System.out.print(rset.getString( 7 ) + "\n");
        }
        System.out.print("\nClosing database connection...");
        conn.commit();
        stmt.close();
        rset.close();
        conn.close();
    }
}
```

Following is the output of the `BuildBeetlesTable` program.

```
venus% java BuildBeetlesTable
Loading JDBC-ODBC driver...
Connecting to Orders database...
Building new Beetles table...
Inserting test row in Beetles table...
   Michael Owen, 123 Elmwood Street, Lake Forest, IL,
   65431, mowen@aol.com, MasterCard
Closing database connection...
```

EXAMPLE 9.8   Modifying a Table with JDBC

PURPOSE

This example shows how to modify a table with JDBC.

DESCRIPTION

This program modifies the structure of the Beetles table, updates the test record in that table, displays the modified table contents, and then deletes the test record.

SOLUTION

JDBC Modify Table

```
import java.util.Calendar;
import java.sql.*;
import java.io.*;

class ModifyBeetlesTable {
  public static void main( String args[] )
          throws SQLException, IOException {
      try {
        Class.forName("sun.jdbc.odbc.JdbcOdbcDriver");
      } catch(ClassNotFoundException e) {
        System.exit(1);
      }
```

```
System.out.print("\nConnecting to Beetles table...\n\n");
String url = "jdbc:odbc:OrdersDriver";
Connection conn =
    DriverManager.getConnection(url,"rPasenko","mpf98eub");
Statement stmt = conn.createStatement();
System.out.print("Modifying Beetles table...\n\n");
String updateString =
    "ALTER TABLE Beetles ADD ORDERNO VARCHAR(12)";
stmt.executeUpdate(updateString);
Calendar cal = Calendar.getInstance();
String orderNo = String.valueOf(cal.get(cal.MONTH)+1) +
                String.valueOf(cal.get(cal.DAY_OF_MONTH)) +
                String.valueOf(cal.get(cal.YEAR)) +
                String.valueOf(cal.get(cal.HOUR)) +
                String.valueOf(cal.get(cal.MINUTE)) +
                String.valueOf(cal.get(cal.SECOND));
updateString = "UPDATE Beetles SET ORDERNO = " +
                orderNo + " WHERE NAME='Michael Owen'";
stmt.executeUpdate(updateString);
ResultSet rset = stmt.executeQuery("SELECT * FROM Beetles");
System.out.print("Displaying table contents...\n\n");
while (rset.next()) {
   System.out.println("    " +
        rset.getString("name") + ", " +
        rset.getString("address") + ", " +
        rset.getString("city") + ", " +
        rset.getString("state") + "\n    " +
        rset.getString("zip") + ", " +
        rset.getString("email") + ", " +
        rset.getString("creditCard") + ", " +
        rset.getString("orderno") );
}

System.out.print("\nDeleting test record...\n\n");
updateString = "DELETE FROM Beetles WHERE NAME='Michael Owen'";
stmt.executeUpdate(updateString);
System.out.print("Closing connection...\n\n");
conn.commit();
stmt.close();
rset.close();
conn.close();
   }
}
```

The following are the results of the `ModifyBeetlesTable` program.

```
venus% java ModifyBeetlesTable
Connecting to Beetles table...
Modifying Beetles table...
Displaying table contents...
   Michael Owen, 123 Elmwood Street, Lake Forest, IL
   65431, mowen@aol.com, MasterCard, 179917556
Deleting test record...
Closing connection...
```

EXAMPLE 9.9   Adding Database Functionality to the Order Applet

PURPOSE

This example demonstrates database updates with JDBC.

DESCRIPTION

This example extends the Order applet from Example 6.13 so that it includes database functionality. In this version, the applet writes each order to the Order database.

SOLUTION

We extend the Order class in Example 6.13, The OrderDialog class will be replace by a new class JdbcOrderDialog.

JDBC Order Dialog

```java
import java.util.Calendar;
import java.awt.event.*;
import javax.swing.*;
import java.sql.*;
import java.io.*;

public class JdbcOrderDialog extends OrderDialog {

  public JdbcOrderDialog(JFrame owner) {
    super(owner);
  }

  protected ActionListener makeButtonHandler() {
    return new JdbcButtonHandler();
  }

  class JdbcButtonHandler implements ActionListener {
    public void actionPerformed(ActionEvent evt) {
      JButton button = (JButton) evt.getSource();
      String label = button.getText();
      if ("Ok".equals(label)) {
        try {
          insertNewOrder();
        } catch( IOException IOex ) {}
        dialogPanel.reset();
        setVisible(false);
      }
    }

    public void insertNewOrder() throws SQLException, IOException {
      System.out.print( "Loading JDBC OCI driver...\n\n\n" );
      try {
        Class.forName( "sun.jdbc.odbc.JdbcOdbcDriver" );
      } catch (ClassNotFoundException e) {
        System.exit( 1 );
      }
```

```
      String url = "jdbc:odbc:OrdersDriver";
      Connection conn = DriverManager.getConnection(url,"rpasenko","mpf8eub");
      Statement stmt = conn.createStatement();
      String creditCard = null;
      if (dialogPanel.visaBox.isSelected()) {
         creditCard = "Visa";
      } else if (dialogPanel.mcBox.isSelected()) {
         creditCard = "MasterCard";
      } else if ( dialogPanel.discoverBox.isSelected() ) {
         creditCard = "Discover";
      }

      Calendar cal = Calendar.getInstance();
      String orderNo = String.valueOf(cal.get(cal.MONTH)+1) +
                  String.valueOf(cal.get(cal.DAY_OF_MONTH)) +
                  String.valueOf(cal.get(cal.YEAR)) +
                  String.valueOf(cal.get(cal.HOUR)) +
                  String.valueOf(cal.get(cal.MINUTE)) +
                  String.valueOf(cal.get(cal.SECOND));

      String insertString;
      insertString = "INSERT INTO Beetles VALUES( " +
                  "'" + dialogPanel.nameField.getText()    + "'," +
                  "'" + dialogPanel.addressField.getText() + "'," +
                  "'" + dialogPanel.cityField.getText()    + "'," +
                  "'" + dialogPanel.stateField.getText()   + "'," +
                  "'" + dialogPanel.zipField.getText()     + "'," +
                  "'" + dialogPanel.emailField.getText()   + "'," +
                  "'" + creditCard                         + "'," +
                  "'" + orderNo                            + "')";
      stmt.executeUpdate(insertString);
      stmt.close();
      conn.commit();
      conn.close();
   }
 }
}
```

The JdbcOrderDialog class extends the OrderDialog class in Example 6.13. The new method insertNewOrder() opens a database connection, builds an SQL string for inserting an order in the Beetles table, executes the SQL command, and then closes the database connection and other JDBC resources.

We have now introduced most of the basic aspects of JDBC. For more complete coverage of JDBC, see [Hamilton et al. 1997]. ▪

9.3.2   Common Object Request Broker Architecture

The Common Object Request Broker Architecture (CORBA) is an open, distributed object computing infrastructure being standardized by the Object Management Group (OMG), an industrial consorium that comprises 500 software vendors, developers, and users.

CORBA simplifies the development of distributed applications by providing a unified view of all distributed systems. The CORBA application framework provides interoperability between objects in heterogeneous distributed environments, where the objects can be implemented in different languages, such as Java, C/C++, Ada, and COBOL.

The basic architecture of CORBA resembles that of RMI. The participants in a CORBA application are similar to participants in a Java RMI application.

Server: An object that provides services to objects residing on remote hosts.

Service contract: An interface that defines the services provided by the server.

Client: An object that uses services provided by objects residing on remote hosts.

Stub: An object that resides on the same host as the client and serves as a proxy, or surrogate, of the remote server.

Skeleton: An object that resides on the same host as the server, receives requests from the stubs, and dispatches the requests to the server.

The center piece of CORBA is the *Interface Definition Language* (IDL). The CORBA clients and servers can be implemented in different languages. The service contract interface of a CORBA server is defined in a language-neutral fashion, using IDL. The IDL compliers translate the interfaces written in IDL to various implementation languages, such as Java and C/C++. The IDL compilers also generate stubs and skeletons in various implementation languages.

A key component of the CORBA architecture is the *Object Request Broker* (ORB). The ORB defines the mechanism and interfaces that enable objects to make requests and receive responses in a distributed environment. The ORB provides an infrastructure allowing objects to communicate independently of specific platforms and implementation languages. The basic structure of a CORBA application is shown in Figure 9.10.

A CORBA application consists of a set of collaborating objects. When a client requests a service, the ORB will first locate a server that implements the requested service. The ORB is also responsible for sending the arguments and call information to the server, invoking the method on the server, and sending the results back to the client. The client need not be concerned with the server object's location, programming language, or operating system.

Figure 9.10

The basic structure of a CORBA application.

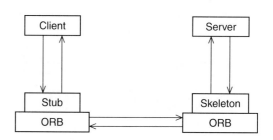

CORBA provides flexibility and interoperability in today's increasingly complex computing environment. It lets programmers choose the most appropriate operating system, execution environment, and programming language to use for each component that they are constructing. Moreover, CORBA allows the integration of Java applications with existing applications. In a CORBA-based solution, legacy components can be modeled by using IDL. Thus CORBA is a giant step on the road to interoperability in distributed object-oriented applications.

A complete discussion of CORBA is beyond the scope of this book. For more information on CORBA see [Orfali and Harkey 1998].

CHAPTER SUMMARY

- Distributed applications consist of components that reside on different network hosts.

- Sockets are the endpoints of two-way connections between two distributed components that communicate with each other. A connection must be explicitly established by both parties. There are two kinds of sockets: client sockets and server sockets. A client socket can be used to send and receive data. A server socket waits for requests for connections from clients. Server sockets can be created only by Java apps, not by applets. Client sockets can be created and used by both Java apps and applets.

- Remote method invocation (RMI) makes the network "transparent." It allows distributed components to be manipulated (almost) as if they were all on the same host. Programmers need not deal at all with interhost communications. They are handled implicitly by the run-time environment supporting the remote method invocation. The key participants of RMI architecture are the following.

Server: An object that provides services to objects residing on remote hosts.

Service contract: An interface that defines the services provided by the server.

Client: An object that uses the services provided by objects residing on remote hosts.

Stub: An object that resides on the same host as the client and serves as a proxy, or surrogate, of the remote server.

Skeleton: An object that resides on the same host as the server, receives requests from the stubs, and dispatches the requests to the server.

Clients and servers are written by programmers, whereas stubs and skeletons are automatically generated by the RMI compiler from the server code.

- Java database connectivity (JDBC) allows Java applications to interface with relational databases, which are widely used today. A wealth of information is stored in relational databases. Through JDBC, Java applcations can access information stored in existing databases and share information with applications written in other languages. Using JDBC involves establishing a connection with a database, using the `DriverManager` and `Connection` classes; using `Statement` objects to pass SQL commands to a DBMS; and processing the results of an SQL query, which are captured as `ResultSet` objects.

▪ The Common Object Request Broker Architecture (CORBA) is an object-oriented framework that supports interoperability among objects written in different languages and running on different platforms. CORBA support is available for most programming languages, including Java, and platforms used for industrial applications. CORBA is especially useful in interfacing applications developed in modern languages, such as Java and C++, with legacy systems.

EXERCISES

9.1 Use sockets to implement a two-way chat application consisting of a server and two clients. The client program has a graphical user interface that consists of

- a text area for typing outgoing messages;
- another text area for displaying incoming messages;
- a Send button for sending outgoing messages;
- a Clear outgoing messages button;
- a Clear incoming messages button; and
- a Quit button.

9.2 Enhance Exercise 9.1 to support multiple clients.

9.3 Use RMI to implement Exercises 9.1 and 9.2.

9.4 Develop a distributed version of the tic-tac-toe game in Section 8.3 [p. 392], using sockets or RMI. It should allow two players on different hosts to play the game remotely.

9.5 Develop a distributed version of the multiplayer tic-tac-toe game in Exercise 8.4 [p. 406], using sockets or RMI. It should allow multiple players on different hosts to play the game remotely.

9.6 Develop a distributed version of the drawing pad in Exercise 7.1 [p. 367], using sockets or RMI. Several drawing pad clients can run simultaneously on different hosts. Drawings by all the clients should be displayed on the same canvas and should be visible to all the clients.

Epilogue

Java technology is continuously and rapidly evolving. It is also rapidly gaining acceptance in the industry. In this book, we could touch on only part of the core features of Java. There are many other exciting features of Java, and efforts are currently underway to develop new Java-based technologies. They promise to make Java suitable for a wide range of tasks in building the information infrastructure in the years ahead. The following are some of these technologies.

JavaBeans and Enterprise JavaBeans

JavaBeans is the platform independent, component architecture for the Java application environment, which allows applications to be assembled from ready-made components, known as *beans*. It is intended for use in developing or assembling network-aware solutions for heterogeneous environments—within an enterprise or throughout the Internet. Enterprise JavaBeans (EJB) extends JavaBeans by letting container-based objects communicate with each other via a network. Containers are software receptacles that know how to communicate with and manage beans and provide services such as persistence management, transactions, concurrency, and security.

Java Media Framework

The Java Media Framework supports the integration of audio and video clips, animated presentations, two-dimensional graphics and imaging, speech input and output, three-dimensional models, and telephony. By providing standard players and integrating these supporting technologies, the Java Media Framework enables developers to produce and distribute compelling, media-rich content.

The Java Media Framework consists of the following packages.

Java Sound: Supports audio mixing, audio capture, MIDI sequencing, and MIDI synthesis.

Java Speech: Supports command and control recognizers, dictation systems, and speech synthesizers.

Java Telephony: Supports platform-independent computer-telephony applications.

Java 2D: Supports advanced two-dimensional graphics and imaging capabilities, encompassing line art, text, and images in a single comprehensive model.

Java 3D: Supports constructs for creating and manipulating three-dimensional geometry and for constructing the structures used in rendering that geometry.

Java Advanced Imaging: Supports sophisticated, high-performance image processing capabilities such as image tiling, regions of interest, and deferred execution.

Java Cryptography Extension

The Java Cryptography Extension (JCE) supports operations such as encryption, key generation and agreement, and Message Authentication Code (MAC) generation. It is an essential component in applications such as electronic transactions.

Jini

Jini connection technology enables users to connect virtually any consumer and enterprise device to a network from any location by removing the compatibility, reliability, and administration constraints that have traditionally impeded the successful deployment of heterogeneous networks.

For more information on these and other Java technologies, access

```
http://java.sun.com/
```

Summary of the APPLET Tag

The `<applet>` tag is used to embed a Java applet in an HTML page. The `<applet>` tag has the following form:

```
<applet
    [ align = alignment ]
    [ alt = alternate-text ]
    [ archive = archived-file ]
    code = applet-filename
    [ codebase = applet-url ]
    height = pixel-height
    [ hspace = horizontal-pixel-space ]
    [ name = applet-name ]
    [ vspace = vertical-pixel-space ]
    width = pixel-width
>
[ <param name = param-name₁ value = param-value₁ > ]
...
[ <param name = param-nameₙ value = param-valueₙ > ]
[ alternate-html-content ]
</applet>
```

The attributes `code`, `width`, and `height` are required. The rest are optional. The attributes of the `<applet>` tag are summarized in the following table.

Attribute	Description
codebase	Specifies the base URL of the applet. It is a relative path to the directory containing the current HTML document. The default value is the same directory as the current HTML document.
code	Specifies the class name of the applet. The location of the class file is specified by the `codebase` attribute.
width	Specifies the width of the applet's display area in pixels.
height	Specifies the height of the applet's display area in pixels.
alt	Specifies alternative text that should be displayed by browsers that understand the `<applet>` tag but do not support Java.
name	Specifies a name for the applet instance, making it possible for applets on the same page to communicate with each other.
align	Specifies the applet's position with respect to surrounding text.
vspace	Specifies the top and bottom margins in pixels.
hspace	Specifies the left and right margins in pixels.
param	Specifies the parameters to the applet. Each parameter is specified by a name–value pair. The `param` attribute may occur multiple times.
archive	Specifies a comma-separated list of Java archives (JAR files) containing classes and other resources.

The *alternate-html-content* section specifies alternative text that should be displayed by browsers that do not understand the `<applet>` tag.

Summary of Documentation Tags

Documentation comments are special comments in Java source code that are delimited by `/**` and `*/`. They are processed by the `javadoc` utility to generate API documentation. The tags that can be used in the documentation comments are summarized as follows.

`@author` *name*

Adds an *Author* entry to the generated docs when the `-author` option of `javadoc` is used. A doc comment may contain multiple `@author` tags or multiple names per tag.

`@deprecated` *description*

Adds a comment indicating that this method has been deprecated since the specified version. The first sentence of the `@deprecated` description should tell the user when the method was deprecated and what can be used as a replacement. An `@link` tag should be included that points to the replacement method.

`@exception` *name description*

Adds an exception description to the *Exceptions* section of the generated API documentation. An `@exception` tag should be included for each checked exception declared in the throws clause of a method. It is synonymous with the `@throws` tag.

`@link` *name*

Inserts a link that points to the specified name. Multiple link tags can be used.

`@param` *name description*

Adds a parameter description to the *Parameters* section of the generated API documentation. A `@param` tag should be included for each parameter of a method.

@return *description*

Adds a *Returns* section to the generated API documentation that describes the return value of a method. The @return tag should be used for all methods except methods that return void or constructors.

@see *text*

Adds a text entry. No link is generated.

@see *package. class#member*

Adds a link that points to a specific name in the API documentation.

@see <a href=*url*>*text*</a>

Adds a link to the specified URL.

@serial *description*

Describes the serializable fields.

@since *text*

Indicates the release or version number in which the feature was first introduced.

@throws *name description*

Synonymous to the @exception tag.

@version *text*

Adds a *Version* section for specifying the version of the software that contains this class or member when the -version option of javadoc is used. Only one @version tag is allowed per doc comment.

Summary of Java Naming Conventions

The following is a summary of the naming conventions used in Java. Using these conventions can help produce more readable code and avoid name conflicts.

Package Names

The first identifier of a package name consists of two or three letters that name an Internet domain, such as `com`, `edu`, `gov`, `mil`, `net`, `org`, or a two-letter ISO country code such as `uk` or `jp`. The following are some examples:

```
com.sun.java.corba
org.npr.pledge.driver
uk.ac.city.rugby.game
```

When defining package names for local use, you should begin the first identifier with a lowercase letter. The first identifier should not be `java`, because it is reserved for standard Java packages.

Class and Interface Names

Descriptive nouns or noun phrases should be used for class type names and interface type names (adjectives that describe a behavior can also be used as interface names). In addition, capitalize the first letter of each word and use mixed case. The following are some examples:

```
HttpSessionContext
HelloServlet
ServletInputStream
```

```
Thread
PrintStream
Runnable
Cloneable
```

Method Names

Verbs or verb phrases should be used for method names. In addition, method names should consist of mixed case, with a lowercase first letter. The first letter of any subsequent words should be capitalized. The following are examples:

```
write
play
showContent
```

Other conventions for method names include the following.

- When using a method to get or set an attribute thought of as variable `Var`, use `getVar` and `setVar`. Examples are `getDate` and `setDate`.
- When a method tests a boolean condition `Cond` about an object, it should be named `isCond`. An example is `isInterrupted`.

Field Names

Field names (other than those that are final) should have names that are nouns, noun phrases, or abbreviations of nouns. They should be in mixed case with a lowercase first letter and the first letters of subsequent words capitalized. Examples include `buf`, `pos`, `count`, and `bytesTransferred`.

Constant Names

When naming the constants in interface types and the final variables of class types, you should use a sequence of one or more words (or other appropriate parts of speech), acronyms, or abbreviations. In addition, components should be all uppercase, and they should be separated by the underscore character (_). Examples include `MIN_VALUE`, `MAX_VALUE`, `MIN_RADIX`, and `MAX_RADIX`.

Local Variable and Parameter Names

Local variable and parameter names are often short sequences of lowercase letters that are not complete words, such as

- an acronym, such as `bg`, for a variable holding a `Color` object used for the background;
- an abbreviation, such as `buf`, for a variable referring to a buffer; and
- a mnemonic term, such as `in` and `out`, for input and output streams.

One-character local variable or parameter names should be used only for temporary and loop control variables, or where a variable holds an undistinguished value of a type. Acceptable one-character names are:

Name	Type
b	byte
c	char
d	double
e	Exception
f	float
i	integer
j	integer
k	integer
l	long
o	Object
s	String
v	any type

You should not use local variable or parameter names that consist of only two or three uppercase letters, as they may conflict with the initial country codes and domain names of unique package names.

Glossary

abstract class   A class that contains at least one abstract method. Abstract classes cannot be instantiated; they must be extended by a class that implements the abstract methods. See also *abstract method*.

abstract method   A method that has no implementation. The implementation is deferred to subclasses.

Abstract Windows Toolkit (AWT)   A core Java package that provides the basic support for building graphical user interfaces. See also *Swing*.

abstraction   The principle of characterizing the behaviors, or functions, of a module in a succinct and precise description known as the contractual interface. See also *contractual interface*.

aggregation   A special form of association in which one class is a part of or belongs to another class. It represents the *has-a* or *part-of* relationship. See also *composition*.

app   See *Java app*.

applet   See *Java applet*.

appletviewer   A command-line utility in JDK for viewing Java applets.

application framework   A set of cooperating classes that represent reusable designs of software systems in a particular application domain. It is a semicomplete application written in a specific programming language.

ASCII   The default character encoding of the United States, officially known as ISO-8859-1, in which all characters are encoded in a single byte.

association   A general binary relationship among classes. See also *aggregation* and *composition*.

auxilary class   A class that is nonpublic and is solely used for implementing other classes.

bag   An unordered collection of elements that may contain duplicates. Bags are also known as multisets.

bytecode   The instructions of the Java Virtual Machine (JVM). The Java compiler compiles Java source code to Java byte-code and stores this resulting code in files with the extension `.class`. See also *Java Virtual Machine*.

cast   (of types) The explicit conversion of one data type to another. Also known as *coersion*.

class   A set of objects with similar characteristics or behaviors. A class characterizes the structure of states and behaviors that are shared by all of its instances.

client   A module that uses the services provided by another module.

cohesion   A measurement of the functional relatedness of the entities within a module.

Common Object Request Broker Architecture (CORBA)   An object-oriented framework that supports interoperability among objects written in different languages and running on different platforms.

compiler   A computer program that translates, or compiles, the source code of a program into machine code, allowing the machine code to be directly executed by the operating system and the hardware.

composition   A stronger form of aggregation, which implies exclusive ownership of the component class by the aggregate class. See also *aggregation*.

concurrent program   See *multithreaded program*.

constructor   An instance method of a class that is invoked with the `new` keyword with the purpose of creating an object. In Java, a constructor has the same name as its class.

contractural interface   A service contract between a module that provides one or more services and its clients.

coupling   A measurement of the interdependency among modules.

CRC cards   A useful technique for deriving complete analysis models. A CRC card is simply a 3 × 5 inch index card describing a class, its responsibilities, and its collaborators.

critical region   A code segment that should be accessible only by one thread at a time.

Decorator A design pattern that attaches additional responsibilities to an object dynamically. Decorators provide a flexible alternative to subclassing for extending functionality.

deserialization The process of restoring an object that has been serialized, and all the objects that are directly or indirectly referenced by the object. See also *serialization*.

design pattern A schematic description of reusable designs. Each pattern describes a recurring problem and the core of the solution to that problem.

distributed application An application that consists of multiple autonomous programs residing on different computers, or hosts, in a computer network and cooperating with one another.

double-buffering A technique used in animation to reduce flickering. Also known as *off-screen drawing*.

downcast Explicit cast of a reference type to one of its subtypes. See also *cast*.

dual application/applet A Java program that can be invoked as either an applet or an application. In either case, program behavior will be identical.

dynamic binding The binding of a method invocation to a specific implementation at run time instead of at compile time.

encapsulation The principle of separating the implementation of an object from its contractual interface and hiding the implementation from its clients. See also *contractual interface*.

event The occurence of a stimulus that can trigger a state transition. See also *state-chart*.

exception An unexpected condition in a program that prevents the program from continuing normally.

extended class See *inheritance*.

extension (of classes) See *inheritance*.

extension (of interfaces) A weak form of inheritance, in which an interface may extend multiple interfaces by inheriting all the features declared in them and declaring additional features. See also *inheritance*.

factorization The process of deriving generic components by identifying recurring code segments that implement the same logic, and capturing this logic in a generic component that is defined once.

Factory Method A design pattern that defines an interface for creating an object but lets the subclasses decide which class to instantiate and how.

framework See *application framework*.

garbage collection A mechanism that automatically detects and deallocates unreferenced or unreachable objects (i.e., garbage).

generic component A program component, usually in the form of a class or package, that can be adapted and used in different contexts without modification.

helper class See *auxilary class*.

heterogeneous network A computer network that consists of computers with different CPUs running different operating systems, such as the Internet.

hiding The introduction of a field or a static method in a subclass that has the same name as a field or a static method in the superclass. See also *overriding* and *overloading*.

hook method A placeholder for context-specific behavior that is implemented differently for each specific context. Hook methods are used in design patterns such as Template Method and are often abstract. See also *Template Method*.

hypertext A form of text file that contrasts sharply to *linear* text, the form of text seen in almost all printed media, such as books and newspapers, that is intended to be read linearly from the beginning to the end. A hypertext document consists of a set of *nodes* that may contain text, graphics, and/or audio/video clips, and a set of *links* between the nodes that are related in some way. A hypertext document is read by following the links but not in a prescribed linear order.

Hypertext Markup Language (HTML) An application of the Standard Generalized Markup Language (SGML) for writing hypertext documents. It is the standard language supported by Web browsers.

Hypertext Transfer Protocol (HTTP) The standard protocol used by Web browsers to transfer HTML documents.

inheritance The relationship among classes and interfaces that models the *is-a* relationship in the real world; the aspect of the *is-a* relationship that permits the reuse of class definitions. When class C2 inherits from, or extends, class C1, class C2 is known as a subclass or an extended class of class C1, and class C1 is known as a superclass of C2. The extension relationship among interfaces and the implementation relationship between a class and interfaces can be considered as a weak form of inheritance. See also *single inheritance* and *multiple inheritance*.

inner class A class that is declared inside another class.

instance field Instance fields are per-object fields that are owned by each instance.

instance method A method that accesses instance fields or invokes other instance methods.

interface A special form of class that declares features but provides no implementation. An interface declares only constants and abstract methods. See also *abstract method* and *abstract class*.

interpreter A computer program that directly parses and executes program source code without generating machine code.

Iterator A design pattern that uses abstract iterators to iterate through different concrete collections in a uniform way.

Java app (application) A full-fledged Java program with full access to system resources.

Java applet A Java program that is embedded in Web pages with restricted access to system resources to prevent break-ins to the hosts that run the applets.

Java chip A CPU that uses Java byte-code as native machine code.

Java Collections Framework A set of interfaces and classes that support storing and retrieving objects in collections of varying structures, algorithms, and time–space complexities.

Java Development Kit (JDK) A collection of tools for developing and running Java programs.

Java Run-Time Environment (JRE) A subset of JDK that contains the tools for running Java programs.

Java Virtual Machine (JVM) An abstract computing machine that executes Java byte-code. It can be implemented as interpreters, JIT compilers, or Java chips— hardware implementations of the JVM. See also *bytecode*.

javac The command that invokes the Java compiler.

javadoc A JDK utility that builds a full set of reference documentation from tags that are embedded in programs.

Just-In-Time (JIT) compiler A compiler that compiles Java byte-code to native machine code "on the fly" and then executes the native machine code.

levels of abstraction The principle of ordering abstractions into different levels through inheritance. See also *inheritance*.

list An ordered collection of elements in which the elements are indexed sequentially starting from 0. Lists are also known as sequences.

literal The representation of the constant values of types.

macro process An iterative software development process that includes the following phases: conceptualization, analysis and modeling, design, implementation, and maintenance.

map An unordered collection of key-value pairs. Maps are also known as functions, dictionaries, or associative arrays.

marker interface An empty interface that is intended to signify that all classes implementing the interface share certain common properties.

message passing   The mechanism by which objects communicate. A message consists of an object (the recipient), a method, and optional parameters.

microprocess   A development process that consists of successive iterations of the following phases: identify the classes; identify the semantics (i.e., attributes and behaviors of the classes); identify the relationships among the classes; define the class interfaces; and then implement the classes.

modularity   The principle of decomposing complex systems into highly cohesive and loosely coupled modules. It is intended to control the complexity of large-scale systems through the use of the divide-and-conquer technique.

multiple inheritance   A form of inheritance that allows a class to have multiple superclasses. Java allows only single inheritance among classes. However, Java allows multiple inheritance for interface extension and interface implementation. A class may implement multiple interfaces, and an interface may extend multiple interfaces.

multithreaded program   A program that is capable of running several threads simultaneaously. Also known as a *concurrent program*.

narrowing (of types)   Conversion of a type of a larger range to a type of a smaller range.

object   Anything in the real world that can be distinctly identified. Objects have unique identity, states, behaviors, and relationships with other objects.

object-oriented analysis and modeling   The task of describing the essential and relevant aspects of the problem domain and the problems to be solved in terms of objects, classes, and their relationships. See also *object* and *class*.

overloading   The ability of allowing different methods or constructors with different signatures of the same class to share the same name. See also *overriding* and *hiding*.

overriding   The introduction of an instance method in a subclass that has the same name, signature, and return type of a method in its super class. The implementation of the method in the subclass replaces the implementation of the method in the superclass. See also *instance method, overloading*, and *hiding*.

package   A mechanism for organizing large programs into logical and manageable units. A package may contain classes, interfaces, or other packages.

parameter passing   The way parameters are passed to method invocations. In Java, all parameters are passed by value.

platform independence   (of programs) The ability to run programs on different platforms without having to modify the programs.

polymorphism   The ability of dynamically interchanging modules without affecting clients.

polymorphic assignment   A form of assignment supported by object-oriented programming languages, where the right-hand-side expression of an assignment can be an object of many different types, as long as the type is a subtype of the type of the left-hand-side expression of the assignment. See also *polymorphism* and *subtype*.

polymorphic method invocation   Refers to method invocations that can be bound to different implementations at run time. This occurs when a method is overridden in subclasses.

porting programs   Conversion of the source code of programs to allow them to be run on different platforms.

primitive type   One of `boolean`, `byte`, `short`, `int`, `long`, `char`, `float`, and `double`. A primitive type variable holds a value of that type. See also *reference type*.

process   A heavyweight flow that executes concurrently with other processes. See also *thread*.

reusable component   See *generic component*.

reference type   A class type, an interface type, or an array type. A reference type variable holds an indirect reference to an object or array.

remote method invocation (RMI)   A distributed object model in which the methods of remote Java objects can be invoked from other Java programs, possibly residing on different hosts.

serialization   The process of writing an object, and all the objects that are directly or indirectly referenced by the object, to a stream. See also *deserialization*.

set   An unordered collection of elements in which no duplicates are allowed.

signature   The signature of a method or constructor, consisting of the sequence of types of its parameters.

single inheritance   A form of inheritance in which each class may inherit from only one superclass. See also *multiple inheritance*.

Singleton   A design pattern that ensures that a class has only one instance and provides a global point of access to it.

skeleton   An object that resides on the same host as the server, receives requests from client stubs, and dispatches the requests to the server.

socket   An end point of logical connections between hosts that can be used to send and receive data.

state (statechart)   A condition or situation during the life of an object during which it satisfies some condition, performs some actions, or waits for some events. See also *statechart*.

State (design pattern)   A design pattern that allows an application to dynamically associate behavior with a given object, based on that object's state.

state transition   A relationship between two states indicating that an object in the first state (the source state) will perform certain actions and enter the second state (the destination state) when a specified event occurs and conditions are satisfied. See also *statechart*.

statechart   A diagram that depicts the flow of control using the concepts of states and transitions.

static field   Per-class fields that are shared by all the instances of the same class.

static method   A method that accesses only static fields.

Strategy   A design pattern that defines a family of algorithms, encapsulates each one, and makes them interchangeable.

stub   An object that resides on the same host as the client and serves as a proxy, or surrogate, of the remote server.

subclass   See *inheritance*.

subtype   A relationship among types. Type T1 is a subtype of type T2 if every legitimate value of T1 is also a legitimate value of T2. T2 is also known as the supertype of T1.

superclass   See *inheritance*.

supertype   See *subtype*.

Swing   An extension of AWT that provides extensive support for building sophisticated and high-quality graphical user interfaces. See also *Abstract Windows Toolkit*.

synchronization   A mechanism to ensure that, while a thread is executing the statements in a critical region, no other threads can execute that same critical region at the same time.

Template Method   A design pattern that defines the skeleton of an algorithm in a method, deferring some steps to subclasses using hook methods, thus allowing the subclasses to redefine certain steps of the algorithm. See also *hook method*.

testing   An activity in software development that is intended to discover bugs.

thread   A single sequential flow of control within a program. A thread is a lightweight flow that executes concurrently with other threads within the same process. See also *process*.

type compatibility   Two types are compatible if values of one type can appear wherever values of the other type are expected, and *vice versa*.

type conversion   The conversion of one data type to another.

Unicode   An international standard of 16-bit character sets that consists of encodings of characters of most languages used in the world today. Java characters are in unicode.

Unified Modeling Language (UML)   A graphical notation for describing object-oriented analysis and design models.

unit testing   An activity that tests each component, usually a class, independently. See also *testing*.

Universal Resource Locator (URL)   A mechanism to uniquely identify every resource (e.g., document, program etc.) on the Internet. A URL consists of the *transfer protocol*, the *host name*, the *path*, and the *port number*. See also *Hypertext Markup Language*.

widening (of types)   Conversion of a type of a smaller range to a type of a larger range.

Java Resources on the Web

- The Java technology home page:

  `http://java.sun.com/`

- The Java Developer Connection:

  `http://developer.java.sun.com/index.html`

- The Java language specification:

  `http://java.sun.com/docs/books/jls/html/index.html`

- Sun's Java education services:

  `http://suned.sun.com/usa.html`

- Java programmer's FAQ:

  `http://www.faqs.org/faqs/computer-lang/java/programmers-faq/`

- The World Wide Web Consortium:

  `http://www.w3.org/`

- The Gamelan Java directory:

  `http://www.gamelan.com/`

- The Java boutique:

  `http://javaboutique.internet.com/`

Bibliography

Alexander, C. (1979). *The Timeless Way of Building.* Oxford University Press.

Alexander, C., et al. (1977). *A Pattern Language—Towns, Buildings, Construction.* Oxford University Press.

Böhm, C., and Jacopini, G. (1966). Flow diagrams, turing machines and languages with only two formation rules. The *Communications of the ACM*, 9:366–371.

Booch, G. (1987). *Software Engineering with Ada*, 2d ed. Benjamin/Cummings.

Booch, G. (1994). *Object-Oriented Analysis and Design with Applications*, 2d ed. Benjamin/Cummings.

Bowman, J., Emerson, S., and Darnovsky, M. (1996). *The Practical SQL Handbook: Using Structured Query Language.* Addison-Wesley.

Campione, M., and Walrath, K. (1998). *The Java Tutorial—Object-Oriented Programming for the Internet*, 2d ed. Addison-Wesley.

Coplien, J. (1992). *Advanced C++—Programming Styles and Idioms.* Addison-Wesley.

Darwen, H., and Date, C. (1997). *A Guide to the SQL Standard*, 4th ed. Addison-Wesley.

Dijkstra, E. (1968). Go to statement considered harmful. *The Communications of the ACM*, 11:147–148.

Ellis, M., and Stroustrup, B. (1990). *The Annotated C++ Reference Manual.* Addison-Wesley.

Fowler, M. (1997). *Analysis Patterns—Reusable Object Models*. Addison-Wesley.

Gamma, E., et al. (1995). *Design Patterns—Elements of Reusable Object-Oriented Software*. Addison-Wesley.

Goldberg, A. (1985). *Smalltalk-80: The Interactive Programming Environment*. Addison-Wesley.

Goldberg, A., and Robson, D. (1983). *Smalltalk-80: The Language and Its Implementation*. Addison-Wesley.

Hamilton, G., Cattell, R., and Fisher, M. (1997). *JDBC Database Access with Java, A Tutorial and Annotated Reference*. Addison-Wesley.

Harbison, S. (1992). *Modular-3*. Prentice-Hall.

Lea, D., ed. (1997). *Concurrent Programming in Java—Design Principles and Patterns*. Addison-Wesley.

Lindholm, T., and Yellin, F. (1996). *The Java Virtual Machine*. Addison-Wesley.

McGraw, G., and Felten, E. W. (1997). *Java Security—Hostile Applets, Holes, and Antidotes*. John Wiley & Sons.

Meyer, B. (1992). *Eiffel: The Language*. Prentice-Hall.

Meyer, B. (1997). *Object-Oriented Software Construction*, 2d ed. Prentice-Hall.

Orfali, R., and Harkey, D. (1998). *Client/Server Programming with Java and CORBA*, 2d ed. John Wiley and Sons.

Pinson, L. J., and Wiener, R. S. (1991). *Objective C: Object-Oriented Programming Techniques*. Addison-Wesley.

Raggett, D., et al. (1998). *Raggett on HTML 4*. Addison-Wesley.

Schneier, B. (1996). *Applied Cryptography*, 2d ed. John Wiley & Sons.

Shaw, M., and Garlan, D. (1996). *Software Architecture—Perspective On An Emerging Discipline*. Prentice-Hall.

Stroustrup, B. (1994). *The Design and Evolution of* C++. Addison-Wesley.

Stroustrup, B. (1997). *The* C++ *Programming Language*, 3d ed. Addison-Wesley.

The Unicode Consortium (1996). *The Unicode Standard, Version 2.0*. Addison-Wesley.

Walrath, K., and Campione, M. (1999).*The JFC Swing Tutorial*. Addison-Wesley.

Zachary, G. P. (1994). *Show-Stopper*. Free Press.

Index